CPG Series of Comparative Constitutional Law, Politics and Governance

Edited by the
German-Southeast Asian Center of Excellence for Public Policy and Good Governance

Vol. 2

Henning Glaser (ed.)

Norms, Interests, and Values

Conflict and Consent in the Constitutional Basic Order

Nomos

Die Deutsche Nationalbibliothek lists this publication in the Deutsche Nationalbibliografie; detailed bibliographic data is available in the Internet at http://dnb.d-nb.de

ISBN 978-3-8487-0432-3 (Print)
978-3-8452-4738-0 (ePDF)

British Library Cataloguing-in-Publication Data
A catalogue record for this book is available from the British Library.

ISBN 978-3-8487-0432-3 (Print)
978-3-8452-4738-0 (ePDF)

Library of Congress Cataloging-in-Publication Data
Glaser, Henning (ed.)
Norms, Interests, and Values
Conflict and Consent in the Constitutional Basic Order
Henning Glaser
370 p.
Includes bibliographic references.

ISBN 978-3-8487-0432-3 (Print)
978-3-8452-4738-0 (ePDF)

1. Edition 2015

Preface

This second volume of the *CPG Series of Comparative Constitutional Law, Politics and Governance* on "Norms, Interests, and Values – Conflict and Consent in the Constitutional Basic Order" is the product of related projects of the German-Southeast Asian Center of Excellence for Public Policy and Good Governance (CPG) in particular including its second annual conference on this topic at Lebua at State Tower Hotel in Bangkok.

The approach is comparative with a range of selected country studies presenting some of the currently most relevant constitutional systems in Europe and Asia, namely Belgium, Germany, Hungary, Indonesia, Italy, the Netherlands, Pakistan, Singapore, Taiwan, Thailand, and Turkey as well as the dominantly Confucian influenced parts of South-East Asia as a distinct socio-political space characterized by particular patterns of political conflict and consent.

Particular thanks is, first and foremost, owed to the authors for their time and efforts to make this collection possible. Their analyses and reflections from a broad variety of vantage points are most appreciated.

For his opening of the second annual conference we have to thank HE Prof. Dr. Suchart Thada-Thamrongvech, Minister of Education of the Kingdom of Thailand, representing the Prime Minister.

Furthermore, this publication was only made possible due to the constant support of our work by a number of individuals and institutions. Since many years now, our Center of Excellence, CPG, which is formed by the universities of Frankfurt am Main, Münster and Passau as well as Thammasat University as a joint institute located at Thammasat University in Bangkok, is enabled by the generous support of the German Foreign Ministry, the Federal Foreign Office, the German Academic Exchange Service (DAAD) as well as Thammasat's Faculty of Law being the host of CPG.

Not only to them but also to the scholars representing CPG as an inter-regional academic institution great thanks is extended, namely, among many others, Assoc. Prof. Narong Jaiharn, Dean of Thammasat University's Faculty of Law, Prof. Dr. Ingwer Ebsen (Frankfurt), Prof. Dr. Dr. h.c. Dirk Ehlers (Münster) and Prof. Dr. Robert Esser (Passau) who all care for the wellbeing of our institution with greatest efforts.

Warmest gratitude is extended to those who tirelessly contributed to make the publication of this collection possible, namely Dr. Duc Quang Ly, Siraprapa Chalermphao, Dr. Sabine Carl, Terence Freibier, Sarah Popp, and Konstantin Trott.

Henning Glaser

Table of Contents

Crisis, Conflict and Consensus in the Constitutional Basic Order – An Introduction

Henning Glaser

The topic of the this volume is the foundational consensus manifested in the constitutional basic order, the question how it is challenged by conflict and crisis and the way constitutional systems experience and respond to it. Touched upon is the fundamental and yet opaque zone of ordering where the socio-political and the legal-constitutional sphere are closely intertwined. This intersection becomes most visible in the moments of conflict and crisis, which lucidly reveal its nature with respect to the foundation, integrity and continuance of each order. Here, central problems of constitutional and political theory are affected. Such issues include the conception of sovereign power, the constituent power and constitutional change, legitimacy and hegemony in the constitutional order, the identity of the constitutional subject and the integration of the political community, the inherent tension between domination and pluralism, liberty and militant democracy, just to name a few of them.

However, a thorough examination of this fundamental dimension of social, political and legal ordering is an endeavor which is too immense to be exhaustively addressed even from only one of the various related disciplinary perspectives. This collection thus restrains to present some selected country studies to invite further discussion. Some of the as to that relevant constitutional systems in Europe and Asia, namely *Belgium*, *Germany*, *Hungary*, *Italy*, *Indonesia*, *the Netherlands*, *Pakistan*, *Singapore*, *Taiwan*, *Thailand and Turkey* will be covered. Consideration will also be given to the Confucian influenced parts of Southeast Asia as a distinct socio-political space characterized by particular patterns of political conflict and consent. Most of these country studies represent constitutional systems which currently experience a more or a less severe crisis of their constitutional basic order. The only two countries enjoying a remarkably stable constitutional basic order among the presented cases are Singapore and Germany. Insofar, the focus of interest lies in the existing mechanisms to prevent or to deal with such challenges, whereas the value of these defensive mechanisms is assessed quite differently in the respective papers (see the contributions of *Thio*, *Esser*, and *Wittreck*).

In general, the presented collection reflects on a timely and current phenomenon which at the same time belongs to some of the 'eternal' issues and problems of constitutional law and political ordering.

A. Contentious Constitutional Politics Pertaining to the Fundaments of Order as a Sign of the Times

The initial optimism toward new democracies that emerged during the 1990s in Asia, Latin America and Africa – most strikingly embodied by *Fukuyama's* claim of the "end of history" – has trailed off among political observers and scholars.[1] The actual signs seem to indicate the presence of fundamental constitutional conflict and crisis in countries and regions all over the globe.

Long established constitutional democracies in Europe like Belgium (see the paper of *Adams*) and Italy (see *Luther*), especially some of those countries severely hit by the Euro-crisis such as Greece, have been joined in recent years by the United States and Canada in encountering escalating difficulties to constructively deal with emerging political divisions over the basis of constitutional law. The same is true for many of the younger European democracies, like Bulgaria, Hungary (see *Toth*), Romania, the Ukraine and Turkey (see *Inceoğlu*). Asian countries such as Pakistan (see *Siddique*), Malaysia, Thailand (see *Glaser*) and Taiwan (see *Hwang*) seem to be captured by a persisting division over the constitutional basic order. Meanwhile, countries like India and Indonesia (see *Machmudi*) at least show signs of potentially critical tensions affecting the societal and constitutional basic consent.

In some of these countries like Hungary, Turkey or Thailand constitutional conflict and national division are directly related with attempts to restate the constitutional order by constitutional reform/ amendment. The constitutional reform in Hungary and Turkey have left the countries deeply divided and at least on the threshold of massive transformation under more (Turkey) or less (Hungary) authoritarian auspices after their constitutional basic order has been replaced or modified respectively. In contrast, Thailand faced a struggle over a constitutional reform project which caused mass protests, political violence

---

1 See Carothers, "The End of the Transition Paradigm," 2002, pp. 5-21.

and radicalization, eventually contributing to a military putsch which prevented the changes from being effective and adjusted the old order with the overarching purpose to preserve it. Even if the junta has for the time being frozen the conflict, the country remains deeply divided, the fundamental consensus a rigidly hegemonic friction. This foreshadows a possibility of future outbreaks and crisis of an even higher scale, if the divisive issue stays unsettled or spirals out of control.

Similarly shaped by protracted constitutional conflicts is the situation in a range of Middle Eastern countries. A good deal of the hopes created by the 'Arab Spring' quickly turned into skepticism of how dissenting political views could be harmonized by integrative and enduring constitutional settings. Failure to do so led to a state of severe crisis in countries like Egypt, Iraq, Libya and Syria, bringing some of them to the brink of civil war. Concurrently, other countries, such as Jordan and Israel, whose rule can be upheld only by massive security regimes, are held in a seemingly inescapable conflict related to the fundamental consensus.

In many of these countries the long-term stability of political order is at stake in one way or another, while the respective constitutional order seems unable to provide sufficient options for adjustment. However, despite the usual associations with the term 'crisis' many countries seem to live with a protracted constitutional crisis for a long time, making it a somewhere normal part of the political setting, without hope for a clear break and compromised restatement. In other countries, severe and protracted constitutional conflicts may be seen as a transformative period of the constitutional and political discourse necessary to rebuild the social contract or acknowledging long existing, yet suppressed streams of political formation, which are gaining increasing relevance under changed circumstances.

In sum, a significant number of political communities in the contemporary world are facing severe conflicts about how they should be ordered and governed, about which fundamental norms and constitutional design should enjoy priority, and how challenges to the basic conflict should be addressed. Notable in this context is the fact that in the contemporary world the quest for an appropriate political order is increasingly formulated in terms of constitutionalism – be it by those in power or those who challenge it.[2] Indeed, the recent increase of internal tension and struggle for political ordering appears to be articulated in the language of constitutional law in a more and more mea-ningful way than ever before, even if this does not exclude the possibility of massive, violent conflict in the respective settings. Equally notable is the fact that a supposed uniform model of constitutional governance (as a subject of national consent) does not exist. This contravenes the mentioned paradigm of the 1990s according to which constitutional systems would achieve a lasting equilibrium and evolve toward a supposedly uniform model of western-style constitutionalism, rule of law and democracy representing the goal for development for all the transforming nations around the globe. *Carothers*, more than a decade ago deconstructed this transition paradigm, aiming at its core assumptions "that any country moving away from dictatorial rule can be considered a country in transition toward [western-style] democracy."[3] A closer look at the globally increasing scenarios of conflict and crisis in the constitutional basic order seems to prove him right, not only with respect to the fact that the desired transformation toward the 'one right' model failed to materialize, but also in consideration of the diversity of distinct models of constitutional governance competing for dominance instead. These observations make one realize that beyond the classical distinction between normative, nominal and semantic constitutionalism introduced by *Loewenstein*, and describing a dominant notion of global constitutional development during the Cold War period, today more and more political communities seem to be in sincere search of a constitutionalism on new and own terms. The question is not chaos or order, real (normative) constitutionalism or fake/failed (semantic or nominal) one, but which substantially particular model of constitutional governance prevails in the given context – be it more on the level of compromise or unilaterally imposed hegemonic rule. This opens up a space for contentious constitutional politics at the fundaments of political formation not aiming to avoid or neutralize but to occupy and dominate the constitutional form. This somehow newly emerged pattern of political ordering around the globe, defined by a highly charged competitive and even contentious constitutionalism, deserves to

2 See Hirschl, *Constitutional Theocracy*, 2010, p. 241, who appreciates the "triumph of constitutionalism as the prevalent form of governance" as one "of the most important phenomena in the late 20th and early 21st century politics."

3 Carothers, "The End of the Transition Paradigm," 2002, p. 6.

be appreciated as a specific expression of the post-Cold War period, even if not as one of the most significant signs of our times with respect to consti-tutionalism and politics. Some expressions of the emergence of this more dense and dynamic appearance of contentious constitutional politics in the contemporary world might be highlighted.

Besides the fact that contemporary constitutionalism on a global scale is much more complicated than it has been expected in the beginning of the 1990s, contentious constitutional politics tend to emerge in various regional and global patterns.

For instance, the different role of political ideologies in this context is striking. The older European democracies seem often in-clined to see a manifest decline of ideologically shaped constitutional politics in the wake of an underlying, widely unexpressed consensus across the party lines, in a direction of what might be called 'neoliberal' politics and the corresponding fading of classical party cleavages. Political phenomena of critical impact for the social contract or the basic consti-tutional order actually arise much less in the constitutionally formalized political arena of party politics and inter-agency cooperation in these countries but outside, in the societal space. Here it is precisely this drain of contentious mega-politics from formal constitutional politics which constitutes a growing cognitive dissonance among those groups feeling unrepresented and excluded. As a consequence, it might challenge the fundamental consensus as being manifested by this political-constitutional order which seems to be defined less by fighting for substansive compromise but by carefully avoiding any contentious substance in fundamental issues.[4] In this respect, it might be no accident that two of the contributions to this volume dealing with one of the most stable European democracies examine the constitutional instruments to redress resistance against the basic constitutional order which might spring from dissatisfaction with this kind of post-ideological constitutional politics.

A totally different image emerges when looking at Latin America, where the fundamental principles and the corresponding constitutional

---

4 In this sense a book like Pierre Rosannvallon's *Counter Democracy – Politics in an Age of Distrust*, 2008, hits a nerve. The problem of the counter-formalistic movement against post-ideological stiffness and perceived shallowness is that the informal, mainly street based counter-movements themselves often lack any consistent programmatic frame producing an ideological volatility which might prove detrimental to the initial consensus of these movements.

basic order are heavily affected or even reshaped under the influence of a left, pro-gressive, democratic ideology which, however, meets fierce resistance form the conservative and liberal segments within the respective political orders. The South American *pink tide*, the turn of a great number of coun-tries to the left in the wake of the strongly emerging global and national security paradigm after 9/11 2001, replaces the dominance of the Washington consensus during the 1990s on the continent, including all of its assumptions of universal constitutionalism and a universal transition paradigm.[5]

Another distinct regional development, in terms of conflict and crisis over the constitutional basic order, has arisen in form of the already mentioned Arab Spring and its aftermath where the dominant role in defining constitutional governance is not so much given to the classical political ideologies of the West but those defined by distinctions between secular and religious on the one hand and more liberal-democratic and authoritarian notions of shaping the constitutional basic order on the other hand. While an underlying thread of socialist-islamic notions of social justice runs through most of the political programs in question, all of them are often challenged by ethnic-tribal forms of political ordering. The resulting conflicts in the constitutional basic order pertain to the fundamental priorities and understandings of nearly all constitutional principles and state institutions. This also includes the clash of substantially different legal sources, including universalistic Islamic law, secular state law and particularistic normative orders in the form of tribalism. Particularly interesting is the enduring appeal of secular, populist-nationalist authoritarianism besides all the upcoming shades of Islamic constitutionalism and more western-like notions of secular constitutionalism that express a general potential of this sort of leadership to not only divide but also to gain popular approval and to unite broad segments of the population.

Many of these exemplary dynamics of contentious constitutional poli-tics on a fundamental level are furthermore related to two grand paradigms of global normative ordering in manifold ways: the neoliberal Washington

5 The regional impact of the *pink tide* becomes obvious if one considers the scope of countries affected by it on more or less radical terms ranging from Argentina, Brazil, Chile, Costa Rica, Ecuador, El Salvador, Guatemala, Paraguay, Peru, Uruguay, Venezuela accompanying traditionally socialist countries like Cuba and Nicaragua.

consensus and the post-9/11 security paradigm which link the national, regional and international level in shaping governance. A third catalyzing factor for the actual dynamics of conflict and crisis at the fundaments of political ordering is the resurgence of religions as major formative force of political ordering (see *Machmudi* for Indonesia).[6]

It might be concluded that all these factors and developments generically represent an immense dynamization of the various struggles for dominance in the project of fundamentally ordering the political, in a broad range of countries, with national, regional and international tendencies mutually reinforcing each other. Thus, the issue of conflict and consent in the basic constitutional order is indeed of actual importance, especially where constitutional and political theory have to respond to practical needs, be it in terms of constitution making, institution building, or conflict settlement.[7]

B. Conflict and Crisis in the Constitutional Basic Order – the Fundamental Frame

Despite its topicality, the perspective on conflict and crisis in the constitutional basic order is embedded in a fundamental frame of great abstractness and complexity. A major point of reference of this volume is the constitutional basic order or basic structure respectively. This term, especially important for instance in the German or Indian constitutional doctrine, refers to something more specific than just the constitutional order or all constitutional law in sum, but the "unquestionable core"[8] or, in the words of *Carl Schmitt*, the "fundamental political decision" of the political community pertaining to the normative fundament and the central institutions and principles of the constitutional order.[9] Correspondingly, talking about the basic constitutional order in terms of conflict and crisis is not to take an interest of simply any constitutional dispute or failure, but

6 See Hirschl, *Constitutional Theocracy*.

7 Also in this respect things have become more complicated compared to the 1990s where the failed state scenario represented the dominating approach in which conflict and crisis in the constitutional basic order have been themed.

8 See Albert, "The Cult of Constitutionalism," 2012, p. 390; see also Simson, "Zur Theorie der Legitimität," 1971, p. 459. The term 'basic structure' became popular with the Indian Supreme Court's 'basic structure doctrine'.

9 Schmitt, *Constitutional Theory*, 2008 (1928).

only those pertaining to the normative fundaments shaping the very identity of the political community.

More than other parts of constitutional law, the basic structure is normally embedded in a whole dimension of narratives, symbols and myths which legitimize, stabilize and concretize the entire legal structure. In this sense, the basic structure is particularly rooted in interwoven historical trajectories, communal experiences, preferred values and virtues and canonic interpretations of history reinforcing them.

In positive constitutional law, the basic structure is often most prominently expressed in the constitution's preamble, in the most fundamental provisions pertaining to the form of state and government or the basic rights; further, in provisions regulating constitutional amendments (exempting the basic structure from changes), and, eventually, in the mechanisms of militant constitutionalism providing a defense against acts being detrimental to the constitutional basic order. In some constitutions, the basic structure might cover both, the 'efficient' and the 'dignified' part of the constitution to speak with *Bagehot*, the one pertaining to institutions commanding 'real' power and the one regulating institutions which enjoy high esteem without such power but represent central political values and preferences.[10]

Due to its centrality it might be desirable or functional to place the basic structure, to a certain degree, beyond the ordinary contentious constitutional discourse "to take certain questions 'off the table' and thereby limit normal [...] politics to questions that do not challenge that fundamental consensus."[11] As far as this is true, it does not mean that critical questions pertaining to the interpretation of, or being relevant for, the basic structure should necessarily be excluded from the constitutional discourse by political style or the rules of militant constitutionalism. This applies at least to more liberal settings: some constitutional orders prefer to strictly assume that the basic structure is virtually off limits of any discussion banning them from public debate.[12] A certain mode to address

10 See Bagehot, *The English Constitution*, 1963 (1867). Such dignified parts of the constitution belonging to the basic structure or being disputed to belong to it might be constitutional institutions or confessions representing particular religious ties for example.

11 Kautz et al., "Introduction: The Idea of Constitutionalism," 2009, p. 3.

12 A good example is the Malaysian *Sedition Act*. The act inherited from British colonial rule – similar acts can be found in many former British colonies – criminalizes speech with "seditious tendency", in particular those which would

the social contract and constitutional basic structure in public debate, however, is practiced in almost all countries, especially those which rigidly protect it by exempting it from critical or non-affirmative debate. This is the case where the basic structure is subject of 'constitutional patriotism' as 'constitutional faith', often even appearing in the form of a nearly ritually reproduced constitutional mantra of quasi-moral quality and expression which might be required by social convention or, directly or indirectly, even by law. [13] Normatively forming the core of the constitutional order, the basic structure, including its embeddedness in the narrative and symbolic dimensions, often provides a valuable yet underrated analytical tool. Following *Loewenstein*, who lucidly envisioned the analysis of constitutionalism in terms of *cratology*, for the study of power within the realm of constitutional law[14] it is specifically the basic structure which seems to be worth being identified as the most promising subject of that sort of studies. For the one who looks for the architecture of political power in terms of constitutional law, the basic structure seems to ideally provide the constitution's sound formula to understand the factual power flow, its sources, channels, transformers, amplifiers, and necessary resistors. It is all the more surprising that the basic structure is rarely themed as a distinct normative complex. It mostly appears as either an empty space of constitutional macro analysis or a simplification in essentialist terms when it comes to appeal to a common policy goal, or to teleologically attest to a presumed political inferiority of non-Western countries. In European discourses on the basic structure, the focus often lies in the shared common denominator of the Ius Publicum Europaeum. The latter consists of a merely abstract set of constitutional concepts like democracy, separation of powers, rule of law and rights. Nevertheless, it

---

"bring into hatred or contempt or to excite disaffection against" the government or engender "feelings of ill-will and hostility between different races". In effect, it prohibits to critically address those parts of the Malaysian constitution which are considered to form the basic structure and the social contract respectively. Despite some exceptions from seditious behavior acc. sect. 3 (2) the act effectively bans nearly any critical, even if constructively meant and formulated comment on this hegemonic basic consent with a punishment up to three years in prison with a very high conviction rate while, according to sect. 3 (3), uphold by the Federal Court, "the intention of the person charged at the time he did or attempted [a seditious act, …] shall be deemed to be irrelevant".

13 See Levinson, *Constitutional Faith*, 2011.

14 See Loewenstein, *Political Power and the Governmental Process*, 1957, a book which is revealingly titled in its German translation as 'constitutional theory'.

has an effective legal-political function for and due to the membership in the European Union and the Council of Europe. Moreover, there is growing interest in analyzing unity and diversity of the European constitutional orders from comparative perspectives in more detail including the project to unfold the historical identity of a joint cultural-political heritage. From this perspective, the particularities of the respect-tive basic structures might find more interest and be related more closely to the shared normative deep structure of Europe's constitutional law. An interesting case in point is the (non-binding) report of the Venice Commission of the Council of Europe on the new Hungarian Constitution – in this volume critically discussed by *Toth*. Here the con-stitution of a member state of the Council of Europe was critically measured against those rules forming the minimum European requirements for the constitutional basic structure *à la Europeanne*. However, especially when looking east, western observers of non-western constitutional systems sometimes overlook the fact that the same constitutional elements often have a different function in the architecture within European and non-European constitutions. While the nexus of civil and political rights and representative democracy is an essential part of the basic structure of European systems, many non-European systems provide rights and mechanisms of electoral democracy as important parts of their respective constitutional design, *just only not* as the interwoven fabric of the constitutional core.[15] In sum, the constitutional basic structure of a particular political community seems not only to be more complex, dynamic and country-specific than often acknowledged but nothing less than the crux of the whole constitutional and political order. Therefore it is the most critical part of the legal and political system to be exposed to conflict and crisis. Thus, the understanding of severe constitutional and political crisis necessarily requires a sound understanding of the basic structure, especially from a comparative point of view.

Finally, conflict and crisis of the constitutional basic order are understood here as being equivalent to the challenge or failure of the underlying fundamental consent. This relation deserves some exploration. First, it may be said that those constitutions which are normatively more meaningful are *inclined* to fully express what can be called the 'social contract or 'fundamental consensus'. Insofar, the constitutional basic

15 See Glaser, "Multiple Constitutionalizations – 'Constitutionalism and Good Governance in European-Asian Perspectives'," 2014, pp. 45 ff.

order/structure can be seen as manifestation of the fundamental consensus in form of constitutional law. Therefore, severe conflict pertaining to it is raising questions about the fundamental consensus. Due to its vagueness the term, however, is difficult to operationalize.

Insofar, it is interesting to recall *Schmitt's* definition of the constitutional core, which he calls "the constitution" in distinction to "constitutional law" which is, in his view, "only possible because the essence of the constitution is not contained in a statue [...]. Prior to the establishment of any norm, there is a fundamental political decision by the bearer of the constitution-making power."[16]

While *Schmitt* refers to an underlying political concept of the written constitution as its very essence and condition, he purportedly avoids the term 'consensus'. Without engaging in the vast classical literature dealing critically with the theory of the social contract[17], of which *Schmitt's* account is a part, it is indeed interesting to ask about the nature and impact of the fundamental consensus (and the corresponding societal fundament of the constitutional basic structure) with reference to the specific notion of force in *Schmitt's* formulation, embedded in his favorite term 'decision'. While it seems evident that no political order is able to exist without a certain "underlying basic consent"[18], the term has to be concretized, what be-comes particular interesting in the light of this notion of force and with reference to the fact that any political order inevitably includes dissent and conflict pertaining to its normative fundaments.[19] While it is not possible to deeply explore the nature of the fundamental consensus here, it is helpful to recognize the triangle of *consent, force and dissent* as a constitutive frame for the fundamental dynamics of (re)producing constitutional and political orders.

Especially the existence of a certain kind of dissent pertaining to the constitutional basic structure might even have also productive, stabilizing and integrative functions and thus form a condition for success of constitutional orders, which embrace a sort of diversity in their very

16 Schmitt, *Constitutional Theory*, p. 77.

17 See Urbinati, "Representative Democracy and its Critics," 2011, pp. 23-49.

18 Dahl, *A Preface to Democratic Theory*, 1956, p. 132, fn. 14.

19 See Foucault, *The History of Sexuality: An Introduction*, 1978, p. 95: „Where there is power, there is resistance."

foundation:[20] "The strength of the constitutional fabric consists in the interweaving of different threads […]"[21] but even of those which might oppose each other. In other words: Whatever the nature of this consensus[22], it does not rest on the friction-less harmony of a once for all established compromise. Rather, its 'result' will remain fluid and to a certain degree even partly inconsistent whereas the dynamic evolving from the resulting tensions will determine its possible stability or weakness.[23] However heterogeneity in the constitutional fabric includes the potential that its diverging normative 'threads' and the social and political forces linked to them strive for dominance. As long as this is staged within the frame of the 'original truce' and the established constitutional basic order, this contributes to the phenomenon of constitutional change. If it goes be-yond, if some 'threads' transcend the original truce, attempting to use the constitutional setup for the purpose of substantially restating it, constitutional conflict and crisis emerge.

The constitutional basic order, in this sense, can be further understood not only as reflecting a dynamic social contract which is at least partly based on the *fiction* of a coherent fundamental consensus, but at least also

---

20 See Denninger, "Nachwort," 1998, p. 143 f.; Sunstein, *Why Society Needs Dissent*, 2003, p. 211. Unrealistic expectations towards the consistency of the fundamental consent might on the other hand only create a vulnerable rigidity or vanishing affection of the people in supporting the system. See Wefer, *Kontingenz und Dissens. Postheroische Perspektiven des politischen Systems*, 2004, p. 88.

21 Tully, *Multiplicity. Constitutionalism in an Age of Diversity*, 1995, p. 197. See also Harris II, "Constitution of Failure. The Architectonics of a Well-Founded Constitutional Order," 2010, pp. 66-87.

22 Practically, a kind of basic consent seems to be not only based on very diverging yet pronounced points of view, but also exists beyond this dimension of 'informed' and explicit consent. In this other dimension, what can be described as an expression of a certain fundamental consensus depends on notions of non-decision-making and docility supported by opportunism, force, more passive reflexes of belonging and loyalty, or reciprocity. See Neidhardt, "Formen und Funktionen gesellschaftlichen Grundkonses," 2000, p. 18, and with a different accentuation also *Habermas'* Theory of Communicative Action distinguishing between an apriori-background consensus and a discursive argumentative consent. Habermas, *Der philosophische Diskurs der Moderne*, 1985, p. 375.

23 In Western societies the co-existence of such different and partly strongly diverging political ideologies like conservatism, liberalism and progressive democracy within the normative fabric of Western societies and constitutions is a good example for both, the possible strength or failure of the respective order.

as partly expressing a *hegemonic* construct. It faces its greatest challenge where former counter-hegemonic normative forces gain the constitutional position to rewrite the constitutional order in their favor revealing the volatile character of the foundational consent and the influence of force on its construction and preservation.

Works cited

Albert, Richard, "The Cult of Constitutionalism," *Florida State University Law Review* 2 (2012): 373-416.

Bagehot, Walter, *The English Constitution*, introduced and published by R. H. S. Crossman, Ithaca, New York: Cornell University Press, 1963 (1867).

Carothers, Thomas, "The End of the Transition Paradigm," *Journal of Democracy* 1 (2002): 5-21.

Dahl, Robert, *A Preface to Democratic Theory*, Chicago: Chicago University Press, 1956.

Denninger, Erhard, "Nachwort," in *Sicherheit, Vielfalt, Solidarität. Ein neues Paradigma des Verfassungsrechts?*, Symposium zum 65. Geburtstag Erhard Dennigers am 20. Juni 1997, ed. Johannes Biezer and Hans-Joachim Koch, Baden-Baden: Nomos 1998, pp. 137-150.

Foucault, Michel, *The History of Sexuality: An Introduction*, trans. Robert Hurley, Harmondsworth: Penguin, 1978.

Glaser, Henning, "Multiple Constitutionalizations – 'Constitutionalism and Good Governance in European-Asian Perspectives'," in *Constitutionalism and Good Governance. Eastern and Western Perspectives*, ed. Dirk Ehlers, Henning Glaser and Kittisak Prokati, Baden-Baden: Nomos, 2014, pp. 13-61.

Habermas, Jürgen, *Der philosophische Diskurs der Moderne*, Frankfurt a.M.: Suhrkamp 1985.

Harris II, William F., "Constitution of Failure. The Architectonics of a Well-Founded Constitutional Order," in *The Limits of Constitutional Democracy*, ed. Jeffrey Tullis and Stephen Macedo, Princeton, NJ: Princeton Univ. Press, 2010, pp. 66-87.

Hirschl, Ran, *Constitutional Theocracy*, Cambridge, MA: Havard University Press, 2010.

Kautz, Steven, Arthur Melzer, Jerry Weinberg and M. Richard Zinman, "Introduction: The Idea of Constitutionalism," in *The Supreme Court and the Idea of Constitutionalism*, ed. Steven Kautz, Arthur Melzer, Jerry Weinberg and M. Richard Zinman, Philadelphia: University of Pennsylvania Press, 2009, pp. 1-11.

Levinson, Sanford, *Constitutional Faith*, Princeton and Oxford: Princeton University Press, 2011 (1988).

Loewenstein, Karl, *Political Power and the Governmental Process*, Chicago: University of Chicago Press, 1957.

Neidhardt, Friedhelm, "Formen und Funktionen gesellschaftlichen Grundkonses, " in *Bundesverfassungsgericht und gesellschaftlicher Grundkonsens*, ed. Gunnar Volker Schuppert and Christian Bumke, Baden-Baden: Nomos, 2000, pp. 15-30.

Rosannvallon, Pierre, *Counter Democracy – Politics in an Age of Distrust*, Cambridge: Cambridge University Press, 2008.

Schmitt, Carl, *Constitutional Theory*, London: Duke University Press, 2008 (1928).

Simson, Werner von, "Zur Theorie der Legitimität," in *Festschrift für Karl Loewenstein: aus Anlass seines achtzigsten Geburtstags*, ed. Henry Steele Commager, Günther Doeker, Ernst Fraenkel et al., Tübingen Mohr Siebeck, 1971, pp. 459-473.

Sunstein, Cass R., *Why Society Needs Dissent*, Cambridge, MA: Havard University Press, 2003.

Tully, James, *Strange Multiplicity. Constitutionalism in an Age of Diversity*, Cambirdge: Cambridge University Press, 1995.

Urbinati, Nadia, "Representative Democracy and its Critics," in *The Future of Representative Democracy*, ed. Sonja Alonso, John Keane and Wolfgang Merkel, Cambrideg, Cambridge University Press, 2011, pp. 23-49.

Wefer, Matthias, *Kontingenz und Dissens. Postheroische Perspektiven des politischen Systems*, Wiesbaden: Vahlen, 2004.

Conflict and Consent in the Constitutional Order of Italy: Lessons for (and from) Thailand?

Jörg Luther

A. Constitutional History as a Starting Point for Comparative Dialogue

The argument of this conference could have been formulated from a Western point of view that consent and order are not necessarily synonymous with societal harmony. If we look from Asia to modern Western societies, conflict seems to precede and stay with consent, especially in the constitutions of the post-authoritarian European democracies what have the shared value of preventing totalitarianism.

Even from the Italian point of view, conflicts played a fundamental role during the nation building process. The Italian State was founded around 150 years ago as a national unitary state governed by a constitutional and confessional monarchy. The national history of Italy was early on characterized by tensions and more or less open conflicts between supporters of monarchists and republicans, secularism and Catholicism, the industrial North and the agrarian South, liberalism and authoritarianism, right wing fascism and left wing socialism or communism, military interventionism and pacific neutralism etc. These conflicts have medieval roots in the European clash between Emperors and Popes, later in the diatribes between Guelphs and Ghibellines that have inspired the classic theories of monarchy and republic in the classical thought of Dante and Machiavelli. This specific "divisivity"[1] of Italy is what historians and politicians rediscover from time to time as a fundamental element of the national political culture. This is also the case of the "transition" post 1989. The shift from proportionality and extreme multipartitism to a majoritarian electoral system with an imperfect bipolarism has rendered the divisivity more visible, increasing the main areas of conflict outlined in the following analysis.

---

1 Nucci and Loggia, eds., *Due nazioni. Legittimazione e delegittimazione nella storia dell'Italia contemporanea,* 2003.

But does it make sense to study the Italian constitution in Thailand? Thailand is proud to be the least colonized country of South-East Asia.[2] Even if the "Phra Thammasat" has been integrated by civil and commercial codes drafted under Belgian advisers,[3] it is perceived as a country that prefers Buddhist harmony to divisive political conflict.[4] The "physique de la servitude", described by *Montesquieu* as a natural condition of the Asian cultures, has not precluded Thailand to become one of the first Asian countries open for ideas of Western "constitutionalism" and democracy.[5]

Still today, teachers of constitutional comparative law are sceptical about the perspectives of a truly intercultural dialogue. European and Asian political empires and legal cultures are often seen as having more differences than similarities. So what can Thailand and Italy learn from each other? Could Thailand learn to live with political conflicts through institutions of democracy and the rule of law? Could Italy learn the virtues of duty and harmony? Notwithstanding the enormous social, cultural and economical differences between them, there are many similarities between *Thaksin Shinawatra* and *Silvio Berlusconi*, as echoed by *Tom Ginsburg's* recent study on the "postpolitical" constitution of Thailand.[6] Indeed, constitutionalism is no longer a national devise, but a worldwide common learning process that is promoted both by the European Union and by the ASEAN Charter commitment for "adherence to the rule of law, good governance, the principles of democracy and constitutional government" (Article 2 [2g] ASEAN Charter). The experiences of globalization demand for new common patterns of law and politics under constitutions that are devoted not simply to upholding the authority of national states and powers, but also to facing the new societal challenges of inclusion, innovation and security. *Andrew Harding's* play for a "sympathetic

2 See Mezzetti, *Teoria e prassi delle transizioni costituzionali e del consolidamento democratico*, 2003, p. 801.

3 See Hooker, *A Concise Legal History of South-East Asia*, 1978, pp. 25 ff., 183 ff.

4 See Engel, *Tort, Custom and Karma*, 2010, pp. 153 ff.

5 See Tania Groppi, "The Codification of Rights in the Thailand Constitution: A Comparative Point of View," 2007, accessible at http://www.unisi.it/dipec/en/agora.php; Harding and Leyland, *The Constitutional System of Thailand*, 2011, p. 12, favours the Westminster model.

6 See Ginsburg, "Constitutional Afterlife: The Continuing Impact of Thailand's Post-Political Constitution," 2009, pp. 83 ff.

engagement" with the "New Asian Constitutionalism"[7] suggests that there are not just technologies of power framing in circulation. European and Asian countries can learn from each other about the interdependence of economic, cultural and constitutional development.

The exchange of constitutional experiences is impossible without a clear understanding of the relevant theories of the constitution. In order to design the lines of "conflict" and the institutions of "consent" within the constitutional order of a country, the Italian science of constitutional law is used to distinguish the written constitution of 1947 from its substantial counterpart and context, the so called "material constitution" or "the material and spiritual forces that hold together a social and political organisation in stable relationships."[8] This material constitution is the basis of the constitution making power and the condition of the validity, primacy and stability of the written constitution. It can be seen as a sort of basic constitutional order. The dynamics of the material constitution are studied both by political and by legal sciences, but constitutional history seems to be the best way to approach both the written constitution and its context.[9] The following pages will therefore start from a reading of the Italian constitution text in its historical context from a (merely virtual) contemporary Thai perspective. The paper will end with an experimental reading of the Constitution of Thailand from an Italian perspective.

B. The Original Basic Consensus: From the Failure of Monarchy to the Myth of "Resistenza"

"Italy is a democratic republic, founded on work. Sovereignty belongs to the people, which exercises it in the forms and within the limits of the Constitution." (art. 1) The constitutional discourse starts with the name of Italy, originally a geographical denomination that expanded during Roman Empire from Calabria in the south of the peninsula to the northern provinces *(italicae)*. Since the revolutions of the modern age, Italia is the name of a "nation", an allegorical personification of the spirit of

7 Harding, "Asian Law, Public Law, Comparative Law Stir-Fry: Theory and Method Considered," 2008, pp. 19 ff.

8 Mortati, *La costituzione in senso materiale*, 1998; See also Crisafulli, "Costituzione," 1975, pp. 1030 ff.

9 See Pinelli and Dogliani, "Italien," 2007, pp. 273 ff.

citizenship.[10] The Italian national state was founded much later, in 1861, when the powerful Kingdom of Sardinia transformed itself through annexations and plebiscitary acts in the Kingdom of Italy. From a formal point of view, no revision occurred to the constitutional statutes adopted during the European revolutions of 1848, just the entitlement of the laws to the King was changed to "by Grace of God and the will of the Nation".[11] The very short "statute" of the constitutional monarchy had been made by the advisers of the House of Savoy, but interpreted by Cavour and the liberal elites as a flexible constitution based on elastic principles. The guarantee of the catholic religion as the "sole religion of the State" (art. 1) could not avoid the incorporation of the State of the Pope in 1871. The "Monarchical Representative Government" (art. 2) was more closed to the French type of a King that "reigns and governs", but became *de facto* a semi-parliamentary form of government with a parliament that could weaken the powers of the King, holding responsible the ministers he appointed and getting re-elected by the people in case of dissolution. The constitution was flexible and the British model of democratization was not excluded. Since no freedom of association was granted, fascism could establish an authoritarian and totalitarian regime based on corporatism.

The failure of the monarchy was caused by the refusal to defend the constitution against the fascist coup d'état in 1922 through a declaration of the state of emergency as requested by the government. On the one hand, the King did not exercise veto powers in order to prevent the fascist dictatorship and signed even the laws for the persecution of Hebrews (1938). He accepted the titles of "Emperor of Ethiopia" as an outcome of the war of Abyssinia (1936), of "First Marshal of the Empire", the same title conferred to Mussolini in derogation to the supreme command clause of the Statute (art. 5), and of King of Albania (1939), before entering into second World War (1940). On the other hand, the King supported in 1943

---

10 Dante, *Purgatorio*, canto 6: "Ahi serva Italia, di dolore ostello, nave sanza nocchiere in gran tempesta, non donna di province, ma bordello! (76ss.). – Ché le città d'Italia tutte piene son di tiranni, … (124)." [Ah! servile Italy, grief's hostelry! A ship without a pilot in great tempest! No Lady thou of Provinces, but brothel!" – "For all the towns of Italy are full of tyrants, ..."]

11 See Colombo, *Storia costituzionale della monarchia italiana*, 2001; Martucci, *Storia costituzionale dallo Statuto Albertino alla Repubblica (1848-2001)*, 2002; Volpe, *Storia costituzionale degli italiani*, 2009; Ghisalberti, *Storia costituzionale d'Italia 1848-1948*, 1974.

another coup d'état, ordered the arrest of *Mussolini* and established a government in the south at Brindisi that still excluded the antifascist opposition and continued war with Germany and Japan. He left the army without any command when the government negotiated a ceasefire with the US-troops, so that Germany occupied the country and created a concurring Italian Social Republic in Verona faced by "Resistenza".

When the King agreed to suspend his own power and appointed his son and successor as "Luogotenente del Regno" (Lieutenant of the Reign) during the election of the new constituent assembly in 1944, the monarchy was still supported by *Churchill* and the US-government. The situation in the country was completely changed by the so called "three wars": the war against the foreign occupying forces, the war of antifascism against fascism and the war of the working class against capitalism.[12] The national identity was destroyed, the Patria was no longer the land of the fathers, just a land of nobody. The constitution making procedure was the only way to find a road back to peace and to find a new "resurgence" (Risorgimento). The elections for the assembly were combined with a referendum about the monarchy itself. The King tried to influence the choice by his unilateral decision to abdicate in favour of his son Umberto, but a thin majority of the people opted for the Republic favoured by most liberal, socialist, communist and catholic forces within the Committees of the National Liberation.[13] When Umberto left the country, the referendum was perceived as the beginning of a new era founded on the failure of monarchy and the myth of "Resistenza".[14] The transitory and final provisions of the Constitution prohibited any royal descendants from returning to Italy, a provision that was abrogated only in 2002.

The basic consensus of the new constitutional order implemented the will to learn from the failure of the monarchical Statute, to live in peace with the Catholic Church and to reshape institutions and society moving away from fascism. The Constituent Assembly was not controlled by a single party and reached an historic compromise between catholic, liberal,

---

12 See Pavone, *Una guerra civile: Saggio storico sulla moralità della Resistenza*, 1991.

13 See Franceschini, Guerrieri and Monina, (eds.), *Le idée costituzionali della Resistenza*, 1997. See also the projects of Galimberti and Trentin in http://www.dircost.unito.it/altriDocumenti/documenti.shtml#XX_secolo.

14 Nevertheless, the constitution making assembly rejected the proposal to recognize the right to resistance, see Buratti, *Dal diritto di resistenza al metodo democratico*, Milano 2006.

socialist and communist components that was upheld even when the left wing parties have been excluded from government. The new Constitution of 1947 lasted longer than the Statute of 1848 and declared new fundamental principles for a democratic republicanism with the purpose to unite all parties. In order to be more flexible, the new Constitution created instruments of self-guarantee such as the Constitutional Court and a specific procedure of revision. In order to rationalize the parliamentary form of government, to stabilize the government and to prevent the degenerations of parliamentarism, the new President was authorized to represent unity, to nominate the members of government and to decide on the dissolution of parliament. The centralism of the executive and legislative power was reduced through the creation of regional authorities and the independence of the judiciary was increased through the independence of the High Council of the Judiciary. The main part of the basic consensus was construed through the system of constitutional rights established within the first part of the constitutional texture, including social and political rights.

C. A Republic Founded on Labour: From Social Rights to Financial Crisis

The democratic Republic was founded on labour, not necessarily directed to a socialist form of state, but also not to a capitalist form of society. The Italian constitution declared not just principles of social justice, but more social rights than other Western European constitutions. The Republic recognized on the one hand the "inviolable" rights of the human being not restricted to liberties, even "in the social groups where he expresses the own personality", on the other hand "imperative duties of political, economical and social solidarity" (art. 2). Social rights are grounded in "equal social dignity" and a specific guarantee of substantial freedom and equality: "It is the duty of the Republic to remove those obstacles of an economic and social nature which, really limiting the freedom and equality of citizens, impede the full development of the human person and the effective participation of all workers in the political, economic and social organization of the country." (art. 3 sect. 2) Effective participation has long been construed as participation through conflict, justifying strikes even for political objectives and within public services.[15]

The first social right is the right to work: "The Republic recognizes the right of all citizens to work and promotes those conditions which will make this right effective. Every citizen has the duty, according to his possibilities and individual choice, to carry out an activity or a function which contributes to the material or spiritual progress of society." (art. 4) The right to work can not be legally enforced as a right to get an employment, but a great political question today is whether the choice of the legislator to grant a right to be reintegrated into work in case of unlawful dismissal (except for small enterprises) has to be reversed in order to promote more flexibility in the workforce. This right to get reintegrated is not directly from the constitution, but was created in the "Statute of workers" (1970) in order to resolve social conflict at the time. Still a decade ago, a referendum that aimed to set a payment in lieu of actual reintegration failed.[16]

The social conflicts are necessary and allowed, but work and capital imply both economic and social duties and have to contribute to the progress of society. They have to serve society, as specified by a clause that precedes the right of property: "Private economic initiative is free. It cannot be conducted in conflict with public weal or in such manner that could damage safety, liberty, and human dignity. The law determines appropriate planning and controls so that public and private economic activity is given direction and coordinated to social objectives." (art. 41) The partially Europeanized economic constitution is based on principles of freedom of investments and of freedom of competition, but the fundamental principle is work, not the market. This choice has been criticized and the last government presented a constitutional reform proposal in order both to enlarge the freedom of initiative to a freedom of economic activity and to establish a duty of loyal cooperation between citizens and public administration.[17]

---

15 Corte costituzionale, sent. 124/1962, 290/1974.

16 Corte costituzionale, sent. 46/2000.

17 See Luciani, "Unità nazionale e struttura economica. La prospettiva della Costituzione repubblicana," 2011, pp. 636 ff., available also at http://www.associazionedeicostituzionalisti.it/sites/default/files/bandigare/Relazione%20Luciani-1.pdf.

The history of social rights in Italy has shown that those rights have always been a source of social conflicts and political competition, being conditioned by the choices of the law and budget makers. Nevertheless there has been a large consensus at least on the principles of social justice and even the Constitutional Court has taken them seriously, declaring unconstitutional legislative exclusion from benefits related to social rights such as health care, social security etc.[18]

The human development indices for the fulfilment of economic and social rights show Italy leading for the right to health (2d) and increasing life expectation, but it is less advanced for the right to education and the right to work.[19] There is still a gap between northern and southern regions, urban and rural local services. The constitutional revision of 2001 has therefore reserved to the State legislation the "determination of the basic level of benefits relating to civil and social entitlements to be guaranteed throughout the national territory."

Nevertheless, social rights and substantial equality have a specific financial impact and need enforcement of the duties of solidarity. "The system of taxation shall be based on criteria of progression." (art. 53) The Constitutional Court has tried to limit its activism when declaring *lacunae* in spending laws, but the constitution did not provide sufficient limitations and guarantees against the expansion of public debt. Italy joined the monetary union being highly indebted, mostly to its own citizens (public debt/PIL 1981: 60,1 %, 1991: 98,6%, 1994: 121,8 %) and reaching a consensus that public debt has to decrease steadily. The financial crisis has rendered it impossible to prosecute this trend of stabilization (2007: 103,6%, 2011: 120 %). In order to resolve the monetary crisis, the European Union has recommended and the parliament has decided to follow the German, Swiss and US-States model of a constitutional reform that creates guarantees for of substantial equilibrium of public finances (balanced budget), but no political party would promote a plan of public

---

18 See Colapietro, *La giurisprudenza costituzionale nella crisi dello Stato sociale*, 1996; Giorgis, *La costituzionalizzazione dei diritti all'uguaglianza sostanziale*, 1999; Salazar, *Dal riconoscimento alla garanzia dei diritti sociali*, 2000; Bifulco, *L'inviolabilità dei diritti sociali*, 2003 .

19 See ESRF-2 Index and Component Rights, http://hdr.undp.org/en/reports/global/hdr2010/seminars/title,20003,en.html.

debt reduction that could compromise the economic growth and the social welfare of the nation.[20]

D. Democracy and the Catholic Church: From "Christian Democracy" to Postsecular Conflicts

Catholicism, socialism and liberalism were in agreement for a social state with market economy, yet the principal constitutional quandary regarding the role of religion in the state still remained. The compromise formula with elements of "separation and cooperation" reached by the constitution makers was included in the fundamentals of the constitution:

> The State and the Catholic Church are, each within its own order, independent and sovereign. Their relations are regulated by the Lateran Treaties. Changes to the Treaties accepted by both parties do not require the procedure for constitutional amendment. (art. 7)
>
> All religious confessions are equally free before the law. Religious confessions other than Catholic have the right to organize in accordance with their own statutes, in so far as they are not in conflict with Italian laws. Their relations with the State are regulated by law on the basis of an accord between the respective representatives. (art. 8)

Nevertheless, the Lateran Treaties negotiated with the fascist government in 1929 – when the State was still based on Catholicism as the religion of the State – were revised only in 1984, when the hegemony of the party of Christian Democracy – the holder of the relative majority – began its decline. An agreement with the Buddhist Union was signed in 2007 but ratified only in 2012 by the legislature and as yet, no negotiations have been started with Islamic confessions that still have to face political resistance wherever they ask to build a mosque.

However, the conflicts between the different religions have been less intensive than the ideological conflicts between the catholic clergy and

20 The new Article 81 of the Constitution orders that the state budget must maintain "balance between revenues and spending, keeping in mind averse and favourable phases within the economic cycle." The impact on social rights is highlighted now for example by Tega, "I diritti sociali nella dimensione multilivello tra tutele giuridiche e politiche e crisi economica".

laicist movements and parties. The church authorities defended religious values as guidelines in elections and threatened religious sanctions for choices considered repugnant to catholic ethics, especially in bioethics. The laicism is fighting for the secularization of civil law and against the privileges of the clergy, particularly against tax exemptions. On the one hand, the liberal call for relativism has been denounced as a support for anti-humanitarian ideologies close to totalitarianism. On the other hand, the call for religious truth and absolute values even during election campaigns has been considered detrimental to democracy. The church lost the referendums against the laws that permitted divorce and abortion, the laicist radical party lost the referendum against the law that restricted artificial insemination.

The Constitutional Court has recognized freedom of conscience and laicality (laicità) as a supreme principle of the constitutional order that can even override the Lateran Treaties,[21] but the administrative judges upheld the administrative regulations that impose the exhibition of the catholic religious symbol of crucifix in public schools where normally also elections are hold.[22] Nevertheless, if the crucifix has to be upheld as a symbol for Christian values on the basis of laicality, school education shall conserve respect for neutrality towards religion and help to understand that it symbolizes first of all human dignity.

In any case, there is no political majority for a legislative decision in favour of or contrary to the exhibition of the crucifix. Since the dissolution of the leading party of "Democrazia Christiana" (Christian Democracy) in the 1990s, political Catholicism is represented by a plurality of parties acting in both camps of the new political bipolarism. There is still a bipartisan catholic majority in parliament for legislation with specific religious interest, but there is not a clear catholic majority for a stable government of the majoritarian democracy.[23]

The constitutional compromise designed a "separation without a wall" and "cooperation without interference". Today there might be a "post-

---

21 Corte costituzionale, sent. 203/1989.

22 European Court of Human Rights, Lautsi vs. Italian Republic, 18 March 2011, http://www.echr.coe.int/echr/resources/hudoc/lautsi_and_others_v__italy.pdf.

23 See Rusconi, *Der säkularisierte Staat im postsäkularen Zeitalter*, 2010; Zagrebelsky, *Scambiarsi la veste: Stato e Chiesa al governo dell'uomo*, 2010; Associazione italiana dei costituzionalisti, *Annuario 2007: Problemi pratici della laicità agli inizi del secolo XXI*, 2008; Ferrari, *La libertà religiosa in Italia. Un percorso incompiuto*, 2012.

secular" constellation with persisting conflicts between religions and laicist forces, but neither a new marriage nor a definitive divorce between the State and the Catholic religion can be foreseen. There is first of all a common crisis of vocations, because the church and the political class are both in search of regeneration.

E. The Struggle for a new Electoral Law: From a Consociativist "First" to a Majoritarian "Second" Republic?

Italy has a long history of electoral reforms and electoral law is considered the most flexible part of constitutional law. Proportionality was introduced in 1919, but changed under fascism in 1924 through a rule that provided a 2/3 majority of seats to the most voted list if supported by more than 25 % of the valid votes. The Constituent Assembly was elected again on the basis of a proportional system without correctives. In 1953 another reform law granted a majority of 65% of the seats to the list or to the coalition that would have reaches 50 % of the valid votes, but the rule was never implemented and was later abrogated.

For a long time, the proportional system has been considered appropriate for the so called "consociative democracy" with a multiparty system and large coalitions in more or less short living governments, always guided by the Democrazia Christiana. These coalitions were initially based on a "*conventio ad excludendum*" against extreme leftist or rightist parties that could not be excluded from parliament but only from government. In the seventies, even the communist party cooperated by supporting a government of national unity with the mission to face terrorism.

In 1991 a referendum eliminated the 65% quorum requested for direct election of members of Senate and created by this way a mixed system, majoritarian for two-thirds and proportional for about one-third of the seats of the Senate. This system has been revised and extended by the legislator to the first chamber election. In 2000, a referendum for definitive abolition of proportionality failed. In 2005, a new reform again designed a proportional system which corrected by both "barring" clauses and the award of a "majority premium" (of 340 of 630 seats in the first Chamber and 55% of the seats in each regional constituency of the Senate) for the list or coalition that obtains most valid votes. The lists are blocked and have to indicate a candidate for the premiership. No more individual preferences can be expressed.

The result of these reforms and similar innovations in regional and local elections has been a complete change of the party system from multipartitism to an imperfect bipolarism in a so called "second Republic".[24] The traditional parties that negotiated the constitutional compromise, Christian Democrats, the Socialist and Communist party are no more represented in Parliament and new parties with more populist identity[25] (regionalist: Lega; enterprise: Forza Italia; postfascist: Alleanza Nazionale; postcommunist: Rifondazione communist; judicialist: Italia dei valori; anti-partitocracy: Movimento 5 Stelle) have been founded and merged (Partito democratico, Popolo della libertà). The new bipolarism has weakened the centre and maintained the right/left divisions, but the cohesion of the coalitions has not been strengthened.

On the one hand, democratic alternation has become more frequent. New generations have entered into politics and a greater variety of parties has attempted to gain popular support. The duration of governments has increased. On the other hand, elections have become more a rite of punishment or jubilation for the leaders than a discussion of the issues. A personalization of power has taken place, but the work of parliamentarians is perceived as less dignified and the form or style of government has been perceived to become more and more presidential.[26] The number of deputies creating new groups (and parties) in parliament or joining the so called "mixed group of independent members of parliament" is rising. The use of the vote of confidence is more frequent and the majorities within the two chambers are often diverging. The hope to give more power to electors and to facilitate innovation is contrasted by the fear of giving less security to minorities and having a less inclusive society. Elections still have a high participation score, but the presidency of the first chamber is no longer reserved to the main group of opposition.

We don't know whether the shift from multiparty consociativism towards majoritarianism still has a sufficient consensus, but the reform of 2005 is perceived by most constitutional lawyers as unconstitutional and even the political parties today agree on the need of a new legislation.

Since the Italian system of constitutional justice focussed on incidental control over legislation and the final decision on elections validity is

---

24 Sartori, *Seconda Repubblica? Si, ma bene*, 1992.

25 See Tarchi, *L'Italia populista: dal qualunquismo ai girotondi*, 2003.

26 See Pizzorusso, *La Costituzione ferita*, 1999; Giovine, ed., *La presidenzializzazione degli esecutivi nelle democrazie contemporanee*, 2007.

reserved to the parliament itself, the Constitutional Court is practically unable to control the constitutionality of the existing electoral laws. The Constitutional Court did not permit two referenda for the abrogation of the reform of 2005 because electoral laws are constitutionally necessary and the abrogation of abrogated laws could not imply a revival of the abrogated legislation. On that occasion, the Court used a diplomatic *obiter dictum* for declaring itself not empowered to control the constitutionality of the law of 2005, notwithstanding "the necessity to carefully take into consideration the problematic aspects, especially the allocation of a majority premium in the House of Deputies and the Senate without any minimum of votes and/or seats to be reached."[27] The message is clear, but even analogous messages regarding media regulations lack of sufficient guarantees of pluralism and of equal access during electoral campaign (*par condicio*) had only partial success.[28]

The future of the electoral law will be decided again by political parties. The coalition supporting the government of Mr. *Monti* has reached a fragile consensus for a reform in favour of a proportional system similar to the German and Spanish ones, based on regional constituencies and a distribution of seats that would exclude minor parties (with barring effects from 5 to 7 %). The electoral reform would be connected with a constitutional reform: The number of members of parliament would be reduced, the second Chamber would be rendered more an instrument of territorial representation (Senato federale) and the prime minister would get more power and could be removed only by a vote in parliament that gives a majority to a successor.[29] The so called second Republic of the majoritarian rule could be transformed into a third Republic based on an electoral system more similar to the other systems on the European continent. But the new consensus has been weakened by Mr. *Berlusconi's*

---

27 Corte constituzione, sent. n. 13/2012.

28 See Venice Commission, *Opinion on the Compatibility of the Laws "Gasparri" and "Frattini" of Italy with the Council of Europe Standards in the Field of Freedom of Expression and Pluralism of the Media*, 2005, available at http://www.venice.coe.int/webforms/documents/?pdf=CDL(2005)009rev-e.

29 The Government's initiative AS 2941 (4 October 2011), available at http://www.riformeistituzionali.it/documentazione/riforme-istituzionali/le-riforme-costituzionali/le-iniziative-del-governo.aspx

recall of the option of a French-styled semi-presidential form of government.[30]

F. The Separation of Politics From Justice: From Partitocracy to Juristocracy?

Italy is a civil law country with ordinary and administrative courts very similar to the French model. The career of judges and public prosecutors is separated from the career of other lawyers. Their independence was developed by reforms and ideas of the self-government of the Association of Judges since 1907[31], but reversed by the fascist regime that obtained the anticipated retreatment of the President of the Supreme Court (Corte di cassazione). The Constitution of 1947 has recognized judiciary as "an order that is autonomous and independent of all other powers" (art. 104). The Superior Council of the Judiciary shall be mainly elected by the judges and empowered to decide on recruitment, career, disciplinary sanctions and other questions involving independence. Public prosecutors have the duty to carry out all criminal proceedings (art. 112) and have been rendered independent from the Ministry of Justice.[32]

---

30 The elections of 2013 gave a majority of seats in the first Chamber to a coalition that reached less than 30 %, but no majority in the second Chamber.

31 For the historical role of one the fathers of the Constitution in the struggle for indipendence see Barbera, "Calamandrei e l'ordinamento giudiziario: una battaglia su più fronti," 2006, vailable at www.forumcostituzionale.it.

32 For history see Bruti Liberati and Pepino, *Autogoverno o controllo della magistratura. Il modello italiano di Consiglio superiore?*, 1998; Guarneri, *Magistratura e politica in Italia. Pesi senza contrappesi*, 2003; Violante, *Magistrati*, 2009; under legal aspects Ferri, *Magistratura e potere politico: la vicenda costituzionale dei mutamenti del sistema elettorale e della composizione del Consiglio*, 2005; Associazione italiana dei costituzionalisti, *Annuario 2004. Separazione dei poteri e funzione giurisdizionale*, 2008; Zanon and Biondi, *Il sistema costituzionale della magistratura*, 2008; Campanelli, ed., *Controllare i giudici? (Cosa, chi, come perché). Atti del convegno di studi (Lecce, febbraio 2008)*, 2009; Violante, *Magistrati*, 2009; Pace et al., (eds), *Problemi attuali della giustizia in Italia*, 2010; Piana and Vauchez, eds., *Il Consiglio superiore della magistratura. Le istituzioni pubbliche in Italia*, 2012. See also within the Council of Europe Raffaele Sabato, "Judiciary and Media," 2011, available at http://www.venice.coe.int/webforms/documents/default.aspx?pdffile=CDL-UDT %282011%29006-e

The rule of law, translated into the "principle of legality", has made some progress under the republican constitution, notwithstanding magistrates have been killed by the mafia and through terrorism.

Tensions between the political class and judiciary have grown at such times as when judges challenged the corruption and illicit forms of financing political parties, practises stimulated by a referendum that abolished direct public funding and favored the absence of specific legal rules for parties, yet still organized as non recognized private associations. The degeneration of parliamentarism into "partitocracy" and the moral death of the so called "first Republic" were denounced in the nineties during the so called "tangentopoli" moment when the majority of parliamentarians were involved in criminal proceedings for corruption and illegal financing of political parties.[33]

The constitutional mechanism for separating politics from justice entered in crisis and the constitutional regulation of parliamentary immunity changed (art. 68). Politicians protested for a syndrome of "political justice" and criticized judicial decisions even without reading the motivation behind the rulings. Prosecutors and judges defended their action through the mass media and have even entered into parliamentary careers. Judicial proceedings have been extensively reported in mass media by non-specialist journalists and weakened the governments both of Mr. *Berlusconi* and Mr. *Prodi*.

The Constitutional Court gets involved by constitutional controversies between one house of parliament and a single court whether the immunity of members of parliament should be extended to libel and slander committed outside the parliament buildings.[34] The Court should decide even on the admissibility of a vote of non-confidence adopted by the parliament against the Minister of Justice[35] and declared unconstitutional two legislative acts that ordered the suspension of all criminal proceedings regarding the presidents of the constitutional authorities (Presidency of the Republic, Constitutional Court, Council of Ministers, Chambers).[36] Being

33 See Ricolfi, *L'ultimo parlamento: Sulla fine della prima Repubblica*, 1993.

34 Corte costituzione, sent. n. 10,11/2000.

35 Corte costituzione, sent. n. 7/1996.

36 Corte costituzione, sent. n. 24/2004 and 262/2009, see Luther, "Das Gesetz als Mittel zur Prozessverschleppung, die Politisierung der italienischen Justiz und die Grenzen europäischer Rechtsstaatlichkeit," 2005, pp. 350 ff; Luther, "Ein erneut verfassungswidriges Gesetz als Vorlage zur Verfassungsreform in Italien?," 2009, pp. 553 ff.

composed by judges chosen by the judges of the superior ordinary and administrative courts, the Constitutional Court itself was accused of not being neutral.

The conflict has paralyzed not only the reforms of the judiciary that preserves impartiality, promotes quality and reduces the excessive length of procedures, (which are frequently censured by the European Court of Human Rights and the Council of Europe[37]) but also the search for a legal framework of political activity that prevents corruption, promotes political correctness in cases of conflicts of interest[38] and reduces the costs of politics lowering the number and the payments for members of parliament.

A recent decision of the European Court has stated the non conformity with EU-law of the Italian law containing restrictions of civil liability of the State in respect of the judicial interpretation of law and the assessment of facts or evidence.[39] The Court has underlined that cases of judicial arbitrariness need to be determined by the legislator, but the governmental reform proposal was amended in such a way that all kinds of "evident violations of law" could render magistrates directly liable and the national association of magistrates expressed deep concern for the independence of the judges.

The conflict is ongoing[40] and both political parties and judges are loosing consensus meanwhile the administration of justice is lacking efficiency The growing need for a better reputation of the political class and a more efficient judiciary could improve a common need for a new culture of information and new forms of dialogue promoted by the President of the Republic acting as President of the Superior Council of the Judiciary.

---

37 See only *Interim Resolution CM/ResDH (2010) 224 - Execution of the Judgments of the European Court of Human Rights Concerning the Excessive Length of Judicial Proceedings in Italy*, 2010, available at https://wcd.coe.int/ViewDoc.jsp?id=1715973&Site=CM.

38 Pertici, *Il conflitto di interessi*, 2002. For an English translation of the so called Frattini Law n. 215/2004 see http://www.venice.coe.int/docs/2004/CDL(2004)093rev-e.pdf.

39 Judgment of the Court (Third Chamber) of 24 November 2011, European Commission v. Italian Republic. Case C-379/10.

40 The sentence of the Supreme Court in the Berlusconi case in 2013 risks to reverse the government of Mr. Letta.

G. The National Unity and Territorial Conflicts: From Regionalism to Federalism?

> The Republic, one and indivisible, recognizes and promotes local autonomies; implements in those services which depend on the State the fullest measure of administrative decentralization; accords the principles and methods of its legislation to the requirements of autonomy and decentralization. (art. 5)

> The Republic safeguards by means of appropriate measures linguistic minorities. (art. 6)

When the constitution was made, separatist movements operated in Sicily and Sardinia and three bilingual areas close to the frontiers (French: Vallée d'Aoste, Austrian: Südtirol, Slovenian: Friuli) demanded specific guarantees and obtained a special regional status through constitutional laws. Italian Regionalism was an intermediate solution between the unitary state and federalism, but the creation of the other 15 ordinary Regions was not a priority in the political agenda governed by strongly centralized political parties.[41] The objectives of welfare urged first of all to integrate north and south, which faced an economic gap in development that today still has not been closed. The original text of the Constitution of 1947 contained a specific clause for the question of the Italian "mezzogiorno"[42] : "To make provision for specific programmes, particularly for the development of Southern Italy and the Islands, the State allocates by law special contributions to single regions." The state preferred to administer itself the "Cassa per il Mezzogiorno" (1950) and the "ordinary" regions were definitely established only in the seventies.

The expectations on regionalism have expanded, but the legislative powers of the regions have been curtailed by restrictions imposed by the national government and legislator on the basis of the "national interest"

41 For legal aspects see Martines et al., *Lineamenti di diritto regionale*, 2008; Caretti and Tarli Barbieri, *Diritto regionale*, 2007; D'Atena, *Diritto regionale*, Torino 2010; in English Simone Pajno, "Regionalism in the Italian constitutional System," 2009, avaiable at www.dirittoequestionipubbliche.org/page/ 2009_n9 /05_studi-08_S_Pajno.pdf, and Bilancia et al., "The European Fitness of Italian Regions," 2010, avaiable at http://www.on-federalism.eu/attachments/063_ download.pdf.

42 For history see Salvemini, *Scritti sulla questione meridionale (1896-1955)*, 1955; Gramsci, *La questione meridionale (1919-1926)*, 1985.

and this has rarely been resisted by the Constitutional Court. The regional legislation could involve only administrative law, not civil or criminal law and procedure. The regions could only partially improve the economic and social development through new planning instruments for land use and public services, especially in the health sector. The Europeanization has strengthened the powers of regions, but northern regions have received more benefits from European funds than southern ones. The cooperation between regions was guaranteed mainly through the Standing Conference for Cooperation between the State, the regions and the autonomous provinces, a cooperative body of the regional governors presided by the head of national government established to discuss issues of regional interest.

In the nineties a new regional party, the Lega Nord (Northern League) demanded the creation of macro-regions and institutions of federalism, in 1996 and 1997 even through symbolic acts of secession of a land named "Padania".[43] Administrative reforms delegated more powers to the regions. The constitutional reform of 1999 introduced a model of direct election of the President of the region and a new procedure for the reform of the regional "statute", similar to the procedure of constitutional revision. Another constitutional reform in 2001 changed the chapter of the Constitution on territorial autonomies and even the concept of the Republic, no more identical with the State: "The Republic is composed of the Municipalities, the Provinces, the Metropolitan Cities, the Regions and the State." (art. 114) The legislative competencies have been revised in a form similar to a federal constitution, with a new residual competence in favour of the regional legislators and without a general limitation in favour of national interest. Nevertheless a specific exclusive competence of the State has been created in favour of the uniformity of public services related to fundamental rights (art. 117 sect. 2, let. m "determination of the essential level of benefits relating to civil and social rights to be guaranteed throughout the national territory"). A new principle of subsidiarity has been recognized and financial autonomy, moderated by an equalization fund and a state power to support the economic development of specific local authorities, has been strengthened (art. 119).[44] In order to

43 See Luther, "Die Verfassung in Zeiten des Übergangs," 2002, pp. 353 f.
44 See law n. 42/2009; Scozzese et al., eds., *Il federalismo fiscale*, 2009; Palermo et al., *Federalismo fiscale: Una sfida comparata*, 2011.

grant further opportunities of "asymmetric federalism"[45], "additional special forms and conditions of autonomy" in matters of Judges of Peace, education and environment can be transferred upon request (art. 116). Another constitutional reform for the creation of a Federal Senate with more territorial representation failed in 2005 (see par. 9) but is still part of the agenda of government as well as the question whether to abolish the intermediate level of administration of the provinces.

The constitutional reform has not yet been completely implemented and federalism remains a controversial issue. On the one side, it is perceived as an instrument of disaggregation – the Belgium experience is a warning – and as an escape from solidarity, a threat both for national unity and local autonomy, especially within metropolitan areas. On the other side, federalism could still become an instrument for upholding unity in diversity and for making solidarity sustainable, even if it is suspected to increase the public debt. In any case, the success of the Italian search for federalism depends upon the ability of the new regional authorities to offer better protection to local identities as well as to the virtues (or vices) of the traditional Italian "municipalism". Better administration and more stable finances of local government, especially the reform of provinces are main issues of the agenda of the national government today.

H. The Enlarged Basic Consensus: Europeanism and International Pacifism

> Italy rejects war as an instrument of aggression against the freedoms of others peoples and as a means for settling international controversies; it agrees, on conditions of equality with other states, to the limitations of sovereignty necessary for an order that ensures peace and justice among Nations; it promotes and encourages international organizations having such ends in view. (art. 11).

The constitutional assembly criticized the loss of territories and colonies as decided by the Peace Treaty and preferred to not favor Europe in a way that could hinder the formation of the North Atlantic Treaty Organization (NATO). Nevertheless, the European Union has long had strong bipartisan

45 See Palermo et al., eds., *Asymmetries in Constitutional Laws. Recent Developments in Federal and Regional Systems*, 2009.

consensus in Italy, from the first pamphlets of Altiero Spinelli and the Resistenza to the draft of a European Constitution Treaty signed in Rome and preceded by a referendum held in 1989.[46]

There are of course ideological differences and conflicts. Europeanization is sometimes perceived as a preference for economic freedoms detrimental for Italian social rights, or for a version of secularism incompatible with the invocation of God or of a Christian-Judaic heritage in the Union treaties, or as a promotion of juristocracy rather than bipartisan politics, or as a form of federalism that could strengthen the existing regions but weaken future devolutions. The asymmetric benefits of the Euro currency, the costs of asylum seekers and refugees coming from the Mediterranean and the French and German hegemony are endured, but the European peace and reconciliation is the sweet fulfilment of an old Italian dream. The first Communities have been founded in Rome and the Union has been anticipated by the emigration of workers from Southern Italy to Germany and other countries of Northern Europe. The French philosopher *Michel Foucault* observed that the Union has absorbed the dreams of a new (Holy or Secular) Roman Empire and traditional Italian federalists could argue that European federalism is just the first step towards a universal federalism.

The Constitutional Court has marked the separation of the national legal order from the European one and the existence of "counter-limits" for European integration in order to keep the Union adherent to the supreme principles of the Italian constitution.[47] Since 1984, the Italian

46 See the contributions of the Italian Association of Constitutionalists, *Annuario 1999: La Costituzione europea*, 2000; *Annuario 2005: L'Integrazione dei sistemi costituzionali europeo e nazionali*, 2007; Foundation CaRiPLo, *Verso la Costituzione europea*, 2001; Bifulco et al., eds., *L'Europa dei diritti*, 2001; Amato et al., (eds), *Genèse et destinée de la Constitution européenne: commentaire du Traité établissant une Constitution pour l'Europe à la lumière des travaux préparatoires et perspectives d'avenir*, 2008; Bassanini and Tiberi, *Le nuove istituzioni europee. Commento al Trattato di Lisbona*, 2010; Cantaro, ed., *Il costituzionalismo asimmetrico dell'Unione*, 2010; Guarino, *Ratificare Lisbona?*, 2008; Lucarelli and Patroni Griffi, *Dal Trattato costituzionale al Trattato di Lisbona*, 2009; Morbidelli and Donati, eds., *Una Costituzione per l'Unione europea*, 2006; Ziller, *Il nuovo trattato europeo*, 2007.

47 Corte costituzionale, sent. n. 98/1965; 183/1970 (Frontini), 170/1984 (Granital), 232/1989 (Fragd). See Corte costituzionale, ed., *La Corte costituzionale tra diritto interno e diritto comunitario*, 1991; Corte costituzionale, *Diritto comunitario europeo e diritto nazionale*, 1996; Corte costituzionale, *Diritto*

constitutional jurisprudence can be considered friendlier to Europe than the German one. In 2001, a constitutional reform translated the jurisprudence in a specific guarantee of relative primacy: "Legislative powers shall be vested in the State and the Regions in compliance with the Constitution and with the constraints deriving from EU-legislation and international obligations."

The legislator has made specific organizational and procedural provisions for the adaption of the national to European law,[48] but Italian judges and administrations still frequently ignore European Union law. The European integration policies have been strongly supported by the Italian presidents and even the recent creation of the technocratic government of Mr. *Monti*, mandated to face the financial crisis, can be considered an evidence of a spirit of Europeanism that accepts sustainable sacrifices.[49]

Furthermore, the Italian foreign policy making is strongly related to European values when acting for the ban of the death penalty, when promoting international human rights instruments and supporting a seat for the European Union within the Security Council of the United Nations. Italy is even one of the first members of the Council of Europe with Venice serving as the seat of the Council's Commission of "Democracy through Law". By effect of the constitutional reform of 2001, the Constitutional Court controls whether national legislation is compatible with the European Convention of Human Rights as construed by the jurisprudence of the Strasburg Court.[50]

The internationalization of the Italian legal order even has other aspects. The participation in NATO activities has often been controversial (e.g., in former Yugoslavia, Kosovo, Iraq, Afghanistan), but Italian military and police forces have been willing participants in multinational, EU- and UN-peacekeeping missions since the mid 20th Century.[51]

---

comunitario e diritto interno, 2008. Furthermore Cartabia, *Principi inviolabili e integrazione europea*, 1995; Falzea et al., eds., *La Corte costituzionale e le corti d'Europa*, 2003.

48 Law n. 11/2005.

49 On the other hand, the protesting "Five Stars Movement" of M. Grillo (25 % at the elections of 2013) demands for a national referendum on further integration steps.

50 Corte costituzionale, sent. n. 348, 349/2007.

51 For constitutional questions see Dogliani and Sicardi, eds., *Diritti umani e uso della forza. Profili di diritto costituzionale interno e internazionale*, 1999;

The meaning of the "repudiation of war" clause (art. 11) is of course controversial between supporters of a more soft or legal pacifism and a more radical or moral pacifism. The clause has facilitated the legal recognition of a right to objection against obligatory military service, but can not mean a prohibition of obligatory or voluntary military defence. The Constitutional Court has decided that military service and civil service are equal alternatives for the fulfilment of the sacred duty of "defence of patria" (art 52). That means not simply the defence of fatherland and of Italian citizens, but also that any military mission has to bring benefit to the constitutional values of international peace and justice integrating Italy in the international community. [52] The constitutional duties of political solidarity (art. 2) do not end at the frontier and the duty to bear arms can be extended even to non-citizens. [53] The internationalization and supra-nationalization of the tasks of military forces goes hand-in-hand with the "constitutionalization" of the military power itself: "The regulations of the armed forces are based on the democratic spirit of the Republic". (art. 52) The democratic spirit means complete subordination under civil power and guarantees of legality and constitutionality, including the respect for the human rights of soldiers and the civilian population. A military coup d'état has therefore never taken place in the history of the Italian Republic, because the constitutional values and the European integration prevented a similar choice that would imply the end of the Constitution.

I. The Development of the Italian Constitution: Success of Constitutional Justice and Failure of Constitutional Reform

The historical outline has shown that conflict and consent both coexist in the constitutional order of Italy. The Constitution has organiyed a pluralism of fundamental principles, fundamental rights, democratic institutions and legal orders to guarantee a sufficient overlapping consensus inside and outside of Italy. Of course, the many conflicts involve the Constitution itself, but the basic consensus is still valid and

---

Luther, "Military Law in Italy," 2003, pp. 427 ff; Vergottini, *Guerra e costituzione. Nuovi conflitti e sfide alla democrazia*, 2004.

52 Corte costituzionale, sent. n. 467/1991.

53 Corte costituzionale, sent. n. 172/1999.

has been enlarged towards Europeanism and international pacifism. In regards to these conflicts, constitutional law is a battle ground not only for interpretations and implementation choices, but also for reforms. From this point of view, the long life of the Italian constitution could be attributed not only to the above mentioned consociativism, but also to a success of constitutional justice and to the failure of radical constitutional reform ambitions.

The Constitutional Court has contributed to the creation of a culture of constitutional interpretation that has not always produced respect for its decisions in the short run, but maintained hope for justice in the long run. Citizens don't have direct access to it and they can't defend directly their fundamental rights, which leads to a large amount of popular referenda. In cases of alteration of the governing majority, the Court has been suspected to be more politically "conservative" and anti-majoritarian. The supporters of federalism have advocated a power for regions to participate actively in the choice of constitutional judges, but all attempts of the majority to arrange a "court packing" have failed. On the other hand, the decisions on constitutional review of legislation, often referring to a general rule of reasonableness, have realized a dialogue with the legislators and the judges that helped at least to lower the conflict level. The Court's decisions on conflicts between powers and between state and regions have moderated these kinds of conflicts and promoted loyal cooperation. One condition for this success could have been the abolition of the special jurisdiction over ministers, other conditions such as the absence of dissenting votes and a cosmopolitan dialogue with other Constitutional Courts, even at the supranational level.[54]

As for constitutional reforms, the need to strengthen the executive power and to rationalize bicameralism has been asserted by various bicameral commissions since 1983. In 1991, a message of the President of the Republic to the Parliament considered legitimate even the convocation

---

54 See from the point of view of general constitutional theory Zagrebelsky, *Principi e voti. La Corte costituzionale e la politica*, 2005; Zagrebelsky, *La legge e la sua giustizia*, 2008; Zagrebelsky, *Intorno alla legge. Il diritto come dimensione del vivere comune*, 2009; for a historical overview Cheli, *Il giudice delle leggi: la Corte costituzionale nella dinamica dei poteri*, 1996; for a synthetic introduction Luther, "Die Verfassungsgerichtsbarkeit in Italien," 2007, pp. 149 ff. See also Ferrari and Gambaro, "The Italian Constitutional Court and Comparative Law. A Premise," 2010, pp. 1 ff.; Groppi, "The Italian Constitutional Court: Towards a 'Multilevel System' of Constitutional Review?," 2010, pp. 100 ff.

of a new constituent assembly. The change of the electoral system seemed than to have weakened the Italian Constitution because it has become easier for the government to get a simple majority in the parliament and than to win a referendum in order to change the Constitution.

The parliament preferred nevertheless to establish through controversial constitutional law a specific procedure with mandatory constitutional referendum for the revision of the Constitution of powers, excluding the general principles and fundamental rights, but these procedures were ended by the dissolution of the parliament. Only a few smaller reforms have been enacted. In 2001, the Prodi government obtained a thin majority for a reform of the chapter dealing with regionalism. In 2006, an analogous attempt by the Berlusconi government to strengthen the powers of the Prime Minister, to get a federal Senate and to reform the judiciary and the Constitutional Court did not find a majority in the referendum.[55] A smaller constitutional reform that could reduce the numeric consistence of both chambers (630+315) and create a "federal" Senate could be included in a package with the electoral reform envisaged today, but the temptation to get the President of the Republic elected directly from the people is still possible and could hamper the new consensus.[56]

The failure of constitutional reform in the last decades has weakened the consensus for the old constitution in the newer generations. The new parties have not yet become co-authors of the Constitution and the Presidents of the Republic have widened their powers. The struggle for the interpretation has been surrounded by a struggle for the conservation and defence. On the one side the defenders – including the last founding fathers – praise the social warmth of the old constitution against the tyranny of the new majoritarianism, on the other side the advocates of a more liberal touch desire a new constitution, freed from the weights of catholic and communist compromises. The defenders could say: The more time is running without a reform, the more stability the constitution could gain. The modernizer could answer: The more reforms are invoked and discussed but not carried out, the more the Constitution will lose legitimacy.

55 For the defence Elia, *La Costituzione aggredita. Forma di governo e devolution al tempo della destra*, 2005.

56 The bipartisan re-election of President Napolitano in 2013 was based on an agreement to lance a new special procedure for constitutional reform prepared by a large committee of constitutional experts.

J. Lessons for or from Thailand?

Comparative constitutional law should be an intercultural dialogue that helps to learn from other experiences of development, to deepen the sustainability of legal systems and to uphold the cultural identity of nations and international regions, but also to develop common standards for international constitutionalism starting for example through periodic human rights review. We are not better than, but different and have to learn from each other. Trying therefore to get a look from the Italian perspective at the constitutional history of Thailand, a constitutional lawyer could first of all focus the high number of constitution making procedures and of authoritarian moments in Thailand and ask whether conflict and consent have yet found an stable equilibrium within the constitutional order.

The question of stability involves democracy and the position of the King. The Constitution of 1932 seems to have been inspired by the tradition of European monarchical constitutionalism open for democracy, but it had a veiled constitution making power. The Thai Monarchy could be similar to a European constitutional monarchy with just a symbolic role of "mental representation of the Nation", but it could also play a more political role of a "potestas indirecta", as a political supervisor and arbitrator that stays behind the arena, similar to the role of the Italian President. A European observer would expect him to be, if possible, protector of democracy and the constitution not unlike the Spanish King.

If one looks at the substance of the conflicts analyzed above and taking seriously the texture of the constitutions, the second observation is that the conflict lines are similar, but with some significant differences:

(1) First of all even though the Thai Constitution grants social welfare rights, it does not grant a right to strike. Economy and legislation can impose more restrictions.

(2) Secondly, meanwhile the Italian Court did not accept majority as an argument for lawmakers dealing with religion, the Thai Constitution orders the government both to "patronize and protect Buddhism as the religion of most Thai people for a long period of time" and to promote "good understanding and harmony among the followers of all religions" (sect. 79).

(3) The mixed electoral system of Thailand is based on the one side on a specific constitutional guarantee of proportionality (sect. 93), but similar to the Italian one favors bigger parties and bipolarization between red and yellow shirts and implies risks of majoritarianism and personalisation of

politics. On the other side, the Thai Constitution provides specific guarantees for media freedom and pluralism, including a prohibition that could prevent the control of a party over a newspaper, radio or television (sect. 48).

(4) Some foreign observers have noted a trend towards juristocracy, especially regarding the role and competencies of the Constitutional Court. The National Counter Corruption Commission could be another institution of political justice.

(5) Furthermore there are territorial conflicts and demands for regional autonomy even in Thailand, at least in the border regions in the south, but any federalism seems to be incompatible with the unity implied in monarchy.

(6) Perhaps for the same reason but also within the geographical context of the Southeast Asia, the provisions related to foreign affairs do not imply a principle of supranational integration developing ASEAN or a principle of a regional human rights jurisdiction.

If one looks again at the high number of constitution making procedures, the third observation is that they could have made the success of constitutional justice more difficult and ordinary procedures of constitutional reform less attractive.

If we compare the constitutional textures, we can say that the legal model of the Thai Constitutional Court is converging with the Italian one, but there are still a number of remaining differences. First of all, the Thai Constitutional Court judges are selected by a specific committee (sect. 206) and by the Senate in a way that technocracy prevails over political forces meanwhile the Italian Court entrusts the President of the Republic to find an equilibrium between the choices of the parliament and supreme courts (art. 135). Secondly, the Italian court has only restricted powers of preventive control over the constitutionality of laws (sect. 141, 154), no power to rule whether political parties are acting against the democratic constitutional order with the King as Head of the State unlike Constitutional Courts of Germany, Turkey, South Korea, Taiwan (sect. 65, 68) and no remedy for concrete human rights violations (sect. 232).[57]

57 See Leyland, "Constitutional Design and the Quest for Good Governance in Thailand," 2008, pp. 100 f. For an Italian analysis of the judgment n. 9/2549 see Pecorario, "Thailand Dangerous Coup and Asian Juristocracy: Involution or

Finally, the Italian Constitutional Court has no power to select through its President holders of constitutional offices (sect. 113) or to rule on the ending of the status of a member of parliament or a minister (sect. 91). A comparative dialogue should therefore face questions such as: Are constitutional judges better selected by technocrats or by political parties? Should they decide just on conflicts regarding laws and institutions or also on the exclusion from power of political parties and persons?

As far as constitutional amendments are regarded, further differences between both constitutions should be mentioned.

(1) First, the Thai procedure of amendment of the Constitution (sect. 291) does not use a constitutional referendum like the Italian one (art. 138).58

(2) Second, the procedure can be started by the Government and takes less time. Notwithstanding the mixed electoral system is for 80 % majoritarian, the procedure can therefore be easier used by government majority for unilateral changes. In Italy, the initiative of the government needs not the signature of the President, three months of reflection and allows the opposition to give the last word to the people. The Italian experience of an *ad hoc* procedure for organic constitutional reforms, based on constitutional laws that allowed to be a derogate form of the ordinary procedure were unhappy, because constitutional issues could not have been separated from governmental ones.

(3) Third, the substantial limits of the amendment power differ in texture, being in Italy "the form of Republic" and in Thailand both "the democratic regime of government with the King as Head of the State" and the "form of State". Under the existing constitutions, Italy can't go back to monarchy and Thailand can't go ahead to a Republic, but reforms of

---

Evolution," 2008, pp. 225 ff; Pecorario, "La 'iuristocrazia' asiatica: il golpe bianco della Corte costituzionale thailandese,", 2009, pp. 131 ff.

58 "(1) Laws amending the Constitution and other constitutional laws shall be adopted by each House after two successive debates at intervals of not less than three months, and shall be approved by an absolute majority of the members of each House in the second voting. (2) The said laws are submitted to a popular referendum when, within three months of their publication, such request is made by one fifth of the members of a House or five hundred thousand electors or five region councils. The law submitted to referendum shall not be promulgated if not approved by a majority of valid votes. (3) A referendum shall not be held if the law has been approved in the second voting by each of the Houses by a majority of two-thirds of the members."

institutions such as bicameralism and local or provincial autonomies are common opportunities.

Nevertheless, the list of unchangeable norms is open, but not empty. In Italy at least the sovereignty of the people and the inviolable human rights are excluded from constitutional amendment as well as laicality, international pacifism and other explicitly stated "fundamental principles". Even in Thailand democracy means the "sovereign power" of the Thai people (sect. 3) and leaves place for the "constitutional conventions" (sect. 7) of the people as the ultimate foundation of the democratic monarchy and of the constitution. If fundamental rights are really fundamental, at least the "crystallized promotion and protection" of them (preamble) could be grounded in similar conventions. And if Buddhism is sympathetic with equality and freedom, emphasizing peace, harmony and nonviolence, it can be the supreme source of, if not of law, at least of democratic culture (sect. 79).[59] The constitutions can be changed and customs can be lost or broken, but even the Thai constitution making power could be bound by similar fundamental principles of the constitutional State.[60] Thailand can learn from Italy and Italy can learn from Thailand that progress in constitutionalism is always possible, but not without realism.

Works cited

Amato, Giuliano, Hervé Bribosia and Bruno de Witte, eds., *Genèse et destinée de la Constitution européenne: commentaire du Traité établissant une Constitution pour l'Europe à la lumière des travaux préparatoires et perspectives d'avenir*, Brussels: Bruylant, 2008.

Associazione Italiana dei Costituzionalisti, *Annuario 1999: La Costituzione europea*, Padua: CEDAM, 2000.

Associazione Italiana dei Costituzionalisti, *Annuario 2004: Separazione dei poteri e funzione giurisdizionale*, Padua: CEDAM, 2008.

Associazione Italiana dei Costituzionalisti, Annuario 2005: *L'Integrazione dei sistemi*

59 Harding, "Buddhism, Human Rights and Constitutional Reform in Thailand," 2007, pp. 1ff; Engel and Engel, *Tort, Custom, and Karma*, p. 155.

60 See Häberle, *Europäische Verfassungslehre*, 2011, pp. 232 ff.; for the reception of European constitutional reform experiences in Turkey Luther, "Zu den Möglichkeiten einer türkischen Rezeption neuerer europäischer Verfassungsreformerfahrungen," 2012 (forthcoming).

costituzionali europeo e nazionali, Padua: CEDAM, 2007.

Associazione Italiana dei Costituzionalisti, Annuario 2007: *Problemi pratici della laicità agli inizi del secolo XXI*, Padua: CEDAM, 2008.

Barbera, Augusto, "Calamandrei e l'ordinamento giudiziario: Una battaglia su più fronti," *Rassegna parlamentare* 48 (2006): 359-393.

Bassanini, Franco, and Giulia Tiberi, *Le nuove istituzioni europee: Commento al Trattato di Lisbona*, Bologna: Il Mulino, 2010.

Bifulco, Daniela, *L'inviolabilità dei diritti sociali*, Naples: Jovene, 2003.

Bifulco, Raffaele, Marta Cartabia, and Alfonso Celotto, eds., *L'Europa dei diritti*, Bologna: Il Mulino, 2001.

Bilancia, Paolo, Francesco Palermo, and Ornella Porchia, "The European fitness of Italian Regions," *Perspectives on Federalism* 2 (2010): E-123-174.

Bruti Liberati, Edmondo, and Livio Pepino, *Autogoverno o controllo della magistratura? Il modello italiano di Consiglio superiore*, Milan: Feltrinelli, 1998.

Buratti, Andrea, *Dal diritto di resistenza al metodo democratico*, Milan: Giuffrè, 2006.

Campanelli, Giuseppe, ed., *Controllare i giudici? (Cosa, chi, come perché). Atti del convegno di studi (Lecce, febbraio 2008)*, Turin: Giappichelli, 2009.

Cantaro, Antonio, ed., *Il costituzionalismo asimmetrico dell'Unione*, Turin: Giappichelli, 2010.

Caretti, Paolo, and Giovanni Tarli Barbieri, *Diritto regionale*, 2nd ed., Turin: Giappichelli, 2007.

CaRiPLo Foundation, *Modelli giuridici ed economici per la costituzione europea*, Bologna: Il Mulino, 2001, 7 vol.

Cartabia, Marta, *Principi inviolabili e integrazione europea*, Milan: Giuffrè, 1995.

Cheli, Enzo, *Il giudice delle leggi: la Corte costituzionale nella dinamica dei poteri*, Bologna: Il Mulino, 1996.

Colapietro, Carlo, *La giurisprudenza costituzionale nella crisi dello Stato sociale*, Padua: CEDAM, 1996.

Colombo, Paolo, *Storia costituzionale della monarchia italiana*, Rome: Laterza, 2001.

Corte costituzionale, ed., *La Corte costituzionale tra diritto interno e diritto comunitario*, Milan: Giuffrè, 1991.

Corte costituzionale, ed., *Diritto comunitario europeo e diritto nazionale*, Milan: Giuffrè, 1996.

Corte costituzionale, ed., *Diritto comunitario e diritto interno*, Milan: Giuffrè, 2008.

Crisafulli, Vezio, "Costituzione," in *Enciclopedia del Novecento*, Vol. I, Rome: Istituto della enciclopedia italiana, 1975, pp. 1030 ff.

D'Atena, Antonio, *Diritto regionale*, Turin: Giappichelli, 2010.

Dogliani, Mario, and Stefano Sicardi, eds., *Diritti umani e uso della forza. Profili di diritto costituzionale interno* e *internazionale*, Turin: Giappichelli, 1999.

Elia, Leopoldo, *La Costituzione aggredita: Forma di governo e devolution al tempo della destra*, Bologna: Il Mulino, 2005.

Engel, David M., and Jaruwan S. Engel, *Tort, Custom and Karma*, Stanford: Stanford Law Books, 2010.

Falzea, Paolo, Antonino Spadaro, and Luigi Ventura, eds., *La Corte costituzionale e le corti d'Europa*, Turin: Giappichelli, 2003.

Ferrari, Alessandro, *La libertà religiosa in Italia. Un percorso incompiuto*, Rome: Carocci, 2012.

Ferrari, Giuseppe Franco, and Antonio Gambaro, "The Italian Constitutional Court and Comparative Law: A Premise," *Comparative Law Review* 1 (2010): 1-22.

Ferri, Giampietro, *Magistratura e potere politico: la vicenda costituzionale dei mutamenti del sistema elettorale e della composizione del Consiglio*, Padua: CEDAM, 2005.

Franceschini, Claudia, Sandro Guerrieri and Giancarlo Monina, eds., *Le idee costituzionali della Resistenza*, Rome: Dipartimento per l'informazione e l'editoria, 1997.

Ghisalberti, Carlo, *Storia costituzionale d'Italia 1848-1948*, Rome: Laterza, 1974.

Ginsburg, Tom, "Constitutional Afterlife: The Continuing Impact of Thailand's Post-Political Constitution," *International Journal of Constitutional Law* 7 (2009): 83-105.

Giorgis, Andrea, *La costituzionalizzazione dei diritti all'uguaglianza sostanziale*, Naples: Jovene, 1999.

Giovine, Alfonso di, ed., *La presidenzializzazione degli esecutivi nelle democrazie contemporanee*, Turin: Giappichelli, 2007.

Gramsci, Antonio, *La questione meridionale* (1919-1926), reprint Rome: Editori Riuniti, 2005.

Groppi, Tania, "The Italian Constitutional Court: Towards a 'Multilevel System' of Constitutional Review?," *Journal of Constitutional Law* 3 (2010): 100-117.

Guarino, Giuseppe, *Ratificare Lisbona?*, Florence: Passigli, 2008.

Guarneri, Carlo, *Magistratura e politica in Italia.* Pesi senza contrappesi, Bologna: Il Mulino, 2003.

Häberle, Peter, *Europäische Verfassungslehre*, 7th ed., Baden-Baden: Nomos, 2011.

Harding, Andrew, "Buddhism, Human Rights and Constitutional Reform in Thailand," *Asian Journal of Comparative Law* 2 (2007): 1-25.

Harding, Andrew, "Asian Law, Public Law, Comparative Law Stir-Fry: Theory and Methods Considered," in *Asian Constitutionalism in Transition, A Comparative Perspective*, ed. Tania Groppi, Valeria Piergigli and Angelo Rinella, Milan: Giuffrè, 2008, pp. 19-43.

Harding, Andrew, and Peter Leyland, *The Constitutional System of Thailand*, Oxford: Hart, 2011.

Hooker, M. B., *A Concise Legal History of South-East Asia*, Oxford: Oxford University Press, 1978.

Leyland, Peter, "Constitutional Design and the Quest for Good Governance in Thailand," in *Asian Constitutionalism in Transition*, ed. Tania Groppi, Valeria Piergigli and Angelo Rinella, Milan: Giuffrè, 2008, pp. 69-105.

Luciani, Massimo, "Unità nazionale e struttura economica. La prospettiva della Costituzione repubblicana," *Diritto e società* 4 (2011) : 636-719.

Lucarelli, Alberto, and Andrea Patroni Griffi, *Dal Trattato costituzionale al Trattato di Lisbona*, Naples: Edizioni scientifiche italiane, 2009.

Luther, Jörg, "Die Verfassung in Zeiten des Übergangs," *Jahrbuch des öffentlichen Rechts* 50 (2002): 331-359.

Luther, Jörg, "Military Law in Italy," in *European Military Law Systems*, ed. Georg Nolte, Berlin: de Gruyter, 2003, pp. 427-516.

Luther, Jörg, "Das Gesetz als Mittel zur Prozessverschleppung, die Politisierung der italienischen Justiz und die Grenzen europäischer Rechtsstaatlichkeit," *Europäische Grundrechte-Zeitschrift* (2005): 350-357.

Luther, Jörg, "Die Verfassungsgerichtsbarkeit in Italien," in *Verfassungsgerichtsbarkeit in Westeuropa*, ed. Christian Starck and Albrecht Weber, Vol. I, 2nd ed., Baden-Baden: Nomos, 2007, 149 ff.

Luther, Jörg, "Ein erneut verfassungswidriges Gesetz als Vorlage zur Verfassungsreform in Italien?," *Europäische Grundrechte-Zeitschrift* (2009): 553-558.

Luther, Jörg, "Zu den Möglichkeiten einer türkischen Rezeption neuerer europäischer Verfassungsreformerfahrungen," *Jahrbuch des öffentlichen Rechts* (forthcoming).

Martines, Temsitocle, Antonio Ruggeri, and Carmela Salazar, *Lineamenti di diritto regionale*, 7th ed., Milan: Giuffrè, 2008.

Martucci, Roberto, *Storia costituzionale dallo Statuto Albertino alla Repubblica (1848-2001)*, Rome: Carocci, 2002.

Mezzetti, Luca, *Teoria e prassi delle transizioni costituzionali e del consolidamento democratico*, Padua: CEDAM, 2003.

Morbidelli, Giuseppe, and Filippo Donati, eds., *Una Costituzione per l'Unione europea*, Turin: Giappichelli, 2006.

Mortati, Costantino, *La costituzione in senso materiale*, Milan: Giuffrè, 1940, reprint 1998.

Nucci, Loreto di, and Ernesto Galli della Loggia, eds., *Due nazioni: Legittimazione e delegittimazione nella storia dell'Italia contemporanea*, Bologna: Il Mulino, 2003.

Pace, Alessandro, Sergio Bartole and Roberto Romboli, eds., *Problemi attuali della giustizia in Italia*, Naples, Jovene, 2010.

Pajno, Simone, "Regionalism in the Italian constitutional System," *Diritto & Questioni Pubbliche* (2009): 625-642.

Palermo, Francesco, Carolin Zwilling and Karl Kössler, eds., *Asymmetries in Constitutional Laws. Recent Developments in Federal and Regional Systems*, Bozen: EURAC, 2009.

Palermo, Francesco, Elisabeth Alber, and Sara Parolari, *Federalismo fiscale: Una sfida comparata*, Padua: CEDAM, 2011.

Pavone, Claudio, *Una guerra civile: Saggio storico sulla moralità della Resistenza*, Turin: Bollati Boringhieri, 1991.

Pecorario, Alessio, "Thailand Dangerous Coup and Asian Juristocracy: Involution or Evolution," in *Asian Constitutionalism in Transition*, ed. Tania Groppi, Valeria Piergigli and Angelo Rinella, Milan: Giuffrè, 2008, pp. 225-237.

Pecorario, Alessio, "La 'giuristocrazia' asiatica: Il golpe bianco della Corte costituzionale thailandese," *Rivista di Studi Politici S. Pio V*, (2009): 131-157.

Pertici, Andrea, *Il conflitto di interessi*, Turin: Giappichelli, 2002.

Piana, Daniela, and Antoine Vauchez, eds., *Il Consiglio superiore della magistratura. Le istituzioni pubbliche in Italia*, Bologna: Il Mulino, 2012.

Pinelli, Cesare, and Mario Dogliani, "Italien," in *Handbuch Jus Publicum Europaeum*, ed. Armin von Bogdandy, Pedro Cruz Villalon, Peter M. Huber, Vol. I, Heidelberg: C.F. Müller 2007, pp. 273-326.

Pizzorusso, Alessandro, *La Costituzione ferita*, Bari: Leterza, 1999.

Ricolfi, Luca, *L'ultimo parlamento: Sulla fine della prima Repubblica*, Rome: La nuova Italia scientifica, 1993.

Rusconi, Gian Enrico, ed., *Der säkularisierte Staat im postsäkularen Zeitalter*, Berlin: Duncker & Humblot, 2010.

Salazar, Carmela, *Dal riconoscimento alla garanzia dei diritti sociali*, Turin: Giappichelli, 2000.

Salvemini, Gaetano, *Scritti sulla questione meridionale (1896-1955)*, Turin: Einaudi, 1955.

Sartori, Giovanni, *Seconda Repubblica? Si, ma bene*, Milan: Rizzoli, 1992.

Scozzese, Silvia, Franco Pizzetti, and Veronica Nicotra, eds., *Il federalismo fiscale*, Rome: Donzelli Editore, 2009.

Tarchi, Marco, *L'Italia populista: dal qualunquismo ai girotondi*, Bologna: Il Mulino, 2003.

Vergottini, Giuseppe de, *Guerra e costituzione. Nuovi conflitti e sfide alla democrazia*, Bologna: Il Mulino, 2004.

Violante, Luciano, *Magistrati*, Turin: Einaudi, 2009.

Volpe, Giuseppe, *Storia costituzionale degli italiani*, Turin: G. Giappichelli, 2009.

Zagrebelsky, Gustavo, *Principi e voti. La Corte costituzionale e la politica*, Turin: Einaudi, 2005.

Zagrebelsky, Gustavo, *La legge e la sua giustizia*, Bologna: Il Mulino, 2008.

Zagrebelsky, Gustavo, Intorno alla legge. *Il diritto come dimensione del vivere comune*, Turin: Einaudi, 2009.

Zagrebelsky, Gustavo, *Scambiarsi la veste: Stato e Chiesa al governo dell'uomo*, Bari: Laterza, 2010.

Zanon, Nicolò, and Francesca Biondi, *Il sistema costituzionale della magistratura*, Bologna: Zanichelli, 2008.

Ziller, Jacques, *Il nuovo trattato europeo*, Bologna: Il Mulino, 2007.

The Protection of State Interests and the Constitutional Order in German Criminal Law

Robert Esser

A. Basic Outlines, Functions and the Necessity of Protecting State Interests in Criminal Law

I. Introduction

The democratic order of a state struggles daily for public support. It is challenged by extreme, sometimes seemingly appealing views and convictions. In this war of opinions, democratic rule needs to prevail by means of arguing and persuading, not by punishing those who threaten it. However, the need to protect state interests by means of criminal law does arise in certain circumstances.

The German legislature has chosen to adopt a rather restricted approach to enacting criminal legislation to protect the state. Even if there is a penal norm protecting state interests, it is hardly ever applied.[1] That is due on the one hand to the lack of complaints and on the other hand due to the strict interpretation applied to the penal norms protecting state interests. This strict approach is demanded by the German Federal Constitutional Court (*Bundesverfassungsgericht* – BVerfG) in order to ensure a cohesive existence of the right to free speech and the state's interest to protect its dignity and identity. That marks a sharp contrast to the situation in other countries where criminal law is often applied to protect the dignity and identity of the state rather than trying to protect these interests by using the power of convincing arguments.

The best protection for the state and its institutions is the acceptance of the constitutional order by its citizens. The rule of law, as being part of this constitutional order, needs the support and acceptance of a sufficiently

---

1 Overall, there were for example 16 court decisions concerning Sec. 90a German Penal Code (StGB), thereof 5 being heard by the Federal Court of Justice (*Bundesgerichtshof*), the highest German criminal court: www.dejure.org, jurisprudence concerning Sec. 90a StGB.

high number of citizens. With the loss of this crucial support, liberalism and democracy cannot be restored, not even with the extraordinary measures allowed during a state of emergency provided for by many constitutions.[2]

II. The Function of Criminal Provisions Protecting the State

The protection of the state and its institutions is a crucial element of internal stability of society. That is why legal provisions concerning crimes against the state have a highly stabilizing symbolic meaning.

These "crimes against the state" laid down in the German Criminal Code (StGB) stress the democratic values of the state and thus provide an orientation for the citizens. In Germany, this was important especially during the aftermath of World War II as well as during the time immediately following the reunification in 1990.

As a liberal state, the Federal Republic of Germany is based on the citizens' identification with the values typified in the state symbols. These symbols thus constitute an important instrument of integration.[3]

The protection of the state by criminal law consequently is also an instrument of integration that has come to great importance especially during the conflict-laden process of "internal legal unity"[4] in reunified Germany.

Laws against criminal offences meant to protect the state and its institutions are part of the so called "symbolic criminal law" which has no great relevance in jurisdictional practice. Its intention is merely to help create a national identity.

The symbolic meaning of the crimes against the state is stressed by the location of the relevant sections in the German Penal Code. The relevant sections stand right at the beginning of the Special Part of the German Penal Code. On the other hand, it has to be mentioned that in Germany the

---

2 See Laufhütte and Kuschel, in *Leipziger Kommentar zum StGB*, 2007, Introduction to Sec. 80, para. 22; Quaritsch, *Probleme der Selbstdarstellung des Staates*, 1977, p. 11 (uses the term "Permanente Massenloyalität").

3 Decisions of the German Constitutional Court (BVerfGE), Vol. 81, p. 293, concerning the national flag.

4 Roggemann, "Von Bären, Löwen und Adlern – zur Reichweite der §§ 90a und b StGB,“ 1992, p. 937.

crimes against the state are not included in the curriculum of most state law exams organized by the federal states.

III. Necessity of Having "Crimes Against the State" in the Penal Code

Parts of the German juristic literature radically postulate the abolition of crimes against the state.[5] Others qualify Sec. 90a StGB as being a "*relict of a – speaking of criminal-policy aspects – obsolete necessity to punish*".[6] The question is thus whether a protection of the state by means of criminal law is needed.

A lack of self-defence of the state against humiliation and degrading treatment encumbers the willingness of ordinary citizens to engage in the protection of the state and the constitution – they will abstain from actively endorsing it.[7] In the end, the existence of the state is endangered; the citizens no longer trust in the state's ability to defend itself. Another effect of unhindered defamation of the state would be the diminishing of the sensibility of real and well-founded warnings of real dangers absolutely crucial to the survival of democracy. Defamation of the state and of the constitution attacks democracy by its mere existence and thereby harms internal peace and stability.[8]

The consequences of a lack of protection of the state by criminal law in the eyes of its citizens and the outstanding importance of the state interests for the people`s well-being show that the protection of the state itself, its organs and its institutions by means of criminal law is necessary. Germany's historical experience also reflects the necessity of a "well-fortified democracy"[9], e.g. the necessity of protection of the state by criminal law.

However, criminal law cannot substitute the political discussions and debates with elements of society hostile towards the constitution, but has

---

5 See Maurach and Schroeder and Maiwald, *Strafrecht: Besonderer Teil*, 2012, § 82 IV, para. 29.

6 Lippold, "Die Staatssymbole – ihre rechtliche Begründung und ihr strafrechtlicher Schutz," 1992, p. 51.

7 See Schroeder, "Probleme der Staatsverunglimpfung," 1979, p. 90.

8 See Würtenberger, "Satire und Karikatur in der Rechtsprechung," 1979, p. 311.

9 Laufhütte and Kuschel, in *Leipziger Kommentar zum StGB*, Introduction to § 80, para. 21.

to follow the *ultima ratio*-principle, e.g. only punishing criminal offences endangering the existence of the state and its institutions.

B. Criminal Offences Against the State and Protected Interests in the German Criminal Code

I. Overview

The German Penal Code (*Strafgesetzbuch – StGB*) distinguishes between various criminal offences directed against the state and its institutions: the crimes against peace, high treason, the crime of endangering the democratic rule of law (title 1, Sec. 80-92b StGB), treason and the crime of endangering the external security (title 2, Sec. 93-101a StGB), crimes against foreign states (title 3, Sec. 102-104a StGB) and finally crimes against the national defence (title 5, Sec. 109-109k StGB).[10]

High treason threatens the territorial integrity and the constitutional order of the Federal Republic of Germany and the federal states (*Länder*). The criminal offences included in chapter 3, crimes endangering the democratic rule of law, are meant to punish those kinds of endangerment of the internal security of the Federal Republic which are not executed by means of high treason but by other methods. They are meant to protect the state from subversive espionage, illegal propaganda and sabotage of the security forces as well as protecting the state and its institutions from being gravely humiliated.[11]

The principle of protection is applicable to a number of crimes against the state (Sec. 5 No. 1-4 StGB). This means that criminal offenders will be held responsible in Germany regardless of their citizenship or the location where the crime was committed. That does not apply to crimes where possible offenders necessarily need to be Germans with their permanent residence within the territorial applicability of the German Penal Code, e.g. the territory of the Federal Republic of Germany (see Sec. 5 No. 3 *lit.*

10 See Maurach and Schroeder and Maiwald, *Strafrecht: Besonderer Teil*, § 82 II, para. 9; compare for the UK, the US, Canada and Australia: Head, *Crimes Against The State – from Treason to Terrorism*, 2011.

11 See Sternberg-Lieben, in *Strafgesetzbuch, Kommentar*, 2014, Introduction to § 80, para. 3.

a StGB).[12] Within the offences against the state, the German Penal Code differentiates between the various protected interests and the ways and means of committing the crimes.

II. Protected Interests

The German Criminal Code enumerates the following protected interests:

1. Integrity of the Federal Republic of Germany (Sec. 92 para. 1 StGB)

The integrity of the Federal Republic of Germany is protected against any form of undermining.

> Section 92 German Criminal Code
>
> Definition of Terms
>
> (1) Within the meaning of this law, a person undermines the continued existence of the Federal Republic of Germany if he causes the end of its freedom from foreign domination, the abolition of its national unity, or the secession of one of its constituent territories.
>
> (2) Constitutional principles, within the meaning of this law, shall be
>
> the right of the people to exercise state power in elections and ballots and through particular organs of legislative, executive and judicial power and to elect Parliament in general, direct, free, equal and secret elections;
>
> the subjection of legislation to the constitutional order and the subjection of the executive and judicial power to law and justice;
>
> the right to form and exercise a parliamentary opposition;
>
> the possibility of dissolving the government and its responsibility to Parliament;
>
> the independence of the courts; and
>
> the exclusion of any government by force and arbitrary rule.

---

12 See Sternberg-Lieben, in *Strafgesetzbuch, Kommentar*, Introduction to §§ 80 ff., para 12.

(3) Within the meaning of this law

efforts against the continued existence of the Federal Republic of Germany shall mean efforts by supporters who actually work toward undermining the continued existence of the Federal Republic of Germany (subsection (1) above);

efforts against the security of the Federal Republic of Germany shall mean efforts by supporters who actually work toward undermining the external or internal security of the Federal Republic of Germany;

efforts against constitutional principles shall mean efforts by supporters who actually work toward abolishing, suspending the application of or undermining a constitutional principle (subsection (2) above).

Undermining as defined in Sec. 92 I StGB means:

- Abolition of the freedom from foreign domination (Sec. 92 para. 1 Var. 1 StGB), i.e. depriving the Federal Republic of Germany of its legal or factual sovereignty, e.g. the transformation of the Federal Republic into a protectorate or a satellite state.[13]
- Destruction of the territorial integrity (Sec. 92 para. 1 Var. 2 StGB): i.e. infliction of the territorial integrity of the Federal Republic of Germany, e.g. its transformation into a confederation of separate states or the transformation of a single federal state (*Land*) into a sovereign state.[14]
- Separation of an integral part of the territory of the Federal Republic of Germany (Sec. 92 I Var. 3 StGB).

2. Constitutional Order

When Sec. 80 ff. of the German Penal Code (StGB) mentions the “constitution” as a protected interest, they do not refer to the *text* of the

---

13 See Fischer, *Strafgesetzbuch*, 2014, § 92, para. 3.

14 See Sternberg-Lieben, in *Strafgesetzbuch, Kommentar*, § 92, para. 4.

German Basic Law (*Grundgesetz*) itself, but to the constitutional order, e.g. the sum of all important principles of German political life.[15]

3. Principles of the Constitution

The term “principles of the constitution” refers to what the Basic Law calls “liberal democratic order”[16] being an order “that constitutes the rule of law based on the self-determination of the (German) people governed by the will of the majority and freedom and equality while excluding any rule by force or decree”.[17]

The *principles of the constitution* are:

> Sec. 92 para. 2 No. 1 StGB: The principle of sovereignty of the people, the principle of – indirect – democracy, the principle of separation of powers and the principle of democratically held elections (Art. 20 para. 2, 28 I, 38 I, 79 para. 3 GG),
>
> Sec. 92 para. 2 No. 2 StGB: the integrity of the rule of law,
>
> Sec. 92 para. 2 No. 3 StGB: the right to form and exercise a parliamentary opposition,
>
> Sec. 92 para. 2 No. 4 StGB: the principle of parliamentary responsibility, e.g. the principles of law laid down in the constitution regulating the relation between government and parliament,[18]
>
> Sec. 92 para. 2 No. 5 StGB: the independence of the courts (Art. 97 GG),
>
> Sec. 92 para. 2 No. 6 StGB: the exclusion of any rule by force or decree.

---

15 See Maurach and Schroeder and Maiwald, *Strafrecht: Besonderer Teil*, § 82 II, para. 12.
16 Laufhütte and Kuschel, in *Leipziger Kommentar zum StGB*, § 92, para. 3.
17 Decisions of the German Constitutional Court (BVerfGE), Vol. 2, p. 12.
18 See Sternberg-Lieben, in *Strafgesetzbuch, Kommentar*, § 92, para. 10.

4. Security of the Federal Republic of Germany

External security includes the defence of the territory of the Federal Republic, the defence of the Federal Republic by means of intelligence, questions of alliance, and the balance of military, political and economical power. It does not include diplomatic relations. *Internal security* means a state of relative stability regarding the integrity of the Federal Republic and its constitution in the face of violent actions by domestic groups or forces.[19]

5. Foreign States, Sec. 102-104a StGB

Foreign states are protected by the German Penal Code as well: Foreign heads of state, members of foreign governments and heads of diplomatic missions are protected against assaults against life or limb (Sec. 102 StGB) and against insults (Sec. 103 StGB).[20] It is furthermore prohibited to destroy, damage, render unrecognizable or to commit insulting mischief with a flag of a foreign state or a national emblem of a state (Sec. 104 StGB). The crimes mentioned in Sec. 102-104a StGB are only punishable if the Federal Republic of Germany maintains diplomatic relations with the other state and reciprocity is guaranteed and was guaranteed at the time of the act[21] (Sec. 104a StGB; objective condition for the act to be punishable[22]).

To prosecute the offender, the Federal Government needs to authorize the criminal prosecution (Sec. 104a, 77e StGB; prerequisite for criminal prosecution). With the Sec. 102-104a, the German Penal Code intents to protect foreign states including their institutions and facilities as well as to

19 See Maurach and Schroeder and Maiwald, *Strafrecht: Besonderer Teil*, § 82 II, para. 15.

20 See Bavarian Administrative Court – Bayerischer VGH, *Neue Juristische Wochenschrift (NJW)* (2011), p. 793 (Satirical criticism of the Catholic Church as potential insult of the Pope as head of state of the Vatican City State); Decisions of the German Federal Administrative Court (BVerwGE), Vol. 64, p. 55, *Neue Juristische Wochenschrift (NJW)* (1982), p. 1008 (calling the Chilean government a "gang of murderers").

21 See Eser, *Strafgesetzbuch, Kommentar*, 2014, § 102, para. 1.

22 See Maurach and Schroeder and Maiwald, *Strafrecht: Besonderer Teil*, § 91 IV, para. 10.

protect the interests of the Federal Republic of Germany in having good diplomatic relations with other states.[23]

6. Protection of the Reputation of the Institutions of the Federal Republic of Germany

Sec. 90 German Criminal Code (StGB)

Defamation of the President of the Federation

(1) Whosoever publicly defames the President of the Federation, in a meeting or through the dissemination of written material (section 11 (3)) shall be liable to imprisonment from three months to five years.

(2) In less serious cases the court in its discretion may mitigate the sentence (section 49 (2)) unless the conditions of section 188 are met.

(3) The penalty shall be imprisonment from six months to five years if the act constitutes an intentional defamation (section 187) or if the offender by the act intentionally supports efforts against the continued existence of the Federal Republic of Germany or against its constitutional principles.

(4) The offence may only be prosecuted upon the authorisation of the President of the Federation.

Sec. 90 StGB intents to protect both the personal integrity of the Federal President and the reputation of the office itself (*contested*[24]). The personal integrity is subject to protection only as long as the Federal President is in office. Beyond the stated motives, Sec. 90 StGB is also meant to protect the state itself and its constitutional order. The protected interest in Sec. 90 StGB is not the ability to make decisions of the Federal President, but the symbolic meaning of his office.[25] The Federal President is protected against any form of disparagement, e.g. a grievous humiliation. Sec. 90 StGB protects the President against disparagement in private matters as well, as a separation between private and official matters seems

---

23 See Eser, *Strafgesetzbuch, Kommentar*, Introduction to §§ 102-104a, para. 2.

24 Dissenting: Maurach and Schroeder and Maiwald, *Strafrecht: Besonderer Teil*, § 84 IV 3, para. 84.

25 See Laufhütte and Kuschel, in *Leipziger Kommentar zum StGB*, § 90, para. 1.

impossible.[26] The disparagement must be grievous. Sloppy or distasteful statements may not fulfil the criteria of grievous disparagement.[27] It must be noted that the Federal President – due to his heavily exposed position in the political system – will be subject to even severe political criticism about the way he fulfils his presidential duties.[28] The disparagement has to be committed in public, during a meeting or by publishing a written statement. The offender is punished even more severely if he commits a disparagement that amounts to defamation (Sec. 187 StGB) or if he intentionally gives his support to efforts against the continued existence of the Federal Republic of Germany or against its constitutional principles. Authorization from the Federal President (Sec. 77e StGB) is needed to commence criminal prosecution (Sec. 90 IV StGB; prerequisite for criminal prosecution).

> Section 90a German Criminal Code (StGB)
>
> Defamation of the state and its symbols
>
> (1) Whosoever publicly, in a meeting or through the dissemination of written materials (section 11 (3))
>
> insults or maliciously expresses contempt of the Federal Republic of Germany or one of its states or its constitutional order; or
>
> insults the colours, flag, coat of arms or the anthem of the Federal Republic of Germany or one of its states
>
> shall be liable to imprisonment of not more than three years or a fine.
>
> (2) Whosoever removes, destroys, damages, renders unusable or defaces, or otherwise insults by mischief a publicly displayed flag of the Federal Republic of Germany or one of its states or a national emblem installed by a public authority of the Federal Republic of Germany or one of its states shall incur the same liability. The attempt shall be punishable.
>
> (3) The penalty shall be imprisonment of not more than five years or a fine if the offender by the act intentionally supports efforts against the continued existence of the Federal Republic of Germany or against its constitutional principles.

---

26 See Steinmetz, in *Münchener Kommentar, StGB*, 2012, Vol. 3, § 90, para. 6 f.

27 See Laufhütte and Kuschel, in *Leipziger Kommentar zum StGB*, § 90, para. 3.

28 See Steinmetz, in *Münchener Kommentar, StGB*, § 90, para. 8.

The superficial intention of Sec. 90a StGB is to protect the reputation of the Federal Republic of Germany, the states, the constitutional order and particular national emblems from degrading actions.[29] The real function of Sec. 90a StGB is to ensure the existence of the Federal Republic, its states and its constitutional order.[30]

This interpretation relates to the fact that Sec. 90a StGB is located in title three of the first chapter (endangering the democratic rule of law). Protected objects are the Federal Republic, its states and its constitutional order. The protection is furthermore extended to the national colours (Art. 22 para. 2 GG), the national flag (Art. 22 para. 2 GG) and the anthems of the Federal Republic and its states. The function of state symbols is to provide the state as an abstract political being with a physical and visible element.[31] The state symbols thus represent the state itself. That is why the defiance of state symbols is at the same time the defiance of the state itself.[32]

Criminal offences punishable by Sec. 90a para. 1 No. 1 StGB are the insult or malicious defamation of the Federal Republic, its states and its constitutional order.[33]

Insult is defined as an especially crude statement which is designed to humiliate either through the extraordinary crudeness of its expressions or the allegation of a particularly disreputable state or attitude of the Federal Republic or its states.[34]

---

29 The Federal Republic is not entitled to receive damages under civil libel legislation for insults suffered, see Hamburg District Court (LG), *Zeitschrift für Urheber- und Medienrecht – Rechtsprechungsdienst (ZUM-RD)* (2003), p. 48.

30 See Laufhütte and Kuschel, in *Leipziger Kommentar zum StGB*, § 90a, para. 1; partly dissenting Würtenberger, "Satire und Karikatur in der Rechtsprechung," 1983, p. 1146.

31 See Würtenberger, "Kunstfreiheit und Staatsverunglimpfung," 1979, p. 311.

32 See Volk, "Der Strafschutz für Staatssymbole und die Freiheit der Kunst," 1984, p. 444.

33 See Laufhütte and Kuschel, in *Leipziger Kommentar zum StGB*, § 90a, para. 2.

34 See Fischer, *Strafgesetzbuch*, § 90a, para. 5; see also BGH, *Neue Zeitschrift für Strafrecht (NStZ)* (2003), p. 145 („Bimbesrepublik", „käuflicher Saustall"); BGH, Judgment of 24 August 1977, 3 StR 229/77 („Staat der Verbrecher und Vaterlandsverräter"); Dresden Regional Court (OLG), Decision of 10 March 2009, 3 Qs 18/09 („Freiheit statt BRD!"); BayObLG, Decision of 23 October 1995, 3 St 3/95 3a, b, *Neue Zeitschrift für Strafrecht – RechtsprechungsReport (NStZ-RR)* (1996), p. 135 (Defendant alleged that the German government had intentionally killed political opponents).

Defamation means the insult of the state by value judgement or statement of fact, judging the state unworthy of the citizen's respect.[35]

The defamation has to be committed *maliciously*. The criminal offender acts maliciously when acting with an extraordinarily hostile attitude, when neglecting the possibility of using less insulting expressions or when ignoring sources of information clearly contradicting his statements.[36]

Criminal offence punishable by Sec. 90a para. 2 StGB is the defamation of the said symbols; e.g. a grievous disparagement, for example booing when the national anthem is intonated[37] or maliciously making fun of the text of the national anthem.[38] Burning the German flag is also an offence punishable under Sec. 90a para. 2 StGB. The situation is the same in Austria.[39] In contrast, in the Unites States, burning the American flag is not a crime punishable under federal law: In reaction to some flag-burnings in the 1960s in response to the Vietnam War, Congress passed the Flag Protection Act in 1968. The law was overturned by the U.S. Supreme Court in 1989.[40] A second attempt by Congress to enact legislature prohibiting the burning of the flag was overturned by the Supreme Court in 1990.[41] The only way to prohibit the burning of the flag under American law is by amending the Constitution. The proposed amendment[42] was passed by Congress several times, but fell short of the required majority in the Senate each time.[43]

Propagating the non-violent removal of the constitutional order does in itself not constitute an offence punishable under Sec. 90a StGB.[44]

---

35 See Schroeder, "Probleme der Staatsverunglimpfung," p. 92; see as an example Adminstrative Court (VG) Weimar, *Thüringer Verwaltungsblätter (ThürVBl)* (2007), p. 46 (Playing songs of the Nazi-Band "Landser" as defamation).

36 See Schroeder, "Probleme der Staatsverunglimpfung," p. 92.

37 Hamm Regional Court (OLG), *Goltdammer's Archiv für Strafrecht*, Vol. 101 (1963), p. 28.

38 District Court Baden-Baden (LG), *Neue Juristische Wochenschrift (NJW)* (1985), p. 2431.

39 § 248 para. 2 Austrian Criminal Code (öStGB).

40 U.S. Supreme Court, *Texas v. Johnson*, 491 U.S. 379 (1989).

41 U.S. Supreme Court, *United States v. Eichman*, 496 U.S. 310 (1990).

42 So-called Flag Desecration Amendment.

43 It was last rejected by the Senate on 27 June 2006 (S. J. Res. 12).

44 BVerfG, Decision of 9 July 2008, 1 BvR 519/08.

> Section 90b German Criminal Code
>
> Anti-constitutional defamation of constitutional organs
>
> (1) Whosoever publicly, in a meeting or through the dissemination of written materials (section 11 (3)) defames a constitutional organ, the government or the constitutional court of the Federation or of a state or one of their members in this capacity in a manner detrimental to the respect for the state and thereby intentionally supports efforts against the continued existence of the Federal Republic of Germany or against its constitutional principles, shall be liable to imprisonment from three months to five years.
>
> (2) The offence may only be prosecuted upon the authorisation of the constitutional organ or member affected.

The superficial intention of Sec. 90b StGB is to protect the reputation of the said constitutional institutions and their respective members. Its real intention is to protect the existence of the Federal Republic of Germany and its constitutional order. Sec. 90b StGB is not meant to protect the individual credit of the institution's members.[45]

Protected interest is not the affected person's credit, but the constitutional order of the Federal Republic.[46] Protected objects are the legislative institutions (*Bundestag* and *Bundesrat*[47]), the government, and the Federal Constitutional Court as well as the constitutional courts of the states and their respective members.[48]

The criminal offence punishable by Sec. 90b StGB consists of disparaging the said objects which is designed to diminish the state's credit. This means that a concrete threat to the reputation of the Federal Republic of Germany has to be caused by the disparagement.[49] Evidence of the said threat is usually difficult to produce. The criminal offence has to be committed in public, in a meeting or by publishing written statements. To be punished, the criminal offender needs to intent to destabilize the existence of the Federal Republic of Germany or its constitutional order.

---

45 See Laufhütte and Kuschel, in *Leipziger Kommentar zum StGB*, § 90b, para. 1.

46 See Steinmetz, in *Münchener Kommentar, StGB*, § 90b, para. 1.

47 See Fischer, *Strafgesetzbuch*, § 90b, para. 2 and § 105, para. 2.

48 See Sternberg-Lieben, in *Strafgesetzbuch, Kommentar*, § 90b, para. 2.

49 Düsseldorf Regional Court (OLG), *Neue Juristische Wochenschrift* (NJW) (1980), p. 603.

III. Particular Problem: Credit of the State as Protected Interest

It seems doubtful today that the protected interest of the crimes against the state covers the "credit of the state". Only Sec. 90, 90a StGB might protect the credit of the state. The interests protected by those norms are only superficially the credit of the state and its institutions; their real goal is to protect the existence of the state and its constitution.[50] Whereas the personality and human dignity of human beings can be directly affected by diminishing someone's credit, the state as a derived and abstract organ does not possess a genuine "stately dignity".[51] Consequently, the credit of the state itself cannot be of any relevance to criminal law in any democratic state.

By diminishing its credit, the state itself is not harmed, only its existence might be endangered. This means that the state as a whole, consisting of institutions, functions and office bearers, is endangered indirectly by refusal of acceptance by its citizens.[52] That is why the protection of the credit of the state itself is not in the interest of criminal law; the reputation of the state can only be protected as an "entitlement to acceptance" by its citizens.

C. Limits of Protecting the State by Means of Criminal law: Fundamental Rights and Civil Liberties

An effective protection of the state and of its fundamental constitutional principles may lead to a restriction of individual rights and civil liberties, e.g. the freedom of opinion and the freedom of arts and science.[53]The protection of democracy eventually collides with the freedom of opinion (Art. 5 para. 1 Sent. 1 German Basic Law – GG) of its political adversaries.

---

50 See Schroeder, "Probleme der Staatsverunglimpfung," p. 90.

51 Häberle, "Die Menschenwürde als Grundlage der staatlichen Gemeinschaft," 1987, p. 847.

52 See Roggemann, "Von Bären, Löwen und Adlern," p. 938.

53 See Maurach and Schroeder and Maiwald, *Strafrecht: Besonderer Teil*, § 82 IV, para. 29.

The protection of the reputation of the state, its institutions and state symbols collides with the freedom of arts (Art. 5 para. 3 sent. 1 Alt. 1 GG) and the freedom of opinion (Art. 5 para. 1 sent. 1 GG).

The protection of state secrets collides with the freedom of information (Art. 5 para. 1 GG), the freedom of the press (Art. 5 para. 1 sent. 2 GG) and the freedom of sciences (Art. 5 para. 3 sent. 1 Alt. 2 GG).

I. Freedom of opinion (Art. 5 para. 1 sent. 1 GG)

The term "opinion" is to be seen in a wider context.[54] It includes value judgments as well as statements of fact (*contested*).[55] Based on the interdependency-theory[56] by the Federal Constitutional Court (*Bundesverfassungsgericht*), the freedom of opinion demands a restrictive interpretation of the single elements of the offence laid down in Sec. 90a StGB.[57] This especially applies to the political struggle. As the Federal Court of Justice (*Bundesgerichtshof*) states, this is due to the fact "*that the content of Art. 5 I GG emanates from the need of protection of criticism of power and remains to be seen in this context.*"[58] That is why there always has to be an evaluation of every single case regarding the consideration between the freedom of opinion on the one hand and the protected interests on the other hand.[59] Furthermore courts must not imply any meaning to the said statement not intended to be expressed by it; in the case of ambiguity of statements, courts have to rule out the less incriminating meaning with convincing arguments before convicting the offender.

---

54 Decision of the German Constitutional Court (BVerfGE), Vol. 61, p. 9; Herzog, in *Grundgesetz (GG)*, 2011, Art. 5 para. 1, 2 GG, para. 51 ff.

55 See Jarass and Pieroth, *Grundgesetz für die Bundesrepublik Deutschland (GG)*, 2011, Art. 5, para. 3.

56 See Roggemann, "Von Bären, Löwen und Adlern," p. 941.

57 See Fischer, *Strafgesetzbuch*, § 90a, para. 13; BVerfG, *Neue Zeitschrift für Strafrecht (NStZ)* (1985), p. 450; Roggemann, "Von Bären, Löwen und Adlern," p. 941.

58 Decisions of the German Constitutional Court (BVerfGE), Vol. 81, p. 294; 93, 266 (293); BGH, *Neue Zeitschrift für Strafrecht (NStZ)* (2003), p. 146.

59 BVerfG, *Neue Juristische Wochenschrift (NJW)* (1999), p. 205; Güntge, in *Strafgesetzbuch* (*StGB*), 2009, § 90a, para. 7.

II. Freedom of the Press/Freedom of the Broadcast Media

The freedom of the press and the freedom of the broadcast media can be limited and restricted by the so called "common laws", as laid down in Art. 5 para. 2 GG. The term "common laws" does include the Penal Code as well.[60] Within the so called press-content-crimes, which are defined by the punishability being created by the content of the writing,[61] there are reported cases of violations against Sec. 90, 90a[62] and 90b StGB, as well as violations against Sec. 86 StGB [63] which prohibits the spread of propaganda.

III. Freedom of Arts (Art. 5 para. 3 sent. 1 Alt. 1 GG)

The freedom of arts does not underlie either the restrictions imposed by Art. 5 para. 2 GG, or those imposed by Art. 2 para. 1 GG. However, it can be limited and restricted by other constitutionally protected interests. Every case has to be evaluated regarding the consideration between the different constitutional values, so that both can be guaranteed as widely as possible.[64]

The Federal Constitutional Court decided that the importation of a piece of art cannot be prohibited unless it poses a direct and imminent threat to the existence of the Federal Republic of Germany.[65]

---

60 See Jarass and Pieroth, *Grundgesetz*, Art. 5, para. 91.

61 Bayerisches Oberstes Landesgericht (BayObLG), *Neue Juristische Wochenschrift (NJW)* (1987), p. 1711.

62 *See* Löffler, *Presserecht, Kommentar zu den deutschen Landespressegesetzen mit systematischen Darstellungen zum pressebezogenen Standesrecht, Anzeigenrecht, Werbe- und Wettbewerbsrecht, Vertriebsrecht, Urheber- und Verlagsrecht, Arbeitsrecht, Titelschutz, Jugendmedienschutz und Steuerrecht*, 2006, § 20 Landespressegesetz (LPG), para. 53; BGH, *Neue Zeitschrift für Strafrecht – RechtsprechungsReport (NStZ-RR)* (1999), p. 10, dissenting: Bayerisches Oberstes Landesgericht (BayObLG), *Neue Zeitschrift für Strafrecht – RechtsprechungsReport (NStZ-RR)* (1996), p. 135; BayObLG, *Neue Juristische Wochenschrift (NJW)* (1987), p. 1711; BVerfG, *Neue Juristische Wochenschrift (NJW)* (2001), p. 596.

63 See Löffler, *Presserecht*, § 20 LPG, para. 53; BGH, *Neue Juristische Wochenschrift (NJW)* (1986), p. 331.

64 See Jarass and Pieroth, *Grundgesetz*, Art. 5, para. 91; Decisions of the German Constitutional Court (BVerfGE), Vol. 30, p. 193.

65 Decisions of the German Constitutional Court (BVerfGE), Vol. 33, p. 71.

The Federal Constitutional Court also restrictively interprets the criminal offences protecting the national flag and the national anthem. This restrictive interpretation does especially apply to caricatures, as it is "*common to this genre to exaggerate, to distort and to alienate*"; thus the satirical "*means are of a greater importance than the content of the piece itself*".[66]

Similarly, the criminal offence of defamation of the Federal Republic may not lead to a criminalization of criticism of the state. However, Sec. 90a para. 1 StGB complies to the Basic Law.[67]

D. BVerfG, Judgement of 28 November 2011 ("Elser"-case)

The following case of denigration of the German state (Sec. 90a para. 1 No. 1 StGB) was the subject of a ruling by the Federal Constitutional Court recently:[68]

In Berlin the play "*Georg Elser – alone against Hitler*" was premiered in 2008. *Georg Elser* was a member of the resistance against the National Socialism (1933-1945). In 1939 he carried out a bomb attack against the dictator *Adolf Hitler* in Munich. The time-bomb should have exploded during *Hitler's* speech at the Bürgerbräukeller. The attempt failed because *Hitler* had to leave earlier than planned, but eight other people were killed. After the premiere of the play leaflets titled "*Georg Elser – hero or murderer?*" were handed out. The leaflet dealt with the assassination attempt against *Hitler*, which "*caused the death of eight innocent persons.*" *Elser* was called a "*militant communist*" and put on par with Red Army Faction (RAF) terrorists. Nevertheless, in the Federal Republic of Germany "*forces students to idolize Elser and thus ridicules the victims of the attack*". A member of the management board of the local National-Democratic Association (NPD) took responsibility for the publication. Therefore she was convicted for denigration of the German state according to Sec. 90 para. 1 StGB. The Local Court was of the opinion, that the leaflet expresses a hostile attitude towards the FRG and its constitutional order, which opposes national-socialist-ideas. Thus she was convicted of denigration of the state. The Local Court (*Amtsgericht*) – as

66 Decisions of the German Constitutional Court (BVerfGE), Vol. 81, p. 295.
67 BVerfG, *Neue Juristische Wochenschrift (NJW)* (2001), p. 596.
68 BVerfG, *Neue Juristische Wochenschrift (NJW)* (2012), p. 1273.

the Regional Court (*Oberlandesgericht*) as well – considered the freedom of expression not to be relevant, because of the intensity of the denigrating statements. The convict lodged a constitutional complaint, because she considered the verdict to be a violation of her freedom of expression. The Federal Constitutional Court (BVerfG) followed her arguments and quashed the verdict.

The Court was of the opinion, that the text of the leaflet mainly represented the opinion of the applicant. The freedom of expression is not guaranteed without any limitations. It may be restricted by a general law. But because of the weight of this basic right, it has to be ensured, that not the content of an opinion is forbidden by a limiting statute, but only the way of communicating the opinion by violating other rights. As only the dignity of *persons, not of the state* is protected by basic rights, the necessary intensity to legitimate the restriction of the freedom of expression is only reached, if the statement in question seems to be capable of putting at risk the state's existence, the functioning of its institutions or peacefulness.

That is not the case as to the content of the leaflet: It deals with the historical events concerning the assassination attempt in 1939. The interpretation of this special incident is different from the evaluation by – what they call – "*the System of the Federal Republic of Germany.*" The main statement is that a "*no murderer of innocent people shall serve as model.*" The leaflet neither fights the constitutional order, nor does it put at risk the existence of the state or its institutions or a peaceful living. Rather, it stays at the level of mere polemic.

E. Conclusion

Protecting the state by the means of criminal law is necessary to guarantee the existence of the state. However, extending the reach of this protection by criminal law may lead to a criminal law that is itself contradictory to the constitution.

Works cited

Eser, Albin, in *Strafgesetzbuch, Kommentar*, (est.) Adolf Schönke und (cont.) Horst Schröder, 29th ed., München: C.H. Beck, 2014.

Fischer, Thomas, *Strafgesetzbuch*, 61st ed., München: C.H. Beck, 2014.

Güntge, Georg-Friedrich, in *Strafgesetzbuch* (StGB), ed. Helmut Satzger, Wilhelm Schluckebier, and Gunter Widmaier, 2nd ed., München: Carl Heymanns, 2014.

Häberle, Peter, "Die Menschenwürde als Grundlage der staatlichen Gemeinschaft," in *Handbuch des Staatsrechts der Bundesrepublik Deutschland*, ed. Josef Isensee and Paul Kirchhof, Vol. 1, Heidelberg: C.F. Müller, 1987, pp. 815-861.

Head, Michael, *Crimes Against The State, From Treason to Terrorism*, 1st ed., Burlington: Ashgate Publishing Company, 2011.

Herzog, Roman, in *Grundgesetz* (GG), (est.) Theodor Maunz and Günter Dürig, 61st ed., München, C.H. Beck, 2011.

Jarass, Hans D. and Bodo Pieroth, *Grundgesetz für die Bundesrepublik Deutschland* (GG), 11th ed., München: C.H. Beck, 2011.

Laufhütte, Heinrich Wilhelm and Kuschel, Annette, in *Leipziger Kommentar zum StGB*, 12th ed., Berlin, De Gruyter, 2007.

Lippold, Rainer, "Die Staatssymbole – ihre rechtliche Begründung und ihr strafrechtlicher Schutz," *Kritische Vierteljahresschrift für Gesetzgebung und Rechtswissenschaft* (KritV) (1992): 38-51.

Löffler, Martin, *Presserecht, Kommentar zu den deutschen Landespressegesetzen mit systematischen Darstellungen zum pressebezogenen Standesrecht, Anzeigenrecht, Werbe- und Wettbewerbsrecht, Vertriebsrecht, Urheber- und Verlagsrecht, Arbeitsrecht, Titelschutz, Jugendmedienschutz und Steuerrecht*, 5th ed., München: C.H. Beck, 2006.

Maurach, Reinhard, Friedrich-Christian Schroeder, and Manfred Maiwald, *Strafrecht Besonderer Teil, Teilband 2, Straftaten gegen Gemeinschaftswerte*, 10th ed., Heidelberg: C.F. Müller, 2012.

Quaritsch, Helmut: *Probleme der Selbstdarstellung des Staates*, 1st ed., Tübingen, Mohr Siebeck, 1977.

Roggemann, Herwig, "Von Bären, Löwen und Adlern – zur Reichweite der §§ 90a und b StGB," *Juristenzeitung* (JZ) (1992): 934-942.

Schroeder, Friedrich-Christian, "Probleme der Staatsverunglimpfung," *Juristische Rundschau* (JR) (1979): 89-93.

Steinmetz, Jan, in *Münchener Kommentar, StGB*, 2nd ed., München: C.H. Beck, 2012.

Sternberg-Lieben, Detlev, in *Strafgesetzbuch, Kommentar*, (est.) Adolf Schönke and (cont.) Horst Schröder, 29th ed., München, C.H. Beck, 2014.

Volk, Klaus, "Der Strafschutz für Staatssymbole und die Freiheit der Kunst," *Juristische Rundschau (*JR) (1984): 441-445.

Würtenberger, Thomas, "Kunstfreiheit und Staatsverunglimpfung," *Juristische Rundschau* (JR) (1979): 309-314.

Würtenberger, Thomas, "Satire und Karikatur in der Rechtsprechung," *Neue Juristische Wochenschrift (*NJW) (1983): 1144-1151.

The Banning of Parties: Remedy for or Symptom of a Crisis?

Fabian Wittreck

A. Introduction: Banning the NPD While Pointing at the NSU – two Shadows From the Past

On December 3, 2013, German authorities tried it again. Legal representatives of the *Bundesrat*[1] submitted a request asking for the banning of the right-wing party *Nationaldemokratische Partei*[2] to the *Bundesverfassungsgericht*[3] in Karlsruhe.

This topic has *two* case histories. First, one has to mention the ill-fated attempt to ban the very same organization in 2003 (we will return to this trauma under B. 3.). Second, the present request can only be properly understood if one takes into consideration the painful unveiling of the terrorist activities of the *Nationalsozialistischer Untergrund*[4] beginning in the November of 2011. It was an especially unpleasant awakening for the German public when it became clear that a right-wing group comprising a core of at least three persons (*Uwe Mundlos*, *Uwe Böhnhardt*, and *Beate Zschäpe*) had not only murdered at least ten people in a killing spree that ranged from 2000 to 2007, but got away with it undetected.[5] To make things worse, police and intelligence authorities were simply unable to identify the extremist motives of the serial killings which had been dubbed "*Dönermorde*" (lit. "doner kebab murders") by the German press in a fit of especially bad taste. As nine of the victims were of Turkish or Greek descent (the last was a young female police officer shot in Stuttgart in 2007; this case still confounds investigators), the law enforcement

1 Lit. "Federal Council", the First chamber of the German Federal Parliament consisting of members sent by the respective governments of the German *Länder*, i.e. states.

2 Lit. "national democratic party", mostly known under the acronym *NPD*.

3 Lit. "Federal Constitutional Court".

4 Lit. "National socialist underground network", abbreviated as *NSU*.

5 Cf. Schmincke and Siri, eds., *NSU-Terror: Ermittlungen am rechten Abgrund. Ereignis, Kontexte,* 2013.

authorities investigated in the direction of organized crime among immigrants. The German public is struggling to come to terms with the whole affair, with hopes especially resting on the criminal proceedings against the surviving member of the NSU *Beate Zschäpe* and her assumed accomplices in Munich.[6] Meanwhile, dim references hinting at some kind of connection between the NSU and NPD functionaries gave a strong motive for the fresh attempt of the *Bundesrat* to ban the latter. According to a popular notion, the detection of a (strong) "missing link" able to prove the entanglement of the NPD leadership with the NSU murder series would lead to a successful quest to ban the party. So far however, such a comforting piece of evidence, literally catching the neofascist party red-handed, is still elusive.

The case gives reason to take a closer look at the instruments in German public law that can be wielded against parties that are hostile to the constitution. This paper will start with a short exploration of the legal framework (B.). Afterwards, it will present the hitherto existing case-law of the Federal Constitutional Court (C.). As a conclusion, it will be important to realize the deep ambivalence of the outright banning of political parties under a democratic constitution (D.).

B. The Legal Framework for Banning Political Parties in Germany

This present paragraph consists of three sections. The first will shed light on the broader context of the concept of "militant democracy," of which the banning of parties is only one application (I.). The second and third will portray the "law in the books" (II.) and the "law in action" (III.) concerning the banning of parties respectively.

I. The Principle of "Militant Democracy" Under the Basic Law

The German Federal Constitution or *Grundgesetz* (lit. "Basic Law") of 1949 has often been described as a "learning" or adaptive constitution.[7] As

6 See Melissa Eddy, "Trial Begins for a Neo-Nazi Suspect in Germany," *The New York Times*, 7 May 2013, p. A4.

7 See Hassemer, "Die lernende Verfassung," 2010, pp. 15 ff. – For a reliable translation of the Grundgesetz see Tschentscher, transl., *The Basic Law*

a matter of fact, it has to be understood as a two-pronged reaction to the (assumed) shortcomings of the short-lived democratic constitution of 1919 ("*Weimarer Reichsverfassung*") as well as the massive breach of civilization committed by the National Socialist regime from 1933 to 1945. Sharing the widespread assumption that the weakness of the former contributed to the takeover of the latter, the framers of the *Grundgesetz* took care to endow the young German democracy with effective weapons against any revival of Nazism (as well as any second Communist spring). Recalling the well-known device of the French revolution "no freedom for the enemies of freedom" (*Saint Just*), the *Grundgesetz* comprises the following instruments intended to prevent any repetition of a demise of democracy:[8]

According to Article 9, para. 2, associations whose aims or activities contravene the criminal laws, or are directed against the constitutional order or the concept of international understanding, may be prohibited. As this power pertains to the Federal and state ministries of the Interior, it is used fairly often, recently mostly against Islamist factions.[9]

According to Article 18, whoever abuses the freedom of expression, in particular the freedom of the press (paragraph [1] of Article 5), the freedom of teaching (paragraph [3] of Article 5), the freedom of assembly (Article 8), the freedom of association (Article 9), the privacy of correspondence, posts and telecommunications (Article 10), the rights of property (Article 14), or the right of asylum (Article 16a) in order to combat the free democratic basic order shall forfeit these basic rights. As this forfeiture and its extent have to be decided upon by the Federal Constitutional Court, Article 18 has not once been successfully implemented.[10]

According to Article 21, para. 2, parties that, by reason of their aims or the behavior of their adherents, seek to undermine or abolish the free democratic basic order or to endanger the existence of the Federal

---

(Grundgesetz). The Constitution of the Federal Republic of Germany (May 23rd, 1949), 2002.

8 See Thiel, "Germany," 2009, pp. 109 ff. Cf. the contributions in Sajó, ed., *Militant Democracy*, 2004.

9 See the recent contribution of Baudewin, "Das Vereinsverbot," 2013, pp. 1049 ff.

10 There were four – abortive – attempts: See Wittreck, "Artikel 18," 2013, para. 28 ff.

Republic of Germany shall be unconstitutional. Again, only the Federal Constitutional Court shall rule on the question of unconstitutionality.[11]

According to Article 98, para. 2, if a federal judge infringes the principles of the Basic Law or the constitutional order of a *Land* in his official capacity or unofficially, the Federal Constitutional Court, upon application of the *Bundestag*, may by a two-thirds majority order that the judge be transferred or retired. In the case of an intentional infringement it may order him dismissed. As with the forfeiture under Article 18, no case law exists regarding this "*Richteranklage*" (lit. "impeachment of judges").[12]

The list could go on.[13] More important than the details, however, is the critical evaluation of the concept of "militant democracy" in its entirety. Under close scrutiny, three major faults or drawbacks become discernible.

At first, the whole concept rests on a historical narrative which is – to put it mildly – truncated at least. The Weimar Republic did not shipwreck due to a lack of legal instruments prone to be used against its enemies from the Left as well as the Right.[14] It came to grief because it lacked the personnel willing to man those defenses. This reluctance was especially pronounced among the German judiciary, which proved to be – according to a famous coeval phrase – "blind in the right eye." The "*Richteranklage*" of Article 98 bears witness of the fact that the framers of the Basic Law were still aware of this failure, even though it may afterwards have been neglected in the handling of Germany's past.[15]

Secondly, it would be grossly misleading to attribute the marginal vulnerability of the postwar Federal Republic to extremism of every description to the legal concept of "militant democracy" (or to the legal framework of the *Grundgesetz* at all). The stability of the German

---

11 A dense German abstract is presented by Morlok, "Das Parteiverbot," 2013, pp. 317 ff. For an English overview see – besides Thiel, "Germany," – the paper of Niesen, "Anti-Extremism, Negative Republicanism, Civic Society: Three Paradigms for Banning Political Parties," 2002, available at http://www.germanlawjournal.com/index.php?pageID=11&artID=164.

12 See Wittreck, *Die Verwaltung der Dritten Gewalt*, 2006, pp. 159 ff.

13 See once more Thiel, "Germany," pp. 117 ff.

14 The *Gesetze zum Schutze der Republik* (lit. "laws for the protection of the republic") of 1922 (RGBl. 1922 I, p. 585 ff.) and 1930 respectively enabled the authorities to ban associations; in a couple of cases they even allowed for the death penalty, see Jasper, *Der Schutz der Republik. Studien zur staatlichen Sicherung der Demokratie in der Weimarer Republik 1922-1930*, 1963.

15 See Wittreck, "Verwaltung," pp. 58 ff., 71 f.

democracy first and foremost rests on economic prosperity and social balance; in their absence, the instruments of militant democracy would prove to be depressingly unable to cope with the widespread adherence to an extremist world view as it occurred in the final stage of the Weimar Republic. Generally, the occupation with the Sociology of Law teaches humility concerning the impact of the law on reality.

Lastly, one has to mention the fundamental contradiction of the concept of "militant democracy." If a democracy governed by the rule of law resorts to illiberal measures like the forfeiture of fundamental rights (cf. Article 18 of the Basic Law above), it endangers its very essence. By banning opponents it has to acknowledge the failure of those measures it relies on: open debate, the contest for the best ideas and the notion of the self-reliant design of our environment.

II. The Privilege of Prohibition: Text and Commentary

The phrase "privilege of prohibition" may seem odd at first glance. But Article 21, para. 2 of the Basic Law is indeed termed "*Parteienprivileg*" (lit. "parties' privilege") in the German discussion. The term becomes perspicuous if the provision on the banning of parties is compared with the one pertaining to the banning of associations (Article 9, para. 2 of the Basic Law, see above). While an Islamist mosque association may be dissolved by the appropriate ministry of the Interior, only the Federal Constitutional Court is authorized to declare the unconstitutionality of parties. Moreover, prior to this declaration, any other German authority is prohibited from treating a party as if it *was* unconstitutional. A typical case unfolds as follows: The NPD files an application to use some public facility (e.g. the town hall for a party convention), which is repudiated with reference to its assumed unconstitutionality. The ensuing routine annulment of this denial by the administrative courts may be embarrassing to the German public; however, it is the inevitable consequence of the previously mentioned privilege. The border is marked by the permission of the intelligence services to survey parties and to *designate* them or parts thereof as unconstitutional in the annual *Verfassungsschutzbericht* (lit. "report of the office for the protection of the constitution").[16]

The pivotal provision for the banning of parties under German law is Article 21, para. 2 of the Basic Law:

> Parties that, by reason of their aims or the behavior of their adherents, seek to undermine or abolish the free democratic basic order or to endanger the existence of the Federal Republic of Germany shall be unconstitutional. The Federal Constitutional Court shall rule on the question of unconstitutionality.

The banning procedure is spelled out in detail in the Law on the Federal Constitutional Court.[17] The application may be filed by the *Bundestag*, the *Bundesrat*, or the Federal Government (Article 43, para. 1 BVerfGG). The government of a *Land* may act as an applicant only in the case of a party confined to the *Land* in question (Article 43, para. 2 BVerfGG). In the present case, the fact that only the *Bundesrat* brought itself to file proceedings raised some concern in the German public; *Bundestag* and Federal Government were (and still are) doubtful concerning the outcome of the motion.[18]

The application initiates a two-stage process. In a first step (the "*Vorverfahren*", lit. "preliminary proceedings"), the Constitutional Court will give the persons entitled to represent the party (according to Article 44 BVerfGG the legal representatives are determined by the party's statutes or the general legal provisions) the opportunity to make a statement within a specified period. Afterwards, it will decide whether the application is to be rejected as inadmissible or insufficiently founded, or whether proceedings are to be held (Article 45 BVerfGG). As we will see, the previous attempt to ban the *NPD* did not initially stumble at this point

---

16 Cf. the judgment of the Federal Constitutional Court of 9 October 2013 on the surveillance of a Parliamentarian (English press release: http://www.bundes verfassungsgericht.de/pressemitteilungen/bvg13-060en.html).

17 Gesetz über das Bundesverfassungsgericht (Bundesverfassungsgerichtsgesetz – BVerfGG) according to the announcement of 11 August 1993 (Bundesgesetzblatt /Federal legal bulletin I, p. 1473), last amended as of 12 July 2012 (Bundesgesetzblatt I, p. 1501). – See the provisions in the appendix to this paper.

18 See Kim, "Hands Off Germany's Neo-Nazi Party," *The New York Times*, 18 Dec 2012, *available at* http://latitude.blogs.nytimes.com/2012/12/18/hands-off-germanys-neo-nazi-party/.

– the application made it to the main proceedings, where it failed ignominiously (see below C. III).[19]

The results of these proceedings are finally governed by Article 46 of the BVerfGG. Pursuant to para. 1 of the provision, the Federal Constitutional Court shall declare that the political party is unconstitutional if the application proves to be founded. According to para. 2, the declaration may be confined to a legally or organizationally independent section of a party. Finally, the declaration shall be accompanied by the dissolution of the party or the independent section of the party and the prohibition of the establishment of a substitute organization (para. 3, cl. 1). Moreover, in this instance the Federal Constitutional Court may direct that the property of the party or the independent section of the party be confiscated for use by the Federation or the *Land* for public benefit (para. 3, cl. 2).

The fate of parliamentarians of the unconstitutional party is governed by the *Bundeswahlgesetz* (lit. "Federal Election Law", known in short as BWahlG). Article 46, para. 4 of this document stipulates that

> the deputies shall lose their membership of the Bundestag, and their successors on the list shall lose their candidacy, if they have been members of that party or party section during the period between the filing of the application (Article 43 of the Law on the Federal Constitutional Court) and the pronouncement of the decision (Article 46 of the Law on the Federal Constitutional Court)." The provision is highly controversial in Germany, as the Basic Law does not contain an explicit vindication of this far-reaching sanction.[20]

Finally, the provision of Article 14, para. 4 of the Law on the Federal Constitutional Court (BVerfGG) is of special importance for the banning proceedings. It imposes the necessity of a supermajority of two thirds of the members of the cognizant Second Senate of the *Bundesverfassungsgericht* (cf. Article 14, para. 2, and Article 13 No. 2 BVerfGG) for any decision which is disadvantageous for the respondent (i.e.: the party). As the senates of the *Bundesverfassungsgericht* are sitting in a

---

19 Cf. Hanschmann, "Federal Constitutional Court To Review NPD Party Ban Motion," 2001, available at http://www.germanlawjournal.com/index.php?pageID=11&artID=104.

20 See only Morlok, "Artikel 21," 2006, para. 153.

composition of eight judges each,[21] "two thirds" actually has to be read as "six out of eight" or "three-fourths," which means that three opposing judges are able to freeze any decision made against a party under scrutiny. This is exactly what happened in 2003 when the Court ruled that the denial of the (implicit) application of the *NPD* to discontinue the proceedings would be such a "disadvantageous" decision, so that the (minority) of three judges who deemed the lawsuit fatally flawed (see below C. III) could outplay the majority of five judges who still saw a chance to mend the procedural defects.[22]

III. The Privilege of Prohibition: Living Law

The reader who has followed up to this point may be amazed about the lack of any substantive rule or standard for the unconstitutionality of the party in question. Indeed, the *Bundesverfassungsgerichtsgesetz* remains mute regarding that aspect. If we want to know what Article 21, para. 2 of the Basic Law means by "seek[ing] to undermine or abolish the free democratic basic order" (the second alternative of "endanger[ing] the existence of the Federal Republic of Germany" may be discarded as insignificant), we will have to take a closer look at the pertinent judicature of the Federal Constitutional Court.

The Court conducted two major acts of sharpening the content of the provision of Article 21, para. 2 of the Basic Law. First, it had to find a yardstick able to distinguish between all-out enemies of the constitution and those merely advocating the reform of the latter. This attempt to seal the "essence" of the Basic Law has resulted in the famous definition of the *freiheitliche demokratische Grundordnung* (lit. "free democratic basic order") which the Court already found in its ruling on the *SRP* (see below C. I):[23]

The free democratic basic order can be defined as an order which excludes any form of tyranny or arbitrariness and represents a

21 Cf. Article 2, para. 2 BVerfGG.

22 BVerfGE 107, 339 (356); see Rensmann, "Procedural Fairness in a Militant Democracy: The 'Uprising of the Decent' Fails Before the Federal Constitutional Court," 2002, pp. 1122 ff, available at http://www.germanlawjournal.com/index.php?pageID=11&artID=332.

23 BVerfGE 2, 1 (12 sqq.); translation by Thiel, "Germany,", p. 116.

governmental system unter a rule of law, based upon self-determination of the people expressed by the will of the existing majority and upon freedom and equality. The fundamental principles of this order include at least: respect for the human rights given concrete form in the Basic Law, in particular for the right of a person to life and free development; separation of powers; responsibility of government; lawfulness of administration; independence of the judiciary; the multi-party principle; and equality of opportunities for all political parties.

Secondly, even open opposition to the constitutional values enshrined in this definition is no viable base for the banning of a peculiar party, as long as it contains itself to the mere advocacy of differing principles. Prerequisite of a ban is "[a]n actively combative, aggressive attitude against the existing order […]; [the party] has methodically to affect the functioning of the order, and aim for the abolition of this order over time."[24] This threshold is obviously transgressed in the case of the use of force attributable to party officials. However, even corresponding preparations or exhortations are sufficient – if they can be ascribed to the party in question. This last prerequisite leads us to the case law on the banning of parties.

C. Experiences with the Banning of Political Parties in Germany

Once again, the following paragraph has three sections. The first two are covering two successful applications to ban parties in the early Fifties; they were both filed in the same week, but required remarkably varying time spans to decide upon. Their comparison may act as a portent of the difficulties the Court encountered in the proceedings: While the banning of the open Neo-Nazi *SRP* was beyond any discussion (I.), the proscription of the *KPD* proved to be a bone of contention (II.). The same is true – after a substantial hiatus – for the ill-fated attempt to ban the *NPD* in 2003 (III.).

24 BVerfGE 5, 85 (141); translation again by Thiel, "Germany," p. 124.

I. Socialist "Reich" Party (SRP – 1952): Matter of course

The application to ban the *Sozialistische Reichspartei* (lit. "Socialist Reich Party") was filed on 19 November 1951 by the German Federal Government. The proceedings did not even last for a year: On October 23rd, 1952, the Federal Constitutional Court declared the unconstitutionality of the *SRP*, ordered its dissolution and issued a ban on the formation of any replacement organizations.[25] Anticipating this move, the party had already dissolved itself in September 1952.

The *SRP* ban was beyond any doubt. The party consisted of prominent members of the former *Hitler* party *NSDAP* (*Nationalsozialistische Deutsche Arbeiterpartei* or "National Socialist German Workers' Party"), and used its language, terminology, and programmatic positions. Moreover, it was organized according to the notorious *Führerprinzip* (lit. "leader's principle") meaning a autocratic top-down structure aligning itself with the will of its founders, among them former *Wehrmacht* officer *Otto Ernst Remer* (notorious for his role in hamstringing the ill-fated attempt to overthrow *Hitler* in the coup of 20 July 1944).[26] Organizations like the *Reichsjugend* (lit. "Reich Youth") or the demand of a "solution to the 'Jewish question'" just underscored the unmistakable NSDAP heritage which left the court practically no choice.

II. German Communist Party (KPD – 1956): Matter of Contention

The move to ban the *KPD* discloses a rather different picture. Once again, the court was ultimately left with no choice, but this had nothing to do with the merits of the case. The application was filed on 23 November 1951 by the Federal Government – apparently *Adenauer* intended to demonstrate some kind of "banning equilibrium" by taking action against persistent Nazis and communists at the same moment (thus effectively equating both factions). While the court had no qualms about banning the

---

25 BVerfGE 2, 1 (abbreviation for *Entscheidungen des Bundesverfassungsgerichts*, i.e. "Decisions of the Federal Constitutional Court"). – A translation in the semi-official series of translations published by members of the court does not exist.

26 BVerfGE 2, 1 (23 ff.) regarding the party's leaders. See also Hansen, *Die Sozialistische Reichspartei (SRP). Aufstieg und Scheitern einer rechtsextremen Partei*, 2007.

SRP, it was remarkably scrupulous about the correspondent verdict aiming at the *KPD*: The ban was not issued until 17 August 1956. What made the judges hesitate, and what finally made them issue the ban? To start with the latter, it simply was the Federal Government or – to be precise – the majority of the *Bundestag* backing this government. As the cognizant First senate of the *Bundesverfassungsgericht* proved reluctant to advance with the proceedings, the law on the Federal constitutional court was amended to transfer the competence for the banning of parties to the Second senate. Just six weeks before this shift of jurisdiction became effective, the First senate reached its verdict against the *KPD*.[27]

What was the hurdle? First, one has to mention that the West German communist party started as a serious political factor – the *KPD* deputy *Karl Renner* was a voice carrying weight in the body framing the Basic Law, and the party was represented in the first *Bundestag* after 1949 (with a vote of about 1.3 million people). Moreover, the party officials played the card of German unity by pointing to the fact that a ban would be perceived as a vote against the Eastern German model of political organization which the *KPD* represented.[28]

Nevertheless, the Federal constitutional court issued a verdict banning the KPD. The judgment is one of the longest in the court's history – fatiguing passages on Marxism/Communism, culminating in the expected result of the last-mentioned ideology's incommensurateness with the free democratic basic order intended by the Basic Law.[29] *Sub specie* "actively combative, aggressive attitude" the KPD came to grief due to its famous appeal to "overthrow" the "Adenauer regime".[30] Thus, the party provided the pivotal arguments for its prohibition in the style of free home delivery. After the verdict, an order of criminal proceedings against communists (or people labeled as such), further prohibitions, and detentions ensued.

Nowadays, a vast majority of historians and constitutional lawyers criticize the banning of the KPD.[31] A famous biting remark of a German lawyer goes as follows: It would have been better to let the KPD die the

---

27 BVerfGE 5, 85.

28 BVerfGE 5, 85 (104 f., 125 ff.).

29 BVerfGE 5, 85 (147-207).

30 BVerfGE 5, 85 (297): "Mit dem Angriff gegen das 'Adenauer-Regime' beabsichtigt die KPD zugleich einen Angriff gegen die freiheitliche demokratische Grundordnung."

31 Instead of all see Stolleis, *Geschichte des öffentlichen Rechts in Deutschland*, 2012, pp. 159 f., 310 f.

calm death of a politically unsuccessful than to slay her with the sharp sword of Article 21.[32] To illustrate this lack of political success, one may point at the election returns of the KPD: they withered to a mere 2.2 per cent in the *Bundestag* of 1953[33], prompting the question whether a party obviously unable to reach its aim of "overthrowing" the government could be banned at all.[34]

III. National Democratic Party (NPD – 2003/2014): Matter of Confidence

The question of feasible political success of the party in question (in other words: the dangers emanating from it) could have been raised in the case of the *NPD* as well (in the recent national election of September 2013, the party netted a rather unimpressive result of 1.3 per cent; at present, it has available seats in two of the *Landtage* or state parliaments). However, the proceedings came to a hard landing without even reconsidering the questions of the NPD's political success or its "actively combative, aggressive attitude" against the "free democratic basic order." What had happened? The proceedings started on 30 January 2001 (application of the Federal Government) and accordingly 30 March 2001 (joint applications of *Bundestag* and *Bundesrat*). After inaugurating the main proceedings,[35] the highest judges were appalled to learn that key witnesses (*Auskunftspersonen*, lit. "respondents") who should be interrogated during a sitting of the court were in fact informants (*Vertrauensleute*, abbreviated as *V-Leute*, lit. "people of confidence") of the miscellaneous offices for the protection of the constitution.[36] This dual capacity of the respondents raised the question if the *NPD* had any aims and positions of its own or

---

32 See Zweigert, "Drei Jahre KP-Verbot," 1959, p. 677: Es wäre „nicht nur eleganter, sondern auch politisch weiser gewesen, diese Partei den leisen Tod der Erfolglosen sterben zu lassen, statt sie mit der blanken Waffe des Art. 21 GG zu erschlagen".

33 BVerfGE 5, 85 (100 f.).

34 The Federal Constitutional Court is nonambiguous: BVerfGE 5, 85 (143) emphasizes the irrelevance of the inimical party's prospects of success.

35 BVerfG, Decision of 1 October 2001. See Hanschmann, "Federal Constitutional Court," *available at* http://www.germanlawjournal.com/index.php?pageID=11&artID=104.

36 BVerfGE 107, 339 (346 ff.); cf. also BVerfGE 104, 370: The senate abolished the scheduled hearings after learning about the dual capacity of the respondents.

was a simple instrument of the state acting as a puppeteer. A minority of three judges voted for the second alternative and came to the conclusion that the proceedings had to be suspended for good as there was no longer any chance for a fair trial.[37] The majority of four judges (the eighth had left office during the course of the proceedings) opposed,[38] but had to succumb due to the voting rule already mentioned.[39] As the decision *not* to suspend the proceedings would have been disadvantageous for the party, it had to be taken with the supermajority of six out of eight judges, which those who opted for proceeding further clearly missed.[40] The embarrassing failure of the motion was unanimously classified as a triumph of the *NPD* (even if it was no acquittal in a technical sense).[41] Bearing this in mind, the German public is especially anxious about the new motion (the same is true with respect to Public Law teachers[42]).

D. Conclusion: The Banning of Political Parties as a Two-Barreled Gun

What is after all the quintessence of the German experience concerning the banning of parties? First of all, the ban is an instrument that may easily backfire, as the *NPD* case amply demonstrates. Second, it is a rather clumsy instrument whose effectiveness lags behind the political currents of the day, as may be learned from the *KPD* case. Third, it is an instrument whose use may make sense in a very unique historical situation, as is highlighted by the *SRP* case: If just after the downfall of a tyranny a small but well-organized faction tries to put the wheel of history into reverse, a (young) democracy founded on the cancellation of this very ideology may be wise to take resort to force and ban this openly revisionist party. A mature democracy, on the contrary, is not well advised to use the same instruments (with the exception, perhaps, for groups using violence). In banning its opponents, democracy risks descending to the level of those very enemies.

---

37 BVerfGE 107, 339 (356 ff., 360 ff.).

38 BVerfGE 107, 339 (378 ff.).

39 See Rensmann, "Procedural Fairness,"

40 BVerfGE 107, 339 (356 ff.).

41 See Flemming, *Das NPD-Verbotsverfahren. Vom „Aufstand der Anständigen" zum „Aufstand der Unfähigen"*, 2005.

42 See only Morlok, "Fragen des Rechts und der politischen Klugheit – Zur aktuellen NPD-Parteiverbotsdebatte," 2013, pp. 69 ff..

Works cited

Baudewin, Christian, "Das Vereinsverbot," *Neue Zeitschrift für Verwaltungsrecht* (2013): 1049-1054.

Flemming, Lars, *Das NPD-Verbotsverfahren. Vom „Aufstand der Anständigen" zum „Aufstand der Unfähigen"*, Baden-Baden: Nomos, 2005.

Hanschmann, Felix, "Federal Constitutional Court To Review NPD Party Ban Motion," German Law Journal 17 (2001), available at http://www.germanlawjournal.com/index.php?pageID=11& artID=104.

Hansen, Henning, Die Sozialistische Reichspartei (SRP). Aufstieg und Scheitern einer rechtsextremen Partei, Düsseldorf: Droste, 2007.

Hassemer, Winfried, "Die lernende Verfassung," in 60 Jahre Grundgesetz, ed. Norbert Kartmann, Wiesbaden: Hessischer Landtag, 2010, pp. 15ff.

Jasper, Gotthard, *Der Schutz der Republik. Studien zur staatlichen Sicherung der Demokratie in der Weimarer Republik 1922-1930*, Tübingen: Mohr-Siebeck ,1963.

Morlok, Martin, "Fragen des Rechts und der politischen Klugheit – Zur aktuellen NPD-Parteiverbotsdebatte," *Zeitschrift für Rechtspolitik* (2013): 69-71.

Morlok, Martin, "Das Parteiverbot," *Jura* (2013): 317-325.

Morlok, Martin, "Artikel 21," in *Grundgesetz-Kommentar*, ed. Horst Dreier, Vol. II, 2nd ed., Tübingen: Mohr Siebeck, 2006, pp. 327-403.

Niesen, Peter, "Anti-Extremism, Negative Republicanism, Civic Society: Three Paradigms for Banning Political Parties," *German Law Journal* 3 (2002), available at http://www.germanlawjournal.com/index.php?pageID=11&artID=164.

Rensmann, Thilo, "Procedural Fairness in a Militant Democracy: The 'Uprising of the Decent' Fails Before the Federal Constitutional Court," *German Law Journal* 4 (2002): 1117-1136.

Sajó, András, ed., *Militant Democracy*, Utrecht: Eleven, 2004.

Schmincke, Imke and Jasmin Siri, eds., *NSU-Terror: Ermittlungen am rechten Abgrund. Ereignis, Kontexte, Diskurse*, Bielefeld: transcript, 2013.

Stolleis, Michael, *Geschichte des öffentlichen Rechts in Deutschland*, Vol. IV, Munich: C.H. Beck, 2012.

Thiel, Markus, "Germany," in *The 'Militant Democracy' Principle in Modern Democracies*, ed. Markus Thiel, Farnham/Burlington: Ashgate, 2009, pp. 109-145.

Tschentscher, Axel, transl., *The Basic Law (Grundgesetz). The Constitution of the Federal Republic of Germany (May 23rd, 1949)*, Würzburg: Jurisprudentia, 2002.

Wittreck, Fabian, "Artikel 18," in *Grundgesetz-Kommentar*, ed. Horst Dreier, Vol. I, 3rd ed., Tübingen: Mohr Siebeck 2013.

Wittreck, Fabian, *Die Verwaltung der Dritten Gewalt*, Tübingen: Mohr Siebeck, 2006.

Zweigert, Konrad, "Drei Jahre KP-Verbot," *Juristenzeitung* (1959): 677.

Constitutional and Socio-Political Dynamics in Belgium and the Netherlands

Maurice Adams

A. Introduction: Theme and Method

Political Power and the Governmental Process, by *Karl Loewenstein*, is one of those rare pieces of 20th century scholarship that explicitly study the practical significance of constitutions. *Loewenstein* was interested in "the concordance of the reality of the power process with the norms of the constitution."[1] He noted the lack of attention for this topic and was very aware of the fact that a constitution does not operate automatically once it has been adopted: "A constitution is what power holders and power addressees make of it in practical application." [2] So what about the dynamics between constitutional law and socio-political practice, or between the formal and material validity of a constitution? Under what conditions can we speak of a constitution that is fully embraced in practice, to the benefit of a nation and of the well being of its population? *Loewenstein*, a Jewish émigré from Nazi Germany who became an American citizen, was troubled by these questions, and was after the 2nd World War one of the few scholars to study conflict and stability in the basic constitutional order in a more systematic way. To be sure, there is, today, more attention than ever before for the types of – interdisciplinary – questions Loewenstein asked[3], but this doesn't preclude the fact that, at least in European academic circles, a specifically legal or normative approach is still dominant.[4]

In this chapter I will study the dynamics between constitutional law and its socio-political environment by focusing on the two jurisdictions with which I am most familiar, i.e., Belgium and the Netherlands. Both

1 Loewenstein, *Political Power and the Governmental Process*, 1965, pp. 147-148.
2 Loewenstein, *Political Power and the Governmental Process*, p. 148.
3 The work of for example Tom Ginsburg c.s. is relevant here. See, e.g.: *The Endurance of National Constitutions*, 2009 (together with Z. Elkins and J. Melton).
4 Bogdandy, "Comparative Constitutional Law: a Contested Domain," 2012, p. 28.

countries, situated in the North-western part of Europe and neighbouring each other, are relatively small and highly affluent. They partly speak the same language. Yet they could not be more different in terms of constitutional culture.[5]

Comparative law can be of particular significance here. Indeed, comparatists must immerse themselves in at least two legal systems. However, such an 'involved' activity does not come naturally. It means that you have to deal with, and convey information about, legal systems whose 'language' (metaphorically understood) you do not necessarily speak, i.e., systems with specific institutions and unexpressed codes, their own history(y)(ies), ideolog(y)(ies) and self-image(s); systems you have not normally been trained, educated or disciplined in, and with which you are therefore not naturally or intimately connected. This process of trying to understand, and convey to the reader, foreign legal systems (or some of their elements) demands a particular approach because it goes far beyond mere fact-finding and the regular (i.e., purely national) way of interpretation and understanding the law, where one almost self-evidently and implicitly engages in its social context. In any case, the problems that the law addresses, as well as the solutions that it intends to provide them, are very much connected to the socio-political environment from which these problems and solutions arise. Therefore, comparative law *explicitly* calls for being able to relate to the socio-political and cultural context of the topic or issue that is being studied[6], and do so in a way that is comprehensible to the reader. Comparison can moreover sharpen the powers of description of each of the jurisdictions under consideration here because sensible – real![7] – comparison asks to describe and analyze these systems *vis-à-vis* each other (contrasting and connecting).

---

5 Borrowing from David Nelken, I understand the term constitutional culture, in its most general sense, as one way of describing relatively stable patterns of behaviour and attitudes towards constitutional norms. Nelken, "Defining and Using the Concept of Legal Culture", 2007, p. 113.

6 On this, see Adams, "Doing What Doesn't Come Naturally. On the Distinctiveness of Comparative Law," 2011, pp. 229-233. Also Lasser, "The Question of Understanding," 2004, pp. 200-202 and Bell, "Legal Research and the Distinctiveness of Comparative Law", 2011, pp. 155-176.

7 This seems to be lacking many times; but as Shapiro in 1981 already noted, comparative law should nevertheless be something more than mere 'auslandrechtkunde': "For the most part [comparative law] has consisted of showing that a certain procedural or substantive law of one country is similar to or different from that of another. Having made the showing, no one knows quite

For these reasons, comparison and contextualisation is thus indeed what can be of particular help when we want to better understand the dynamics between a constitution and its socio-political environment. But lawyers are used to studying constitutions merely as legal phenomena, and political scientists, if they do so at all, tend to study constitutions exclusively as social phenomena.[8] The explicit aim in this text is to integrate these two approaches. "[K]nowledge of the constitutional text alone equate[s], [not] even nearly, to an understanding of political reality", some colleagues wrote a few years ago. "[B]ut", they added, "it is a necessary condition of that understanding."[9] This indicates reciprocity, and what we should pay attention to is how political reality and constitutional law inform and influence *each other*.

B. Some Facts About Constitutions and Constitutionalism in Belgium and the Netherlands

I. Belgium[10]

Belgium today has some 10.6 million inhabitants, and is a small and affluent country. It is notorious for its many politically and constitutionally salient divisions: linguistically, ideologically, culturally, regionally, economically, etc. The proliferation of these divisions recently resulted in the country experiencing a profound political and institutional

what to do next. Or, alternatively, comparison consists of presenting descriptions of a number of legal systems side by side, again with no particular end in view." Shapiro, *Courts. A Comparative and Political Analysis,* 1981, p. vii. This of course doesn't preclude that even the sheer description of a foreign legal system will inevitably, albeit implicitly, make the researcher reflect about her own legal system. Benda-Beckmann, "Ethnologie und Rechtsvergleichung," 1981, p. 310.

8 Cfr. Harding and Leyland, "Comparative Law in Constitutional Contexts," 2007, pp. 322-323.

9 Finer, Bogdanor and Rudden, *Comparing Constitutions*, 1995, p. 5.

10 An English version of the text of the Belgian Constitution can be found on: http://legislationline.org/documents/section/constitutions. This paragraph builds on Adams, "Disabling Constitutionalism," 2014, pp. 279-302.

crisis, having no federal government for 541 (!) days,[11] a world record apparently.

Belgium is organized around two dominant language and cultural communities (*demoi*): the Dutch-speaking part in the north (called Flanders, with a population of some 6.1 million people, referred to as Flemings) and the French-speaking part in the south (called Wallonia, making up 55% of the land in the country and with 3.4 million residents known as Walloons). A language border, officially marked by the legislator in 1962-63 and entrenched in 1970 in Section 4 of the Constitution,[12] separates the two communities and has resulted in a rigid division of the country into linguistic areas. The fact that within such an area a language is recognized as the main official language means that it is also the language of administration, government, education and justice. As a result, Dutch is the official language in the north and French in the south. However, Brussels, with some 1.1 million inhabitants, has been constitutionally recognized as a bilingual area – Dutch and French-speaking – but has a predominantly francophone population.[13] In effect, some 60% of the Belgian population is Dutch-speaking and some 40% French-speaking. Constitutional recognition has also been granted to a small German-speaking part of the country (bordering Germany and with some 75,000 residents).

In addition, there are a limited number of municipalities – situated on the language border and also bordering the so-called Brussels-Capital Region (see below) – where a substantial number of Dutch and French-speaking people reside and where language facilities are granted to those who speak the 'minority' language, i.e., the language that is not the

11 Since 26 April 2010. The federal government was installed on 6 December 2011. The government formation process of 2007 took 194 days. The most recent government formation process (2014) took 139 days.

12 Since in the context of this chapter this is a telling provision, I quote the text in full: "Belgium comprises four linguistic regions: the Dutch-speaking region, the French-speaking region, the bilingual region of Brussels-Capital and the German-speaking region. Each municipality of the Kingdom forms part of one of these linguistic regions. The boundaries of the four linguistic regions can only be changed or corrected by a law passed by a majority of the votes cast in each linguistic group in each House, on condition that a majority of the members of each group is present and provided that the total number of votes in favor that are cast in the two linguistic groups is equal to at least two thirds of the votes cast."

13 Historically Brussels was a Dutch-speaking city. Nowadays, during office hours, with many Flemish commuters coming to work there, it is a bilingual city.

official language.[14] They can use the language of their choice in matters relating to, e.g., administration, schooling of children (6-12 years old) and justice. These municipalities are called 'facility municipalities' and are also obliged to communicate with these citizens in the language of the 'minority' language speakers' choice. So, too, do all forms and official communications have to be available in – depending on the language area in which a municipality is situated – either Dutch and French, or German and French. However, in communications between such a municipality on the one hand and the regional or federal authorities under which the municipality resorts on the other hand, the official language is the norm, as it is for communications *within* the municipal administration itself. In other words, language facilities are a service for the citizens and not for the administration. To be sure, individual linguistic liberty is protected in Section 30 of the Constitution (and has been since 1831, when Belgium was established as an independent State), and the aforementioned arrangements are only applicable in the relation between the citizens and the state; the choice of language used in private and social life, including commercial activities, is in principle free.

Belgium, as Section 1 of the Constitution has stated since 1993, "is a federal state composed of Communities and Regions." Belgian federalism is organized, as is clear from this provision, on the basis of a double subdivision into Communities and Regions, [15] each having its own legislative and executive jurisdiction. By way of several state reforms[16] there has, since 1970, been a progressive transfer of powers from the federal level to these Communities and Regions. Between them on the one hand and the federal level on the other hand, there is no legislative hierarchy; all can enact legislation, for which they are exclusively

---

14 Which in practice might well be the majority language, since the official language is based on a dated language count. As a result, where, for example, French is not the official language, this does not rule out the possibility that sometimes the majority of the population in these municipalities are first and foremost French-speaking. This can especially be the case in the municipalities surrounding Brussels.

15 In this text I use capitals whenever I refer to these officially recognized *C*ommunities and *R*egions and their competences. When these capitals are not used I refer to the non-official, i.e., colloquial, meaning of the words.

16 Five in all: 1970, 1980, 1988-89, 1993 and 2001. At the time of this chapter's composition there the legislation for sixth state reform, had yet partly to be laid down in legislation and implemented.

competent, and all legislation enacted by the Communities and Regions is on a par with federal legislation.

There are three constitutionally recognized Communities, of which the so-called Flemish and French Communities are the most prominent ones. There is also a small German-Speaking Community in the eastern part of the country. The Communities are mainly competent in relation to specific subject matters of cultural concern to the respective Dutch, French and German-speaking populations in Belgium. However, they also have exclusive jurisdiction over what are termed personal matters: certain aspects of health care, family policy, education, and such like. This competence is territorially defined: it stops at the language border.[17] For example, the Flemish Community is not competent in the French Community. The situation in Brussels, however, is an exception to the territorial rule. There the Flemish Community has competence in these matters with regard to the Dutch-speaking residents, and the French Community with regard to the French-speaking ones. To give but one example: it is the Flemish Community that has competence with respect to schools in Brussels that teach in Dutch, and the French Community with respect to schools that teach in French.

Belgium is further divided into three Regions: the Flemish, the Walloon and the Brussels-Capital Regions. These Regions are mainly and exclusively competent in certain economic matters in their respective areas: environment, agriculture, energy, employment policy, public transport, international cooperation connected to these competences, area development and planning, etc. There is no German Region; it is the Walloon Region that has competence in the German-speaking part of Belgium.

Complementing this federalized structure, the federal government and bicameral federal parliament have decision-making powers extending across the whole country, especially concerning issues that are not expressly left to the Regions or Communities. So, although the Regions

---

17 Although there still is political disagreement on the issue of territorial competence: some French-speaking politicians claim that the competences of the Communities are personally rather than territorially defined. This would imply that the French Community would be competent with respect to the French-speaking population of Flanders. There is however an authoritative line of case law by the Belgian *Cour constitutionnelle* as well as the *Conseil d'Etat* that confirms the principle of territoriality in this context, although there are exceptions to this.

and Communities have significant competences, federal institutions retain a fair share of powers. Key issues like social security, police, immigration, foreign policy, justice and fiscal policy are still, to a large extent, in the hands of the federal government and parliament.

The federal government depends on a majority in parliament; Belgium is thus a parliamentary democracy (as well as a mainly ceremonial monarchy). In federal parliament, which has competence towards the constitution, there is a clear Dutch-speaking majority: 62 of the members of the Chamber of Representatives belong to the French-speaking language group, while 88 belong to the Dutch-speaking language group; in the Senate the numbers are 29 and 44 respectively. From a numerical point of view, Dutch-speaking members of parliament could impose their will on the minority of francophone parliamentarians. In reality, of course, things are not quite that simple in a federation whose main organisational principle is language. Not only has linguistic parity been mandatory, in the Federal Council of Ministers since 1970 (Section 99 Constitution), decisions that concern the organisation of the state moreover have to be taken by a two-thirds majority in federal parliament, as well as by a majority in each of the two language groups in this parliament (the requirement is described in Section 4 of the Constitution and referred to throughout). Interestingly enough this can be done without constitutional amendment, but by so-called "special legislation"; it is a technique that is prescribed for most Belgian institutional reforms. So while a two-thirds majority can change the Constitution itself after a complicated and lengthy procedure, institutional reform must meet even stricter demands, even if such reform follows a 'regular' legislative procedure. Consequently, institutional reforms are impossible without a special majority in federal parliament, and 31 members of the federal Chamber of Representatives or 15 members of the federal Senate can block them. To put it differently, an institutional reform can never be achieved against the will of a majority in one of the language groups, even if this majority is representative of a minority in Belgium (as is the case with the French-speaking language group in federal parliament).

Moreover, whenever a 75% majority of one of these language groups in one of the chambers of federal parliament declares that the relations between the different communities in Belgium may deteriorate as a result of a federal legislative proposal (as long as they are not dealing with budgets and do not concern laws requiring a special majority), the legislative procedure will be postponed (Section 54 Constitution). This is known as the *alarm bell procedure* and the idea behind it is to prevent one of the language groups in federal parliament from pushing through a legislative proposal against the will of the other language group in parliament. When the alarm bell is raised, the Council of Federal Ministers, which is composed on the basis of linguistic parity, must then, within 30 days, advise parliament on the issue concerned. As can readily be imagined, such a procedure puts enormous pressure on the federal government and if it cannot come to an agreement, it will almost certainly fall, with representatives of the two language groups subsequently having to negotiate a new government on a subject about which there is fundamental disagreement. Thus, the alarm bell procedure has preventive or dissuasive quality and the political factions in parliament will not easily raise the alarm.[18]

Belgium's transition in the 1970s and 1980s, from a unitary state to a federal one, ultimately resulted in judicial constitutional review being accepted, initially solely in order to resolve conflicts of competence between the different levels of government. As there was no hierarchy of legislative instruments enacted by the various entities of the Belgian state, conferring those powers could cause conflicts of competence between the Communities/Regions and the federal state. To resolve these conflicts, it was felt that a constitutionally created body was needed, as leaving this to the parliaments would lead to a situation where Belgium would become

---

18 This alarm bell mechanism exists next to the so-called *conflict of interest* procedure, which is applicable between the different entities of the Belgian federal state. More specifically it is about a conflict that arises when the profession of competences by one of the parliaments of the Communities, Regions or Federation is believed to be harmful to the interest of one or more of the other entities (thus possibly contravening federal loyalty, as laid down in Section 143 of the Constitution). When, after consultations between the different entities no solution for the conflict is forthcoming, the case is sent to a "consultation committee", composed of 12 members of the federal, Regional and Community governments, which has to find an agreement. If it does not, the issue is tabled again in the assembly where it was first dealt with (after which another assembly might initiate the procedure again). This procedure can delay a legislative procedure for quite some time. A similar procedure exists for conflicts of interest between the different governments.
Of course, since this procedure concerns the different autonomous entities of the Belgian federal state, the political consequences are not necessarily as drastic when compared to the alarm bell procedure (which, as we saw, deals within one and the same level of the Belgian federal state): the continued existence of any of the governments is not dependent on a political majority in a parliament to which it does not depend on.

ungovernable. Instead of assigning this role to the existing courts, the initiators of a constitutional amendment of 1980 chose to set up a special court, the so called *Cour d'arbitrage* (Court of Arbitration), which would adjudicate on disputes between the various legislatures of the federal Belgian state.[19] The *Cour d'arbitrage* could thus check whether legislation introduced by the Federal state, or the Communities or Regions was in line with the competences that were assigned to them by the Belgian constitution.

The twelve bench seats were evenly divided between Dutch-speaking and French-speaking Belgians, with at least one of the judges required to have an adequate knowledge of German. But the originators of the *Cour d'arbitrage* also paid particular attention to the background of these judges: three judges from each language group are former politicians, i.e., they must have served in a legislative assembly for at least five years. Through their (former) work as parliamentarians, they are presumed to have developed the requisite skills needed to bring their knowledge of political sensitivities in order to apply them to their judicial duties.[20] The other judges are recruited from the group of jurists from the Court of Cassation or the Council of State, professors of law at Belgian universities, or clerks (called 'legal secretaries') within the Court itself. The purpose of this mixed composition, was to render the principle of judicial constitutional review palatable to the legislature. In addition, these judges are appointed by the King on the recommendation of one of the (elected) Houses of Federal Parliament, in an effort to partially obviate the presumed 'democratic impediment' to constitutional review by the judiciary: namely that of unelected judges reviewing and nullifying legislation created by the people's chosen representatives. Moreover, the required two-thirds majority for appointment proposals was intended to make the *Cour d'arbitrage* reflect as accurately as possible the political and ideological movements in the country.

---

19 On this Adams and Schyff, "Political Theory Put to the Test. Comparative Law and the Origins of Judicial Constitutional Review," 2010, available at http://www.bepress.com/gj/vol10/iss2/art8, and Peeters, "Expanding Constitutional Review by the Belgian 'Court of Arbitration'," 2005, pp. 475-479.

20 These court officials were not required to be jurists (unlike the other judges). It should be noted that appointing 'political' judges to the Belgian constitutional court did meet with criticism because of the lack of independence and impartiality this would allegedly bring about.

As said, the *Cour d'arbitrage* was originally only authorised to verify whether legislation enacted by the federal government, the Communities, or the Regions was in accordance with the constitutional division of legislative powers. In time, however, this jurisdiction gradually came to expand. For instance, since 1989 the Court was also required to determine whether the right to equal treatment, the right not to be discriminated, and the right to freedom of education were violated (encapsulated in the Sections 10, 11, and 24 of the Belgian Constitution respectively). Finally, the Court's formal powers were extended to include all provisions of Title II of the Belgian Constitution ("On Belgians and Their Rights"). As a consequence, the *raison d'être* of the Court is no longer the federalisation of the Belgian state alone, but also the judicial protection of its citizens and their fundamental rights. Eventually, the name *Cour d'arbitrage* was changed to *Cour constitutionnelle* (Constitutional Court) in order to do justice to its present powers.

In sum, Belgium can, on the one hand, be characterised by what might called warehouse federalism: a polity in which the different constituent parts of the state are competent in different matters, sometimes even in the same geographical area (i.e., Brussels). On the other hand, Belgium's layout is also characterized by what might be called a blocked constitution, i.e., a constitution on whose basis a minority can freeze any decision concerning institutional and constitutional reform. As far as state reforms and related matters are concerned, it is almost as if the majority is structurally in a minority position; it is a constitutional paradox.[21] Today, all this makes for eight parliaments and eight governments,[22] next to ten provinces and a constitutional court, and also one King (and two Queens!).

---

21 Velaers, "De crisis van de staat en de achillespees van het staatsrecht," [The crisis of the state and the achilles heel of constitutional law], 2011, p. 24.

22 Each government comes with a parliament. The parliaments are: Federal Parliament (which is the only one with two chambers), Flemish Parliament (for both the Flemish Region and Community); Parliament of the Walloon Region; Parliament of the French Community; Parliament of the German-Speaking Community; Parliament of the Brussels-Capital Region; Combined Assembly of the Common Community Commission; Assembly of the French Community Commission; and Assembly of the Flemish Community Commission. The last four parliaments/assemblies are composed of the same people, each time exerting other competences. Depending on the definition of parliament, the count may differ from the one given here. *H. Vuye*, for example, refers to nine parliaments, counting Federal Parliament, because of its two Chambers, double. Vuye, "België: een Staat in hervorming of in ontbinding?," [Belgium: a State in reform

II. The Netherlands[23]

The situation could not be more different in the Netherlands. This is remarkable in light of the fact that the two countrie once were one. After the Napoleonic wars, the United Kingdom of the Netherlands was established in the Low Countries in 1815. This Kingdom encompassed both the northern provinces that nowadays constitute the Netherlands and the southern provinces that nowadays constitute Belgium. Support for the policies of the first monarch of the United Kingdom, King William I, was far less strong in the south than it was in the north. In the south, Roman Catholics and liberals pursued greater liberty in shaping their own identities. The Roman Catholics sought freedom of religion from the Protestant north, while the liberals wanted better representation: southern underrepresentation in the States General, i.e., the parliament based in the northern provinces, was indeed sorely felt by many in the region. In addition, the francophone population found it hard to stomach William's Dutch-language politics. Matters eventually came to a head when, in 1830, the pursuit of liberty sparked a revolution, and the southern part of the country seceded from the northern part.

Nowadays, the Netherlands is a small unitary country, with some 17 million inhabitants. Just like Belgium it is highly affluent and densely populated. It is also a (mainly) ceremonial monarchy.[24] The Netherlands has traditionally, and for a long time already, been a country of minorities, especially in religious and political terms. This also shows in electoral results: since the introduction of universal suffrage in 1917, no political party has ever been able to succeed in winning a parliamentary majority.[25]

Parliament, which consists of two chambers, is situated in The Hague. The so-called Second Chamber is the more political one of the two, and consists of 150 members, who are elected once every four years – if there

---

or in corruption?], 2008, pp. 719-724. To avoid making matters even more complex, I will disregard the ten provinces (each of which also have an assembly) and the 589 Belgian municipalities.

23 An English version of the text of the Dutch Constitution can be found on: http://legislationline.org/documents/section/constitutions.

24 A useful and more detailed overview about Dutch political history and institutional shape can be found in Andeweg and Irwin, *Governance and Politics of the Netherlands*, 2009.

25 See Andeweg and Irwin, *Governance and Politics of the Netherlands*, 2009, pp. 22-23.

are no new elections in between, as a result of government collapse – through a system of proportional representation. The First Chamber, also informally called Senate, consists of 75 members who are elected every 4 years by the members of the provincial councils (i.e., 12 councils with 564 members in total, accounting for 12 provinces). Its election, however, does not coincide with elections for the Second Chamber. The position of Senator is moreover a part time one, for one day a week, with no parliamentary assistance. Its members come from all sectors of society. Although having more or less the same powers of governmental oversight as the Second Chamber, the First Chamber has no right of legislative initiative or even amendment, but nevertheless has to approve of legislation accepted by the Second Chamber. It can only fully accept or reject this legislation, making for a rather intricate and complicated relation between the First and Second Chamber. Constitutional convention has it that the First Chamber is supposed to mainly look at technical issues of legislative quality (chamber of reflexion), but once in a while it behaves more politically. Its existence and legitimacy has been a matter of debate for years already, especially when it contravenes the Second Chamber on political topics.[26] Just like Belgium, next to being a monarchy, the Netherlands is a parliamentary democracy, which means that the existence of the government is dependent upon a majority in parliament (especially the Second Chamber).

Dutch constitutionalism can be described as being a rich tapestry of customs and documents.[27] Two national documents nevertheless stand out in this regard. On the one hand, there is the *Charter of the Kingdom of the Netherlands* (1954), and on the other hand, we find the *Constitution of the Kingdom of the Netherlands* (the first version dating back to 1813, but with its last major revision in 1983). Of the two, the Charter is the less known, but the higher in terms of legal hierarchy nonetheless. It states that the Kingdom consists of equal partners, i.e., the Netherlands, Aruba, Curacao and Sint Maarten (the latter three islands being situated in the

---

26 On this Adams, "De nieuwe Belgische Senaat en het wetgevingsproces: kamer van reflectie of doublure? Enkele beschouwingen in het licht van de Nederlandse situatie," [The new Belgian Senate: Chamber of reflexion or duplication? Considerations with a view to the Dutch situation], 1996, pp. 230-238.

27 See Schyff, *Judicial Review of Legislation. Constitutionalism Personified in the United Kingdom, the Netherlands and South Africa*, 2010, par. 37 (on which this alinea is partly based).

Caribbean), and regulates the relations between these constituent entities of the Kingdom. The Dutch Constitution itself however, is only applicable to the Netherlands and foresees a decentralised unitary state. I will focus here on this last document, which is in effect the most important and prominent one.

The constitutional dispensation of the Netherlands can reasonably be seen as that of a democratic *rechtsstaat*.[28] This means that the Dutch democracy is not intended to be left to its own devices completely, but that it is expected to operate within the recognised boundaries of a *rechtsstaat*, i.e., in terms of protecting fundamental rights through a bill of rights (ranging from classical to socio-economic rights, prominently encapsulated in Chapter 1 of the Dutch Constitution) and respecting people's liberty.

Deserving special attention here, and in strong contrast to Belgium, is that the Dutch Constitution explicitly forbids judicial constitutional review.[29] The debate regarding constitutional review in the Netherlands is indeed an old, yet undecided one. It is also informative and typical of Dutch constitutional culture and design. As just stated, the Dutch Constitution was adopted in 1814 and was revised on a number of occasions since then.[30] Importantly, the revision of 1848 saw constitutional review prohibited by Section 115(2), which stated that "statutes are inviolable". This provision was included at the insistence of the government at the time and was contrary to the opinion of a State Commission entrusted with revising the Constitution, as the latter favoured constitutional review by the judiciary. Nonetheless, the prohibition became a standard feature of the Dutch Constitution, as *J.R. Thorbecke*, who chaired the State Commission and was a noted supporter of constitutional review, warned it would be.[31] As a matter of fact, it survived all constitutional revisions since 1848. However, while not affecting its function, its formulation was changed in the most recent revision in 1983. The prohibition is now included in Section 120 and

---

28 See about this also Schyff, *Judicial Review of Legislation,* par. 35.

29 See on this also Adams and Schyff, "Constitutional review by the judiciary. A Matter of Politics, Democracy or Compensating Strategy?," 2006, pp. 399-414.

30 For an overview, see Sap, *The Netherlands Constitution 1848-1998. Historical Reflections*, 2000.

31 See Thorbecke, *Bijdrage tot de herziening van de Grondwet* [Contribution to the revision of the Constitution], 1921, p. 60.

provides that "[t]he constitutionality of statutes and treaties shall not be reviewed by the judiciary."

Yet, it may not be deduced from the above that the Dutch judiciary may never review legislation for compatibility with higher norms. This is because the revision of the Constitution in 1953 recognized the power of the judiciary to review legislation for compatibility with international treaties. Section 94 states in this regard that "legislative regulations in force within the Kingdom shall not be applicable if such application is in conflict with provisions of treaties that are binding on all persons or in conflict with resolutions adopted by international institutions."

When read together, Sections 94 and 120 lead to a rather peculiar situation. On the one hand the judiciary is barred from testing the constitutionality of statutes, but not from reviewing legislation that enjoys a lesser legal position than statutes, as Section 120 only applies to statutes in the sense of 'acts of parliament'. For example, the judiciary may review delegated legislation for compatibility with the Constitution, but not to the extent that the enabling statute is questioned. Testing the constitutionality of delegated legislation may then not be used as an excuse to test the constitutionality of the legislation from which it stems. On the other hand however, the judiciary may, on the basis of Section 94, review all forms of legislation for compatibility with international treaties and resolutions. In practice, this usually means that classical rights guaranteed in international treaties are applied, but not socio-economic rights, bar a few exceptions, as the latter rights are usually judged to be not directly enforceable.[32]

This chequered situation has been the topic of much debate. Interestingly, a report drafted in 1966 by the Interior Ministry's Section for Constitutional Affairs recommended that the prohibition on constitutional review be partially lifted to allow the judiciary to test legislation in respect of the classical rights guaranteed in the Constitution.[33] It was felt that such rights provided their bearers with greater protection than rights guaranteed in international law, and therefore deserved the benefit of judicial protection: international law was seen as only providing minimum norms, and therefore, did not adequately protect rights.

---

32 See Prakke, Reede and Wissen, *Handboek van het Nederlandse staatsrecht* [Handbook Dutch Constitutional law], 2001, p. 238.

33 *Proeve van een nieuwe Grondwet* [Attempt of a new Constitution], 1966.

The debate regarding the introduction of constitutional review by the judiciary gained momentum with the publication in 1969 of the second report of the State Commission, called upon to render advice in respect of the Constitution (and the Electoral Law).[34] The Commission considered the recommendation, by the Interior Ministry's Section for Constitutional Affairs, that the prohibition be partially lifted. It took note of the arguments commonly used against constitutional review. For example, the point was raised that constitutional review calls upon the judiciary to make *political decisions*, instead of entrusting this task to the legislature where it is normally considered to belong.[35] Furthermore, lifting the prohibition would potentially endanger judicial independence, as appointments to the bench could then become the object of political contestation and influence.[36] It was also considered that judicial review of international treaties presented a different case altogether and could consequently not be used as a base from which to argue for constitutional review. This was founded on the argument that the judicial review of international treaties was geared towards engendering respect for minimum norms across a variety of legal systems, whereas constitutional review was much "closer to home", as it were.[37] In other words, constitutional review would amplify the role of the judiciary in the *trias politica* to an unacceptable extent, thereby encroaching on the domain preserved for the legislature. These arguments are very much in line with those that dominated the European continent after the French Revolution and that found favour with numerous Dutch academics, namely that good governance amounted to a clear *separation* of powers.[38] In this case, this would mean a separation between the legislature and judiciary – each to its own.

Nonetheless, the State Commission came to the conclusion by 11 votes to 6 that constitutional review of classical rights had to be allowed. The point was made that such review was necessary to strengthen the position of the individual in relation to the government. Classical rights were

---

34 Cals and Donner, *Tweede Rapport van de Staatscommissie van advies inzake de Grondwet en de Kieswet* [Second Report of the State Commission concerning an advice for a new Constitution and the Electoral law], 1969.

35 See Cals and Donner, *Tweede Rapport*, p. 39.

36 See Cals and Donner, *Tweede Rapport*, p. 39.

37 See Cals and Donner, *Tweede Rapport*, p. 39.

38 Cfr. Brewer-Carias, *Judicial Review in Comparative Law*, 1989, p. 252; Cappelletti, *The Judicial Process in Comparative Perspective*, 1989, pp. 193-194.

judged as the proper vehicle for this, as their primary function lay in keeping government intrusion at bay when it came to personal freedom. However, the successive government supported the minority of the State Commission in opposing the introduction of constitutional review by the judiciary. Political reluctance sealed the fate of reform, and as mentioned, the 1848 prohibition on constitutional review survived the 1983 constitutional revision, albeit with a different formulation.

This did not bring the debate to an end though. In 1988, the President of the District Court in The Hague, sitting in summary proceedings, gave a ruling in a case that achieved a large amount of attention.[39] The case related to three statutes on education, which were amended by the so-called 'Harmonisation Law'. This statute retrospectively limited state funding (i.e., scholarships) for students. An application was brought requesting the Court not to apply the statute, as it violated the general principle of legal certainty. It was argued by the applicants that although Section 120 prohibited constitutional review by the judiciary, it did not explicitly bar the judiciary from reviewing legislation against (unwritten) general legal principles not included in the Constitution – such as that of legal certainty *in casu*. The Court, however, rejected this argument. Section 120 could thus not be sidelined in this manner.

In addition, the applicants also averred that the Harmonisation Law violated the principle of legal certainty, as guaranteed in Section 43(1) of the aforementioned Charter of the Kingdom of the Netherlands of 1954. As said, the Charter, which acts as a basic law, states that the Kingdom of the Netherlands is composed of three equal partners, namely the Netherlands, Aruba, Curacao and Sint Maarten. It is distinct to the Constitution, as the latter applies only to the Netherlands as such. Moreover, the Charter is technically the highest law in the Netherlands. Interestingly enough, the Charter, in contrast to the Constitution, does not explicitly prohibit the judiciary from testing the constitutionality of statutes from being reviewed by the judiciary, yet also does not explicitly empower the judiciary to effect such review. The District Court in The Hague judged the absence of a prohibition as reason enough to engage in constitutional review of the Harmonisation Law. It consequently held that the Harmonisation Law did indeed violate the students' rights when tested against the Charter and consequently refused to apply the offending

39 Pres. District Court's Gravenhage, 11 August 1988, *Nederlands Jurisprudentie* [Dutch case law] 1989, p. 489.

provisions. This amounted to introducing constitutional review by the judiciary.

The matter was eventually lodged with the Supreme Court of the Netherlands (*Hoge Raad*). The Supreme Court joined the court *a quo* by noting that Section 120 could not be interpreted to allow the judicial review of legislation against general legal principles. Contrary to the District Court however, the Dutch Supreme Court took the view that the Constitution excluded any possibility of reviewing legislation in the light of any higher rule whatsoever, bar the exception of international law in Section 94 of the Constitution of course. The Court also pointed out that, during the revision of the Constitution in 1983, the legislature discussed the question whether it was desirable to abolish the rule in Section 120 prohibiting constitutional review by the judiciary, and that no fundamental objections had been raised against it. The Court went on to conclude that the rule prohibiting constitutional review by the judiciary, including extra-constitutional legal norms, was therefore entirely consistent with the "traditional position"[40] occupied by the courts in the institutional structure of the Dutch state. The ultimate judgment on the meaning of the Constitution should accordingly be entrusted to the *democratically-elected legislature*. The Supreme Court noted though that the need for civil society to be protected against the government had increased since 1983, but that it was not for it to exceed its boundaries in this respect. In other words, positive law had to prevail, which meant upholding and applying the prohibition on constitutional review contained in Section 120 of the Constitution. The Supreme Court proceeded to overturn the finding by the court *a quo* that the Harmonisation Law could be tested against the guarantee of legal certainty contained in Section 43(1) of the aforementioned Charter. The Court also stated that although the Constitution contained an express bar to constitutional review by the judiciary, the absence of a similar provision in the Charter could not be interpreted as allowing judicial review by implication. The Court explained that such a turn of events would neither accord with the intention embodied in the Charter, nor would it accord with the principle in the Kingdom of the Netherlands of avoiding judicial review of compliance with constitutional documents. The prohibition on constitutional review by the judiciary in Section 120 of the Constitution

40 Pres. District Court's Gravenhage, 11 August 1988, *Nederlands Jurisprudentie* [Dutch case law] 1989, p. 489.

could thus not be outflanked by testing the contested legislation against the Charter instead.

This decision did – again – revive the debate in the Netherlands regarding constitutional review by the judiciary. In 1991 the Dutch government presented a policy note to, *inter alia*, the Supreme Court for its considerations in an advisory opinion.[41] The central question, according to the government, no longer revolved around *whether* constitutional review had to be introduced, but centred on the *form* that it had to take. The Supreme Court supported the idea of lifting the prohibition on constitutional review in respect of a number of, mostly classical, rights.[42] The Supreme Court also supported the idea of de-concentrated judicial review, in other words, empowering *all judges* to carry out constitutional review, instead of reserving this function for a few selected judges or a special constitutional court. However, differences of opinion led the government to not proposing a constitutional amendment. The government in 1997 again asked the Supreme Court for its opinion on constitutional review, but again failed to act, and in 2002 submitted a policy note to the legislature.[43] This time, it noted that although much could be said against constitutional review by the judiciary, it nonetheless had a slight preference towards the introduction of de-concentrated review. The timing largely coincided with a proposal to amend the Constitution, which was tabled by a prominent opposition member of the Dutch legislature.[44] This proposal built on earlier arguments that sought to allow the courts to conduct judicial review. It was also met with some success; but in order to amend the Dutch Constitution, the proposal had to satisfy the usual criterion of passing two readings.[45] The first reading implies that both houses of the legislature accept the proposal with a simple majority, after which the proposal is subsequently reconsidered in a second reading after a general election. The proposal becomes a constitutional amendment if passed by a two-thirds majority in both houses during this second reading. At the moment, the Second as well as First Chamber of the Dutch

41 *Nota inzake rechterlijke toetsing* [Policy note concerning judicial review], 1991.

42 Published in 7 *NJCM-bulletin* 1992, p. 243.

43 Tweede Kamer vergaderjaar 2000-2001 [Second Chamber of Parliament, meetings of 2000-2001], 27, 460, no. 1.

44 Tweede Kamer vergaderjaar 2001-2002 [Second Chamber of Parliament, meetings of 2001-2002], 28, 331, no. 2. Cfr. Tweede Kamer vergaderjaar 2002-2003 [Second Chamber of Parliament, meetings of 2002-2003], 28, 331, no. 9.

45 Section 137 of the Constitution.

parliament have accepted the proposal – the First Chamber with a single vote majority! – and so the first reading is complete. It is however at this very moment widely agreed upon that the proposal will not pass the second reading, and that as a result judicial constitutional review will thus not be introduced in the Netherlands in the near future. As all this shows, one might characterise the Dutch constitutional order as rather open, thereby strongly emphasizing parliamentary democracy.

C. A Possible Explanation for Belgian and Dutch Politico-Constitutional Design

I. Theory

How can Belgian and Dutch constitutional culture and accompanying design be explained? *Arend Lijphart's* political theory could well offer an explanation for the specific institutional configuration of both politico-constitutional systems, and also of the behavior of the actors shaping these configurations. *Lijphart* has termed his theory 'consociational democracy'.[46] It means "government by elite cartel to turn a democracy with a fragmented political culture into a stable democracy."[47]

A consociational democracy is most often found in societies, as is clear from the definition just cited, that are strongly divided. It was generally assumed that political stability was beyond reach for such societies, but *Lijphart* has demonstrated that this *nec plus ultra* is not untenable for them; political *in*stability is thus not a predestined terminus for fragmented or disunited societies. The potentially destabilizing effects of division are on the contrary likely to prompt the established political actors to search for pragmatic ways to deal with societal cleavages. Alternative methods of political accommodation, contrary to regular majoritarian politics, are thus explored, and the different segments in society actively strive for

---

46 On this, see in particular his *The Politics of Accommodation. Pluralism and Democracy in the Netherlands*, 1968; *Democracy in Plural Societies: A Comparative Exploration*, 1977; and *Democracies: Patterns of Majoritarian and Consensus Government in Twenty-one Countries*, 1984. See, too, Adams and Schyff, "Political Theory Put to the Test. Comparative Law and the Origins of Judicial Constitutional Review," 2010, available at http://www.bepress.com /gj/vol10/iss2/art8.

47 Lijphart, "Consociational Democracy," 1969, p. 216.

cooperation, consensus and stability: they seek to find each other and to cherish common ground as much as possible. Political differences between the ruling groups are, as a result, not politicized or exaggerated and a substantial number of the political leaders cooperate in governing the country, thus neutralizing destabilizing tendencies. This also prevents major political groups from becoming estranged from the political system. As a result, although political decision-making in consociational democracies is strongly affected by the interplay of past and present political and other tensions, in practice, so the theory goes, it operates in a way that defuses these tensions and encourages compromise.

The hallmarks of a consociational democracy are broad government coalitions, political proportionality (in elections and representative bodies, but also in advisory bodies, the civil service, etc.), mutual rights of veto in political decision-making, and 'pillarisation'. Pillarisation is a term that describes the vertical organization of a society along traditional ideological, religious, and/or politico-economic divides. Pillarised societies are divided in several smaller segments or pillars according to different religions or ideologies. All of these pillars have their own social institutions (broadcast companies, newspapers, schools and universities, sports clubs, mutual sickness funds, etc.) and resources, with each group retaining autonomy of how to use them.

The Dutch and Belgian societies for the greater part of the twentieth century play an important part in (the development of) Lijphart's views and theories. They were both deeply ideologically divided between liberals and socialists, and between Catholics and Protestants (in the Netherlands) and between Catholics and non-confessional groups of society (in Belgium). According to *Lijphart*, Dutch society from the 1960s onwards was a classic example of both a pillarised society and a consociational democracy. And he considered Belgium "the most thorough example of a consociational democracy."[48] Both Belgium and the Netherlands have nevertheless developed into completely different political and constitutional cultures. What is common however, is that although in both countries the pillars have crumbled as religious division have weakened (although more in the Netherlands than in Belgium), elite

48 Lijphart, "Introduction: The Belgian Example of Cultural Coexistence in Comparative Perspective," 1981, p. 1 (italics added). See also Lijphart, *Democracy in Plural Societies*, pp. 223-238.

compromise still remains a key operational devise.[49] Indeed, when essential societal issues cannot be resolved or addressed via the regular political channels, for example because of a potential structural political deadlock between the political factions in parliament, other elitist bodies are many times empowered to cut the knots.[50] The issue of judicial constitutional review, dealt with in the previous paragraph, is again telling here.

II. Belgium

It might be good to mention here that the demise of the Belgian federal government in 2007, which was mentioned previously in this chapter, was the direct result of a decision by the Belgian Constitutional Court on a highly sensitive issue: the constituency of Brussel-Halle-Vilvoorde (BHV), which for the federal elections comprised the central bilingual district of Brussels and some neighboring parts of Dutch-speaking Flanders (where as a matter of fact many French-speaking Belgians live), together containing some 1.6 million inhabitants. It has been a politically exceptionally difficult issue for decades. In 2003 the Constitutional Court ruled that, after the 2002 electoral reform which was the result of a hard-fought political compromise, this constituency contravened the equality and non-discrimination clauses of the Constitution, because it was the only constituency in the country that did not come with a single monolingual province. As a result of this 2002 reform, voters in parts of Flanders could vote for French-speaking politicians. The Court declared unconstitutional parts of the law concerning this compromise,[51] also stating that a solution for this situation had to be reached before the 2007 federal elections. A

---

49 See Hague and Harrop, *Comparative Government and Politics*, 2007, p. 115.

50 On this, see, e.g., Guarneri and Pederzoli, *The Power of Judges. A Comparative Study of Courts and Democracy*, 2002, pp. 161-180. Hirschl too refers to this work (p. 33).

51 Judgement 73/2003 of 26 May 2003. To be found in Dutch, French and German on: www.const-court.be/public. See Sinardet, "From consociational consciousness to majoritarian myth: Consociational democracy, multi-level politics and the case of Brussel-Halle-Vilvoorde," 2010, pp. 346-369 and Lindemans, "Het probleem Brussel-Halle-Vilvoorde. Analyse van een staatsrechtelijke doos van Pandora," [The problem Brussel-Halle-Vilvoorde. Analysis of a constitutional Box of Pandora], 2005-2006, pp. 473-504.

solution, however, was not reached, and its contention made the post-election coalition negotiations very difficult. In November 2007, the Dutch-speaking members of parliament almost unanimously voted to split up the constituency. This was the first time ever a single language group did so in view of a sensitive issue like this, which put a lot of pressure on the relations between the different language groups. The dire prospect of the *conflicts of interest*[52] and *alarm bell*[53] procedures loomed largely, and the 'conflicts of interest' procedure was actually resorted to. This caused considerable delay in resolving the issue, institutionally and otherwise. In 2010 the government fell again, before agreement on this topic between the different political factions was reached.[54]

What may not be immediately obvious to outsiders, however, is that the difficulties surrounding this electoral district have to do with territorial-linguistic claims. Due to the constituency's hybrid nature, the Dutch-speaking Flemish political parties wanted it to be split, which would create two separate electoral districts: one for the Brussels Region and one district for the Province of Flemish Brabant. This would prevent the francophone political parties from attracting French-speaking voters outside of bilingual Brussels and put a brake on the frenchification of parts of Flanders (especially in the municipalities surrounding Brussels) something so greatly feared by the Flemish.

This is a highly sensitive issue in Belgian politics and society. Brussels has, over the centuries, developed from a Dutch-speaking city into a French-language enclave in Flanders. The legislative fixation in 1962-63 of the language border (which was based on the language count of 1947), was meant to stop the frenchification of Brussels and its surrounding area. The border was not to be based on language counts anymore. The granting of linguistic facilities and rights to the French-speaking population in some municipalities was to compensate for this. The frenchification, however, didn't stop, resulting today in French-speaking majorities in officially Dutch-speaking municipalities. The debate as it unfolds today is

52 See footnote 18.

53 See main text surrounding footnote 18.

54 All this provokes the question whether the 2007 and 2010 elections in the aforementioned constituency were conducted in a legally correct manner. Opinions differ. The issue was, however, negotiated in the 2011 government formation, and a settlement was reached. In July 2013, the particulars were being put in legislation.

partly put in terms of whether or not the language facilities were introduced as a temporary measure to give the French-speaking population the opportunity to learn to speak Dutch (of which many Dutch speakers say has been to no avail), or introduced as some sort of fundamental right which almost by definition cannot be temporal (as many of the French speakers claim).

III. The Netherlands

Consider the Netherlands now. Dutch society and its institutions have long availed themselves of channels, other than judicial constitutional review, to deal with social or political conflicts and interests, including the protection of fundamental rights. Whereas previously, societal problems were solved within the pillars, today, pivotal organizations dealing with these problems include, next to parliament, the Council of State, the Social and Economic Council, the Auditor's Office, the Scientific Council for Government Policy, the High Council of the Judiciary, Ombudspersons, and other public advisory, controlling or decision-making bodies ('poldering' bodies).[55] This fact might somehow tone down one of the essential arguments put forward in the aforementioned proposal to introduce judicial constitutional review in the Netherlands, namely, that it would be more beneficial to have an extra link in the chain to create new legislation or regulation and essentially that an extra-legislative check is necessary to secure proper checks and balances.[56]

In any case, what is important to note here, is that in the Netherlands there has been, for many years, talk of a mild or moderate constitutional culture, and of a strong distance between constitution and politics: "It is virtually impossible to find any politician in The Hague [the seat of Parliament, MA] who would want to win or lose a political debate on the

---

55 The Council of State for example advises, next to being the highest administrative court, on the legislative quality (including the constitutionality) of pending bills.

56 *Parliamentary Proceedings* II, 2001-2002, 28 331, No.3, pp. 13-15. More particularly, it is argued that the dwindling influence of the parliament makes judicial constitutional review necessary in order to safeguard or enforce the protective function of the law. But from a systemic perspective, there would not appear to be a dearth of checks and balances in the Netherlands, despite the courts not being able to review the constitutionality of legislation.

ground that a certain topic would be contravening the Dutch Constitution."[57] As a result, there are very few people, besides those who belong to the inner circle of constitutional specialists that consider themselves as the 'guardians of the constitution.' Concerning significant topics, Dutch constitutional life is developing next to the written Constitution, in constitutional customary law for example, with all the dubiety that accompanies this last source of constitutional law. To give but a few examples: the development and limitation of the monarch's power is predominantly arranged without the Constitution, as such, being amended; even stronger: the Constitution is to a large extent silent about this topic. The same is true for cabinet formation proceedings, which are arranged by means of constitutional convention. Also, nothing can be found about political parties or the independence of the judiciary in the Dutch Constitution, and there is no word whatsoever in the Constitution about the European Union or about the 'rule of law', neither is there any inspiring preamble or prelude. In addition, to give a last example, the independence of both Chambers of parliament is only implicitly acknowledged, through the Section that states that each Chamber chooses its own chair (Section 61). The Constitution is however not only a rather sober document, but its role in everyday political and constitutional life is more limited than that of some if not most other constitutions, so much so that in some respects one might even speak of a 'constitutional illiteracy' on behalf of the political class. This conclusion can be based on the very scant use of the Constitution during parliamentary debates, as well as the lack of enforceability before the country's courts (see above in pararaph B.II.).

IV. Contrasting

The contemporary constitutional and institutional structures of Belgium and the Netherlands, as set out previously in this chapter (see paragrapgh B), can indeed be understood or explained from the point of view of consociationalism. In Belgium, federal government coalitions usually have a fairly broad support base with a minimum of three coalition partners

---

57 Besselink, "Constitutionele klimatologie," [Constitutional, climatology], 1998, p. 212. Also about Dutch constitutional culture Tang, *Grondwet en grondwetsidee* [*Verfassung* and the idea of a constitution], 1998, pp. 373-375.

(and often more), and it is clear that changes in the country's institutional set-up cannot possibly be decided by a simple majority in parliament; there are moreover many institutionalized mechanisms in place to reach political consensus or pacification on these issues. For this reason, Pinder has defined consociational arrangements as "institutions and procedures that encourage consensus rather than allowing the will of those who represent a simple majority of the population to prevail."[58] Majority-type democracy, from this point of view, is "the antithesis of consociational democracy."[59] All this means that the Belgian Constitution has a rigid and highly politically salient nature, being expressly called upon in public and political discourse; possibly with the Constitutional Court as leverage or as a background threat, especially whenever the relations between the two communities that make up the country are at stake.

And although the Netherlands is also essentially ruled by elites, and in this respect still has a distinctly consociational flavour to it, its constitutional culture is nonetheless rather different from the one that is prevalent in Belgium. In the Netherlands, the accommodation of political conflicts is arranged by many means, but not through evoking constitutional law. In line with *Lijphart's* reasoning, it could well be argued that the renowned late 20th-century Dutch 'polder model' (consultation model) is an offshoot of a consociational democracy. The phrase 'polder model' has uncertain origins, but is mostly used to describe the typically Dutch version of consensus politics, developed in the 1980s and 90s in socio-economic affairs.[60] It is a short hand, referring to the typical Dutch 'polders'[61], for an institutionalized form of cooperation and consensus seeking between political actors, social partners and other societal organizations. The term was, however, also quickly adopted for a broader meaning, i.e., pragmatic elite consensus decision-making in the face of diversity and plurality in general. So, following the gradual dissolution of the old 'pillarised' way of organizing Dutch society, the Dutch system of political decision-making found new, distinctly non-

---

58 Pinder, "Multinational Federations," 2007, p. 9.

59 Lijphart, "The Belgian Example of Cultural Coexistence in Comparative Perspective," p. 1.

60 See Woldendorp, *The Polder Model: From Disease to Miracle? Dutch Neo-Corporatism 1965 – 2000*, 2005, p. 28.

61 A 'polder' is a low-lying piece of land, which was originally flooded by water and was later won as land. It is enclosed by embankments to prevent the land from flooding. It is a very typical (though not exclusive) Dutch phenomenon.

judicial ways to channel potential bottlenecks in the political decision-making processes; ways which were completely different from the ones that prevailed in Belgium.

As a result of all this, Dutch constitutional culture is not really marked by the use of legal and normative (i.e., 'binding') language, which is so typical for Belgian constitutional discourse. We might thus typify Dutch constitutional culture as relativistic and the two aforementioned constitutional documents – i.e., the Charter and the Constitution – can best be understood as more general maps as opposed to robust guarantees in the service of the democratic *rechtsstaat*. This is even more so, since courts in the country generally show great restraint in their dealings with higher law (as the European Convention on Human Rights for example).[62] The Constitution does not function as a strong normative document; it is rather a codification of political practice than the other way round.[63] The Dutch Constitution as such, as is also generally agreed upon, is moreover rather uninspiring; a construction with no character, the builders of which were rather provident and drifty.[64] All this of course does not necessarily mean that political life develops arbitrarily. It might also mean that political and social practice are intimately in tune with the constitution (and the democratic values it expresses). And since the Netherlands is generally regarded as a tolerant and democratic nation, the Dutch might as well praise themselves with such a situation. If that is a correct evaluation, it would not be unfair to state, with Loewenstein, that the Dutch constitutional suit fits very well and is moreover actually worn.[65] The question of course is if this is a correct evaluation indeed.

D. Consociational Troubles

Do Belgian and Dutch constitutional layouts promote societal consensus and stability? The short answer to this question is that both its track

---

62 See Schyff, *Judicial Review of Legislation*, par. 40.

63 As Dutch scholar Van der Hoeven already in 1958 observed, in his seminal *De plaats van de grondwet in het constitutionele recht* [The place of the written Constitution in constitutional law], 1958.

64 See Tang, "Een Grondwet voor de politieke samenleving" [A constitution for a political society], 2008, pp. 91 and 94.

65 See Loewenstein, *Political Power and the Governmental Process*, p. 148.

records are not optimal. I will in this paragraph elaborate on this, and again split up my analysis in a Belgian and a Dutch part.

I. Belgium

Constitutional design in Belgium, as much as it fosters cooperation, structurally hinders accommodation techniques. As it develops, consociationalism can harden or rigidify pre-existing group differences[66], and it is clear that the Constitutional Court is not necessarily conducive to accommodation. At least two problems stand out.

The first can be found on the level of political parties and elite estrangement. In a consociational democracy, Stephen Holmes has aptly observed, the political elites must both represent and not represent their constituencies: "They must hold their followers' loyalty, but not reproduce their uncompromising attitudes in national negotiations. Such cross-sectarian cooperation among elites requires 'a strengthening of the political inertness of the non-elite public and their deferential attitudes to the segmental leaders.'"[67] The trouble is that in Belgium this seems hardly possible since *national* political parties no longer exist. Since the 1960s Belgium has had regional political parties, and today quite a few of these parties have no ideological counterpart on the other side of the language border. And even when they do (as is the case with the Christian-democratic, liberal and social-democratic political parties) they are split on many important issues. Today, the discursive focus of politics and of public opinion is almost exclusively geared towards the regional level and its sentiments. Federal politicians are first and foremost representatives of their respective regions in which they are elected. This makes for a not necessarily Belgian minded political elite with hardly any Belgian

---

66 Pildes, "The Legal Structure of Democracy," 2008, p. 333.

67 Holmes, *Passions and Constraint. On the Theory of Liberal Democracy*, 1995, p. 212 (referring to Lijphart). Peters describes this as follows: "The federal nature of Belgian politics means that the party leaders must be thinking about their role in the context of a multi-level governance arrangement, and must conceptualise their role as the cement that binds the various elements of the system together." Peters, "Consociationalism, Corruption and Chocolate: Belgian Exceptionalism," 2006, p. 1081.

identity.[68] All this has removed incentives for moderate consensual and electoral politics, and has resulted in a big gap between regional electoral pledges and the reality of national politics. This gulf has been widened by a split media landscape,[69] and the fact that since the 1990s it is possible to form different or asymmetrical regional and federal government coalitions.[70] Consociationalism asks for the willingness and ability to compromise and reach consensus between the language communities, but before that is possible, in Belgium, "elected politicians wanting to govern at the federal level must first solve the problems that they have created themselves."[71]

The second consociational fault line, which lines up to the first one in that both stimulate calls for more, in this case, Flemish autonomy (and in both cases the solutions desired become part of the problem for consociationalist theory and politics), has to do with the specificity of Belgian federalism. Federalism is mostly intended to bring the separate

68 *Deschouwer* therefore talks about distrust at the top: the elite does not trust the system, because the political system is perceived to benefit the other more. Deschouwer, *The Politics of Belgium. Governing a Divided Society*, 2009, p. 233.

69 Which, if it even reports on this issue, gives a very one-sided and even partial account of events and political life on the other side of the language border. Sinardet and Temmerman, "Political journalism across the language border: communicative behaviour in political interviews by Dutch- and French-speaking journalists with Dutch- and French-speaking politicians in federal Belgium," 2008, pp. 110-138.

70 See Deschouwer, *The Politics of Belgium*, p. 233-236. Goethem, *Belgium and the Monarchy. From National Independence to National Disintegration*, 2010, pp. 269-271. *B. Guy Peters* rather neutrally observes that "there is not necessarily a greater identification of the public with Belgium as an entity than with the constituent parts." He adds that the regions have become the arena in which the conflict between both parts of Belgium are played out. Peters, "Consociationalism, Corruption and Chocolate: Belgian Exceptionalism," pp. 1083 and 1084.

71 Deschouwer, *The Politics of Belgium*, p. 237. I believe that this is the core of one of the main criticisms of consociationalism by *Donald Horowitz*: the granting of autonomy to different communities not necessarily promotes attitudes and behavior that promotes stability. Horowitz, "Constitutional Design: an Oxymoron?," 2000, pp. 253-284 and "Constitutional Design: Proposals versus Processes," 2002, pp. 15-36. For an excellent overview of the debate between *Lijphart* and *Horowitz*, see Choudhry, "Bridging comparative politics and comparative constitutional law: Constitutional design in divided societies," 2008, pp. 15-26. See also, Andeweg, "Consociational democracy," 2000, pp. 509-536.

units of a state together.[72] The Belgian variety of federalism however has the exact opposite aim of separating its two main components;[73] Belgian federalism is thoroughly bipolar. While federalism tends to work well when there are more than two basically equal partners, "[Belgian federalism] is the juxtaposition of two peoples moving in different directions."[74] As a result, social tensions among the groups can easily worsen, since 'the problem' can always be traced to "the same other":[75] political parties belong to one language group, as do members of parliament (including the accompanying veto mechanisms), federal government is based on linguistic parity, etc. This is even more so since the rather far-reaching allocation of competences to the Regions and Communities highlight the differences rather than the commonalities between the two main Regions and language groups. To put it in financial terms, the fact that there are significant financial transfers from one economically solid region – Flanders – to the economically less well off region – Wallonia – has a profound impact on Flemish public opinion. Many would reason that the financing region should also have a more decisive say in the other's state of affairs and in their institutional and constitutional relations (i.e., how they relate to each other).[76] However, as we have seen, decision-making on the future of the Belgian state, including its financial allocation mechanisms,[77] always involves the other veto player who is perceived to be radically different. And since calls for

72 Interestingly, *Lijphart* himself seems to have recognized this early one: "A multiple balance of power among the segments of a plural society is more conducive to consociational democracy than a dual balance of power or hegemony by one of the segments, because if one segment has a clear majority its leaders may attempt to dominate rather than cooperate with the rival minority." Lijphart, *Democracy in Plural Societies*, p. 55.

73 Belgian federalism might have this in common with Canada or Spain, or possibly the United Kingdom (devolution).

74 As former prime minister *Tindemans* said in 1971: *Parliamentary Proceedings*, Senate, 7 July 1971, p. 2368.

75 Deschouwer, *The Politics of Belgium*, p. 235.

76 See Goethem, *Belgium and the Monarchy*, p. 271.

77 Which are not fully federalized: the division of competences between the two Regions and Communities does not always come with the full fiscal autonomy necessary for employing these competences; the financing mechanisms remain in federal hands. On this Swenden and Jans, "'Will It Stay or Will It Go?' Federalism and the Sustainability of Belgium," 2006, p. 885.

more autonomy tend to come from the Dutch-language part of the country, this 'other' is also a linguistic minority.

But how long will this situation last? "Prediction is difficult, especially concerning the future", *Niels Bohr* reportedly once said. The complexity of the Belgian situation makes predicting an even more hazardous challenge than it normally is. From the perspective of this chapter, the one million dollar question is whether Belgium's constitutional and institutional set-up is conducive to societal stability and peace (and in line with this: whether Belgium will survive its seemingly permanent political crisis). So far it seems as if it has indeed been conducive to societal stability: Belgium is not marked by riots and violent uprisings between the different communities. And even the relative instability of Belgian governments can be seen as systemically functional because governmental break-up might also be understood as one of the means of reducing the possibilities for political deadlock and blockage.[78] Even so, there are indications that in Belgium consociational strategies can no longer be fully relied upon. For example, the cries for more autonomy have in recent years led to the rise of a strong democratic nationalist political party in Flanders, NV-A (*Nieuw Vlaamse Alliantie*, New Flemish Alliance), which is currently part of the Flemish and Federal government coalition. The NV-A would appear to have replaced the more extremist and separatist right-wing *Vlaams Belang* (Flemish Interest) as the voters' favourite *nationalist* political party; until recently the latter did rather well in elections, but politically it has remained a marginal force because of its xenophobic views of foreigners and the resulting exclusion of any government coalition.[79] It is also at heart an opposition party. The current enormous success of the NV-A might be a sign of a changing political constellation – separatism is becoming a real issue in political discourse; maintenance of the status quo does not appear to be the only option any longer, at least not for the Flemish part of the country, nor is it realistic given the institutional and historical weaknesses of the Belgian state.[80]

78 See Peters, "Consociationalism, Corruption and Chocolate: Belgian Exceptionalism," p. 1088.

79 In 2004 some of its satellite organisations were convicted for racist crimes. See Adams, "Geen woorden maar daden? De vrije meningsuiting van het Vlaams Blok" [Not words, but actions. Freedom of opinion of the Flemish Interest], 2004, pp. 189-196.

80 See Goethem, *Belgium and the Monarchy*, p. 276.

And although demands for more autonomy seem to come mainly from the Dutch-speaking side of Belgium, these demands are highly relevant to the French-speaking part. Previously, when tensions ran high and one of the actors insisted on institutional reform, the other side perceived that as a quasi-obligation to negotiate a solution for the problem concerned.[81] Today however, the positions are hardening and some development towards more federalization seems to be the unavoidable next step.

Logically, a desire to coalesce implies a need for it.[82] So in the light of what has been said so far, we might well wonder why Belgium does not split up. The most convincing explanation for the current situation is Brussels. There are at least two elements that are relevant here. The first is the economically vital position of Brussels: it is a significant place of employment for many people from out of Brussels. Breaking up comes at considerable cost, possibly too high to even seriously consider. The second element is the emotional element: although nowadays Brussels is essentially a French-speaking city, geographically surrounded by Flanders, historically it is of Dutch-speaking origin. The frenchification of Brussels, which started in the mid-nineteenth century, is a "romantic" source of frustration for many. "If Flanders were not to claim or need Brussels, the structure of Belgium could be much less complicated. Both communities see Brussels as their (capital) city and that is what has created the double federation of Regions and Communities."[83] In the meantime, tensions continue to build up and Flemish calls for more autonomy are becoming stronger and stronger, and the willingness to federally cooperate in a consensual manner seems to be losing ground.

The Belgian Constitution has institutionalized political distrust and instability, by installing a kind of disintegrating federalism. As a result it has not been capable of installing a sense of nationhood – with mutual respect and common interests between the (populations of the) different communities – or *Verfassungspariotismus* in its nationals.[84] The Belgian

81 See Deschouwer, "And the Peace Goes On? Consociational Democracy and Belgian Politics in the 21st Century," 2005, p. 906.

82 As Lijphart himself admits in "The Wave of Power-Sharing Democracy", 2002, p. 43.

83 Deschouwer, *The Politics of Belgium*, p. 244.

84 See Lemmens, "De Belgische Grondwet, een model voor Europa? Over natie en identiteit," [The Belgian Constitution; A model for Europe? About nation and indentity"], 2005, p. 185. Elazar puts it like this: "Federalism can exist only where there is a considerable tolerance of diversity and willingness to take

Constitution is an encumbering one, and the type of decision-making it encourages can hardly serve as the 'germ of a nascent sense of political community' or promote the general interest beyond the regional interests.

II. The Netherlands

In the Netherlands, consociational structures and pillarisation have been waning for quite some time already – because of secularization and emancipation –, but new social cleavages have arrived instead. The composition of Dutch society has been changing significantly through immigration in the last few decades, especially as a result of the influx of new ethnic and religious minorities, Muslims in particular.[85] This presents the country with many pressing issues surrounding integration, even more so since these immigrants, in many instances, turn out to be members of disadvantaged groups. The pressures were amplified by e.g. the murder of politician *P. Fortuyn* in 2002 and of public commentator *T. Van Gogh* in 2004. As Andeweg and Irwin make clear, the elitist character of Dutch politics has, as a result, been under increasing attack in the last decade or so: political competition seemed to intensify with no guaranteed voters available anymore (a result of depillarisation), the rise of the populist right, and calls for a more direct democracy have been multiple.[86] There have however hardly been any institutional or political reforms.

In the same vein, the Dutch Constitution still has no role to play in the process of societal integration and in creating political stability: in the Netherlands constitutional relativism still prevails, even in the context of fundamental rights, and even though this relativism might not be adapted to contemporary Dutch society anymore. To give but a few examples in the context of ethnic integration and diversity: the judicial section of the Dutch *Conseil d'État* (*Raad van State*), the highest administrative court in the country, has for some time already been limiting the rights of refugees to a considerable and impressive extent (also when compared to other European countries!). The same is true for the right to family

---

political action through the political arts of negotiation even when the power to act unilaterally is available." Elazar, *Exploring Federalism,* 1987, p. 181.

85 On this see Andeweg and Irwin, *Governance and Politics of the Netherlands*, pp. 44 ff.

86 See Andeweg and Irwin, *Governance and Politics of the Netherlands*, p. 51.

reunification, i.e., a legally recognized reason for immigration in many countries, enabling a family to immigrate to a country where one (or more) of their family members already resides. Although the Netherlands, in these contexts, has been convicted for contravening human rights law on several occasions already, there has been hardly any policy or judicial change. The 2010 Government, in its coalition agreement, even stated that there would be a "restrictive and selective" policy, where possible, concerning migration, even if that would mean changing the European Convention of Human Rights.[87] Such policy can certainly be understood as a response to the aforementioned attacks on elite political culture and the increase of political competition.

Let it be clear that we are not dealing here with a 'mere' normative issue ("Fundamental rights should of course be upheld!"), but with an issue that is explicitly instrumentally relevant too: what does it do with human beings when they are – or feel – excluded from full citizenship, are treated as outsiders or bestowed with marginality? What loyalty can one then expect from the community in which they are present? What kind of unrest and social instability will be the result of this? These are questions that are rarely asked. What is nevertheless important and necessary is to create and support a political and moral climate where everyone has a change to make something out of his or her life. This is what Rosanvallon refers to as 'relational equality' or 'equality as social relation'[88]; a form of equality that is not only dealing with the distribution of wealth, but on the basis of which it is also possible to recognize and acknowledge the individual as a full member of a society. There is a clear role for a type of constitutionalism here, which can be conducive in recognizing full equality and thereby enabling loyalty to the democratic *rechtsstaat* (*citoyen*; citizenship). A constitution in this respect represents not just a (incidental political) majority, it also and most importantly defines principles for the whole community. Unfortunartely the Dutch constitution is largely absent in doing so.

87 About all this, see Spijkerboer, "Subsidiariteit 2.0," 2012, p. 252.
88 See Rosanvallon, *La société des égaux*, 2011.

E. Rounding up: Lessons to be Learnt

In *Passions and Constraint*, *Stephen Holmes* writes that a constitution disables political decision-making in that it sets up procedural roadblocks by, for example, introducing supermajority decision-making rules or by enacting bills of rights; the idea is to thereby prevent tyranny and other abuses of power.[89] *Holmes* terms this 'negative constitutionalism'. In a divided society, as in any liberal society, constitutions must fulfill this negative or disabling role.[90] A constitution at the same time can, according to *Holmes*, also assume an enabling role, which he calls 'positive constitutionalism': it can help create the very *demos* which governs itself through the constitutional regime. In this sense a state can also use its powers to achieve cooperation and support. Even stronger, if a divided society also wants to be a free society, negative and positive constitutionalism should be connected to each other. *Choudhry* puts it like this:

> [B]ecause of a history of conflict or a lack of shared existence, the constitution is often the principal vehicle for the forging of a common political identity, which is, in turn, necessary to make that constitutional regime work. To some extent, the constitution can foster the development of a common political identity by creating institutional spaces for shared decision making among members of different ethnocultural groups. Concrete experiences of shared decision-making within the framework of the rule of law, and without resource to force or fraud, can serve as the germ of a nascent sense of political community.[91]

I submit that in both Belgium and the Netherlands negative and positive constitutionalism are not connected and thus cannot be (mutually) reinforcing. Although the Belgian Constitution does play a significant role in channelling and/or constraining the local politico-institutional situation,

---

89 See Holmes, *Passions and Constraint*, xi-xiii, pp. 5-7 and pp. 161-164. Also Choudhry, "Bridging comparative politics and comparative constitutional law," 2008, pp. 5-6.

90 See Choudhry, "Bridging comparative politics and comparative constitutional law," p. 6.

91 Choudhry, "Bridging comparative politics and comparative constitutional law," p. 6. Choudhry adds that a constitution can "constitute a demos by encoding and projecting a certain vision of political community with the view of altering the very self-understanding of citizens."

it does not succeed in taking up an enabling role. The Constitution itself is at best a rational construction, possessing an accidental nature and a complex technicality; it represents a *status quo* and a form of federalism that does not create any Belgian public space. In the Netherlands, the Constitution is fading ever more into oblivion, neglecting its possible enabling role too.

As a result both the Belgian and Dutch Constitutions are in danger of no longer being able to govern the dynamics of the power process and become instead governed by it: a warning of the demise of a state's capacity to effectively act as the agent of its citizens' well being. In such conditions, the constitution runs the risk of falling prey to political manipulation. The democratic *rechtsstaat*, a concept which is given authority and effect through constitutions and constitutionalism, can however not fly on autopilot; it needs maintenance and active direction. The introduction of judicial constitutional review in the Netherlands might be one way of doing this, or the creation of better developed form of constitutional literacy, as might be the installation of a Belgian public space through (re)introducing a federal electoral district for federal parliament.[92]

All this of course raises more general questions of a constitution's normative and practical value, i.e., questions similar to the ones Loewenstein was troubled about and with which I started this chapter: under what conditions are political actors usually prepared to comply with constitutional requirements or take them into account? The answer to questions like this are, I believe, highly contingent and not clear cut; there does not seem to exist an objective set of rules for matching a people and their situation with a set of institutions.[93] Nevertheless, both the Belgian and Dutch cases can, so it seemed, be instructive in telling us a bit more about the constitutional conditions that might be conducive to societal stability. It is however of the utmost importance to generate more knowledge about this, because societal unrest usually comes with an array

---

92 See Sinardet, "Direct democracy as a tool to shape a united public opinion in a multilingual society? Some reflections based on the Belgian case", 2009, p. 59. About this Horowitz, "A Federal Constituency for Belgium: Right Idea, Inadequate Method", 2009, pp. 25-28.

93 See Lutz, *Principles of Constitutional Design*, 2006, p. ix. *Loewenstein* too discards the idea of trying to devise a "perfect theoretical constitution", instead claiming that "an ideal constitution has never existed, and will never exist." K. Loewenstein, *Political Power and the Governmental Process.*

of negative consequences (the possibility of violence being one of them). Democratic politics without positive constitutionalism is in any case troublesome; in the long run no democracy can survive such a state of affairs.[94]

Works cited

Adams, Maurice, "Disabling Constitutionalism", *International Journal of Constitutional Law (I•CON)* 12 (2014): 279-302.

Adams, Maurice, "Doing What Doesn't Come Naturally. On the Distinctiveness of Comparative Law," in *Methodology of Legal Research*, ed. Mark Van Hoecke, Oxford: Hart Publishing, 2011, pp. 229-233.

Adams, Maurice, and Gerhard van der Schyff, "Constitutional review by the judiciary. A Matter of Politics, Democracy or Compensating Strategy?," *Zeitschrift für ausländisches öffentliches Recht und Völkerrecht* 66 (2006): 399-414.

Adams, Maurice, "Geen woorden maar daden? De vrije meningsuiting van het Vlaams Blok," [Not words, but actions. Freedom of opinion of the Flemish Interest], *Rechtsfilosofie en Rechtstheorie* 2 (2004): 189-196.

Adams, Maurice "De nieuwe Belgische Senaat en het wetgevingsproces: kamer van reflectie of doublure? Enkele beschouwingen in het licht van de Nederlandse situatie" [The new Belgian Senate: Chamber of reflexion or duplication? Considerations with a view to the Dutch situation], *RegelMaat. Tijdschrift voor Wetgevingsvraagstukken* 5/6 (1996): 230-238.

Andeweg, Rudy B., and Galen A. Irwin, *Governance and Politics of the Netherlands*, Basingstoke: Palgrave Macmillan, 2009.

Andeweg, Rudy B., "Consociational democracy," *Annual Review of Political Science* 3 (2000): 509-536.

Bell, John, "Legal Research and the Distinctiveness of Comparative Law," in *Methodology of Legal Research*, ed. Mark Van Hoecke, Oxford: Hart Publishing, 2011, p. 155-176.

Benda-Beckmann, Franz von, "Ethnologie und Rechtsvergleichung," *Archiv für Rechts- und Sozialphilosophie* 67 (1981): 310-329.

Besselink, Leonard F. M., "Constitutionele klimatologie," [Constitutional climatology], *Nederlands Juristenblad* 5 (1998): 212-213.

Bogdandy, Armin von, "Comparative Constitutional Law: a Contested Domain," in *The Oxford Handbook of Comparative Constitutional Law*, ed. Michel Rosenfeld and András Sajó, Oxford: Oxford University Press, 2012, pp. 25-37.

---

94 Cfr. Gunsteren, "Het staatsrecht in de politiek," [Constitutional law in politics], 2010, pp. 1111-1114.

Brewer-Carias, Allan R., *Judicial Review in Comparative Law*, Cambridge: Cambridge University Press, 1989.

Cals, J.L.M.Th., and A.M. Donner, *Tweede Rapport van de Staatscommissie van advies inzake de Grondwet en de Kieswet* [Second Report of the State Commission concerning an advice for a new Constitution and the Electoral law], 1969.

Cappelletti, Mauro, *The Judicial Process in Comparative Perspective*, Oxford: Oxford University Press, 1989.

Choudhry, Sujit, "Bridging comparative politics and comparative constitutional law: Constitutional design in divided societies", in *Constitutional Design for Divided Societies, Integration or Accommodation?* ed. Sujit Choudhry, Oxford: Osford University Press, 2008, pp. 3-40.

Deschouwer, Kris, *The Politics of Belgium. Governing a Divided Society*, Basingstoke: Palgrave MacMillan, 2009.

Deschouwer, Kris, "And the Peace Goes On? Consociational Democracy and Belgian Politics in the 21st Century," *West Euroepean Politics* 29 (2005): 895-911.

Elazar, Daniel J., *Exploring Federalism,* Tuscaloosa: University of Alabama Press, 1987.

Elkins, Zachary, Tom Ginsburg and John Melton, *The Endurance of National Constitutions*, Cambridge: Cambridge University Press, 2009.

Finer, Samuel Edward, Vernon Bogdanor and Bernard Rudden, *Comparing Constitutions*, Oxford: Clarendon Press, 1995.

Ginsburg, Tom, Zachary Elkins and James Melton, *The Endurance of National Constitutions*, Cambridge: Cambridge University Press, 2009.

Goethem, Herman van, *Belgium and the Monarchy. From National Independence to National Disintegration,* Brussels: EPA, 2010.

Guarneri, Carlo, and Patrizia Pederzoli, *The Power of Judges. A Comparative Study of Courts and Democracy*, Oxford: Oxford University Press, 2002.

Gunsteren, Herman van, "Het staatsrecht in de politiek" [Constitutional law in politics], *Nederlands Juristenblad* 17 (2010): 1111-1114.

Harding, Andrew, and Peter Leyland, "Comparative Law in Constitutional Contexts," *Comparative Law. A Handbook*, ed. Esin Örücü and David Nelken, Oxford: Hart Publishing, 2007, pp. 313-338.

Hague, Rod, and Martin Harrop, *Comparative Government and Politics*, Basingstoke: Palgrave MacMillan, 2007.

Hoeven, J. van der, *De plaats van de grondwet in het constitutionele recht* [The place of the written Constitution in constitutional law], Zwolle: Tjeenk Willink, 1958.

Holmes, Stephen, *Passions and Constraint, On the Theory of Liberal Democracy*, Chicago: University of Chicago Press, 1995.

Horowitz, Donald L., "A Federal Constituency for Belgium: Right Idea, Inadequate Method," in *Electoral Engineering for a Stalled Federation*, ed. Kris Deschouwer and Philippe Van Parijs (eds.), Re-Bel e-book, 2009, pp. 25-28.

Horowitz, Daniel L., "Constitutional Design: Proposals versus Processes," in *The Architecture of Democracy. Constitutional Design, Conflict Management, and*

Democracy, ed. Andrew. Reynolds, Oxford: Oxford University Press, 2002, pp. 15-36.

Horowitz, Daniel L., "Constitutional Design: an Oxymoron?," in *Designing Democratic Institutions*, ed. Ian Shapiro and Stephen Macedo, New York: New York University Press, 2000, pp. 253-284.

Lasser, Mitchel de S.-O. –L É. "The Question of Understanding", in *Comparative Legal Studies: Traditions and Transitions*, ed. Pierre Legrand and Roderick. Munday, Cambridge: Cambridge University Press, 2004, pp. 197-239.

Lijphart, Arend, "The Wave of Power-Sharing Democracy," in *The Architecture of Democracy: Constitutional Design, Conflict Management, and Democracy*, ed. Andrew Reynolds, Oxford: Oxford University Press, 2002, pp. 37-54.

Lijphart, Arend, *Democracies: Patterns of Majoritarian and Consensus Government in Twenty-one Countries*, New Haven: Yale University Press, 1984.

Lijphart, Arend, "Introduction: The Belgian Example of Cultural Coexistence in Comparative Perspective", in *Conflict and Coexistence in Belgium. The Dynamics of a Culturally Divided Society*, ed. Arend Lijphart, Berkeley (University of California): Institute of International Studies, 1981.

Lijphart, Arend, *Democracy in Plural Societies: A Comparative Exploration*, New Haven: Yale University Press, 1977.

Lijphart, Arend, "Consociational Democracy," *World Politics* 21 (1969): 207-225.

Lijphart, Arend, The Politics of Accommodation. Pluralism and Democracy in the Netherlands, Berkeley: University of California Press, 1968.

Lindemans, Servaas, "Het probleem Brussel-Halle-Vilvoorde. Analyse van een staatsrechtelijke doos van Pandora," [The problem Brussel-Halle-Vilvoorde. Analysis of a constitutional Box of Pandora], *Jura Falconis* 4 (2005-2006): 473-504.

Lemmens, Koen, "De Belgische Grondwet, een model voor Europa? Over natie en identiteit" [The Belgian Constitution; A model for Europe? About nation and indentity"], *Rechtsfilosofie en Rechtstheorie* 2 (2005): 179-185.

Loewenstein, Karl, *Political Power and the Governmental Process*, 2nd edition, Chicago/London: The University of Chicago Press, 1965.

Lutz, Donald S., *Principles of Constitutional Design*, Cambridge: Cambridge University Press, 2006,

Nelken, David, "Defining and Using the Concept of Legal Culture," in *Comparative Law. A Handbook*, ed. Esin Örücü and David Nelken, Oxford: Hart Publishing, 2007, pp. 109-132.

Peeters, Patrick, "Expanding Constitutional Review by the Belgian 'Court of Arbitration'," *European Public Law* 11 (2005): 475-485.

Peters, B. Guy, "Consociationalism, Corruption and Chocolate: Belgian Exceptionalism," *West European Politics* 29 (2006): 1079-1092.

Pildes, Richard, "The Legal Structure of Democracy", in T*he Oxford Handbook of Law and Poli*tics, ed. Keith Whittington, R. Daniel Keleman and Gregory Caldeira, Oxford: Oxford University Press, 2008, pp. 321-339.

Pinder, John, "Multinational Federations," in *Multinational Federations*, ed. Michael Burges and John Pinder, London: Routledge, 2007, pp. 1-16.

Prakke, Lucas, J.L. de Reede, and G.J.M. van der Wissen, *Handboek van het Nederlandse staatsrecht* [Handbook Dutch Constitutional law], Zwolle: Tjeenk Willink, 2001.

Rosanvallon, Pierre, *La société des égaux*, Paris: Le Seuil, 2011.

Sap, Jan Willem, *The Netherlands Constitution 1848-1998. Historical Reflections*, Utrecht: Lemma, 2000.

Schyff, Gerhard van der, *Judicial Review of Legislation. Constitutionalism Personified in the United Kingdom, the Netherlands and South Africa*, Dordrecht: Springer, 2010.

Shapiro, Martin, *Courts. A Comparative and Political Analysis,* Chicago: University of Chicago Press, 1981.

Sinardet, Dave, "From consociational consciousness to majoritarian myth: Consociational democracy, multi-level politics and the case of Brussel-Halle-Vilvoorde," *Acta Politica* 45 (2010): 346-369.

Sinardet, Dave, "Direct democracy as a tool to shape a united public opinion in a multilingual society? Some reflections based on the Belgian case", in *Public Opinion in a Multilingual Society Institutional Design and Federal Loyalty*, ed. Dave Sinardet and Mark Hooghe, Re-Bel ebook 3, 2009, pp. 47-60.

Sinardet, Dave, and Martina Temmerman, "Political journalism across the language border: communicative behaviour in political interviews by Dutch- and French-speaking journalists with Dutch- and French-speaking politicians in federal Belgium", in *Multilingualism and applied comparative linguistics: vol. 2: cross-cultural communication, translation studies and multilingual terminology*, ed. Jeroen Darquennes, Cambridge: Cambridge Scholars Publishing, 2008, pp. 110-138.

Spijkerboer, Thomas, "Subsidiariteit 2.0," in *Amici Curiae. Adviezen aan het Europees Hof voor de Rechten van de Mens* [Amici Curiae. Advice for the European Court of Human Rights], ed. J. Gerards and A. Terlouw, Nijmegen: Wolf Legal Publishers, 2012, pp. 251-260.

Swenden, Wilfired, and Maarten Theo Jans, "'Will It Stay or Will It Go?' Federalism and the Sustainability of Belgium," *West European Politics* 29 (2006): 877-984.

Tang, Ger F. M. van der, "Een Grondwet voor de politieke samenleving," [A constitution for a political society], in *De Grondwet herzien, 25 jaar later* [Rethininking the Constitution; 25 years later], Den Haag: Ministerie van Binnenlandse Zakenpp, pp. 85-112.

Tang, Ger F. M. van der, *Grondwet en grondwetsidee* [*Verfassung* and the idea of a constitution], Arnhem: Gouda Quint 1998.

Thorbecke, Johan Rudolf, *Bijdrage tot de herziening van de Grondwet* [Contribution to the revision of the Constitution], s'Gravenhage: Nijhoff 1921.

Velaers, Jan, "De crisis van de staat en de achillespees van het staatsrecht," [The crisis of the state and the achilles heel of constitutional law], *Rechtskundig Weekblad* 1 (2011): 23-27.

Vuye, Hendrik, "België: een Staat in hervorming of in ontbinding?" [Belgium: a State in reform or in corruption?], *Ars Aequi* 10 (2008): 719-724.

Woldendorp, Jaap J., *The Polder Model: From Disease to Miracle? Dutch Neo-Corporatism 1965 – 2000*, Amsterdam: Thela, 2005.

Hungary's Constitutional Transformation from a Central-European Comparative Perspective*

Gábor Attila Tóth

A. Introduction

More than two decades after the post-communist constitutional transition, Hungary entered the spotlight once again. The winning party in the 2010 elections gained two-thirds of the seats in Parliament, which made constitutional revision exceptionally easy – bypassing political and social deliberation.

The constitution was then changed fifteen times within a year, including a reduction of the Constitutional Court's competencies. Moreover, on April 25, 2011 (Easter Monday), on the first anniversary of the 2010 election, the President promulgated a brand new constitution called the Fundamental Law.

The new document has attracted the attention of scholars, politicians, media and the general public, both at home and abroad. While it is the first newly made constitution to originate from a democratically elected parliament in Hungary, the way the text was drafted as well as the content of the text itself, according to many observers, are in conflict with some of the basic features of democratic constitutionalism.

The objective of this paper is to describe how these constitutional changes are altering the basic structure of the Hungarian state. I first briefly outline the constitutional background of the 1989 revolutionary transition in Central Europe with a focus on Hungary. Second, I show the

---

* This paper is based upon my lecture at the conference "*Conflict and Consent in the Basic Constitutional Order*" of the German-Southeast Asian Center of Excellence for Public Policy and Good Governance and Thammasat University, Bangkok, on 25 February 2012. The text describes the situation as it was at that time. Since then, the Hungarian Constitutional Law has undergone changes. The paper contains extracts from my "From Uneasy Compromises to Democratic Partnership: The Prospects of Central European Constitutionalism," *European Journal of Law Reform*, 2011, pp. 53-69, and my "Hungary's Constitutional Transformation," 2011, pp. 183-203 (with Kriszta Kovács).

basic constitution-making process of Central European states. Third, I show why Hungary became an anomaly in the region and how the flexible constitution and the hostile political climate have challenged its constitutional stability. Fourth, I interpret the result of the 2010 parliamentary elections, called "Revolution in the polling booth" by the winning party, and describe the flaw of the controversial constitutional changes including the limitation of the competencies of the Constitutional Court immediately after the 2010 elections. Fifth, I review the process of the adoption of the new constitution, the Fundamental Law. And finally, painting with a broad brush, I introduce the main features of that new constitution.

Focusing on both the constitution-making procedure and the substance of the text, I provide a brief account of the Fundamental Law's main attributes and its underlying principles. The Hungarian constitutional transformation is a localized story, but it is of global relevance. Therefore I not only examine what the Hungarians have achieved or failed to achieve, but, implicitly, also call attention to what modern societies can learn from the Hungarian trauma.

B. "Velvet Revolutions" in 1989

A quarter-century ago Central European countries including the former Czechoslovakia, Hungary, Poland and Romania, were communist regimes that could be characterized by a single-party system (Hungary, Romania) or a dominant-party system (Czechoslovakia and Poland) without the possibility of competitive elections. The common feature of these states, like any other communist countries, was chronic shortage:[1] an economy of shortage instead of a market economy, a budget deficit instead of a balanced budget, and the lack of democratic institutions rather than a constitutional democracy. Although constitutions formally declared fundamental rights, these were not legally enforceable. The constitutional structures of these states were not based upon the principles of separation of powers and the rule of law. Moreover, the states did not ensure the independence of the judiciary or the press. And, of course, non-

1 See Kornai, *Economics of Shortage*, 1980.

governmental organizations were forced by the repressive regimes to work underground.

The historical turning point for the transformation from authoritarian regime to democracy was 1989. With the exception of only Romania, the dismantling of the communist regime proceeded peacefully, involving at some point roundtable negotiations between delegates of the state party and those of the opposition-in-the-making.[2] *Timothy Garton Ash* described the events with the expression "refolution" combining the term of reform and revolution.[3] Other authors labeled the developments as "coordinated transition" or "negotiated revolution".[4] Moreover, the dissolution of the federal state of Czechoslovakia and the establishment of the Czech Republic and the Slovak Republic, which took place in 1993, is often mentioned as "Velvet Divorce", a reference to the term "Velvet Revolution" that was used internationally to describe the 1989 revolutions.[5] These classifications all express that the Central European single-party systems did not collapse due to a classical revolution, but through negotiations and compromises between the old regime and the democratic opposition. However, the political transition did result in revolutionary changes in the political and constitutional system and did so without a revolution as such.

In his new evaluation, *Timothy Garton Ash* presupposes that the peaceful, negotiated regime changes in Central Europe together with the unification of Germany and the disintegration of the Soviet Union established a new model of non-violent revolution. The ideal type of classical revolution is violent, utopian, class-based, and characterized by a progressive radicalization, culminating in terror… The 1989 ideal type, by contrast, is non-violent, anti-utopian, based on broad social coalitions, and

---

2 *János Kis* characterizes the coordinated transition as an interruption of legitimacy, but continuity of legality. See Kis, *Between Reform and Revolution*, 1998, p. 317. See also, from the critical point of view of democratic theory, Arato, "Dilemmas arising from the Power to Create Constitutions in Eastern Europe," 1994, pp. 165-194.

3 See Garton Ash, "Revolution: The Springtime of Two Nations," 1989, 3-10; Garton Ash, "Revolution in Hungary and Poland," 1989, pp. 9-15.

4 Tőkés, *Hungary's Negotiated Revolution*, 1996.

5 But see the birth of the Czech Constitution from a critical point of view: Petra Gümplova, "Democracy and the Politics in Extraordinary: The Constitutional Making in Czechoslovakia, 1992," available at www.newschool.edu/uploadedFiles/NSSR/Departments_and_Faculty/Political_Science/Recent_Placements/Gümplova-Democracy_Extraordinary.pdf.

characterized by the application of mass social pressure to bring the current power holders to negotiate. It culminates not in terror but in compromise. If the totem of 1789-type revolution is the guillotine, that of 1989 is the round table.[6]

Without doubt, the negotiation was a process led not by the common interests of the parties, but by a clash of values and interests, in which both parties, the Communists and the democratic movements, were compelled to make compromises. We can say that the demand to reach compromises is one of the underlying characteristics of peaceful transitions. The Hungarian Constitutional Court called this "a revolution under the rule of law."[7]

The roundtables, however, did not actually have a mandate for constitution-making. They had no formal authorization to make law for the old regime. Nor did they have popular authorization to make law for the new regime. *János Kis* argues that the roundtables understood their task to be limited to facilitating the run-up to free, competitive elections, and were determined to leave to an elected assembly to give a constitution to the new regime. In order for their decisions to come into legal effect, those decisions must have been sent for enactment to the old legislature. And so the agreements were meant to regulate the transition from the old regime to a new one. Consequently, the roundtables were exceptional bodies having the capacity to start a coordinated process of constitutional change but leaving the completion of the process to an assembly with the democratic mandate they were lacking.[8]

János Kis characterizes the constitution-making profile of the "Velvet Revolutions" as consisting of two stages.[9] In the first stage, a roundtable agreement determines the ground rules of preparing and holding free elections. The second stage takes place when a body of freely elected representatives adopts, in the sovereign people's name, a new constitution.

In the aftermath of the Polish Round Table Agreement, the old constitution was amended in April 1989, and the first democratic

---

6 Garton Ash, "Velvet Revolution: The Prospects," 2009, pp. 20-23. See also, Garton Ash, *Facts are Subversive,* 2009, p. 51.

7 Decision 11/1992. See Sólyom and Brunner, eds., *Constitutional Judiciary in a New Democracy*, 2000, p. 214.

8 Kis, "Introduction: From the 1989 Constitution to the 2011 Fundamental Law," 2012.

9 See Kis, "Introduction: From the 1989 Constitution to the 2011 Fundamental Law," 2012, pp. 1-21.

parliament then reshaped the relations between the legislative and executive branches of the state ("Small Constitution"). The reformed constitution was finally replaced in 1997 by a completely new constitution for Poland. The old constitution of Czechoslovakia was also amended in 1989. The Charter of Fundamental Rights and Basic Freedoms was incorporated in 1991. After the dissolution of the federal state, the Czech Republic and the Slovak Republic adopted a new constitution in 1992. In Bulgaria and Romania, the second step was made in 1991.

By contrast, Hungary is the only nation that did not adopt an entirely new constitution after the fall of Communism. It is true, however, that Hungary has been a constitutional democracy since 1989. Like other countries in the region, the peaceful, co-ordinated political transition resulted in revolutionary outcomes: democratic institutions replaced an authoritarian regime; pluralist society replaced the dominance of communist ideology.

In comparison to the speedy political transformation, the text of the Hungarian constitution was changed only gradually. The 1989 amendments of the old Constitution created the legal frameworks of the new democracy that can be characterized by the main institutions of constitutionalism: a representative government, a parliamentary system, an independent judiciary, ombudsmen to guard fundamental rights, and a Constitutional Court to review the laws for their constitutionality. The most crucial elements of the substantively new Constitution were promulgated on the thirty-third anniversary of the 1956 revolution, two weeks before the fall of the Berlin Wall. According to one of the ground breaking principles, "The Republic of Hungary shall recognize the inviolable and inalienable fundamental human rights; respecting and protecting these rights are primary obligations of the State."[10] This means that the constitutionally protected moral rights are not constituted but only recognized and respected by the constitution-makers.[11]

The first democratic elections in 1990 resulted in a landslide victory for the opposition forces. Conservative rightist parties formed a coalition government relying on a sixty percent majority in Parliament. By the time Parliament was convened on 2 May, the upcoming Prime Minister concluded a deal with the leaders of the liberal opposition party. The deal resulted in an overhaul of the 1989 amendments. The opposition agreed to

10 Art. 8(1) of the 1989 Constitution.

11 See Kis, *Constitutional Democracy*, 2003, p. 119.

limit the number of issues that require two-thirds majority and also agreed on the creation of a constructive vote of confidence system. The 1990 amendments entered into force on June 26, 1990. As part of this agreement the liberal opposition party received the right to nominate a President of the Republic. *Árpád Göncz*, an opposition Member of Parliament, was elected President of the Republic by consensus.

As a consequence, similarly to the other countries in the region, the 1989 and 1990 amendments of the old text created the legal frameworks of the new constitutional democracy. Since the transition, the Constitution has been amended several times, including the 2004 modification that empowered Hungary to join the European Union. However, Hungary did not accomplish the symbolic mission: it failed to adopt a constitution, which would have demonstrated a successful finish of the democratic transition.[12]

C. Constitutional Structures

Today, these Central European countries belong to the class of constitutional democracies. Since the models of the reshaped Central European constitutions were international human rights instruments, as well as the more recent Western constitutions, they were written in the language of modern constitutionalism. This was true in Hungary since the non-violent but drastic change in 1989 created political and legal institutions similar to those already existing in the established liberal democracies.

Members of the legislature are selected through periodically held free elections. The vast majority of the nation's adult population has the right to vote regardless of race, gender or property ownership. The states' constitutions contain enforceable legal provisions rather than a collection of mere good wishes. The purpose of constitutions is seen as limiting the authority of state power.

Each of these constitutions recognizes and protects judicial independence, freedom of the press and the right to establish civil associations. There are constitutional courts – or in Poland, a Tribunal – that safeguard the constitutional values and principles and strike down

12 See Arato, "The Constitution-Making Endgame in Hungary," 1996, pp. 31-39.

unconstitutional laws. Judicial protection of the constitution in all countries is closer to the centralized German model than to the diffuse U.S. judicial review.[13]

The new Central European democracies followed Western European traditions in establishing an adapted parliamentary system instead of importing a United States presidential architecture.[14] The Hungarian constitution copied the German Chancellor-led system including a weak President elected by the parliamentary representatives.[15] The 1989-1990 constitutional amendments made it clear that the Prime Minister heads the executive and the Government is the supreme body of that branch, responsible to the Parliament. Considering only the relation between the legislature and the Head of the State, in normal circumstances the balancing power is the President's limited right of veto.

Since 1990 the Hungarian Constitutional Court has been considered to be the safeguard of fundamental rights and an institutional guarantee of the separation of powers. As in other Central and Eastern European countries,[16] the Constitutional Court was institutionally separated from the ordinary court system[17] and had unique, *erga omnes* constitutional interpretative authority. Under the 1989 constitutional system the broadest competence of the Hungarian Constitutional Court was the abstract constitutional review of legal rules, when there was no case or controversy. Anyone was entitled to bring an action without limitation; there were no deadlines to be observed, nor was the applicant required to

---

13 From a theoretical and critical point of view see Sadurski, *Rights before Courts*, 2005. See also Schwartz, *The Struggle for Constitutional Justice*, 2000; Procházka, *Mission Accomplished*, 2002.

14 See Garlicki, "Democracy and International Influences," 2005, p. 264.

15 In spite of this, several scope-of-authority controversies have revealed a characteristic uncertainty that occurs in the Hungarian and other Central European parliamentary systems. Vindicating real power as the head of state and the depository of national sovereignty sometimes leads to theatrical struggles. From a comparative perspective see Dorsen, Rosenfeld, Sajó and Baer, *Comparative Constitutionalism*, 2003, p. 269.

16 With one exception: after the transition Estonia – following the Scandinavian model – set up a Constitutional Review Chamber in its Supreme Court.

17 The main reason for this was that the transition was characterized by a deep mistrust among the new elites and the masses in the judiciary. The judiciary was considered to be a means of the previous oppression. See Sajó, "Contemporary Problems of the Judiciary in Hungary," 1993.

show any impact or other legally protected interest (actio popularis).18 In the first two decades the great majority of the proceedings fell in this category.

At the same time, the competence of the Constitutional Court in examining constitutional complaints was unusually limited. It could only review individual complaints alleging the judicial application of an unconstitutional law in the course of the proceeding. Thus, in Hungary, in a concrete controversy ending in a judicial decision, only the law applied could be reviewed, not the decision itself. If the Constitutional Court concluded that an unconstitutional law had been applied, the procedure might be re-opened. In the application of the law that was unconstitutional in the concrete case, the Constitutional Court is powerless. There was no legal remedy in cases where fundamental rights were violated as a result of judicial application itself.[19]

Despite this shortcoming, the Constitutional Court was the most important institution in maintaining the constitutional balance of powers. Because of the establishment of a one-chamber legislature, the constitutional system did not contain a limiting upper house. Since Hungary is a unitary state, it could not realize the vertical separation of powers doctrine of federalist states. The constitution-makers introduced a parliamentary system in which the executive and legislative powers were intertwined and the President had strongly limited competencies, even considering his veto powers. Hence, the real constitutional check on the powers of Parliament were the fundamental rights recognized by the 1989 Constitution and the Constitutional Court that interpreted and upheld those rights.

D. Hungarian Failure

As previously mentioned, Hungary is the only nation in the region that did not adopt an entirely new constitution after the fall of Communism. Substantially, the constitution was modern and democratic due to the

---

18 See Sólyom and Brunner, *Constitutional Judiciary in a New Democracy*, 2000, p. 81.

19 Hence, Georg Brunner's conclusion is well founded: "The arrangement for a constitutional complaint constitutes the most unsuccessful provision of the Constitutional Court Act." Brunner, "Structure and Proceedings," 2000, p. 84.

1989-1990 amendments. In formal terms, however, the 1989 Constitution was a mere modification of the Stalinist 1949 Constitution.

Compared to those of other European states, the Hungarian Constitution was easy to amend. The Constitution did not render any provision or principle un-amendable, i.e. *Ewigkeitsklausel*, and it required only the votes of two-thirds of members of parliament. Despite the fact that the Constitution could not be modified or amended by the ordinary law-making procedure according to a simple majority rule, it was regarded as relatively flexible rather than rigid, because one legislative body had the sole power to change the constitutional text. Neither a referendum, nor any other form of ratification (e.g., approval by the subsequent parliament) was required for the adoption of a new Constitution or a constitutional amendment.

According to the 1989 Constitution, with regard to particular rights and constitutional principles (including freedom of speech, freedom of conscience, freedom of association and assembly, the electoral system, etc.), any act substantially affecting those rights had to be approved by a two-thirds majority of the votes of the Members of Parliament present. The two-thirds majority could not only modify the Constitution and the above-mentioned crucial acts, but also elected the President of the Republic, the Supreme Court Chief Justice, the members of the Constitutional Court and ombudspersons.

Hungary made its attempt to bring the post-communist constitution-making process to a conclusion. Prior to 2010, there was only one period, between 1994 and 1998, when the Government was supported by two-thirds of the seats in Parliament. Even though on a number of issues the then ruling parties failed to seek the consent of the opposition regarding certain acts requiring a two-thirds majority, the governing coalition also expressed some willingness to co-operate with the opposition in constitution-making. They modified the procedural guaranties of the Constitution, to the effect that Parliament should decide by a four-fifths majority in the preparatory process on the cornerstones of the new Constitution.[20] Because of the hostile political environment and the

20 Art. 24(5) of the 1989 Constitution: "The majority of four-fifth of the votes of the Members of Parliament is required to pass the parliamentary resolution on the detailed rules on the preparation of the new Constitution." The provision was repealed by a constitutional amendment adopted by a two-thirds majority on 5 July 2010. See below.

divergent constitutional conceptions, the talks in the constitution-making process collapsed in 1997. The ideas of the rival political parties regarding the legal frameworks of the political community were diffuse enough to prevent a consensus on a brand new constitution. This is why although the 1989 Constitution was amended several times (e.g. to empower Hungary to join NATO and the European Union), the conception of fundamental rights and the basic structure of the state under the 1989 Constitution remained untouched until 2010.[21]

The above-mentioned two-thirds rule and the four-fifths procedural amendment incompletely represent a theoretical consideration. According to this, in order to govern the state properly, the simple parliamentary majority does not need to reshape the constitutional architecture or limit fundamental rights. The requirements of a qualified majority are supposed to function as a control over the governing majority in power. It seems to be an exceptional guarantee to protect constitutionalism in Hungary; however, it makes the constitutional balance fragile. Intense co-operation between the parliamentary parties and their strong commitment toward constitutional values are necessary to modernize the constitution. Without such a consensus there is a risk that the Constitution could become the victim of an overwhelming governing majority.[22]

E. Revolution in the Polling Booth – Flow of Modifications of the 1989 Constitution

Hungary's decisive parliamentary election, the sixth since the 1990 founding elections, took place in April 2010. In this election the then opposition party Fidesz won by a landslide, gaining a majority of 68 per cent of the seats with 53 per cent of the votes.[23] It was a majority

---

21 See Arato, "Post-Sovereign Constitution-Making in Hungary," 2010, pp. 19-44.

22 *Zoltán Miklósi* holds that rival parties have a shared responsibility to cooperate in sustaining the constitutional arrangement that regulates the political competition. What's more, in case of disagreement, no party should act alone in fundamental constitutional matters, even if it is fully convinced of the rightness of its position. See Miklósi, "Constitution-Making, Competition and Cooperation," 2012, pp. 59-81.

23 Since Hungary has a mixed – majoritarian and proportionate – electoral system with single member districts, county lists and compensatory lists, a party can

sufficiently large (2/3) to amend the Constitution or rewrite it totally. Both were to happen.

During the election, the necessity of a new constitution was not on the agenda. However, very soon after the 2010 elections the new Prime Minister announced that he would provide a brand new Constitution for the nation. As a first step, the Parliament adopted a proclamation statement of national co-operation,[24] and a governmental ordinance was published which made it compulsory for the proclamation to be prominently displayed in governmental buildings. The proclamation declares:

"[A]fter 46 years of occupation, and 20 confused years of transition, Hungary has regained the right and power of self-determination, [...] In spring 2010, the Hungarian nation gathered its strength once again, and brought about a successful revolution in the polling booth. Parliament declares that it recognizes and will respect this constitutional revolution. [...] Parliament declares that in April's election a new social contract was born. [...] The pillars of our common future will be work, home, family, health and order."[25]

The election results opened the way for a flow of constitutional changes. In first one and a half years of its term, the ruling party adopted a range of constitutional amendments, which are explored below.

I. Representative Organs

Soon after the inaugural sitting of the newly elected Parliament, a symbolic constitutional amendment was adopted to reduce the number of parliamentary deputies. Hungary had a 386-seat parliament, while under the new rules the number of Members of Parliament "shall not exceed 200."

Parliament also reduced the number of local government representatives, and with a constitutional amendment paved the way for the local representative body to name a vice mayor to substitute the

---

secure two-thirds of the parliamentary seats with a little more than 50 per cent of the votes.

24 1/2010. (VI. 16.) *OGY politikai nyilatkozata* [Proclamation of the Parliament].

25 1140/2010. (VII. 2.) *Korm. Határozat* [Governmental Resolution].

mayor. Henceforth, even a non-elected member of the local representative body (e.g. a political ally of the mayor) may be appointed as vice mayor.

Reducing the number of Members of Parliament as well as local government representatives required essential statutory changes in the election system and procedure. Concerning the parliamentary deputies, these statutes were not launched before the 2011 Fundamental Law. However, on a local level the parliamentary majority modified the substantive and procedural statutory rules of the elections and significantly reshaped the boundaries of the electoral constituencies. Local government elections were held based upon these new provisions in October 2010.

II. Administering Justice

In order to speed up court proceedings and to achieve "law and order" in society, a new constitutional provision was adopted. According to this, court secretaries, i.e., lawyers without a judicial appointment, may rule on cases within the competence of local courts, among others cases concerning the detention of those committing minor offences.[26] Although the new addendum declared that when administering justice the court secretaries were independent and answer only to the law, as a result of the new rule, not only judges could decide in legal disputes. Moreover, the court secretaries had the competence to rule on deprivation of personal liberty.

The governing majority also made significant changes with regard to the constitutional status of the public prosecutor's office. In the future the Parliament is to elect the Chief Public Prosecutor by a two-thirds majority instead of a simple one, and the term of the mandate has increased from six years to nine years. The Chief Prosecutor can also be re-elected an unlimited number of times.[27] In addition, Members of Parliament may no longer address interpellations to the Chief Public Prosecutor. According to the reasoning given, the change was intended to reinforce the

---

26 Court secretaries are law school graduates, who after the three-year clerkship pass the state professional exam and a vocational exam. They must serve for at least one year as a court secretary, after which they are eligible for judicial appointment.

27 Based upon the adopted rules, should the Parliament in 2019 fail to elect a nominee because the future governing party does not have a two-thirds majority in Parliament, the current Chief Prosecutor will remain in office.

independence of the Public Prosecutor's Office. However, the means applied do not clarify the constitutional status of the prosecution, which has been unclear since 1989. On the one hand it is not under the jurisdiction of the Minister of Justice, therefore the Minister could not be held responsible for the unlawful actions or omissions of the prosecution. On the other hand the prosecution does not enjoy an independent status like the judiciary, because prosecutors work within a strong hierarchical system with the obligation to obey the orders of higher-ranking prosecutors. With the modifications the governing majority further enhanced legal uncertainty instead of trying to clarify it.

III. Media

Brand new constitutional provisions on freedom of expression have been adopted by the Parliament. The amendments entailed significant changes. Formerly, the Constitution had required the Parliament to adopt a statute on preventing information monopolies by a two-thirds majority of its members. Since this 2010 amendment protecting and promoting media pluralism by adopting a special act has not been a constitutional aim. It has been replaced by the "protection of the diversity of the press",[28] which is not an equally effective guarantee for the goal to be achieved. A lack of a constitutional requirement to adopt an act about prevention of information monopolies may lead to a narrow interpretation of the diversity requirement. It might not include anti-monopoly rules (which are an important means to diversity), but only rules ensuring a diversity of media content. However, as a Recommendation of the Council of Europe Committee of Ministers points out, there is a difference between promotion of structural pluralism of the media, and content diversity.[29] The former refers to a sufficient variety of media outlets provided by a range of different owners, while the latter to a sufficient variety of information, opinions and programs being disseminated by the media and available to the public.

---

28 Art. 61(2) of the 1989 Constitution.

29 See Council of Europe, Committee of Ministers, *Recommendation on media pluralism and diversity of media content*, Rec (2007)2, available at https://wcd.coe.int/wcd/ViewDoc.jsp?id=1089699.

The governing majority introduced a scheme merging the former telecommunications and broadcasting regulatory authorities and it established one powerful Media Authority, providing this with a constitutional status and giving a competence for the Head to issue decrees, which are binding on everyone. The Head of the Authority is appointed by the Prime Minister for a term of nine years, which – under the given circumstances – ensures that the Government has a solid influence on the performance of the Media Authority. Moreover, such a long term of office could ensure that even if the government loses its parliamentary majority in the next elections, the officials it appointed will remain in power for almost a decade.

On the basis of this constitutional amendment, the legislature adopted acts relating to "content regulation" and to procedures and sanctions. According to the Act on institutional changes, the President of the Authority is also the Head of the Media Council,[30] the competence of which is not limited to regulating and controlling broadcast media, but supervises the print and Internet outlets. In parallel to this, the basic approach of the Act on content regulation is to place all media in the same regulatory basket: broadcast, print, and online media (news portal, professional blogs), by extending the content regulatory framework to the print and the new media. This means that not only does the same body oversee the different media providers, but the content requirements are also the same. Last but not least, the Act concerning the procedures and sanctions paves the way for the Media Council to impose large fines on print, online and broadcast media or even to shut down an organ permanently, which could have the effect of discouraging the press from expressing criticism. International bodies like the Organization for Security and Co-operation in Europe, the Council of Europe Commissioner for Human Rights and the European Commission have found the institutional transformations and the restrictions of the press freedom inappropriate.

The OSCE analysis emphasized that although the media legislation represented an attempt to modernize Hungarian media law by responding to the challenges posed by technological change, this was done mainly by extending the traditional regulatory framework to the new communication services. The report criticized the institutional design of the Media

30 The Media Council members are elected by the two thirds parliamentary majority for nine years. Under the given circumstances this results in a one-sided body.

Authority which "may, if deliberately (mis)used for this purpose, create conditions for the realization of the 'winner-takes-most' or indeed 'winner-takes-all' scenario in the current term of Parliament, in defiance of the principle of the division of powers and of the checks and balances typical of liberal democracy."[31]

According to the Council of Europe Commissioner for Human Rights, the provisions regarding appointment, composition and tenure of existing media regulatory bodies, "lack the appearance of independence and impartiality, quite apart from a *de facto* freedom from political pressure or control."[32]

The European Commission expressed concerns about the compliance of media legislation with EU law concerning four issues. These issues comprise extended usage of the obligation of balanced coverage, application of fines to broadcasters legally authorized in other Member States, rules on registration of all media content providers and broadly applicable provision under which media content may not cause offence, even by implication, to individuals, minorities or majorities. Following the intervention of the European Commission, Hungarian Parliament restricted the balanced coverage requirement to broadcasting and limited the range of sanctions with regard to media service providers resident in other Member States. In addition, media legislation was amended so that all media (including press and online media) are subject to subsequent registration with no prior authorization by the Hungarian authorities. And last but not least the ban on offensive content was softened.[33]

---

31 Organization for Security and Co-operation in Europe Office of the Representative on Freedom of the Media, *Analysis and Assessment of a Package of Hungarian Legislation and Draft Legislation on Media and Telecommunications*, September 2010, available at http://www.osce.org/files/documents/1/3/71218.pdf.

32 Council of Europe, Commissioner for Human Rights, *Opinion of the Commissioner for Human Rights on Hungary's media legislation in light of Council of Europe standards on freedom of the media*, CommDH (2011)10, available at https://wcd.coe.int/wcd/ViewDoc.jsp?id=1751289.

33 *Neelie Kroes*, European Commission Vice-President for Digital Agenda welcomed the amendments to Hungarian Media Law. See online at http://europa.eu/rapid/pressReleasesAction.do?reference=MEMO/11/89

IV. Retroactive Legislation

In addition to the media package, in the second half of 2010 the parliamentary majority adopted a constitutional amendment on retroactive tax obligation, which permitted the legislature to retroactively tax incomes received from public funds (from pensions to extra bonuses for former high-ranking government officials) if the income was given contrary to 'good morals' by state organizations.[34] The aim of the new amendment was to create an exception to the prohibition of *ex post facto* laws and the constitutional limits of taxation established by the Constitutional Court. Based upon this constitutional provision, an act was adopted concerning a 98 per cent tax on public sector severance pay above HUF 2 million (approximately Euros 7,300). It was to be applied to the pay received by public sector employees who left their jobs after 1 January 2010.

Several petitioners challenged the Act before the Constitutional Court. The Justices unanimously declared the Act unconstitutional, and annulled it *ex tunc*. The Court did not examine explicitly the constitutionality of the new constitutional amendment, but took this for granted by applying it in the current case. According to the reasoning of the Court, the constitutional amendment makes an exception to the prohibition of retroactive legislation only in cases of incomes paid *contra bono mores*. Despite this, under the challenged Act, the 98 per cent tax was applied to severance pays received legally, in accordance with 'good morals'. The 98 per cent tax was aimed not only at incomes that the new government considered going against 'good morals', such as excessive public sector bonuses, but also at the wages and salaries of public sector workers, such as civil servants and public sector employees (doctors, teachers), that were completely legitimate. In the Court's view, payments received according to former statutory regulations could not be seen as incomes *contra bono mores* and could not therefore be taxed retroactively from the beginning of the year 2010, even under the new constitutional amendment. Moreover, although the constitutional amendment paved the way for the legislature to

---

34 This version of Art. 70/I(2) of the Constitution reads as follows: "In cases of income received from public funds serving as a contribution to public revenues, special taxes may be introduced by statute retroactively as of the beginning of the given tax year if the income was given contrary to good morals by organizations managing state property or by organizations owned mostly by the state or governed by the state."

introduce special taxes on certain incomes, 98 per cent seemed to be a confiscatory tax and was therefore contrary even to the newly enacted Article of the Constitution.[35]

Shortly after the Court decision, the ruling coalition launched a new version of the constitutional amendment allowing any income from public funds to be taxed retroactively up to five years. [36] Besides the constitutional provision, the Parliament voted again for extra tax on certain incomes. The new Act stated that with effect from 2005, public sector employees must pay extra taxes on severance payments which exceed the HUF 3.5 million threshold.[37]

V. Limiting the Constitutional Court

The modifications of the constitutional rules on taxation in order to override a settled constitutional case-law were not the first steps in limiting the role of the Constitutional Court. After the inaugural sitting of the newly elected Parliament, the majority changed the constitutional regulation of the Constitutional Justices' nomination process. Hitherto, the members of the Constitutional Court had been nominated by a special committee consisting of one member of each parliamentary faction and elected by a two-thirds majority of the plenum. Under the new rule the Constitutional Justices can be nominated by a parliamentary committee

---

35 Decision 184/2010.

36 The new version of Art. 70/I (2) of the Constitution reads as follows: "In cases of income received from public funds serving as a contribution to public revenues, statute may retroactively as of the beginning of the fifth tax year before the given tax year, introduce a special tax that shall not reach the amount of the income where this income was given by organizations managing state property or by organizations owned mostly by the state or governed by it."

37 There is a HUF 2 million cap for managers of state-owned enterprises, companies owned by local governments and senior officials in the public sector, including municipalities. In its Decision 37/2011 the Constitutional Court annulled again the retroactive effect of the 98 per cent tax. The decision was based on the Court's competence to protect human dignity. The Court argued that the retroactive effect of the tax was an affront to this right, since it attempted to tax gains on which tax had already been lawfully paid; therefore the law was annulled. Due to the wording of the law, the decision pertains to payments effected in 2010, too, even if they did not fall in the "retroactive" category. Two days after delivering the Decision, Parliament approved a new law, under which a 98 per cent tax can be levied on severance pays given after 1 January 2010.

whose members are appointed from and by the parties according to their share of seats in Parliament. Consequently, even in the nomination process there is no longer a need for consensus. The parliamentary majority is able to nominate candidates without working together with the opposition or even with its own coalition partner. Based upon this constitutional change, the majority nominated and elected two new justices.

Moreover, in June 2011, there was one more amendment to the 1989 Constitution. (At that time the Fundamental Law had already been enacted but not entered into force.) The amendment enlarged the Court's membership from eleven to fifteen, adding up to four justices to the bench. (Five new justices were elected due to a vacant seat.) In sum, seven new justices were elected within one year. Following these amendments the Constitutional Court consists of fifteen members as of 1 September 2011.

When the Constitutional Court declared the 98 per cent tax unconstitutional, the ruling coalition responded by initiating a constitutional amendment that removed some parts of the Constitutional Court's jurisdiction. According to this, the Court is allowed to *review* the constitutionality and *annul* acts affecting the budget, the implementation of the budget, taxes, contribution payments and duties only if they violate the right to life and dignity, the right to protect personal data, the freedom of thought, conscience, religion and the rights connected to Hungarian citizenship. This means that the Court may examine the constitutionality of acts related to the state budget, central taxes, stamp duties and contribution's, custom duties and central requirements related to local taxes only if the petition refers exclusively to the right to life and dignity, the protection of personal data, the freedom of thought, conscience and religion or the rights connected to the Hungarian citizenship. But the Constitutional Court may not assess these acts for example with regard to the principles of non-discrimination, rule of law, proportionality of burden-sharing, and the prevalence of the right to property.

The selection of rights for which there can be constitutional review raises the following questions: Why just these rights and not others? Why for example the right to life and the protection of personal data but not the non-discrimination clause and property rights? In order to understand the motivation behind the selection, there is little point in searching for principled reasons. Hungarian case law reflects that the Constitutional Court has annulled tax and other financial measures by referring to those rights and principles that are missing from the list. Property rights, acquired rights and the so-called reliance interest in maintaining the social benefits were the references of the annulments. The Constitutional Court from the very beginning of its operation has been active in reviewing financial measures. In 1995 the Court issued a series of decisions which blocked the immediate implementation of cuts in the system of child support, sick pay, maternity leave, and other social programs by invalidating several parts of the Economic Stabilisation Act, the government's IMF-required austerity program.[38] Since then the Court has reviewed several tax measures. It annulled the regulation on the expected corporate tax base rate[39] and decided that 'quasi taxation' of family allowance was against the Constitution.[40] Recently the Court found the property tax unconstitutional.[41] These cases were the symptoms of a theoretical separation of power dilemma. If the Constitutional Court without having political responsibility frequently makes a policy choice better left to the governing majority, democratic decision-making is confounded. The government officials gave a definite answer to this problem when they made it clear that they saw no choice but to limit the power of the Constitutional Court. Otherwise the recent 'crisis taxes' imposed on banks, energy companies, foreign retail and telecommunication firms might be deemed unconstitutional. Hungary faced a growing budget deficit and was on the verge of a severe economic crisis. To solve this, the Parliament chose to introduce the series of unconventional, 'windfall taxes' and budget policies instead of structural, social and economical reforms.

Excluding the possibility of a constitutional review regarding financial measures means there will be no consequences for violating the Constitution in those areas. The selection of "protected rights" could bring the Hungarian legal system into conflict with the rights protected by the European Convention on Human Rights and cases that could have been settled at a national level might end in condemnations of Hungary by the European Court of Human Rights. Therefore, as the Venice Commission clearly pointed out, restricting the Constitutional Court's competence in

---

38 See e.g. Decisions 43-45/1995. The Court held that the government's failure to maintain at least a nominal level of social support violates fundamental rights. In addition, the speed with which these programs were modified violated the principle of legal certainty. See the analysis of Scheppele, "A Realpolitik Defense of Social Rights," 2004. See also the strong criticism of Sajó, "How the Rule of Law Killed Hungarian Welfare Reform," 1996, p. 1.

39 Decision 8/2007.

40 Decision 127/2009.

41 Decision 8/2010.

such a way that it would review certain state acts only with regard to a limited part of the Constitution runs counter to the aim of enhancing the protection of fundamental rights in Hungary.[42]

VI. Abolition of the Four-Fifths Rule

In July 2010 the governing party used its two thirds vote to remove the constitutional rule requiring a four-fifths vote to approve the cornerstones of the new constitution.[43]

Consequently, the Parliament suspended key constitutional checks on legislation and facilitated a constitution drafting process that could proceed without opposition involvement.

F. Making the New Constitution

A closer look at the constitutional developments reveals that the above-mentioned constitutional changes were only the first steps in a greater development. Most of the constitutional amendments in fact served a temporary goal.

Donning the mantle of the "2010 revolution", the ruling coalition started to work on a new Constitution. It argued that the period of post-communist transformation should draw to a close, and for this reason Hungary needed a new Constitution. Prime Minister *Viktor Orbán* personally established an advisory council and named its members to elaborate a draft. In addition, the Parliament set up a special parliamentary ad-hoc committee to develop the regulatory frameworks of the new Constitution. Although at the outset all parliamentary parties were represented in this committee, the opposition quit immediately after the Constitutional Court's competence was seen to be curbed. Within a couple of months, the remaining committee had completed its preparatory task

---

42 Venice Commission, *Opinion 614/2011 on three legal questions arising in the process of drafting the new Constitution of Hungary*, (March 25-26, 2011) para 10. See more, below.

43 Arato argues that this provision was unchangeable: one cannot change by 2/3 what only 4/5 can change. Andrew Arato, *Orban's (Counter) Revolution of the Voting Booth and How it was Made Possible*, available at http://www.comparativeconstitutions.org/2011/04/arato-orbans-counter-revolution-of.html.

and published the Regulatory Framework of the Constitution of Hungary. Subsequently, the Parliament discussed this regulatory framework and decided that the document was no longer seen as determining the direction of framing the Constitution, but served as a material in support of the deputies' constitution-making work.[44] Finally, the ruling coalition set up a three-member panel of politicians (instead of the parliamentary committee) to draft the text of the new Constitution.

Meanwhile the Deputy Prime-Minister requested for the Venice Commission to prepare a legal opinion on three particular issues arising in the constitution-making process: (1) the incorporation of the EU's Charter of Fundamental Rights in the planned Constitution, (2) the significance of preliminary constitutional review, and (3) the abolition of the *actio popularis* and the extension of direct individual complaint in constitutional adjudication. In the absence of a draft of the new Constitution, the Commission limited itself to general comments on the three given issues, however, expressing doubts about the process of adoption of the new Constitution: the limited public debate, the lack of transparency of the process, and the tight schedule established for its adoption.[45]

To lend the constitution writing process legitimacy, a National Consultation Body was set up with the aim of sending a questionnaire to every citizen of Hungary. The questionnaire was composed of twelve issues including the relation between fundamental rights and obligations; the restriction of the public debt; the role of the family, public order, labor and health; the need for extra votes for mothers as a proxy for their children; the ban on levying taxes on the expenses related to child rearing; the protection of future generations; the conditions of public procurement; the togetherness of Hungarians across frontiers; the protection of natural diversity and national treasures; the protection of land and water; the need to include the sentencing to life imprisonment into the Constitution, and the obligation to testify before a Parliamentary Commission if a person is summoned. According to unaudited data, approximately 900,000 citizens have filled in and sent back the questionnaires. The answers were in the middle of being processed when the draft new Constitution was submitted to Parliament.

---

44 9/2011. (III. 9.) *OGY határozat* [Parliamentary Resolution].

45 See Venice Commission, *Opinion 614/2011 on three legal questions arising in the process of drafting the new Constitution of Hungary.*

On March 14, 2011 the draft text of the new Fundamental Law was released.[46] The parliamentary agenda ensured five days for the plenary debate about the concept and four days about the details. That meant nine days from start to finish. The date of promulgation (April 25) was chosen to identify the Fundamental Law with the first anniversary of the election victory. It entered into force on January 1, 2012.

The Fundamental Law has been criticized for the lack of transparency and insufficient dialogue with the opposition during the enactment process, as well as for failing to institute substantial professional or open public debate and the hastiness of the constitution-making procedure. On March 25, 2011 the Monitoring Committee of the Parliamentary Assembly of the Council of Europe decided to ask the Venice Commission for an opinion on the new Constitution. The Venice Commission released its detailed opinion on June 20, 2011.[47]

G. The Content of the Fundamental Law

I. Ideology

The Fundamental Law, and especially of its preamble called the National Avowal, changes the characteristics of the Hungarian constitutionalism. The 1989 Constitution established a secular state based upon a pluralistic society. The leading principles were liberty, equality, and democracy. Contrary to this, the Fundamental Law does not meet the requirement of ideological neutrality expected from modern democratic constitutions. The Fundamental Law has its foundations in religious and historical

---

46 The name Fundamental Law implies that the document is only a part of the "historical constitution", not the Constitution of the Republic of Hungary.

47 See Venice Commission, *Opinion 621/2011 on the New Constitution of Hungary.* Subsequently, the Venice Commission issued *Opinion 662/2012 on the elections to Parliament* (June 18, 2012), *Opinion 663/2012 on the judiciary*, *Opinion 664/2012 on freedom of religion and the status of the churches* (March 16–17, 2012), *Opinion 665/2012 on the Constitutional Court* (June 19, 2012), *Opinion 668/2012 on the prosecution* (June 19, 2012), and *Opinion 671/2012 on the nationality issues* (June 19, 2012). In 2012 the Commission commenced to review more acts, i.e., on freedom of information and family protection. This is a reaction to the excessive Hungarian legislation. In 2011 the Parliament adopted 215 acts; from the 2010 elections to January 2012 the total number of Acts of Parliament was 365.

considerations. It was written in the spirit of not just Christianity, but specifically the Roman Catholic faith. This is what the reference to Saint Stephen and the Holy Crown (of St. Stephen) implies: "We are proud that one thousand years ago, our King Saint Stephen established the Hungarian State on solid foundations, and led our country to become part of Christian Europe" and "we acknowledge the nation-preserving role of the Christian faith." The National Creed explicitly mentions "the Holy Crown, which embodies the constitutional continuity of the state and the unity of the nation."

The proponents of the Constitution repeatedly mentioned the Polish Constitution as a model of the Fundamental Law. It is well known that the Polish Constitution refers to Christianity. In a European context, these are unusual and controversial references. However, the social facts and constitutional norms in Poland are different from those in Hungary.

As opposed to Hungary, Poland remains one of the most religious countries in Europe: 89 percent of the population belongs to the Roman Catholic Church, and more than half of the population goes to church. Yet, the Polish Constitution treats believers and non-believers as equals. The Polish text says: "those who believe in God as the source of truth, justice, good and beauty, as well as those not sharing such faith but respecting those universal values as arising from other sources, equal in rights and obligations" and: "our culture is rooted in the Christian heritage of the Nation and in universal human values."

Hungarian citizens are divided by ethical, political, and religious disagreements. According to a recent poll, 44 percent of Hungarians answered that they believed there is a God, 31 percent answered that they believed there is some sort of spirit or life force, and 19 percent answered that they are atheists. Meanwhile, more than half of the population belongs to the Roman Catholic Church, and 20 percent of the citizens are Protestant, but only 10 percent are churchgoers and follow religious norms.

In contrast with the Polish Constitution, however, the Hungarian Fundamental Law does not mention the role of universal secular values or those who respect such values. In this way, it does not simply remember the historical role of Christianity in founding the Hungarian State, but expresses that the Hungarian constitutionalism present is based upon traditional Christian faith. Consequently, it identifies itself with the moral and political foundations of the faith.

II. History

The historical references of the Fundamental Law negate the post-communist era. The text does not mention the republican traditions or look back on the tragic failures of the nation. It is a mythical and romantic account of history. In the sense of the Fundamental Law, 1989 was a beginning of confusion, and the real revolutionary year is 2010 because of the results of the parliamentary elections. It is worth comparing this to the historical narrative of the Polish Constitution, which represents a reflective and critical view by stating that the country that "recovered in 1989" is "mindful of the bitter experiences of the times when fundamental freedoms and human rights were violated in our Homeland."

III. Integrative Function

One of the crucial judgments on the Fundamental Law is that it does not fulfill the integrative function of modern constitutions.[48] It is biased in favor of the winners of the 2010 elections and against everybody else. It provides a mythical historical narrative that goes against the grain of republican traditions. It prefers Catholics to non-believers and followers of other faiths. Of course, Hungary is not exceptional in being a disunited nation.[49] For an important analogy, the so-called red (Republican) and blue (Democratic) political cultures deeply divide the people of the United States of America. In Northern Ireland nationalists and unionist disagree about no less than under which state (the United Kingdom or Republic of Ireland) the country's territory should be governed. In Belgium the Flemish and Walloon communities not only speak different languages, but are unable to find a common political language. Every modern political society with a plurality of moral convictions, world views, and interests must face the question of whether there are principles that all the parties can share notwithstanding of their deep disagreements; if there are, what

48 Here I refer to the idea of constitutional patriotism originated from Habermas, *Eine Art Schadensabwicklung*, 1987, pp. 173-175. See also Müller, *Constitutional Patriotism*, 2007, and Schwartz, "Patriotism or Integrity," 2011, pp. 503-526.

49 For an overview, see Choudhry, ed., *Constitutional Design for Divided Societies*, 2008.

kind of institutional design can help to implement their common political and constitutional goals. In this respect the Hungarian case provides sad lessons on the consequences of a delusive constitutional majoritarianism.

Moreover, the Fundamental Law does not identify the "people" with citizens as subjects of the same legal system; it rather insists that there is "one single Hungarian nation that belongs together," a nation including all ethnic Hungarians regardless of their habitual residence and effective link to the State. According to the Fundamental Law, the "nation [was] torn apart in the storms of the last century." This refers to the historical Hungary as believed to have existed in the Middle Ages, and certainly to those neighboring territories where some two and a half million Hungarians are still living today as a consequence of the post-world-war treaties of 1920 and 1947. Therefore the Fundamental Law treats Hungarians living beyond the borders as members of a nation disunited by the international legal and political order. The constitution that identifies the nation as an "intellectual and spiritual" constitutional community can be understood as a descendant of the East-Central European nationalist ideas and movements from the last two centuries.

IV. Constitutional Checks

The Fundamental Law decreases the independence and the competences of the Constitutional Court. First, the previously changed nomination rules concerning the members of the Court are maintained; the governing majority therefore has absolute freedom to nominate judges. With regards to the election process, the president of the Court will no longer be elected by his fellow justices for three years but by parliamentary majority for twelve years. Second, while the Fundamental Law retains most of the competences of the Court, changes are considerable. Previously every person was entitled to take action for constitutional review against a normative act after its enactment. Now the *ex post* review of the unconstitutionality of legislation is restricted, since the Fundamental Law abolishes this kind of *actio popularis*. In addition, the limitation of the Court's competencies connected with financial matters has been maintained. The Fundamental Law, however, introduces a German-type constitutional complaint, making it possible to complain not only against a normative act but also against the violation of a fundamental right through an individual act, i.e. decisions of the judiciary, based on a normative act. It should be welcome that the mechanism of individual complaint related to a concrete case includes the possibility to challenge the unconstitutional application of a legal norm.

The institutional design is subject to a number of criticisms. Checks and balances seem illusory because people who occupy crucial positions can be appointed for extraordinarily long terms by the current majority. Offices like the head of the state (5+5years), Chief public prosecutor (9 years), the president of the Supreme Court (9 years), the president of the National Judicial Office (9 years), the head of the Budget Council (6 years), the head of the State Audit Office (12 years), constitutional judges (12 years), the president of the National Media and Communications Authority (9 years) are being filled by the current government.[50]

V. Human Rights Protection

The catalogue of fundamental rights has been partly built on the structure of the EU Charter of Fundamental Rights and Freedoms. However, the Rights and Responsibilities chapter, together with the National Avowal and Foundations chapter, includes several provisions that raise serious concerns and controversies. Here are some examples:

The Venice Commission found it problematic that freedom of the press is not formulated as an individual's right, but as an obligation of the state.[51] The Fundamental Law has been criticized since it does not treat same-sex couples as equals. In the Foundations chapter family is defined by a provision under which only a man and a woman can marry. The text lacks any mention of the prohibition of discrimination on the ground of sexual orientation. As to the right to life and liberty, there is a provision in the right to life clause seeking to "protect the fetal life from the moment of conception". Not only reproductive but also therapeutic cloning of human beings is prohibited. While the Fundamental Law does not prohibit capital punishment, it allows compulsory life imprisonment without parole. In addition, everyone has the right to repel any unlawful attack against their person or property, or one that poses a direct threat to the same. The right to asylum is granted only "if neither their country of origin nor another

---

50 Bánkuti, Halmai and Scheppele suggest a similarly strong position on the nature and direction of the constitutional change in their "From Separation of Powers to a Government without Checks," 2011, pp. 237-268.

51 Venice Commission, *Opinion 621/2011*, para 74.

country provides protection" for the asylum-seeker. Finally, as a consequence of the new constitutional and statutory regulation more than 300 religious communities lost their church status while only 32 churches were legally recognized.[52]

H. Conclusions

The constitution agreed upon by the parties in 1989 was based on the principles of liberal democracy and the rule of law. However, the provisions for changing the constitution did not require a sufficiently high approval level to prevent abuses of democracy. Hungary became an anomaly in the region since it was the only nation that did not adopt a brand new constitution after the democratic transition. This way the flexible constitution and the hostile political climate have challenged the constitutional stability.

In 2010-2011 the ruling government has used its two-thirds parliamentary majority to adopt several constitutional changes concerning the representative organs, the media and the Constitutional Court. Recent constitutional transformation fundamentally alters the Hungarian secular constitutional system, and weakens the institutional checks and balances. I introduced the process and the main ideas of the newly adopted Fundamental Law. As I remarked, there was no political consensus about the necessity of constitution-making nor about the content of a new constitution, and the opposition parties did not take part in the preparation process.

---

52 See Act CCVI of 2011 on freedom of conscience and religion, and the legal status of churches, religious congregations and religious communities. This Act was amended soon by the Act VII of 2012. The re-registration of the churches is a matter of agreement with the government and the final decision is in the hands of Parliament. The Venice Commission issued an opinion on 2011 Act. The Commission found that the Act induces, to some extent, an unequal and even discriminatory treatment of religious beliefs and communities, depending on whether they are recognized or not. The Commission recommended redrafting the Act in order to avoid a de-registration process and provisions operating retroactively unless specific reasons can justify it. It also recommended deleting the provision on forfeiture, which constitutes an undue limitation to the right to access to legal-entity status. Venice Commission, *Opinion 664/2012*, paras 92, 110. See also, Uitz, "Freedom of Religion and Churches," 2012, pp. 197-234.

The constitutional crisis is a consequence of the shortage of democratic traditions and the failed collective historical self-examination. Exceptionally in Central Europe, the text of the Fundamental Law represents the "winner-takes-all" concept of democracy. Therefore the new constitution does not unite and integrate but divides the political community. This is why we can conclude that Hungary is a constitutionally disunited nation.[53]

Works cited

Arato, Andrew, "Dilemmas arising from the Power to Create Constitutions in Eastern Europe," in *Constitutionalism, Difference, Identity, and Legitimacy, Theoretical Perspectives*, ed. Michael Rosenfeld, Durham: Duke University Press, 1994, pp. 165-194.

Arato, Andrew, "The Constitution-Making Endgame in Hungary," *East European Constitutional Review* 5:4 (1996): 31-39.

Arato, Andrew, "Post-Sovereign Constitution-Making in Hungary: After Success, Partial Failure, and Now What?," *South African Journal on Human Rights* 26 (2010): 19–44.

Bánkuti, Miklós, Gábor Halmai, and Kim Lane Scheppele, "From Separation of Powers to a Government without Checks: Hungary's Old and New Constitutions," in *Constitution for a Disunited Nation: On Hungary's 2011 Fundamental Law*, ed. Gábor Attila Tóth, Budapest: Central European University Press, 2012, pp. 237-268.

Bogdandy, Armin von, et al., "Reverse Solange: Protecting the essence of fundamental rights against EU Member States," *Common Market Law Review* 49 (2012): 489-519.

Brunner, Georg, "Structure and Proceedings of the Hungarian Constitutional Judiciary" in *Constitutional Judiciary in a New Democracy: The Hungarian Constitutional Court*, ed. Laszlo Solyom and Georg Brunner, Ann Arbor MI: The University of Michigan Press, 2000.

---

53 The future of Hungarian constitutionalism relies on the actions of people in the country and the commitment of the EU. On January 17, 2012 the European Commission of the EU launched accelerated infringement proceedings against Hungary over the independence of its Central Bank and data protection authority as well as over measures affecting the judiciary. As a scholarly reaction to the Hungarian constitutional crisis *Armin von Bogdandy* and his team have come up with the so called Heidelberg Proposal with its suggestion of the adoption of a "reverse" *Solange* doctrine by the Court of Justice of the EU. See Bogdandy et al., "Reverse Solange," 2012, pp. 489-519.

Choudhry, Sujit, ed., *Constitutional Design for Divided Societies: Integration or Accomodation?*, Oxford: Oxford University Press, 2008.

Dorsen, Norman, Michel Rosenfeld, András Sajó, and Susanne Baer, *Comparative Constitutionalism, Cases and Materials*, St. Paul, MN: Thomson-West, 2003.

Garlicki, Lech, "Democracy and International Influences", in *European and U.S. Constitutionalism*, ed. Georg Nolte, Cambridge: Cambridge University Press, 2005, pp. 263-279.

Garton Ash, Timothy, "Revolution: The Springtime of Two Nations," *The New York Review of Books* 36 (1989): 3-10.

Garton Ash, Timothy, "Revolution in Hungary and Poland," *The New York Review of Books* 36 (1989): 9-15.

Garton Ash, Timothy, "Velvet Revolution: The Prospects," *The New York Review of Books* 56 (2009): 20-23.

Garton Ash, Timothy, *Facts are Subversive: Political Writing from a Decade Without a Name*, London: Atlantic Books, 2009.

Habermas, Jürgen, *Eine Art Schadensabwicklung: Kleine Politische Schriften VI*, Frankfurt a.M.: Suhrkamp, 1987.

Kis, János, "Between Reform and Revolution," *East European Politics and Societies* 12 (1998): 300-383.

Kis, János, *Constitutional Democracy*, Budapest/New York: CEU Press, 2003.

Kis, János, "Introduction: From the 1989 Constitution to the 2011 Fundamental Law," in *Constitution for a Disunited Nation: On Hungary's 2011 Fundamental Law*, ed. Gábor Attila Tóth, Budapest: Central European University Press, 2012, pp. 1-21.

Kornai, János, *Economics of Shortage*, Amsterdam/New York: North-Holland, 1980.

Miklósi, Zoltán, "Constitution-Making, Competition and Cooperation" in *Constitution for a Disunited Nation: On Hungary's 2011 Fundamental Law*, ed. Gábor Attila Tóth, Budapest: Central European University Press, 2012, pp. 59-81.

Müller, Jan-Werner, *Constitutional Patriotism*, Princeton: Princeton University Press, 2007.

Procházka, Radoslav, *Mission Accomplished: On Founding Constitutional Adjudication in Central Europe*, Budapest/New York: Central European University Press, 2002.

Sadurski, Wojciech, *Rights before Courts: A Study of Constitutional Courts in Postcommunist States of Central and Eastern Europe*, Dordrecht: Springer, 2005.

Sajó, András, "Contemporary Problems of the Judiciary in Hungary" in *The Social Role of the Legal Profession*, ed. Kahei Rokumoto, Tokyo: International Centre for Comparative Law and Politics, University of Tokyo, 1993, pp. 141-150.

Sajó, András, "How the Rule of Law Killed Hungarian Welfare Reform?," *East European Constitutional Review* 5 (1996): 31-40.

Scheppele, Kim Lane, "A Realpolitik Defense of Social Rights," *Texas Law Review* 82 (2004): 1921-1961.

Schwartz, Herman, *The Struggle for Constitutional Justice in Post-Communist Europe*, Chicago/London: University of Chicago Press, 2000.

Schwartz, Alex, "Patriotism or Integrity? Constitutional Community in Divided Societies," *Oxford Journal of Legal Studies* 31 (2011): 503-526.

Sólyom, László, and Georg Brunner, *Constitutional Judiciary in a New Democracy: The Hungarian Constitutional Court*, Ann Arbor MI: The University of Michigan Press, 2000.

Tőkés, Rudolf L., Hungary's Negotiated Revolution: Economic Reform, Social Change and Political Succession, 1957-1990, Cambridge: Cambridge University Press, 1996.

Uitz, Renáta, "Freedom of Religion and Churches: Archeology in a Constitution-making Assembly," in *Constitution for a Disunited Nation: On Hungary's 2011 Fundamental Law*, ed. Gábor Attila Tóth, Budapest: Central European University Press, 2012, pp. 197-234.

Constitutional Conflict and the Idea of New Constitution in Turkey

Sibel Inceoğlu

Although areas of constitutional conflict in Turkey are diverse, we can say that the basic issues of conflict are based on ethnic identity, faith identity, civil-military relations, independence and impartiality of the judiciary, and the role of presidential office in legislation-executive relations.

In recent years there has been a drive to make a new constitution in order to replace the 1982 Constitution, which was a constitution that was drafted after a coup d'état, by a power that had not been elected. Thus, a new constitution is sought to find solutions to all these issues of conflict as well as to broaden the freedoms. Before the elections of 12 June 2011, all political parties in the Grand National Assembly of Turkey (GNAT) promised a new constitution in their election bulletins. After the elections, the President of the GNAT sent an invitation to all parties in which he stated his intention to set up a Conciliation Commission for the new Constitution.

An historical approach to this matter is needed in order to better understand the above mentioned areas of conflict and the difficulties of reconciliation. In a global environment, solutions are needed which are based on internationally accepted values, the resolution of these issues of conflict will also be attempted in this work.

A. The Effect of History on the Constitutional Conflict

In order to comprehend the areas of conflict, one must know the constitutional history of Turkey. The first constitution of the people of Turkey dates back to 1876. The 1876 Constitution was drafted at the time of the Ottoman Empire, before the foundation of the Republic of Turkey. Both international and domestic factors played roles in the adoption of that constitution. The Ottoman Empire was facing the threat of war from Russia and needed European support. In exchange for such a support, Europe demanded constitutional guarantees especially for the Christian minority population that had lived in the Ottoman lands. In this environment, Turkish intelligentsia and bureaucrats[1] – most of whom had been educated in Europe – convinced the Ottoman Sultan to have a constitution made.

The 1876 Constitution allowed for a National Assembly that was elected by the people and did for the first time, although on a small scale, limit the powers of the Sultan. After a short time, this Constitution was suspended by *Sultan Abdulhamid*, and an authoritarian regime was reestablished. However, in 1908 a popular uprising took place. The Constitution was again put into effect and in 1909 it was amended extensively. [2] These amendments increased the powers of the Assembly, and introduced guarantees for the parliamentary government. It broadened the rights and freedoms of the people. [3]

The second constitution of the people of Turkey was the 1921 Constitution. In World War I, the Ottoman Empire was on the losing side, and much of its territory was lost. The idea of a nation state gained more ground because of the Ottoman government's failure to resist invasion. Under the leadership of *Mustafa Kemal*, the Turkish nation elected an Assembly that was independent from the Ottoman government and that Assembly made the 1921 Constitution. This Constitution abolished the powers of the Sultan and introduced an assembly government regime based on the supremacy of the National Assembly. The principle of national sovereignty was adopted and all powers – legislative, executive and judicial – were concentrated in the hands of the National Assembly. This period belonged to a new state, to be more precise the foundation of the state of the Republic of Turkey.

Following the victory in the independence war, the decision was made to hold the elections. The Republic was proclaimed by the National Assembly, and immediately afterwards the first Constitution of the Republic was drafted in 1924. This Constitution not only adopted the supremacy of the National Assembly, it also possessed the characteristics of a parliamentary government. [4] The period during which the 1924 Constitution was implemented is at the same time the period when the principle of secularism was first adopted. The model of a nation-state that excluded ethnical and cultural diversities was taken as the basis. The

1 See Mardin, *The Genesis of Young Ottoman Thought*, 1962.
2 See Tunaya, *Türkiye'de Siyasal Gelişmeler*, 2001, pp. 121-123.
3 See Tanör, *Osmanlı-Türk Anayasal Gelişmeleri*, 1995, pp. 106-164.
4 See Ozbudun, *1924 Anayasası*, 2012, pp. 16-18.

principle of secularism was from time to time implemented in such a way that restricted the freedom of religious belief. As for the matter of democracy, the political party that had been founded by *Mustafa Kemal* (Republican People's Party, RPP) – except for brief periods when the introduction of a multi-party system was experimented – ruled the country under a single party regime. In those years, the party's mission was to protect the territorial integrity and to create a modern Turkey. In order to attain these objectives, those who governed the country back then, in accordance with the understanding of 1920s and 30s, deemed many undemocratic actions as legitimate measures. However, transition to the multi-party system occurred with the initiative of this same party. In the elections of 1950, the Democrat Party (DP), the opposition political party won and power changed hands. This in fact was a peaceful revolution. [5]

The last two constitutions of Turkey, which are the 1961 and 1982 constitutions, were drafted as the result of military coup d'états. The driving forces behind these two coups were different. The coup in 1960 was made on the grounds that the DP had exploited the religious beliefs, violated the Constitution, and tried to eradicate the opposition. It is true that the DP had violated the Constitution, made anti-democratic laws to intimidate the opposition and engaged in such oppressive practices. Nevertheless, a significant portion of the population did not support the military's actions either. The DP was a political party, for which an important majority of the people had voted, and they saw the military coup and execution of the prime minister and two ministers as illegitimate. This created a breaking point in the country's political life.

Following the military coup d'état, a Constituent Assembly in which the DP was not represented, drafted the 1961 Constitution. In contrast with the way it was made, the 1961 Constitution was in substance a constitution with high democratic and human rights standards. In other words, the 1961 Constitution is a constitution with low input but high output legitimacy. It adopted the classical parliamentary government. Social rights were for the first time included in the Constitution. Rights and freedoms were expanded and guaranteed. A Constitutional Court was founded for the first time. Judicial independence was guaranteed and a strong administrative justice system was designed. Concerns with regard to violations of rights and freedoms can be traced in the 1961 Constitution.

---

5 See Ahmad, *The Making of Modern Turkey*, 1993, pp. 152-120.

A review by the Constitutional Court was intended for the prevention of violations of the Constitution by the majority in the National Assembly whereas a review by the administrative courts was intended to deter the government from violating the laws. In this framework, we can say that the 1961 Constitution had intended to establish a liberal state governed by the rule of law.

The 1982 Constitution which is currently in effect was drafted by a Constituent Assembly. The creation of the document, however, was not democratically representative of the people, as its members had been appointed by the military after the coup of 12 September 1980. This military coup caused trauma in Turkey. Before the 12 September 1980, there was domestic chaos where shootouts between the right wing and left wing militants occurred. Coalition governments were in power and governmental crises frequently arose as the political parties failed to reach an agreement. The right wing parties argued that the 1961 Constitution had expanded the freedoms too much, as the result of which this Constitution became the source of conflict. The military authority that had staged the 1980 military coup expressed the same views. According to them, the 1961 Constitution on the one side had created an atmosphere of excessive freedoms; on the other side, measures that would have ensured stability, security and public order were treated as having secondary importance, and judicial review had excessively limited the government. The 1982 Constitution does fully reflect this background. The Constitution considerably limited rights and freedoms. Pluralism was suppressed, the judicial independence was weakened by giving concessions from the principle of the rule of the law, and the powers of the executive were enhanced to the disadvantage of the legislative power.[6]

Throughout the 30 years during which the 1982 Constitution has been in force, the GNAT amended it 18 times. One of these amendments was annulled by the Constitutional Court.[7] Eventually, 79 of the 177 Articles of the Constitution were amended, and furthermore, some of these 79 Articles were amended more than once. In fact, as nearly half of its provisions have been amended, the Constitution that is currently in force is considerably different from what it was when it was adopted after the coup. Still, however, both its input legitimacy as well as output legitimacy

6 See Tanör, *İki Anayasa 1961-1982*, 2012.

7 For the Constitution of Turkey see http://www.servat.unibe.ch/icl/tu00000_.html, last visited 10 December 2014.

are in dispute. Primarily, the fact that it is a constitution that had been made by putschists damages its legitimacy.[8] The society expects a constitution that is made by the representatives that are elected by it, and with the participation of the people. Secondly, people's demands regarding the content of the Constitution have not yet been realized. Further guarantees for the rights and freedoms, resolution of problems of ethnic and faith identities, securing the independence and impartiality of jurisdiction, putting an end to military influence on politics, and clarification of the role of the presidential office in legislation-executive relations are among the expectations of the society.

Not all of the problems mentioned above do arise from the Constitution, some of them arise from Acts of Parliament. As a matter of fact, the political party that has the majority in the National Assembly and forms the government (Justice and Development Party - JDP) has the power to meet a great many social demands by amending the laws, without any need for ammending the Constitution. Yet, instead of doing this, the JDP has postponed any action until a new amendment to the Constitution can be passed. This of course arouses suspicions about its sincerity in these matters. Besides, maximizing the expectation that the new constitution will resolve all the problems creates constitution fetishism.

B. Conciliation Commission and Constitution-Making Procedure

On the date of 19 September 2011, the President of the GNAT invited all constitutional law professors, and heard their opinions as to how a new constitution should be made.[9] In this meeting three theses were put forward. The first thesis argued that a new constitution could be made only where there is a legal vacuum as in the case of the foundation of a new state or a revolution or coup d'état. Since in this framework, a legal vacuum could not now be deemed to exist in Turkey, it was asserted that a national assembly which is elected under ordinary circumstances cannot make a new constitution.

---

8 Tanör and Yüzbaşıoğlu, *1982 Anayasasına Göre Türk Anayasa Hukuku*, 2002, pp. 29-38.

9 See http://yenianayasa.tbmm.gov.tr/docs/anayasa-hukukculari-ile-toplanti.pdf, last visited 10 December 2014.

The second thesis defended the idea that the national assembly, which is elected under ordinary circumstances, can and should make a new constitution. It was expressed that Turkey should get rid of the 1982 Constitution as soon as possible, which is a product of a coup d'état and which is to a great extent authoritarian.

The first thesis is problematic because it denies the possibility of making a new constitution at ordinary times. However, a will to make a new constitution can emerge under many different circumstances. Hence the examples of Finland, Switzerland and Hungary prove that a new constitution can be made even when the foundation of a new state or a revolution or coup d'état is not in question. The second thesis is based on the idea of getting rid of the 1982 Constitution in response to the demand for a new constitution. It, however, pays little attention to the question of the widest possible popular participation in the process of making the constitution. Yet, the process is as important as the result itself.[10]

On the basis of these arguments, a third thesis was set forth. According to this thesis, the new constitution should be made not by the existing National Assembly, but by a Constituent Assembly (Constitution Assembly) that would be elected solely for this purpose. In the Turkish election system, the number of votes that political parties receive and the number of seats they get in the National Assembly are not proportional. As the result of an election threshold of 10%, parties that receive less than 10% of the votes at the national level are not represented in the National Assembly. Women are represented at only 14% in the present Assembly. Defenders of the third thesis suggested that a "Constitution Assembly" could be elected after adopting an election system that would overcome such drawbacks, and which would impose a quota (40 or 50%) for women. Those who profess the third thesis argued that the very fact that eight persons who had been elected by the people to the National Assembly are still remanded under custody was a shame for Turkish democracy, and that the legislative body should pass an act regarding this

10 See Vivien Hart, "Democratic Constitution Making, Special Report 107," United States Institute of Peace, July 2003, available at http://www.peacemaker.un.org/sites/peacemaker.un.org/files/DemocraticConstitutionMaking_USIP2003.pdf, last visited December 2014; Jon Elster, "The Optimal Design of a Constituent Assembly," College de France, May 2008, available at http:// download2.cerimes.fr/canalu/documents/cerimes/UPL55488_Elster.pdf, last visited 10 December 2014.

matter. It was also expressed by the same group that because of the existing statutory limitations to freedom of expression, freedom of assembly and freedom of political parties, all sections of the society would not be able to contribute to the making of the constitution which was another impediment to democratic participation. It was emphasized that these problems should be resolved before starting the constitution making process.[11]

The political parties that were represented in the National Assembly were reluctant to call an election for a "Constitution Assembly" and, instead, they decided to set up a "Constitution Conciliation Commission" in the National Assembly. It was also decided to have this Conciliation Commission lay down its own procedural rules. In fact, such a commission is mentioned neither in the Constitution nor in the Parliamentary Law of the National Assembly. In other words, there is no legal basis for it. Therefore, the Constitution Conciliation Commission is an ad hoc body.

The first meeting of the Constitution Conciliation Commission was held on 19 November 2011. In the Conciliation Commission, four political parties were represented on equal basis, regardless of the ratio of votes they had received. Considering that small minority groups encountered some problems that are mentioned below, this equal representation of all parties can be deemed as a positive step. On the other hand, the failure to allow representation of the other political parties that remain below the high election threshold of 10% and the fact that only one of the 12 members of the Commission was a woman are significant defects.

The Conciliation Commission laid down its own procedural rules.[12] The Commission meetings can be held if at least one member from three of the parties is present. To make a decision, the approval of all political parties represented in the Commission must be obtained. As it would be considerably difficult to obtain such approval on all matters, taking decisions will obviously not be easy.

---

11 For discussions on the constitution making process in Turkey see "Yeni Anayasa Yuvarlak Masa Toplantıları Dizisi: Yeni Anayasanın Beş Temel Boyutu," *TÜSİAD* 2011, pp. 13-15, available at http://yenianayasa.tbmm.gov.tr /docs/yuvarlak-masa-1.pdf, last visited 10 December 2014.

12 See http://yenianayasa.tbmm.gov.tr/calismaesaslari.aspx, last accessed 10 December 2014.

The Commission was anticipated to perform its duty in four steps. The first step was gathering and assessing data. The second step was the laying down of principles and drafting of the text. The third step was the public announcement of the text and having it discussed in public. The fourth step was reviewing of the draft text under the light of the opinions that have been expressed in society, and presenting it to the National Assembly as a constitutional draft. Amending this motion after it was presented to the National Assembly will possible only if all political parties agree.

It was decided to conclude the data gathering and assessment phase by the end of April 2012. In this framework an internet website was created to enable the people to communicate their opinions to the Commission.[13] Furthermore, oral and written opinions of the small political parties that are not represented in the National Assembly, non-governmental organizations, universities, professional organizations and trade unions were welcomed by the Commission. However, this process lacked transparency, and it is not certain if this will change in the future. For example, at the beginning suggestions of some non-governmental organizations, universities, trade unions and professional organizations were published on the website. Yet, later on, the Commission announced that it had decided not to publish these suggestions in order to protect these organizations from becoming the target of possible reactions.[14] It was decided not to allow the media to attend these meetings, and it was stated that the Commission would consider measures to ensure transparency. It is not known how this transparency would be furnished.

In addition to these, limitations of freedom of speech, assembly and association as well as certain restrictions on the political parties caused people to be reluctant to participate in the constitution making process. Failure to make the necessary amendments to facilitate the people's participation in the constitution making process is a significant drawback.

C. Ethnic Identity and Constitution

With regard to the rights of ethnic groups, fewer problems were experienced in the case of non-Muslim minorities, because they were

---

13 See http://yenianayasa.tbmm.gov.tr/gorusgonder.aspx, last accessed 10 December 2014.

14 See *Milliyet Gazetesi*, 27 January 2012.

under the protection of an international agreement, namely the Lausanne Treaty. As in the case of ethnic groups like the Muslim Kurds, more human rights violations occurred following the adoption of the 1982 Constitution.[15]

Although violence is an unacceptable method for demanding the rights and freedoms, terror did, under the pretext of protection of the rights of the Kurdish ethnic group, continue to be a serious problem from the late 80s until today. Unfortunately thousands of people died in these armed clashes. One of the most significant expectations from the new Constitution is that since it would be a new social contract, it might therefore end these clashes.

Certain minor amendments to the Constitution and to the laws have been made before in favor of the rights of these ethnic minority groups. For example, prohibitions with regard to the use of their mother tongue were lifted. Article 26 of the Constitution on freedom expression, before 2001, reads as follows: "Any language that had been banned by the law cannot be used for expressing the ideas." Laws prohibited oral and written artistic works in Kurdish language. This ban had first been lifted by repeal of the Act, and then the Constitution in 2001 was amended in such a way not to allow for any similar prohibitions or bans. In the 2000s private Kurdish language courses were allowed,[16] and a state television channel that broadcasts in Kurdish language was founded. In 2010, the provision of the Act on the prohibition of the use of any language other than Turkish by political parties in their election propaganda was repealed.[17] However, these reforms did not prove to be sufficient for the terrorist organization that claims to act on behalf of the Kurdish minority group, and they continue to use methods of violence.

The Peace and Democracy Party (PDP), which is the legal political party that defends the rights of the Kurdish minority group, announced its expectations from the new Constitution to the public opinion. PDP's basic demands can be summarized as follows: Recognition of the right of education in mother tongue, an amendment of the Constitutional provision

---

15 See *A Quest for Equality: Minorities in Turkey, Minority Rights Group International*, 11 December 2007, available at http://www.minorityrights.org /4572/reports/a-quest-for-equality-minorities-in-turkey.html, last accessed 10 December 2014.

16 Act of Parliament No. 4963, Art. 2, dated 30 July 2003.

17 Act of Parliament No. 5980, Art. 7, dated 08 April 2010.

that defines citizenship and amending the Constitution in such a way to allow regional autonomy.

Education in the mother tongue is different than the teaching of the mother tongue in education. Whereas the teaching of the mother tongue (or minority language) in education means the teaching of the grammar and other features of that language, education in the mother tongue means a curriculum according to which all subjects are taught in the mother tongue of that ethnic group. Article 42 of the Constitution does not allow this. The Nationalist Movement Party (NMP) reacted against this demand. The main opposition party, RPP, defends teaching of the mother tongue in the state schools as an elective course. In other words, it proposes that teaching of the minority language should be financed by the state, but it does not support education to be given in the mother tongue of the ethnic group. The Justice and Development Party (JDP), however, did not clarify its position on this matter.

When discussing the demand for education in the minority language, integration of the minority groups comes up as an issue that cannot possibly be ignored. That is because a curriculum that is entirely in the mother tongue of the minority group can make teaching the official language more complicated, thus resulting in a society where its members do not speak a common language, problems regarding peaceful coexistence can arise. At this point, alternative solutions for better teaching of the official language that the majority of the people speaks to the minority groups must be considered. In that sense, mixed model education systems, in another words bilingual education which balance the demands of the minority groups and the need for living together in an integrated society must be emphasized.[18] For this reason, in-depth discussions over Article 42 will obviously take place in the National Assembly during the constitution making process. During these discussions it will be helpful to dwell on the alternatives in the international documents on minorities.[19]

---

18 See Organization for Security and Co-operation in Europe (OSCE), *The Hague Recommendations Regarding the Education Rights of National Minorities, High Commissioner on National Minorities*, 1 October 1996, available at: http://www.refworld.org/docid/3dde52563.html, last accessed 10 December 2014.

19 Such as the Framework Convention for the Protection of National Minorities, dated 1. February 1995,CETS No. 157, Art. 12, 13, 14, or the European Charter

In the Constitution citizenship is defined as follows: "Everyone bound to the Turkish state through the bond of citizenship is a Turk" (Art. 66). This definition is criticized for making reference to ethnicity, to be precise to the Turkish identity. Actually, in many constitutions all over the world a definition of citizenship is not even included. The problem can as well be solved without including any such definition. However, the problem does not originate only from the article that defines citizenship. In the Preamble and in 17 articles of the Constitution,[20] the concept of a Turk is referred to as "Turkish citizen," "Turkish state," "Turkish nation," "Turkish history," "Turkish society" and "interests of the Turkish Nation." The PDP suggests using "Turkey" and "Turkeyan (Turkiyeli)" instead of "Turk." Although this proposal might appear as a matter of technicality, in fact it is not. When looked at from an historical perspective, this proposal can be attributed to the occasional past ethnicity based discriminating practices. Therefore, it won't be wrong to say that the proposal reflects a desire for social belonging, and that such a change can help strengthen the feeling of social belonging of different ethnic groups. Nonetheless, it must be stated that the nationalist political parties put up a serious resistance remembering the ethnic nationalism and ethnic strife which had followed the days of the Ottoman Empire's collapse.

Finally, the regional autonomy that is expressed by the PDP is a demand that requires shifting from a unitary state to a regional or federal state. Such a transformation would require all of the provisions of the Constitution about the structure of the state to be reconsidered. The scope of the regional autonomy is not yet clear and distinct. Will the powers of these autonomous entities be as exhaustive as of states of the USA? Or will it be like that of the regional governance of Spain? Or else is a lesser regional autonomy like the one in Italy desired? The collective subconscious of Turkey that had been created in Ottoman times is still very strong. The memory of the trauma that had been experienced during the fall of the Ottoman Empire is always fresh in the minds of the people of Turkey. This fear is deeply felt by all of the political parties in the National Assembly, with the exception of the PDP. Therefore, considering the inclinations of the political parties, the adoption of a federal state is far from the most likely outcome. Similar concerns will also cast a shadow

for Regional or Minority Languages, dated 05 November 1992, CETS No. 148, Art 8.

20 Articles: 5, 7, 9, 41, 42, 59, 62, 66, 67, 69, 76, 81, 101, 103, 104, 134, 174.

over the prospects for other options. Thus, the topic that will be discussed more than others under this title will evidently be regional autonomy. Even though consensus on stronger local administrations and regional administrative autonomy can be deemed possible, the adoption of political autonomy is very unlikely.

D. Faith Identity and Constitution

Discussions about the demands of religious groups for more rights are frequently on Turkey's political agenda.[21] Since some think that religious pluralism during the reign of the Ottoman Empire played a role in its downfall, skepticism against different faiths is deeply rooted in subconscious beliefs. This is one of the reasons why the Muslim Sunni majority of the society put up resistance against such demands. Another point of resistance originates from the fears that radical Islam might take over. That is what lies behind the skepticism of the secular section of the society against the demands of the conservative Muslim population.

Non-Muslim minorities are, as mentioned before, under the protection of the Lausanne Treaty. Their own educational institutes and places of worship are under protection. Still, the foundations of the Christian minority groups encountered ownership problems that arose because of the laws. However, this problem was resolved to a great extent in the 2000's.

The Alevi population in Turkey, which is one of the sects of the Muslim religion, faces serious violations against their rights. Furthermore, those who do not want to observe all the religious rules or those who do not follow any religion also face difficulties. Ultimately, there is a need for a social consensus with regard to all religious believes and conscientious convictions.

The Alevi basically have two major significant demands regarding the Constitution. These can be summarized as follows: Abolition of compulsory religion courses in primary and secondary education, abolition of the Directorate of Religious Affairs or provision of the services of this

21 For the relationship between laicite and democracy in Turkey see Vaner, "Laiklik, Laikçilik ve Demokrasi, Türkiye'den Birkaç Örnekle Birlikte," 2001, pp. 165-196.

directorate to all faith groups on equal basis, and recognition of djemevis (cemevi) as legitimate places of worship.

In the Constitution it is provided that courses of religious culture and moral are compulsory subjects in elementary and secondary schools. Before the 1982 Constitution when the 1961 Constitution was in effect, they were optional subjects.[22] Attendance to these courses was up to the student and parents. According to the current provision,[23] all children must attend religion courses. Non-Muslims like Christians and Jews are exempted from these compulsory courses in practice, but there is no exemption for Muslims, agnostics, skeptics and non-believers or atheists. When we look into the context of this lesson, we see that it is to a great extent a Sunni interpretation of the Muslim religion, while information on Alevi beliefs constitutes a very limited section. Atheism and similar approaches are considered as heresy. Thus an Alevi father and his daughter took this matter to the European Court of Human Rights (ECHR). The ECHR in this case first established that the religious culture and moral course books did not reflect an objective and pluralist understanding, and secondly that the state did not offer to the parents a choice which they would deem suitable for their children. In order to be exempted, they were forced to disclose their beliefs which according to the Court constituted a violation.[24] The Alevi society demanded annulment of this provision of the Constitution.

Another demand of the Alevi society was the abolition of the Directorate of Religious Affairs or the introduction of a provision for the services of this directorate to all faiths on equal basis, and official recognition of the djemevis as legitimate places of worship. The Directorate of Religious Affairs is a state institution that offers services in the field of religion. The responsibility for the maintenance of the mosques and for the activities of the staff therein as well as for the opening and operation of Koran courses belongs to this Directorate. Expenses for all these activities and the salaries of the mosque personnel are paid out of the government budget. State owned properties – land or plots – could be allocated for construction of mosques. Yet, all these services are provided to the members of the Sunni sect. Alevi people pray in djemevis, not in mosques. Djemevis, however, are neither accepted by

22 The 1961 Constitution, Art. 19/4.
23 The 1982 Constitution, Art. 24/4.
24 Hasan Zengin et Eylem Zengin c. Turquie, 9 October 2007, Appl. No. 1448/04.

the state as legitimate places of worship nor do they receive any funds from the government budget. Furthermore, no land is allocated for them to build their places of worship. In this case they demanded one of these two solutions: Either the religious services should not be financed by the state – in other words the Directorate of Religious Affairs should be abolished – or funds should be appropriated to all other faith groups as well.[25]

As a matter of fact, these demands must be met not only for the Alevi population, but also for all other faith groups as well as the non-believers. Among the political parties in the National Assembly, especially the RPP, expressly supports such demands. The ruling party which is supported by the Sunni conservatives is opposed to them.

E. The Governmental System and the Status of the Office of the President

According to the existing provisions of the Constitution, it can be said that in Turkey the parliamentary government system has been adopted. However, unlike the case of classical parliamentary government systems, the President of the Republic of Turkey has significant powers. For example, a great majority of the members of the Constitutional Court are directly or indirectly selected by the President. One fourth of the members of the State Council, the Chief Prosecutor and the Deputy Chief Prosecutor of the Court of Cassation, some members of the Supreme Council of Judges and Public Prosecutors that take crucial decisions about other judges and public prosecutors are selected by the President. Furthermore, the members of the Council of Higher Education (CHE), which has supervisory and administrative powers over the universities, as well as the presidents of universities are appointed by the President of the Republic. The President also retains an important position in the executive branch by virtue of having the power to sign the decrees.

Presidents in Turkey have been always elected by the legislative organ. However after the amendment of the Constitution that was passed in 2007, goes into effect Presidents will be elected by the people. A new

25 See TÜSİAD, *Yeni Anayasa Yuvarlak Masa Toplantıları Dizisi: Yeni Anayasanın Beş Temel Boyutu*, 2011, pp. 24-26, available at http://www.tusiad.org.tr /__rsc/shared/file/YENI-ANAYASA-YUVARLAK-MASA.pdf, last accessed 10 December 2014.

presidential election has not yet been held because the term of office of the existing President did not end.

The real purpose of this radical amendment is not a regime change. In fact, this amendment was the result of a reaction.[26] That is because before the general elections in 2007, the National Assembly could not agree on who to elect the President and because the Constitutional Court did eventually decide that he/she could be elected by the National Assembly at a session where two-thirds of the total number of its members is present. For that reason, a new President could not be elected and the National Assembly had to call early elections. Right before the elections, a constitutional amendment for the election of the President directly by the people was put to the vote. As this motion did pass with a majority of less than two-thirds (less than 367) of the votes, a referendum had to be called. A Referendum was held on the date of 21 October 2007, because 120 days had to elapse after the publication of the text of the amendment in the Official Gazette. It was approved by a majority of 68%. Before the referendum, the general election was held on 22 July 2007, and the number of seats held by the political parties changed. This new distribution of the seats in the parliament allowed the election of the President by the National Assembly before the referendum.

The election of the President directly by the people will have an impact on the existing governmental system. Two different government bodies, i.e. the Parliament and the President, will both have been elected directly by the people. As the basis of their legitimacy would be the same and both will be very powerful, a clash will be inevitable when these two government bodies do not share the same political views.

Despite the significant powers the President of Turkey might have, they are not as strong as they are in France where a semi-presidential system prevails or in the USA where a presidential system prevails.[27] That is why there currently are two different views. According to one view, the presidential or semi-presidential system should be adopted. In other words, the powers of the president, they say, should be increased. According to the other view, the powers of the President should on the contrary be reduced to a symbolic level.

---

26 Constitutional Court judgment, No. 2007/45, dated 1 May 2007.

27 The Turkish governmental system is described as "premier-presidential". Özsoy, *Başkanlı Parlamenter Sistem*, 2009, p. 298.

In Turkey the political differences between the parties are sharp. Furthermore, there is an adverse political environment. Increasing the powers of the President in such an atmosphere can lead to severe disagreements between the legislative organ and the president. Therefore, in Turkey semi-presidential and presidential systems will prove to be very risky. Besides, considering the authoritarian inclinations of the executive branches as well as the inadequacy of the checks and balances system, it is concluded that the accumulation of powers in the hands of one person would likely lead to more authoritarianism.

F. Independence of the Judiciary and the Constitutional Court

The structure of the judiciary in general and of the Constitutional Court in particular was reshuffled as per the 2010 amendments to Constitution. Amendments were also made regarding the guarantees of the judiciary.

Amendments that are claimed to have been made to bestow further independence to the judiciary theoretically included certain improvements; it did not however make it more independent. The Judiciary could not attain independence from the executive branch.[28] Amendments regarding the Constitutional Court made it more dependent on the executive.

The number of members of the Constitutional Court after the latest amendment is 17. Fourteen of them are selected by the President, either directly or indirectly. The President appoints four members directly, and selects the other 10 members from among the groups of three candidates nominated by several institutions. Among such institutions are the High Courts and the Council of Higher Education. Since the members of the Council of Higher Education, which nominates the candidates for three seats, will have also been appointed by the President, in fact the President can be deemed to have been empowered to directly select seven members.

Three member of the Constitutional Court are elected by the National Assembly. However, a qualified majority like two-thirds is not required for this, and thus the leading party need not seek any agreement with the opposition parties for the election of these members of the Constitutional

28 See Inceoglu, "Constitutional Recommendations on Protecting Judicial Independence", 2012, Renewal of the Constitution, Proceedings of the International Round Table organised by IACL/AIDC (Istanbul, 28-29 April 2011).

Court. In fact they can be deemed to have been selected by the Cabinet alone.

As a result, a great majority of the members of the Constitutional Court are elected by the executive branch. As there is currently no variation with regard to political posture between the President and the Cabinet, it is difficult to claim that the Constitutional Court has a pluralist composition.

Such dependence of the Constitutional Court to the executive organ can be attributed to reactance. Particularly the two judgments of the Constitutional Court had drawn the reaction of the ruling party, which had had the majority in the National Assembly that was necessary to amend the Constitution. One of these judgments is the one about the Presidential election that is mentioned at above, and the other one is about the ban of headscarf in universities.[29] In other words, it won't be wrong to say that the constitutional amendments on the structure of the Constitutional Court were the result of the showdown between the Court and the conservative government.

In many democratic countries, the parliaments have a strong say in the selection of the members of the Constitutional Court.[30] Their election by the National Assemblies, with agreement of the different political parties therein strengthens pluralism and impartiality. Unfortunately in Turkey, things didn't develop in this direction and the Court's dependence on the executive power increased.

The social disagreements that are expressed above are reflected in the struggle over the judiciary. For this reason, expectations about the real independence of the judiciary and a Constitutional Court that has a pluralist and impartial structure are of utmost significance. Especially the opposition parties are under the impression that the judiciary is manipulated by the ruling party and therefore frequently express their demand for its independence.

G. Military-Civilian Relations

The 1961 and 1982 Constitution were shaped as the result of military coup d'états. Therefore, the military tutelage had been reflected on their

---

29 Constitutional Court judgement, No. 2008/16, dated 5 June 2008.

30 E.g. Germany, Portugal, Poland, Italy, Spain; see http://www.venice.coe.int/webforms/courts/, last accessed 10 December 2014.

contents. The role of the military is stronger in the 1982 Constitution in comparison with its role in the 1961 Constitution.

The National Security Council (NSC) was first mentioned in the 1961 Constitution. The NSC was introduced in that Constitution under the title for the Council of Ministers, and on a par with it. Members of the NSC were the Ministers that were stated in the law, the Chief of General Staff, the representatives of air and land forces as well as the navy and the gendarme. Article 111 of that Constitution defined the powers of the NSC as follows: "The NSC will communicate the required fundamental recommendations of the Council of Ministers with the purpose of helping the decisions to be taken on and the coordination of matters of national security." In 1971, some amendments were made as the result of the intervention by the Turkish Armed Forces, thus changing the composition of the NSC and increasing its powers. While until then representatives of the military were attending the meetings, after the amendments commanders of these forces were appointed as members of the NSC. Whereas according to the 1961 Constitution the NSC was expressing its opinions to the Council of Ministers, in the new version as amended in 1971, the verb "advise" was used. Regardless of this amendment, it can still be argued that in the 1961 Constitution, the NSC was still a consultative committee.[31]

In the 1982 Constitution, the ministers that would attend the NSC were listed one by one, and any change to it by law was prohibited. The number of these ministers was less than the number of commanders of the forces. The NSC was empowered to take decisions not only on foreign but also on domestic security issues. Furthermore, the 1982 Constitution rephrased the function of the NSC which had previously been referred to as consultative and stated that the Council of Ministers would "primarily take" its recommendations "into account."[32] Eventually, the NSC was transformed into a tool for the military to manipulate civilian politics.[33]

Upon emergence in 1999 of the possibility for Turkey to become an EU member, and in response to the EU demands for democratization, amendments were made to the Constitution. The number of ministers in

31 For the discussions on the characteristics of the NSC's decisions in the 1961 Constitution see Akgüner, *1961 Anayasasına Göre Milli Güvenlik Kavramı ve Milli Güvenlik Kurulu*, 1983, pp. 220-225.

32 Özdemir, *Rejim ve Asker*, 1989, pp. 271-279.

33 See Özbudun, *Türk Anayasa Hukuku*, 2010, pp. 344-346.

the NSC was increased and the Council was again transformed into a consultative organ upon the 2001 amendment to the Constitution. The amendment in 2004 lifted the exemption of the Turkish Armed Forces from the Supreme Council of Public Accounts audits – which is the supreme body that performs financial audits of the administrative organs on behalf of the GNAT. Nevertheless, actual diminishing of the powers of the armed forces has taken time. In the criminal case that was opened in 2008 and which is named as "Ergenekon", some military personnel and some civilians that had allegedly attempted to pave the way for another coup d'état by organizing provocative actions have been put on trial. This process changed the military-civilian relations to a significant extent and put an end to military tutelage. Although from this perspective it is a very positive development, the process has from time to time been used as pretext for remanding the opponents of the government under custody, by associating them with the alleged state within state and military coup attempts. Especially remanding of people like *Ahmet Sik* and *Nedim Sener* – the prominent journalists that had been awarded for their achievements in journalism and defending freedom of speech – under custody justified this belief. These incidents served as instruments for suppressing freedom of speech. The long detention periods, violation of the privacy of the accused individuals as well as their right to a fair trial is raising serious concerns.

This process did trigger two major social expectations. The first one is the exclusion of any provision that grants privileges and instruments to the military authorities for the manipulation of the civil authority from the new Constitution. It can be said that there is hardly any significant difference of opinion among the political parties regarding this matter. Some of the measures regarding this topic are requiring the Chief of Staff to report to the Minister of National Defense instead of directly reporting to the Prime Minister, abolishing of the special courts like the Supreme Military Administrative Court and the Military High Court of Appeal, and granting right of jurisdiction to the civilian courts over military issues.[34]

The second social expectation – which is expressed especially by the opposition parties – on the other hand is reinforcing the guarantees in the new Constitution against violations of the rights and freedoms which have increased after the "Ergenekon" case. In this context, the need for

34 See DISK, "Özgürlükçü-Eşitlikçi Demokratik ve Sosyal Yeni Bir Anayasa İçin Temel İlkeler," 2009, pp. 66-67, 76.

guarantees for freedom of speech, freedom of press and the media, freedom of assembly, right to liberty and security are especially emphasized in addition to the expectations regarding the independence and impartiality of the judiciary.

H. Conclusion

The idea of a new constitution triggered an exciting process. Expectations for solutions regarding the conflicts on issues of faith identity, ethnic identity, independence and impartiality of the judiciary, governance system and for the enhancement of the rights and freedoms in general are very high.

The expectations are certainly not limited to the solution of the points of conflicts that are discussed at above. For example in Turkey, the problems regarding the gender identity are another important issue. Despite the amendments to the Constitution, which were made in 2004 and 2010 to ensure equality of women and men not only in the laws but also in practice, amendments to the laws for putting positive discrimination into force were unfortunately not implemented. Women's involvement in the labor market[35] and in the political decision making mechanisms is still very limited. Women's organizations are struggling very hard to increase the number of women in the National Assembly and in other political decision taking mechanisms. Introduction of general election quotas and other election and selection quotas with regard to the other decision-making bodies are demanded.[36] This method is implemented in 81 other countries, but not yet in Turkey. In the National Assembly for the 23rd legislative term, only 48 of the 550 members were women. In other words less than 10% of the members of the parliament were women. In the National Assembly for the 24th legislative term, which is the current parliament, this number has increased to 77. This figure is still very low, and women are represented at a mere ratio of 14%. Women are expecting to be heard when the Constitution is being amended.

---

35 See http://tuikapp.tuik.gov.tr/isgucuapp/isgucu.zul, last accessed 10 December 2014.

36 See http://www.undp.org.tr/Gozlem3.aspx?WebSayfaNo=526, last accessed 10 December 2014.

Other issues not discussed could include workers and the poor demand more benefits; ecologists demand more guarantees for the protection of the environment; gays and lesbians demand prevention of discrimination against them; university students demand free education for all: and academicians demand university autonomy. It goes without saying many others can be added to this list.

All these demands can be addressed only by ensuring a free and participatory constitution-making process. In order to allow the groups that have demands to freely express themselves, freedoms of association, assembly and expression must be enhanced. They must be able to speak out without fear of intimidation and repercussion. Only by this way issues of social disagreements such as ethnic identity and faith identity can be discussed peacefully, and reconciliation can be achieved. All of these areas of disagreements cannot be resolved just by making a new Constitution. The people can sometimes wrongfully see the Constitution as the source of some problems, which indeed have to be resolved politically through dialogue. Extreme expectations create constitution fetishism.

Works cited

Ahmad, Feroz, *The Making of Modern Turkey*, London/New York: Routledge, 1993.

Akbulut, Olgun, *Barış İçinde Yaşamanın Hukuk Zemini*, Istanbul: XII Levha Publ., 2008.

Akgüner, Tayfun, *1961 Anayasasına Göre Milli Güvenlik Kavramı ve Milli Güvenlik Kurulu*, Istanbul: İstanbul Üniversitesi Siyasal Bilgiler Fakültesi Publ., 1983.

Inceoğlu, Sibel, "Constitutional Recommendations on Protecting Judicial Independence," *Journal of Constitutional Law* 1 (2012): 259-294.

Mardin, Şerif, *The Genesis of Young Ottoman Thought*, Princeton: Princeton University Press, 1962.

Özbudun, Ergun, *1924 Anayasası*, Istanbul: İstanbul Bilgi Üniversitesi Publ., 2012.

Özbudun, Ergun, *Türk Anayasa Hukuku*, Ankara: Yetkin Publ., 2010.

Özdemir, Hikmet, *Rejim ve Asker, Istanbul*: AFA Publ., 1989.

Özsoy, Şule, *Başkanlı Parlamenter Sistem*, Istanbul: XII Levha Publ., 2009.

Tanör, Bülent, *Osmanlı-Türk Anayasal Gelişmeleri*, Istanbul: Der Publ., 1995.

Tanör, Bülent, *İki Anayasa 1961 ve 1982*, Istanbul: XII Levha Publ., 2012.

Tanör, Bülent, and Necmi Yüzbaşıoğlu, *1982 Anayasasına Göre Türk Anayasa Hukuku, Istanbul*: Yapı Kredi Publ., 2002.

Tunaya, Tarık Zafer, *Türkiye'de Siyasal Gelişmeler*, Istanbul: İstanbul Bilgi Üniversitesi Publ., 2001.

Vaner, Semih, "Laiklik, Laikçilik ve Demokrasi, Türkiye'den Birkaç Örnekle Birlikte", in Laiklik ve Demokrasi, ed. İbrahim Ö. Kaboğlu, Ankara: Imge press, 2001, pp. 165-196.

Divided National Identities and Constitutional Changes: The Case of Taiwan

Jau-Yuan Hwang

A. Introduction

Conventional wisdom within political science suggests that democratization can only occur within an established state. In the legal world, the existence of a written constitution presupposes a state as well. In this sense, national identity is considered a precondition for constitutional identity. In the case of Taiwan however, its democratization has proceeded in spite of hotly debated and divided national identities.

This paper discusses the dynamics between national identity and constitutional changes in Taiwan since its democratization in the 1990s. Section B will analyze the change in national identity among the Taiwanese people during the past two decades, featuring the emergence of a new Taiwanese identity in relation to the old Chinese identity. Section C will then examine the constitutional changes in response to this change in national identity and pinpoint the gaps between the constitutional norms and political reality. Section D will explain the possible causes and constraints for the above developments. Section E will further explore the case of Taiwan by proposing some preliminary reflections from the theoretical perspective.

B. Evolution of National Identities in Taiwan: Before and After 1990

From 1895 to 1945, Taiwan was a colony of Japan. Soon after the end of WWII, the Chinese government took control of Taiwan from the defeated Japanese in October 1945, under the authorization of General Order no. 1[1] issued by *Douglas MacArthur* as the Supreme Commander for the Allied Powers on September 2, 1945. Since then, Taiwan has been *de facto*

1 For the text of this order, see http://www.taiwandocuments.org/surrender05.htm, last visited 10 Oct 2013.

administered by the government of Republic of China ("ROC"), in spite of its undetermined international legal status. As a result, Taiwanese national identity took an abrupt turn from a colonized Japanese identity to a newly-imposed Chinese identity after 1945.

From 1949 to 1990, the ROC/KMT ("Kuomintang") government on Taiwan was more like a Chinese government in exile, rather than a government of Taiwan, by Taiwan or for Taiwan. Unsurprisingly, the only national identity allowed and imposed in Taiwan during this time span was the Chinese identity. Taiwanese identity, along with local languages, cultures and political participation were harshly suppressed under martial law during this era.

Beginning from the mid-1980s, waves of social movements for liberalization emerged from the bottom up. Democratization finally arrived in the early 1990s. In September 1986, the first opposition party, the Democratic Progressive Party (DPP) was formally established in spite of the government's threat to suppress it. In July of next year, the longest-ever rule by martial law was finally lifted. Three years later, Taiwan's Constitution was, for the first time, amended to replace the existing provisions of the emergency constitution.[2] As the democratization and constitutional changes moved on in the 1990s, the national identity of Taiwan began to evolve and flourish.

For the past two decades in Taiwan, the question of national identity has involved two separate but related positions: (1) Who are you? Are you a Taiwanese, Chinese or both? (2) What is your preference on the future political relation between Taiwan and China? Namely, are you in favor of Taiwanese independence, unification with China or maintenance of the status quo?

The following two tables illustrate the evolution of different identities with the above two questions among the Taiwanese people since the early

---

2 These emergency provisions were called "Temporary Provisions EffectiveDuring the Period of National Mobilization for Suppression of the Communist Rebellion." These Temporary Provisions (TP) were first enacted in China on April 18, 1948, for the purpose of fighting the civil war against the Chinese Communist Party (CCP). After December 1949 when the ROC/KMT government was defeated and replaced by the PRC/CCP government, these TP, along with the ROC Constitution, were enforced in and only in Taiwan. From 1948 to its termination in May 1991, these TP were revised four times, with the last revision in 1972.

1990s. The columes tagged in gray indicate the highest percentage in each surveyed year.

National Identity	Taiwanese only	Both Taiwanese and Chinese	Chinese only	No response
1992	17.6%	46.4%	25.5%	10.5%
1993	NA	NA	NA	NA
1994	20.2%	44.6%	26.2%	8.9%
1995	25.0%	47.0%	20.7%	7.3%
1996	24.1%	49.3%	17.6%	9.0%
1997	34.0%	41.4%	19.2%	5.3%
1998	36.2%	39.6%	16.3%	7.8%
1999	39.6%	42.5%	12.1%	5.8%
2000	36.9%	44.1%	12.5%	6.5%
2001	41.6%	43.1%	10.6%	4.7%
2002	41.2%	43.7%	9.2%	5.8%
2003	42.5%	43.3%	8.3%	4.7%
2004	41.1%	47.7%	6.2%	5.0%
2005	45.0%	43.4%	7.2%	4.4%
2006	44.2%	44.9%	6.3%	4.6%
2007	43.7%	44.7%	5.4%	5.9%
2008	48.4%	43.1%	4.0%	4.1%
2009	51.6%	39.8%	4.2%	4.4%
2010	52.7%	39.8%	3.8%	3.7%
2011	52.2%	40.3%	3.9%	3.7%
2012	54.3%	38.5%	3.6%	3.6%
2013	57.5%	36.1%	3.6%	2.8%

Table 1: National identity change in Taiwan between 1992 and 2013

Source: Core Political Attitudes Trend Chart, Election Study Center, National Chengchi University, http://esc.nccu.edu.tw/modules/tinyd2/content/pic/trend/People201306.jpg, last visited 10 Oct 2013.

On the issue of Taiwan v. Chinese identity, there has been a steady and clear trend of an emerging Taiwanese identity and a declining Chinese identity. As illustrated in Table 1, the percentage of people in Taiwan identifying themselves as "Taiwanese only" increased rapidly from 17.6%

in 1992 to 57.5% in 2013, more than three-times of growth. It has become the most prevailing identity in Taiwan since 2008. On the contrary, the percentage of "Chinese only" identity went down shaprply from 25.5% in 1992 to mere 3.6% in 2013. Noteworthyly, even after the pro-China and pro-unification KMT government regained its ruling power in May 2008, the divergence between Taiwanese and Chinee identities only became much wider rather than narrower. In spite of the KMT government's official policies of promoting close ties with China, the increase in Taiwanese identity passed the 50% threshold in 2009.

As to the issue of the future political relation between Taiwan and China, Table 2 below indicates a similar trend of change: (Note: Ind. for "Independence"; Uni. for "Unification"; ASAP for "as soon as possible")

Future Status	Ind. ASAP	Toward Ind.	Status quo forever	Status quo now, to be decided later	Toward Uni.	Uni. ASAP	No response
1994	3.1%	8.0%	9.8%	38.5%	15.6%	4.4%	20.5%
1995	3.5%	8.1%	15.6%	24.8%	19.4%	2.3%	26.3%
1996	4.1%	9.5%	15.3%	30.5%	19.5%	2.5%	18.6%
1997	5.7%	11.5%	16.3%	30.5%	17.3%	3.2%	15.4%
1998	5.7%	11.5%	15.9%	30.3%	15.9%	2.1%	18.7%
1999	4.7%	13.6%	18.8%	30.9%	15.2%	2.2%	14.5%
2000	3.1%	11.6%	19.2%	29.5%	17.4%	2.0%	17.3%
2001	2.8%	10.5%	16.4%	35.9%	17.5%	3.7%	13.3%
2002	4.3%	13.8%	15.0%	36.2%	15.7%	2.5%	12.4%
2003	6.2%	14.5%	18.0%	35.0%	11.9%	1.8%	12.5%
2004	4.4%	15.2%	20.9%	36.5%	10.6%	1.5%	11.0%
2005	6.1%	14.2%	19.9%	37.3%	12.3%	1.8%	8.5%
2006	5.6%	13.8%	19.9%	38.7%	12.1%	2.0%	7.9%
2007	7.8%	13.7%	18.4%	36.8%	10.0%	1.9%	11.4%
2008	7.1%	16.0%	21.5%	35.8%	8.7%	1.5%	9.4%
2009	5.8%	15.0%	26.2%	35.1%	8.5%	1.3%	8.1%
2010	6.2%	16.2%	25.4%	35.9%	9.0%	1.2%	6.1%
2011	4.6%	15.6%	27.4%	33.8%	8.8%	1.5%	8.2%
2012	4.8%	15.1%	27.7%	33.9%	8.7%	1.7%	8.1%
2013	5.4%	17.9%	25.6%	32.4%	9.4%	2.1%	7.1%

Table 2: Taiwanese people's attitudes toward independence v. unification between 1994 and 2013

Source: Core Political Attitudes Trend Chart, Election Study Center, National Chengchi University, http://esc.nccu.edu.tw/modules/tinyd2/content/pic/trend/Tondu201306.jpg, last visited 10 Oct 2013.

We may use a more simplified formula to classify the above different attitudes by dividing them into three main categories with positive responses: "pro-unification", "status quo" and "pro-independence". Both categories of "unification as soon as possible" and "toward unification" should be added together and called the "pro-unification" category, while "independence as soon as possible", "toward independence" and "status quo forever" could be attributed to the "pro-independence" category. By this way, we will see a trend showing change very similar to Table 1:

Future Status	Pro-Ind.	Status quo now, to be decided later	Pro-Uni.	No response
1994	20.9%	38.5%	20%	20.5%
1995	27.2%	24.8%	21.7%	26.3%
1996	28.9%	30.5%	22.0%	18.6%
1997	33.5%	30.5%	20.5%	15.4%
1998	33.1%	30.3%	18.0%	18.7%
1999	37.1%	30.9%	17.4%	14.5%
2000	33.9%	29.5%	19.6%	17.3%
2001	29.7%	35.9%	21.2%	13.3%
2002	33.1%	36.2%	18.2%	12.4%
2003	38.7%	35.0%	13.7%	12.5%
2004	40.5%	36.5%	12.1%	11.0%
2005	40.2%	37.3%	14.1%	8.5%
2006	39.3%	38.7%	14.1%	7.9%
2007	39.9%	36.8%	11.9%	11.4%
2008	44.6%	35.8%	10.2%	9.4%
2009	47.0%	35.1%	9.8%	8.1%
2010	49.8%	35.9%	10.2%	6.1%
2011	47.6%	33.8%	10.3%	8.2%
2012	47.6%	33.9%	10.4%	8.1%
2013	48.9%	32.4%	11.5%	7.1%

Table 3: Regrouping summary of the 1994-2013 trend table of Taiwanese people's attitudes toward independence v. unification

Source: Table 2

As indicated in Tables 2 and 3, the percentage of people preferring to maintain the status quo and defer the ultimate decision until later has remained the highest category. However, if we consider those choosing to maintain the status quo forever as "pro-independence", then the total percentage of "pro-independence" category would have exceeded that of "status quo forever" group since 1997, except for 2001 and 2002. A statistically more significant difference of a more than 10% gap between these two groups has emerged and widened since 2008. At the other end of the spectrum, the number of people identifying with eventual unification has steadily dropped from roughly 20% before 2001 to around 10% after 2008.

In summary, it should be safe to draw some observations from the above statistics: since 1996, the Taiwanese identity has undisputedly outweighed the Chinese identity and, since 2008, become the most prevailing national identity among the people of Taiwan. Secondly, Taiwanese people's' attitude toward their future relationship with China remains more mixed and ambivalent. However, there has been an obvious trend among the absolute majority of Taiwanese people that moves away from unification with China and leans toward permanent separation (even if not in the name of formal independence) from China.

In the next section, we will analyze how Taiwan's Constitutional and legal systems responded to such changes.

C. Constitutional Changes Regarding National Identity Since Democratization

I. 1945-1991: Imposed Chinese Identity and a Transplanted Constitution

After WWII, China first took control of Taiwan from the defeated Japanese on behalf of the Allied Powers. In October 1945, China unilaterally extended its own jurisdiction and laws over Taiwan.

Not surprisingly, Taiwan's Constitution was originally promulgated in China in 1947. In December 1947, a new Constitution (hereinafter the 1947 Constitution) took effect in China and was applied to Taiwan as well. Two years later, this Constitution lost its territory of original application as a result of the overthrow of the KMT/ROC government by the CCP/PRC government. After 1949, the ROC/KMT government re-established itself on Taiwan after being ousted by the PRC/CCP government in mainland China. Hence, this short-lived Chinese Constitution has remained and gradually evolved to become, practically and normatively, the Constitution of Taiwan since 1949,[3] though it continued to claim itself as the *Chinese* Constitution for the next four decades.

Despite the fact that Japan's *de jure* sovereignty over Taiwan did not come to end until April 1952 when the San Francisco Peace Treaty tookcame into force, the 1947 ROC Constitution still envisioned its territory to cover both China and Taiwan. Under the 1947 Constitution, both China and Taiwan were considered two parts of the ROC territory. Accordingly in Taiwain, Taiwan was once called the Free China or Free Area, and China was named the "Bandit-Occupied Area." Until 1991, the ROC Constitution employed the model of "One State, Two Areas" to define the Taiwan-China relations. Under this model, only Chinese identity was legally allowed and imposed. The unification pursued by the government would be a matter of domestic affair, instead of international nature.

II. Since 1991: Thriving Taiwanese Identity and a Transformed Constitution

Before 1991, all three representative bodies at the national level in Taiwan consisted mainly of delegates elected in China in 1948. They were allowed to stay in their office for life.[4] Even in the 1980s, the people of Taiwan could elect less than 10% of the total representatives of each body.

---

3 For a brief introduction of Taiwan's post-war constitutional history, see Hwang, *Constitutional Change and Political Transition in Taiwan since 1986: The Role of Legal Institutions*, 1995, pp. 16-71; Ginsburg, *Judicial Review in New Democracies: Constitutional Courts in Asian Cases*, 2003, pp. 111-15.

4 In 1951, all members of the Legislative Yuan (hereinafter LY) were due for re-election in accordance with the 1947 Constitution. Nevertheless the then LY adopted a resolution which extended its members' term for another year. Two similar resolutions were passed in the following two years. In 1954, the Council of Grand Justice, the equivalent of a constitutional court in Taiwan, finally issued Interpretation No. 31 and allowed all members of both the LY and Control Yuan (hereinafter CY) elected in 1948 to remain in office indefinitely. The delegates to the National Assembly simply stayed in office without re-election by their own resolution. For relevant documents, see Chiu, *Constitutional Development and Reform in the Republic of China on Taiwan*, 1993, pp. 19-22.

Domestically, the ROC/KMT government used these institutions and the 1947 Constitution as political tokens to maintain its fabricated claim as the sole legitimate government of China. Since 1991, a series of constitutional reforms have gradually redefined the constitutional identity of Taiwan in relationship to China.

After the martial law decree was finally lifted in 1986, constitutional reforms were initiated to facilitate democratization in the 1990s. This gradual process eventually changed the once self-claimed Chinese Constitution into a truly Taiwanese Constitution, though still carrying the name of the ROC. While the major reforms were the results of amending the large-capital written Constitution, some were achieved by evolution of the small-capital constitution, including constitutional court decisions and political practice of constitutional significance.

1. Transformation of the National Government from the Self-claimed Chinese Government to a Democratic Taiwanese Government

In June 1990, Taiwan's Grand Justices (the equivalent of constitutional court judges) rendered the Judicial Yuan Interpretation No. 261, which required all those senior (Mainlander) representatives elected in China in 1948 to step down by December 31, 1991.[5]

After the said constitutional interpretation cleared the way for further constitutional reforms, in April 1991, Taiwan's Constitution underwent its first formal amendment to accommodate democratization. A set of 10 Additional Articles were added to the 1947 Constitution. These new constitutional amendments mandated, among others, the re-election of the three national representative bodies.[6] Accordingly, general elections for the National Assembly and Legislative Yuan (LY) were held in December 1991 and December 1992, respectively.[7] Since then, Taiwan's national

---

5 Judicial Yuan Interpretation No. 261 (June 21, 1990), available at www.judicial.gov.tw/constitutionalcourt/en/p03_01.asp?expno=261, last visited 10 October 2013.

6 Additional Articles of the Constitution of the Republic of China (May 1, 1991), available at http://www.judicial.gov.tw/constitutionalcourt/p07_2_one.asp?lawno=48&types=all, last visited 10 Oct 2013.

7 A new Additional Article enacted in 1992 changed the composition of the CY. See Additional Article 3 of the Constitution of the Republic of China (May 28, 1992), available at http://www.judicial.gov.tw/constitutionalcourt/ p07_2_one

legislatures have been re-elected on a regular basis. All members of national legislatures are elected exclusively from and by the people of Taiwan. During the amendment process, there once was a proposal to establish so-called “Mainland Representatives,” in order to symbolize the ROC’s virtual representation of China. However, the proposal was dropped and the newly elected national legislatures no longer claimed to represent China at all.

In March 1996, Taiwan went on to hold its first direct, popular presidential election under the 1994 Constitutional Amendments, despite the missile drills and military intimidation by China right before the ballot date. Since then, the President of Taiwan has been directly elected, every four years, by the people of Taiwan only.

The above developments not only marked a watershed in Taiwan’s democratization process, but also reshaped the political and international identity of Taiwan. These general elections formally cut off Taiwan’s self-claimed representation of Chinese people and territory, and thus based the legitimacy of the Taiwan/ROC government exclusively on the political will of the people of Taiwan. The people of China were therefore constitutionally excluded from participation in the formation of the Taiwan/ROC government, as were other foreigners.[8] In this sense, the power base and legitimacy of the present Taiwan government have exclusively relied on the people of Taiwan. After democratization and constitutional changes in the 1990s, the governing authority of Taiwan has transformed into a genuine Taiwanese government and is no longer a Chinese government in exile.

.asp?lawno=52&types=all, last visited 10 Oct 2013. Since then, the members of CY have been appointed by the President with confirmation by the National ssembly. Additional Article 7 of the 2000 Constitutional amendments moved the confirmation power from the National Assembly to the LY, available at http://www.judicial.gov.tw/constitutionalcourt/p07_2_one.asp?lawno=56&types=all, last visited 10 October 2013.

8 For the evolution of Taiwan’s constitutional reforms on its international status, see Chiang and Hwang, “On the Statehood of Taiwan: An Legal Appraisal,” 2008, pp. 57-80.

2. A New Statehood?: New Wine in an Old Bottle

Meanwhile, the 1991 Additional Articles also redefined the territorial jurisdiction of the ROC Constitution to the Taiwan area only.[9] On May 1, 1991, President *Lee Teng-hui* officially announced the unilateral termination of military hostility against China and formally acknowledged the effective control of China by the PRC government since 1949.

On the issue of territory and statehood, Taiwan's Constitution did not take a revolutionary change. The official state title has remained the same ("Republic of China"). The specific constitutional provision for state territory continues to refer to an ambiguous and undefined concept of "existing boundaries" without a clear definition. However, some provisions in the 1947 Constitution do imply that all of mainland China remain within its territory, at least in a formalistic sense. The 1991 Constitutional Amendments also adopted the ambiguous term of "Free Area" to refer to Taiwan and "Mainland Area" for China. On the definition of the people (nationals), the 1991 Constitutional Amendments and related statutes have used the "household registration" to distinguish the Taiwanese people (people of Free Area) from the Chinese people (people of Mainland Area). As applied, the legal effects of the household registration have been virtually identical to those of nationality. Though Taiwan's Constitution has not expressly re-defined its territory, the relevant Amendments and statutes have skillfully redefined and limited its jurisdiction to Taiwan only, and thus excluded China implicitly therefrom.

On the part of small-capital constitution, Taiwan's Constitutional Court once issued a decision (Interpretation No. 328) in 1993[10] and ruled that delimitation of the existing boundaries under the Constitution was a political question beyond the scope of judicial review. It is unclear, however, whether the Constitutional Court intended to let the political process determine this thorny issue by taking it out of constitutional reach. In 1994, Taiwan's Ministry of Foreign Affairs publicly announced that the Taiwan government would no longer compete for the Chinese representation with the PRC government. Accordingly the Taiwan

---

9 Additional Article 10 to the Constitution, May 1, 1991; renumbered to be Additional Article 11 (1994, last amended 2005).

10 Judicial Yuan Interpretation No. 328 (Nov. 26, 1993), available at http://www.judicial.gov.tw/constitutionalcourt/p03_01.asp?expno=328, last visited 10 Oct, 2013.

government would seek a separate but appropriate representation for Taiwan only in the U.N.[11] From the international law perspective, such statement amounted to a redefinition and identification of the ROC as and with Taiwan.

3. A Thriving New National Identity

The most dramatic changes regarding national identity have occurred on the part of individual rights and within the civil society. Before 1990, Taiwanese identity was oppressed. Either political speeches or associations in support of Taiwan independence were banned and criminally published as treasons. In 1992, the Legislative Yuan of Taiwan abolished a statute that criminalized the pro-independence speech. In 1998, the Constitutional Court found unconstitutional a provision of the Assembly Act that prohibited both communist and separatist speeches, by applying the "clear and present danger" test.[12] In June 2008, the Constitutional Court further declared unconstitutional a similar provision in the Civic Organizations Act that prohibited the registration of associations advocating either communism or separation of national territory.[13] Eventually an uninhibited free market of speech emerged to accommodate the rapid booming of Taiwanese identity and to allow the people to make a free and informed choice on Taiwan's future relationship with China.

As far as national identity is concerned, there has existed an obvious gap between the large-capital Constitution and small-capital constitution in Taiwan. On the part of small-capital constitution, the people of Taiwan

11 See Mainland Affairs Council of the Executive Yuan, Taiwan, *Relations across the Taiwan Straits*, Taipei: MAC, 1994, p. 10. This position was later expressly confirmed by the Spokesman of the Ministry of Foreign Affairs, while commenting on Taiwan's efforts in applying for the UN membership. See *Central Daily News*, International Edition, p. 1, (July 17, 1994) [original in Chinese].

12 Judicial Yuan Interpretation No. 445 (Jan. 23, 1998), available at http://www.judicial.gov.tw/constitutionalcourt/p03_01.asp?expno=445, last visited 10 October 2013.

13 Judicial Yuan Interpretation No. 644 (Jun. 20, 2008), available at http://www.judicial.gov.tw/constitutionalcourt/p03_01.asp?expno=644, last visited 10 Oct 2013.

have enjoyed the full-fledged constitutional liberties and rights to pursue their individual or collective identity. The powers and legitimacy of Taiwan's government are also derived from and based on the consent of the Taiwanese people, exclusively. With the large-capital Constitution, Taiwan's Constitution still kept the written texts of Chinese origin intact on paper, particularly the state title and national territory, in spite of the dramatic change in national identity over the past two decades. Under the old clothes of the written Constitution, there has been a flourishing new national identity competing and coexisting with the lingering old one.

D. Gaps Between Norms and Facts: Causes and Constraints

There are several reasons that could explain the gaps between the constitutional norms and the political reality regarding the issue of national identity in Taiwan:

(1) Still two competing national identities: A substantial number of Chinese identity holders now hide their political loyalty behind the mask of "double identities" by identifying themselves as "both Taiwanese and Chinese" at the same time, as suggested by the poll surveys in Table 1.

(2) Lack of a strong consensus on the new national identity: Among the more than 90% of Taiwanese people who hold Taiwanese identity, only a slight majority of them embrace the new identity as their first and only identity. That is far from a strong enough new consensus to replace the old Chinese identity. Nevertheless, as indicated by Table 1, the percentage of people identifying themselves as "Taiwanese only" has risen to about 60%, and appears to follow this pattern in subsequent years. Given the trend, there might be a strong enough consensus on the new national identity in the near future.

(3) High and rigid threshold for constitutional revisions: In Taiwan, in order to amend the Constitution, it would take a super-majority vote of three-fourths of the members of the national legislature present at a meeting with a quorum of two-thirds of the entire legislature. Consequently, amending the Constitution would require a high degree of consensus among nearly all major political parties. On the issue of national identity, such consensus simply did and does not exist in Taiwan.

(4) No real power turnover in the national legislature: Although Taiwan has experienced its first power turnover between 2000 and 2008, its national legislatures have been controlled by the pro-China KMT without any turnover. Since 2008, the KMT has won the Presidential elections

twice and taken a strong pro-China and pro-unification stand. It is worth watching how the incumbent KMT government since 2008 and its China policy would affect the trend of change in Taiwan's national identity.

On top of the above causes that have prevented Taiwan's Constitution from being amended to reflect the changing national identity, there have been external constraints that further deterred Taiwan's Constitution from being so amended, such as China and other international factors. For decades, China has threatened to invade Taiwan, should the latter declare independence. Even the U.S. government has been reluctant to support calls for Taiwan's formal independence, including constitutional amendments to such effects.

E. Reflections on the Models of Constitutional Transformation

I. Consensus on National Identity as a Presupposition of Constitution Making or Revision?

In modern democracies, "we the people" are regarded as both the author and the subject of Constitution. A constitution often presupposes a national or political identity of "we the people," strong or weak. Against this presumption, we may be curious to ask: could a constitution be created or amended without a consensus on national identity among its people? The answer is a clear "yes" in the case of Taiwan.

Over the past two decades, it has been a divided people with two competing identities working together and fighting against each other under a paper-thin Constitution of Taiwan. Transformed by and large, Taiwan's C/constitution has gradually come to acknowledge and then recognize a new reality. It has been "we the *divided* people" that formed the foundation of present C/constitution in Taiwan. In other words, a single set of Constitution has been accommodating two different (and conflicting) imaginations of national identities in Taiwan.

Along this line, we may argue that a strong sense of "we the people" is not necessarily a precondition for the foundation of a constitution. Nor must "we the people" refer to the idea of a preceded, established and even homogeneous nation (ethnos), which is manifested by the cases of the German and French Constitutions.

The U.S. Constitution suggests a weak sense of "we the people" as the foundation of the Constitution. This sense of people would refer to the idea of "citizens" (demos) coming together under a liberal and democratic framework of a constitution. The overlapping consensuses on or shared commitments to the liberal and democratic framework provide the basis for such a thin civic identity of the people.[14]

Compared to the above two models, Taiwan's case is more akin to the latter type of a weak civic identity. However, the idea of "we the people" under the U.S. Constitution still refers to a solid imagined community, collectively committed to a given state. In Taiwan's case, particularly after 1990, the process of democratization and constitutional changes have indeed helped create a weak, civic sense of national identity to sustain a constitutional republic at present. Such identity, however, still falls short of creating an overlapping consensus on the future of a new State.

II. How Should a C/constitution Cope with the Existence of "We the Divided People"?

The process of constitutional change or political transition towards democracy (democratization) could be revolutionary or evolutionary, or, in Samuel Huntington's words,[15] by replacement, transplacement or transformation. In the temporal sense, the evolutionary model often refers to a more incremental and piecemeal process, while the other to an abrupt, one-shot type of change. Historically, the U.S. and France should belong to the revolutionary model, while the U.K belongs to the evolutionary model. During the third-wave democratization, South Korea (in 1987) and the Philippines (in 1986) could be considered examples of revolutionary models, while Taiwan is clearly an evolutionary one.[16]

On the issue of national identity, Taiwan's evolutionary approach has been a deliberate but hardly a voluntary choice. Considering the causes and constraints as stated above, it is understandable that Taiwan did not take the revolutionary approach to settle its internal disputes over national identity once and for all. What remains to be seen is that whether or not

---

14 For more inspiring analyses of these issues, see generally Rosenfeld ed., *Constitutionalism, Identity, Difference, and Legitimacy: Theoretical Perspectives*, 1994.

15 See Huntington, *The Third Wave: Democratization in the Late Twentieth Century*, 1991.

16 For more in-depth analysis, see generally Lerner, *Making Constitutions in Deeply Divided Societies*, 2011; Miller, ed., *Framing the State in Times of Transition: Case Studies in Constitution Making*, 2010.

Taiwan will be able to make any further step toward an eventual solution. Or, given the external constraints, will the current constructive ambiguity turn into a state of destructive paralysis, which would upset Taiwan's free democracy in the long run?

Works cited

Chiang, Huang-Chih and Jau-Yuan Hwang, "On the Statehood of Taiwan: An Legal Appraisal," in *The "One China" Dilemma*, ed. Peter Chow, New York: Palgrave Macmillan, 2008, pp. 57-80.

Chiu, Hungdah, *Constitutional Development and Reform in the Republic of China on Taiwan*, Maryland: School of Law, University of Maryland Occasional Papers 2 (1993): 2-61, 1993.

Ginsburg, Tom, *Judicial Review in New Democracies: Constitutional Courts in Asian Cases*, Cambridge: Cambridge University Press, 2003.

Huntington, Samuel P., The Third Wave: Democratization in the Late Twentieth Century, University of Oklahoma Press, 1991.

Hwang, Jau-Yuan, *Constitutional Change and Political Transition in Taiwan since 1986: The Role of Legal Institutions*, Unpublished S.J.D. Dissertation, Harvard Law School, 1995.

Lerner, Hanna, *Making Constitutions in Deeply Divided Societies*, Cambridge: Cambridge University Press, 2011.

Miller, Laurel E. ed., *Framing the State in Times of Transition: Case Studies in Constitution Making*, D.C.: United States Institute of Peace Press, 2010.

Rosenfeld, Michel ed., *Constitutionalism, Identity, Difference, and Legitimacy: Theoretical Perspectives*, Durham, NC: Duke University Press, 1994.

Constitutionalism and Religious Diversity in Singapore: A *via media* Between Principle and Pragmatism?

Li-ann Thio

A. Constitutional Origins and Moments: Genesis Through Exodus

Given the potentially conflictual nature of relations between the state and religion, in competing for the loyalty of citizen and adherent, and of tensions between and within religious groups, the constitution as the basic law has to negotiate and mediate these tensions. It does so through deploying varied schemes of punitive sanctions, providing facilities for rights remediation and also, adopting more dialogical and reconciliatory approaches to promote sustainable relationships. What is at stake is not merely 'public order', but 'racial and religious harmony' which goes not only to state stability but also to the quality of relationships between disparate faith communities within the polity.

Thus, to understand the constitutional design for negotiating State-Religion relations within the multi-religious,[1] multi-ethnic polity of the island city-state of Singapore, it is necessary to grasp the historical origins of what has been described as an accidental nation.[2]

The genesis of Singapore is located in the plans that the British colonial government had for Peninsular Malaysia as it prepared to withdraw from South-east Asia, and the need to manage matters of race and religion to ensure a social equilibrium. The match that might light the tinder-box was the latent threat of political volatility posed by racial tensions: the overwhelmingly Muslim Malays considered themselves the indigenous

---

1 The 2010 Census of Population reports the religious composition of Singapore as follows: Buddhists and Taoists (44%); Christians (18%), Muslims (15%) and Hindus (5%). It also notes that 99% of Malays in 2010 were Muslims, which marks a high degree of conflation between ethnicity and religion with respect to Malays and Islam: Singapore Department of Statistics Press Release, Census of Population 2010 available at http://www.singstat.gov.sg/news/news/press 12012011.pdf, visited 15 October 2013.

2 See generally Thio, "Control, Co-optation and Co-Operation: Managing Religious Harmony in Singapore's Multi-Ethnic, Quasi-Secular State," 2005, pp. 197-253; Thio, "Chapter 15: Freedom of Religion," 2012, pp. 869-924.

people of the Peninsula[3] who were under siege from Indian and Chinese immigrants, and were particularly threatened by the economic clout of the Chinese. With its predominantly Chinese population, Singapore posed a 'Chinese problem' both in terms of diluting the economic and political strength of the Malays but also, the fear that Singapore might become "a Cuba in Malaya's backyard."[4]

The plan was never that Singapore should be a stand-alone independent nation; it gained self-government in 1959 and by the early 1960s, the local political actors and the colonial British government had decided that Singapore would be incorporated into part of a 'Greater Malaysia'; thus from 1963-1965, Singapore was a constituent state of the Malaysian Federation, until her exodus into independent statehood through consensual secession on 9 August 1965. One primary reason fuelling the decision of the central Malaysian authorities to expel Singapore from the Federation was the politicking of Singapore's first Prime Minister, *Lee Kuan Yew*, to have a 'Malaysian Malaysia' rather than one based on special privileges for one community, that is the Malays as *bumiputera* or 'sons of the soil.'[5]

The trauma of expulsion shocked the Singapore leadership which was soon galvanised into addressing the pressing problems of the day: homelessness, a high unemployment rate, the internal threat of communalism and communism and the external threat of the Indonesian Konfrontasi.[6] Added to that, a discomfited Malay population which had been part of the majority community in the Federation, now found itself a minority group which had to be pacified, particularly given the concerns of the 'kin' state, Malaysia which could internationalize a minority dispute.

---

3 Historically, the Malays were not the first peoples on the Peninsula: the various tribes collectively known as *Orang Asli*, were: Nowak and Muntil, "Btsisi', Blandas, and Malays: Ethnicity and Identity in the Malay Peninsula Based on Btsisi' Folklore and Ethnohistory," 2004, pp. 303-323.

4 Chin Huat Wong, "Weakened Federalism in the New Federation," *The Sun* 25 July 2007.

5 See Mohamad, *The Malay Dilemma*, 1970, arguing that Malays should accept government aid because their non-confrontational nature had allowed them to be subjugated in their own land with British collusion, and to correct Chinese hegemony in commerce.

6 The Indonesians and communists alleged that Malaysia (and later Singapore) was a stooge of British imperialism. See 'Konfrontasi' at http://www.globalsecurity.org/military/world/war/konfrontasi.htm/, visited 15 October 2013.

Demonstrating its signature technocratic pragmatism, the government led by the People's Action Party (PAP) did not convene a constituent assembly to draft a constitution, despite initial indications it would; instead it sought a working document to meet the exigencies of the day. Singapore's Constitution after independence was cobbled together like a patchwork quilt, drawing on the Singapore state constitution buttressed with amendments consequent to political independence.[7] This included making certain provisions of the Malaysian Federal Constitution applicable to Singapore, through the Republic of Singapore Independence Act (RSIA),[8] such as the Part II list of fundamental liberties.

What is of key interest, in terms of religion-state constitutional design and indeed, national identity, is what transpired the following year, when the government convened a constitutional commission mandated with the task of making recommendations on safeguarding minority rights.[9] Without a shared history in terms of a common culture, language, faith or ethnicity, the PAP government sought to sustain social cohesion and to build a sense of solidarity by downplaying the urge to religious or ethnic chauvinism; this was based on constructing a political culture and system open to all citizens, to point not to a shared past but a common future. The commission made recommendations in a report which Parliament debated.

In an expression of aversive constitutionalism, the new Singapore polity defined itself in oppositional terms from the Malaysian constitutional order. Three points of departure are worth highlighting. First, the Singapore Constitution excluded any reference to an official religion, departing from article 3 of the Federal Malaysian Constitution which recognizes Islam as the religion of the Federation. While contemporaneous understanding was that the Malaysian polity was meant to be secular, as a pre-commitment strategy to placate the non-Muslim communities, the confessional clause 'de-secularised' the Constitution to some extent.[10] As Prime Minister *Lee Kuan Yew* noted of Singapore in

7 See Tan, "The Evolution of Singapore's Modern Constitution: Developments from 1945 to the Present Day," 1989, pp. 1-28.

8 Act No. 9 of 1965. This incorporated all the Federal Powers formerly part of the Federal Constitution when Singapore was in Malaysia.

9 See Thio, "The Passage of a Generation: Revisiting the 1966 Constitutional Commission," 2009, pp. 7-49.

10 *Abdul Aziz Bari* notes that a constitution which refers to Islam and mandates public expenditure for religious purposes "could not be said to be an out-and-out secular constitution." Bari, "Islam in the Federal Constitution: A Commentary on

1967, "Alone in Southeast Asia, we are a state without an established church."[11] In contrast to the Proclamation of Malayan Independence of 1957 which invoked the Muslim God and Prophet, the basis for the Singapore founding was an appeal to democracy, the Proclamation being done "on behalf of the people and the Government of Singapore." While the text of the Singapore constitution does not contain an explicit commitment to the principle of secularity, the 1966 Constitutional Commission described Singapore as a "democratic secular state."[12] This has been reaffirmed in numerous ministerial statements and 'soft constitutional documents' such as the 2006 Declaration on Religious Harmony.[13] The Singapore Court of Appeal has described Singapore as having a system based on "accommodative secularism,"[14] as its founders appreciated that a nation with a plural society "based on one race, one language and one religion," would be "doomed for destruction."[15] This commitment to a different model of secularism from the Malaysian one is also evident in the *de facto* preamble to both constitutions contained in soft or non-binding instruments declaring national principles in the form

---

the Decision of Meor Atiqulrahman," 2002, p. cxxix. While the reference to 'Islam' was meant to be ceremonial, today, there is a strong agenda to increasingly treat Islam as a source of public values. For example, then Deputy Prime Minister *Najib* described Malaysia as an Islamic state: "We have never been secular because being secular by Western definition means separation of the Islamic principles in the way we govern a country. We have never been affiliated to that position. We have always been driven by our adherence to the fundamentals of Islam." "Malaysia Not Secular State, Says Najib," *Bernama.com*, 17 July 2007. See also Fernando, "The Position of Islam in the Constitution of Malaysia," 2006, p. 249.

11 Prime Minister Lee Kuan Yew, addressing a Buddhist Convention: "No dominance by religious group over others – Lee," *Straits Times* (Singapore), 5 January 1967, p. 6.

12 *Report of the Constitutional Commission* 1966 (Singapore Government Printers, 1966), para 38.

13 Ministry of Community Development and Sports Press Release, *Declaration on Religious Harmony*, 9 July 2003, text of Declaration annexed at http://www.mcys.gov.sg/MCDSFiles/Press/Articles/press-release-9Jun-inal.html. See Thio, "Soft Constitutional Law in non-liberal Asian Constitutional Democracies," 2010, pp. 766-799; Thio, "Constitutional 'Soft' Law and the Management of Religious Liberty and Order: The 2003 Declaration on Religious Harmony," 2004, pp. 414-443.

14 *Nappalli v Institute of Technical Education* [1999] 2 SLR(R) 529 at [29].

15 Chief Justice Wee Chong Jin, *Report of the Constitutional Commission*, General Introduction, Singapore Government Printers, 1966.

of the Malaysian *Rukunegara* of 1971[16] and the statement of Singapore shared values. While the former identifies a "Belief in God" as a key national principle, a proposal to include a similar commitment was rejected in the Singapore context in these terms:

> Singapore is a secular state. The Government has always maintained a strictly neutral position on matters of religion, and should continue to do so. Each religious group has its own tenets. While many religions enjoin their followers to practise similar virtues, the faiths themselves are fundamentally different. Even if we confine ourselves to those religious aspects which are common, such as belief in God, we will be unable to extend them to the substantial number of Singaporeans who do not belong to any particular religion. The Shared Values should therefore be a secular document, and not include any religious values.[17]

Second, the Singapore Constitution does not conflate ethnicity and religion in the way article 160 of the Malaysian Constitution does, in defining a 'Malay' as one who practises the Muslim religion. The Malaysian approach underscores that Islam is integral to Malay identity, which undermines religious freedom, most clearly demonstrated in politically volatile apostasy cases. Malaysian courts have held that Malays cannot convert out of Islam, without a declaration of apostasy from the religious or *syariah* courts (which has never been issued for ethnic Malays).[18] One High Court judge has gone so far to declare: "A Malay under art 160(2) remains in the Islamic faith until his or her dying days."[19] This statement renders freedom of conscience nugatory. The constitutional

---

16 The Declaration contained five objectives: to secure "a greater unity of all her peoples", to maintain "a democratic way of life", to create "a just society in which the wealth of the nation shall be equitably shared", to ensure a "liberal approach to her right and diverse cultural traditions" and to build a "progressive society" based on modern science and technology. The pursuit of these ends was to be guided by five principles: (i) Belief in God, (ii) Loyalty to King and Country; (iii) Upholding the Constitution; (iv) Rule of Law and (v) Good Behaviour and Morality. Government of Malaysia, *Rukunegara*, 1970.

17 Shared Values White Paper (Cmd 1 of 1991, Singapore Parliament) at [45].

18 E.g., Thio, "Apostasy and Religious Freedom: Constitutional Issues Arising from the *Lina Joy* Litigation," 2006, pp. i-cxvi; Thio, "Jurisdictional Imbroglio: Civil and Religious Courts, Turf Wars and Article 121(1A) of the Federal Constitution," 2007, pp. 197-226.

19 Thamby Chik J, *Lina Joy v Majlis Agama Islam Wilayah* [2004] 2 Malayan Law Journal (MLJ) 119 at 143, para. 58.

ascription of religious identity to one sector of its population by the Malaysian Constitution is distinct from the voluntarist conception of religious freedom in Singapore where "the protection of freedom of religion under our Constitution is premised on removing restrictions to one's choice of religious belief."[20]

Third, the Singapore model of state-religion relations adopts a more expansive vision of religious freedom by deleting a substantive limitation from its religious freedom clause contained in Article 15(1). This reads that "Every person has the right to profess and practise his religion and to propagate it." This is subject to "any general law relating to public order, public health or morality", as stated in Article 15(4). In contrast, the Malaysian article 11, from whence article 15 is derived, is more restrictive and protective (rather than neutral) towards Islam as the 'national religion.' It provides that the right to propagate religion is subject to state law which may "control or restrict the propagation of any religious doctrine or belief among persons professing the religion of Islam." The 1966 constitutional commission reported receiving a memorandum requesting that this restriction "be left untouched". However, the Commission felt unable to recommend this as:

> [W]e are not aware of any law in Singapore which controls or restricts the propagation of any religious doctrine or beliefs among persons professing the Muslim religion and because we think it would be inappropriate and indeed inconsistent that there should be any provision in the Constitution of a democratic secular state such as Singapore expressly singling out a particular religion for special treatment of this nature.[21]

The government evidently accepted its proposal to delete the Malaysian provision mandating anti-propagation legislation. The historical or original intent of the constitution framers was thus to guarantee to Singaporeans a more liberal enjoyment of religious freedom than the truncated Malaysian version.[22]

---

20 *Nappalli v Institute of Technical Education* [1999] 2 SLR(R) 529 at [29].

21 Constitutional Commission, Republic of Singapore, *Report of the Constitutional Commission 1966*, Singapore Government Printers, 1966, para 38.

22 In the Singapore context, the apex Court has accorded primary weight to the intention of constitutional framers: see *Yong Vui Kong v AG* [2010] SGCA 20 at [64]-[69].

Constitutionalism is a commitment against arbitrary power, whether in the form of despotic rule or imposed absolutist principle. It does not in itself require "moral or metaphysical skepticism"[23] though it is "the modern and secular legitimation of government, prior to any legitimation by performance."[24] As a foundational instrument, a constitution articulates the political identity and normative architecture of a polity, its public values, structural distribution of power and shapes the relationship between government and citizens. It is sited where "national history, custom, religion, social values and assumptions about government meet positive law."[25] Secularism is itself a principle of limited government, insofar as it posits a theory of two jurisdictions or sphere sovereignty, limiting religion's interference with civil government and insulating it from undue government interference. Modern constitutionalism rejects non-secular authority as a basis for political authority and displays an anti-theocratic secularism to that extent.

The role and position of religion in a constitution poses a fascinating field of inquiry, given that both religion and law are regulatory systems and competitors for allegiance, as well as sources of identity, authority, systems of knowledge and interpretation. There are a range of models of structuring religion-state relations, from separationist models to models where to varying degrees there is state interaction and cooperation with religion.[26] While theocracies fail to take politics seriously, militant secularist models may fail to take religion seriously. Between the former's union of religion and state and the latter's strict divorce of religion and state, are a range of models which have been described as constitutional theocracies to models of secular constitutionalism which adopt a 'neutral', benevolent or accommodative stance towards religion and religious expression.[27] *Dane* argues that to take both religion and politics, one can neither choose between either, nor reconcile both, but must "find some

23 Walker, "The Idea of Nonliberal Constitutionalism," 1997, p. 176.

24 Friedrich, *Limited Government: A Comparison*, 1974, p. 110.

25 Beer, "Introduction," 1992, p. 2.

26 See Hirschl, "Comparative Constitutional Law and Religion," 2011, pp. 422-440; Durham, "Perspectives on Religious Liberty: A Comparative Framework," 1996, pp. 1-44.

27 See Hirschl, "The Rise of Constitutional Theocracy," 2008, pp. 72-82; Rabb, "'We the Jurists': Islamic Constitutionalism in Iraq," 2008, pp. 527-579.

way, haphazard and tentative, of navigating between them", as a continuing project. [28]

Singapore's unique model of state-religion relations has been described as 'secularism with a soul'. This juxtaposition of the material and metaphysical speaks to the co-operative relationship between state and religion rooted in a conception of secularism which may be anti-theocratic, but not anti-religious, insofar as religion is "allowed to play its role in forging a harmonious and cohesive society."[29] While the Singapore Constitution does not recognise an official role for any religion, which would be oppressive to people outside that faith community who adhere to another faith (be this religious or irreligious faiths like secular humanism), it does explicitly provide for some measure of legal pluralism through affording some protection to the ethnic Malay minority community, which is discussed in further detail below.

When it comes to the constitutional regulation of religious diversity, two primary issues are implicated. First is the imperative of maintaining harmonious relations between diverse religious groups. Second, where the state's interest in maintaining the secular general law poses a threat to the religious freedom of individuals and group autonomy, engaging religion-based claims for recognition, accommodation and exemption. This itself pits 'non-state' law (authoritative norms drawn from sacred beliefs and practices) in competition against state law and political authority.[30]

The desire to be *insulated* from general law and the secular ordering of the state is distinct from demands for *inclusion* within the public sphere, alluding to the need in handling religious diversity to maintain a separate domain where group identity and autonomy is safeguarded, and a common domain in which all citizens may interact and forge a bond of national solidarity that transcends ethnic and religious affiliations.

This paper is structured as follows. Part B sets out the Singapore constitutional order regulating religion-state relations and further elaborates on the nature and content of the 'secularism with a soul' model. It considers where the state accommodates religion, and where it

---

28 Dane, "Constitutional Law and Religion," 1999, pp. 113, 124

29 Senior Minister of State, Zainul Abidin Rasheed, 74 Singapore Parliament Debates 23 May 2002 col 2220. See also Thio (Nominated Member), *Debate on President's Address*, 26 May 2009, on Singapore secularism.

30 See Hirschl and Shachar, "The New Wall of Separation: Permitting Diversity, Restricting Competition," 2009, p. 2236.

recognizes religious exemptions from the operation of the general law as a facet of minority protection. In particular, the Administration of Muslim Law Act (Cap 3) is discussed. It examines how the state views the role of religion and its demands for visibility in the public square and politics, and whether this is considered a threat to democracy, or a facet of religious pluralism which buttresses a free democratic society. It considers case law to see how religious freedom is treated in the balancing process, whether it is optimalized or rendered otiose by adjudicative method, and whether the courts or state have drawn a categorical 'red line' in identifying 'religion' and 'politics'.

Part C examines specific topics showcasing how the state handles religious diversity. It first examines the role of the Constitution in establishing a peace architecture for regulating instances where religious harmony is threatened, either when there is inter-communal conflict or where members of a religious minority group are viewed by society as a larger threat, such as religiously-inspired terrorism. It considers when the state adopts a punitive or legalistic approach, and when it deploys a more dialogical and reconciliatory approach towards handling religious tensions between groups or between religious citizens and the state. In this respect, relevant aspects of the Maintenance of Religious Harmony Act (Cap 167A), the Penal Code (Cap 224) and the Sedition Act (Cap 290) are discussed. Second, it examines claims for exceptional treatment or accommodation with specific reference to the hijab/tudung controversy which involves wearing religious dress in the public sphere. Third, it considers how the state seeks to build consensus to get a religious community to participate in a general law, such as organ donation, which is offensive to religious sensibilities and in the view of some, constitute a violation of religious law or standards. Part IV offers concluding observations on the success of the Singapore experiment in handling religious diversity to the degree it is able to optimalise religious freedom and social stability, and avoid the prospect of state regulation devolving into a form of cultural oppression through statist imperatives.

B. Religion and State – the Singapore Model

I. 'Secularism with a soul': Rejecting Anti-Religious Militant Secularism

Secularism is a protean term which can encompass a range of state-religion models, from the Turkish or French model of laïcité or strict separation, to more accommodationist or cooperationist models. The model of the secular state in Singapore is one which is anti-theocratic, not anti-religious; the source of government authority is not derived from a sacred text or divine sanction, but from the constitution and democratic processes.[31]

In 1989, Foreign Affairs Minister *George Yeo* observed the Government was "secular but it is certainly not atheistic."[32] This evinces a rejection of a thick, atheistic version of secularism. A "thick" secularism constitutes a substantive ideology which, like any other religion, speaks to first order questions of life and death and how human action ought to be guided. Thus, secularism as an anti-religious ideology is rejected in Singapore, where religion is viewed as a "constructive social force" with the caveat that "full respect" is given to other faiths and provided religionists "do not use religion to pursue political causes."[33] Secularism is apprehended not as an ideology critical of religion but as a critique of religious homogenization within a multi-religious society, and the prospect of religious domination of public institutions. The government is not to be "antagonistic to the religious beliefs of the population" and must be "neutral in its relations with the different religious groups, not favouring any of them in preference to the others." It is duty-bound to protect the right of every citizen to choose his own religion and to ensure that no citizen in exercising religious or other rights "infringes upon the rights and sensitivities of other citizens."[34]

Secularism is viewed as a framework to promote the pacific co-existence of the various religious communities in Singapore, the Buddhist, Taoists, Muslims, Christians, Catholics and Hindus, being the main groups. The government's policy is to be even-handed in treating these groups as far as possible, to "hold the ring so that all groups can practise their faiths freely without colliding with one another in Singapore."[35] In matters of welfare provision, the government readily cooperates with religious groups.[36] The state is pragmatic rather than dogmatic in relation

31 Para 5, *Maintenance of Religious Harmony White Paper* (Cmd 21 of 1989).

32 "Govt is secular, not atheistic: BG Yeo," *Straits Times*, 8 October 1989.

33 Para 45, *Shared Values White Paper*, (Cmd 1 of 1991).

34 Para 5, *Maintenance of Religious Harmony White Paper* (Cmd 21 of 1989).

35 Prime Minister Lee Hsien Loong, "Racial and Religious Harmony," National Day Rally Speech, 16 August 2009.

36 See Thio, "The Cooperation of Religion and State in Singapore: A Compassionate Partnership in Service of Welfare," 2009, pp. 33-45.

to what warrants 'separation,' and religious and political leaders have come together in times of national mourning on the same stage to commemorate national disasters.[37] Subject to regulations which relate to matters like noise control, religion is not privatized insofar as religious festivals, such as Hindu Thaipusam[38] are publicly celebrated. In 2011, Singapore had its first public menorah on Orchard Road to celebrate the Jewish festival of Chanukah.[39] *Rabbi Morechai Abergel* from the Jewish Welfare Board stated that this event testified to "the amazing spirit of harmony in Singapore"; a Jewish Frenchman noted "It just shows how different religions can live in harmony in Singapore. The whole world should be like this."[40] This is a form of 'religious diversity as inclusion', the creation of a shared public space where distinct group identity can be manifested.

Singapore is a secular state but a religious society. The government recognizes that for the 80% or more of Singapore who subscribe to a religious belief, their faith is "the source of their sense of morality, social duty and concern for their fellow man."[41] Individual citizens, speaking from religious or irreligious convictions, are free to participate in public square debates and to persuade their fellow citizens.[42] This model of religious pluralism protects viewpoint diversity and freedom of conscience, which is the lifeblood of a democratic society. There is an eternal concern that religious harmony is fragile in Singapore, and needs to be continually nurtured and safeguarded from such threats as aggressive proselytism which disrupts the equilibrium between religious groups, the use of religion for subversive purposes and the unwarranted mixing of 'religion' and 'politics'. With respect to the latter, there is concern that religious leaders not abuse their position to express their political views so

---

37 E.g., the Silkair crash (Zuraidah Ibrahim, "The nation mourns," *Straits Times* (Singapore), 31 December 1997, p. 1) and the 2004 Asian Tsunami (Tracy Sua and Sharlene Tan, "Thousands gather to pray for tsunami victims," *Straits Times* (Singapore) 31 January 2005).

38 See "Thaipusam rules apply to all religious processions," Asiaone, 18 Feb 2011.

39 See "First Public Menorah in Singapore," 25 December 2011, at http://collive .com/show_news.rtx?id=17782

40 "Singapore's first public menorah," *Straits Times*, 22 December 2011, archived at http://160.96.2.211/content/mfa/media_centre/press_room/if/2011/201112/in focus_20111222_03.printable.html?status=1.

41 Para 45, *Shared Values White Paper*, (Cmd 1 of 1991).

42 Thio, "Religion in the Public Sphere of Singapore: Wall of Division or Public Square?," 2008, pp. 73-104.

to galvanise the faithful against the government or its policies.[43] There is also concern that political parties (as they do in Malaysia)[44] may exploit religious sentiments to garner popular support.

In Singapore, this fear has been contained by the reorganization of the electoral system which is dominated by multi-member constituencies known as Group Representation Constituencies (GRC). Under article 39A of the Constitution, teams of 4-6 members compete for a GRC ward, and it is constitutionally stipulated that one of the members be from a minority community, whether Malay, Indian or any other minority. Unlike the Malaysian constitution, the Constitution does not provide a definition of who a Malay is, or that a Malay is necessarily Muslim, as this would be a violation of the voluntarist conception of religious identity constitutionally safeguarded. Instead, article 39(A)(4) provides both subjective and objective criterion in describing a "person belonging to the Malay community" as any person "whether of the Malay race or otherwise, who considers himself to be a member of the Malay community and who is generally accepted as a member of the Malay community by that community."

II. Legal Pluralism and the Constitutionally Mandated Exemption from General Law: The Special Position of Malays (and Their Religion: Islam)

The Constitution itself does not have an anti-establishment clause;[45] thus there is no bar to providing pecuniary or non-financial support for a religion, as the government does in relation to Islam. This is by dint of the constitutional requirement in article 152(2) that the government protects the "special position of the Malays" as the "indigenous people of Singapore", and so safeguard and foster their political, cultural, linguistic, educational, economic and religious interests. It is common knowledge that 99% of Malays are Muslims. Insofar as Islam receives special

43 Paras 19-23, *Maintenance of Religious Harmony White Paper* (Cmd 21 of 1989).

44 A recent call to de-register religion-based parties has provoked strong reaction: see "Ban religious political parties, former minister tells UMNO," *Malay Mail online*, 8 Nov 2013, at http://my.news.yahoo.com/ban-religious-political-parties-former-minister-tells-umno-030700254.html, visited 8 November 2013.

45 Yong Pung How CJ, *Colin Chan v Public Prosecutor* [1994] 3 SLR(R) 209.

treatment, it is by dint of the indigeneity of Malays, not the recognition of a national religion.

Article 152(1) enjoins the government to constantly care for the interests of Singapore's "racial and religious minorities." In requiring special protection for the Malay community, the Constitution leaves the choice of means and programs within the realm of legislative/executive discretion, as opposed to the affirmative action constitutionally mandated in the Malaysian Constitution, such as state-sponsored Islamic educational institutions under article 12(2). In terms of policy, Malays receive special treatment such as, for example, being able to utilize the state's Central Provident Fund System (CPF System) to collect compulsory contributions for the Mosque Building Fund; this special concession was not extended to other religious groups; for example, the Hindu Endowments Board's request that donations be processed through the CPF System was denied.[46] Other concessions include allowing Muslim victims of Severe Acute Respiratory Syndrome (SARs)[47] to be buried in two sealed body bags as opposed to being subject to the public health control measure of cremation. In addition the government, to ensure that Muslims have sufficient places of worship in the process of urban resettlement, adopted a 'one mosque per town' program whereby land is set aside for mosques, whose funding is raised within the Muslim community.[48]

Under article 153 of the Constitution, the legislature is mandated to adopt a law "for regulating Muslim religious affairs and for constituting a Council to advise the President in matters relating to the Muslim religion." This is the authorization for the Administration of Muslim Law Act

46 "It would be no less convenient for Hindus to make their regular contributions ... through the POSB." Dr Ahmad Matter, 42 Singapore Parliament Report, 3 Dec 1982 (Contributions from Hindus for Temples etc and Monies from Muslims for Mosques etc) col. 309-311.

47 See "No wakes for suspected SARs deaths," *Straits Times* (Singapore), 24 Apr 2003, H4.

48 See Statement, Minister for Social Affairs Othman bin Wok, *37 Singapore Parliament Reports 29 June 1977*, (Mosque Building Fund Scheme), col. 62-63: "The Majlis Ugama Islam Singapura supports the policy of the Government in building one new mosque in each new town where the Muslim population is sufficiently large and agrees that this is the most practical way to meet the religious needs of the Muslims as they are resettled in the new towns." This is funded through the Mosque Building Fund Scheme whereby employers are required to pay a small contribution per Muslim employee per month to the fund and recover this from their Muslim employee wages.

(AMLA) (Cap 3) which established the Majlis Ugama Islam (MUIS) or the Islamic Religious Council of Singapore in 1968 as a statutory body. The state is further involved in that while Muslim societies select Majlis members, the Singapore President, advised by the Cabinet, issues these appointments and can terminate these in the public interest. The Singapore President must consult the Majlis before appointing the Singapore Mufti (highest religious leader).

In terms of subject-matter, AMLA demonstrates some degree of legal pluralism in deferring to Muslim sensitivities with respect to personal and customary law, family law, dietary matters, prayer obligations and religious instruction. AMLA lists Muslim-specific offences such as cohabitation outside marriage (section 134); it regulates religious affairs and safeguards cultural particularities pertaining to personal laws, such as permitting polygamy for Muslim. This is banned under the Women's Charter (Cap 353) which was adopted in 1961 and institutionalizes monogamous marriages as a facet of modernity. Notably a religious exemption was carved out for Muslims but not for that part of the Chinese community which practised polygamous unions under Chinese customary law.[49]

State recognition of this brand of local autonomy effectively buttresses patriarchial religious laws, such as those reserving certain public posts for male Muslims alone,[50] or gender discriminatory inheritance laws which stipulates that a male's share is double that of a female's.[51] These are contrary to international human rights obligations such as those adopted under the Convention for the Elimination of All Forms of Discrimination

---

49 See Chan Choy Siong, *14 Singapore Legislative Assembly Debates, Official Report*, November-July (1960-1961): col. 1201. The Chinese were to abide by modern norms which outlawed polygamous marriages under Chinese customary law, while, in deference to religious but not customary beliefs, the Muslim community could retain its Islamic traditions.

50 E.g., the Mufti, Registrar of Muslim Marriages and Kadi: Sections 90(1), 91(1) and 146 of the AMLA.

51 See Part VII, AMLA, For example, Section 117(1) AMLA provides that when a wife dies intestate with her own property, preference is given first to her male children over 21, followed by her husband and then other relatives in this order: daughters, father, mother, brothers, sisters, uncles, aunts, nephews and nieces of the intestate. This shows a preference for male over female relationship in inheritance matters.

against Women (CEDAW), which Singapore acceded to in 1995.[52] Thus, to preserve Muslim communal autonomy, Singapore had to attach reservations to CEDAW provisions such as articles 2 and 6 (modification or abolition of laws and customs that discriminate against women) "where compliance with these provisions would be contrary to their religious or personal laws."

MUIS is charged with such functions as collecting *zakat* (tithes), arranging *haj* (pilgrimages) and *halal* certification. Singapore's brand of secularism is less dogmatic then the Philippines strict separationist model, insofar as a government agency engaged in *halal* certification was considered to violate the Philippines doctrine of 'the separation of church and state' as this was a matter for religious organizations only.[53] Secular civil courts are enlisted to enforce violations such as section 88A of AMLA, in relation to the illegal use of *halal* certification mark, that is, to sell uncertified food as *halal.* Parliamentary debates revealed that the purpose of section 88A AMLA was to serve the public interest in conferring upon MUIS the sole authority to advise and regulate *halal* matters. As *Wong Keen Oon DJ* noted:

> Singapore is a multi-racial and multi-cultural society. Sensitivity towards the practice of the various religions in our society is vital for the growth, peace and stability of Singapore as a nation. Proper respect must be accorded for each other's religious practices to preserve racial and religious harmony. As counsel for MUIS had rightly pointed out, halal food and its certification is very dear to the Muslim community. Muslims in and out of Singapore, including Muslim tourists, will rely on the MUIS halal certification mark when they patronize eating establishments or buy food products. Infringements of the MUIS certification mark, if not checked early, will erode public confidence in and adversely affect the reputation of the MUIS halal certification mark in and out of Singapore. Such

52 See Thio, "The Impact of Internationalisation on Domestic Governance: The Transformative Potential of CEDAW," 1997, pp. 248-350.

53 *Islamic Da'Wah Council of the Philippines Inc v. Office of Muslim Affairs* G.R. No. 153888 (July 9, 2003), judgment available online: http://sc.judiciary.gov.ph/jurisprudence/2003/jul2003/153888.htm. Given the principle of separation of Church and State extant in the Philippines, the state must ensure the Office of Muslim Affairs does not intrude into purely religious matters lest it violate the non-establishment clause and the "free exercise of religion" provision found in Article III, Section 5 of the 1987 Constitution. For further analysis, see Thio, "Courting Religion: The Judge between Caesar and God in Asian Courts," 2009, pp. 52-79.

> infringements are a matter of serious concern and the primary consideration in sentencing would be deterrence, to strongly discourage the offender and the other persons from committing similar criminal acts, which can be lucrative, given the growing Muslim market, and are not easily detected. Where there are large scale infringements or where significant direct harm is caused, it may well lead to custodial sentences.[54]

Part III, AMLA establishes the Syariah Court with jurisdiction over matrimonial and divorce related matters. Evidence may be taken through Muslim oaths and syariah courts are generally immune from judicial review, although civil courts have a supervisory role in ensuring that the terms of AMLA, rather than Islamic law *simpliciter* (derived from divine text and teachings, as opposed to a secular law), is applied. Effectively, this entails the regulation of Islamic law under AMLA which is "an essential statutory adjunct of Muslim law in Singapore,"[55] by a secular court as where the MUIS *fatwa* committee (which gives religious rulings) was informed they had misconstrued Islamic law under AMLA. Civil courts have also held that the rules of natural justice apply to Muslim religious bodies as "It is an important principle of Western as well as Muslim jurisprudence that a person cannot be a judge in his own cause."[56]

Thus, religious courts as creatures of statute have limited jurisdiction as determined by a secular law and cannot apply divine law in an unbounded fashion; they are also subject to some degree of supervision by civil courts.[57] It is no wonder that the advent of British colonialism into Peninsula Malaysia with the introduction of the common law marked the death knell of theocratic rule, in the days where sultans were both religious and political leaders. All laws "including the administration of

---

54 *Public Prosecutor v Angliss Singapore Pte Ltd* [2006] SGDC 70 at [11]. This decision was upheld in *Angliss Singapore Pte. Ltd. v. PP* [2006] 4 SLR 653 (Singapore High Court).

55 *Mohd Ismail bin Ibrahim v. Mohd Taha bin Ibrahim* [2004] 4 S.L.R. 756 (H.C.), at [63]. This related to a question of testamentary disposition under section 14, AMLA. See Hardjoe, "Hukum Faraid and the Application of AMLA as 'The Statutory Adjunct of Muslim Law in Singapore',", *Law Gazette* October 2006, available at http://www.lawgazette.com.sg/2006-10/, last visited 13 November 2013.

56 Rubin J., *Mohd Ismail bin Ibrahim v. Mohd Taha bin Ibrahim* [2004] 4 S.L.R. 756 (H.C.), at [55].

57 "The fine balance of civil and syariah law in Singapore," *Straits Times* (Singapore) (17 February 2008).

Islamic laws had to receive ... validity through a secular fiat." Today, the Islamic law that applies is mediated through general secular legislation and confined to a narrow sphere pertaining to marriage, divorce and inheritance laws only.[58]

However, rather than creating an entirely autonomous space for the Muslim community to operate exempt from general law, Islamic institutions are subject to some degree of national supervision. For example, while the Compulsory Education Act (Cap 51) does not apply to *madrasahs* or Islamic religious educational schools,[59] the state maintains an interest in ensuring minimal standards and by requiring certain academic subjects to be taught alongside religious instruction, to ensure the employability of *madrasah* graduates who do not become religious scholars.[60]

III. State Delineation of 'Religion' and 'Politics'

The government acknowledges that there is no 'bright line' between the overlapping categories of 'religion' and 'politics'; the latter has been judicially defined as "the multitude of issues concerning how Singapore should be governed in the interest and for the welfare of its people."[61] This is an all-encompassing definition and problematical, given the fact, as acknowledged by the government, that faiths like Islam and Christianity deny the possibility of separating faith from all aspects of life.[62]

It appears that what the state defines as a matter of 'politics' into which religion may not intrude is determinative. It is important to note too, the power of the government in a dominant one party parliamentary system. The government in a white paper on religious harmony has identified certain issues which pose legitimate concerns for public policy and also

58 *Che Omar bin Che Soh v PP* [1988] 2 MLJ 55.

59 Para. 6.10, Second Report Periodic Report to the UN Committee on CEDAW (Ministry of Community Development: Singapore, 2001); Kadir, "The Role of Education in Ethnic/Religious Conflict Management: The Singapore Case," 2005, p. 17.

60 "Contrasting views of madrassas in multi-ethnic Singapore," 17 Feb 2009 at http://www.irsyad.sg/?p=728.

61 *Dow Jones Publishing v AG* [1989] 1 SLR(R) 637 at -42].

62 Para 25, *Maintenance of Religious Harmony White Paper* (Cmd No 21 of 1989).

raise moral or religious questions.[63] When it is not a matter of state security, the government recognizes certain issues of conscience, such as abortion and whether a doctor or nurse wants to commit one – on such matters, "religious groups may and do properly take positions and preach to their followers." [64] However, the government rejects pleas for conscientious objection, such as that made by the Jehovah's Witnesses, where this threatens its policy of compulsory military service for all male Singaporean citizens. The government has stated that a refusal to do any form of military service, as required under the Enlistment Act (Cap 93), is not conscientious objection but criminal conduct which is punished with imprisonment. In this case, religious freedom is trumped by considerations of national security as a facet of public order.

IV. Courts and Religious Freedom Cases

Article 15(1) of the Constitution guarantees the right of religious individuals to profess, practise and propagate their faith. This is subject to general law relating to public order, health and morality under article 15(4).

In adjudicating alleged violations of religious freedom by the state against an individual or group, the courts typically declare they are adopting a 'balancing' approach which implies that it identifies and then weighs relevant interests, to determine an optimal balance. While the right to profess a religious faith belongs to the *forum internum* and is immune from state regulation, being a matter of personal self-determination, the state may regulate external expressions of faith through practice and propagation. For example, although the pacifist Jehovah's Witnesses (JWs) have been deregistered under the Societies Act (Cap 311) and materials published by its publishing arm banned under the Undesirable Publications Act (UPA) (Cap 338), it is not an offense to be a JW or to profess the beliefs of what has become an unlawful society;[65] nevertheless,

63 Para 26, *Maintenance of Religious Harmony White Paper* (Cmd nm No 21 of 1989).

64 Para 26(a), *Maintenance of Religious Harmony White Paper* (Cmd nm No 21 of 1989).

65 Yong Pung How CJ in *Kok Hoong Tan Dennis v Public Prosecutor* [1996] 3 SLR(R) 570 at [26].

their religious freedom has been severely truncated. For example, as the JWs are an unlawful society, it would contravene the law for them to meet in a private home to study their sacred book.

In the leading case of *Chan Hiang Leng Colin v Public Prosecutor*, where the deregistration order under the Societies Act and the prohibition order under the UPA was challenged as a violation of article 15, the High Court expressed the issue as one of balancing but basically applied a public order consideration as a 'trump' in displaying a statist orientation which affirms rather than constrains power. While formalistically declaring that he was of "the view that such religious belief ought to have proper protection," action taken consequent to that belief had to "conform with the general law relating to public order and social protection."[66] *Yong* CJ created a statist trump in stating that the "sovereignty, integrity and unity of Singapore are undoubtedly the paramount mandate of the Constitution and anything, including religious beliefs and practices, which tend to run counter to these objectives must be restrained." This approach precludes balancing as it is a categorical approach which denudes article 15 of any real content. This trump was subsequently applied to reject the claim that requiring a JW teacher at an educational institution to participate in a flag-statute ceremony violated his religious freedom, despite the fact that JWs consider such action an act of idolatry. Its bare invocation by the High Court was enough to settle the matter, without any real attempt to balance the competing interests:

> What is in issue is whether in the special circumstances of Singapore, an educational institution is entitled to insist that its teachers encourage students to be good and useful citizens by complying with an implied term in their contracts of employment requiring them to lead their students in the taking of the National Pledge and the singing of the National Anthem during school assembly. With no natural resources of its own, Singapore's success depends on, among other things, the unity of its multi-racial and multi-cultural population [cites Colin Chan].... Surely the Ministry of Education is entitled to take reasonable steps to ensure that future generations of Singaporeans understand the importance of preserving the sovereignty, integrity and unity of Singapore.[67]

---

66 [1994] 3 SLR(R) 209 at [64].

67 *Nappalli v Institute of Technical Education* [1998] SGHC 351 at [46]; this was upheld by the Court of Appeal in [1999] 2 SLR(R) 569.

This is distinct from other jurisdictions where in dealing with similar cases, what is required before a constitutional liberty may be curtailed is that it poses a 'clear and present danger' to a constitutional good such as public order.[68] The Singapore High Court did not adopt the role of guarding fundamental liberties of the vulnerable individual against the state, but invoked the "the danger of allowing absolute freedom of religion which might create a complete denial of a government's authority and ability to govern individuals or groups asserting a religious affiliation."[69] It raised the spectre of the anarchic society rather than the totalitarian state. In deferring to statist considerations, it is not surprising that the courts refused to find a conscientious objector exemption based on the religious freedom guarantee. This approach towards judicial review does little to ameliorate the asymmetries of power between state and individual, in displaying a presumptive bias in favour of state articulated concerns.

Singapore jurisprudence has come a long way since the string of article 15 cases unsuccessfully litigated by the JWs in the 1990s; in an era where a more holistic communitarian approach towards constitutional adjudication is emerging,[70] it is hoped that courts will not invoke statist trumps to peremptorily dismiss a fundamental liberties claim, but will in balancing competing interests do this in a manner which does not render a competing interest "otiose."[71]

C. State Management of Religious Diversity: Specific Topics

I. *The Regulation of Religious Harmony: Legalistic and Relational Approaches*

Public order is a constitutionally identified ground for derogating from religious freedom and certainly all public order threats may, if they escalate to the level of national security threats, be subject to preventive detention orders under the Internal Security Act (Cap 143), which is a

---

68 *Ebralinag v Division Superintendent of Schools of Cebu* GR No 95770, 1 March 1993, 219 SCRA 256 (1993) (Supreme Court, Philippines).

69 [1994] 3 SLR(R) 209 at [78].

70 Thio and Chong, "The *Chan* Court and Constitutional Adjudication: 'A sea change into something rich and strange'," 2012.

71 *AG v Shadrake No. 1* [2011] 2 SLR 445 at [57].

form of anti-subversion legislation mandated under article 149 of the Constitution.

'Religious harmony' where cited as a justification for restraining religious freedom must be a facet of public order, but must go beyond maintaining civil peace or law and order; the term 'harmony' speaks to a quality of relationship or sense of solidarity which punitive state measures or adversarial litigation may harm rather than promote or restore, as an adversarial ethos is more likely to engender alienation rather than reconciliation.

Former Law Minister *S. Jayakumar* noted that social harmony in a non-homogenous or diverse society "cannot be achieved with a laissez-faire system." The general rule of law was important as it made expectations transparent, providing a harmonising standard of law in the face of disparate moral values, set for the "common ground rules of engagement and conflict resolution" and sought to "secure as large common secular space which belongs to all citizens regardless of race, language or religion." [72] As such, "maintaining racial and religious harmony has become an important tenet for us when approaching the rule of law."[73]

1. Legalistic Approach: Punitive Sanctions

A legalistic approach seeks to deal with threats to religious harmony through invoking legal sanctions as a punitive or deterrent measure. The fear that wounded religious sensitivities may erupt into public disturbances is reflected in the list of "Offences relating to religion" in section 295-298 of the Penal Code (Cap 224). These include crimes causes by defiling a place of worship with intent to insult the religion of any class, disturbing a religious assembly or uttering words with deliberate intent to wound the religious or racial feelings of any person. These may be punished by fines or terms of imprisonment ranging from three to five years.

The government has also prosecuted cases under the Sedition Act (Cap 290) in the interests of preserving religious harmony. As a crime against

72 S. Jayakumar, "The Meaning and Importance of the Rule of Law," keynote address, IBA Rule of Law Symposium, 19 October 2007, pp. 18-19.

73 S. Jayakumar, "The Meaning and Importance of the Rule of Law," keynote address, IBA Rule of Law Symposium, 19 October 2007, p. 20.

state security, sedition is a recognised constitutional exception to the article 14 free speech guarantee. The capacious statutory definition of 'sedition' departs from the common law understanding of sedition which entails some form of political violence with a view to "to induce discontent and insurrection, and stir up opposition to the Government, and bring the administration of justice into contempt."[74] Under section 3(1) words with a "seditious tendency" include those which direct "hatred or contempt" against the Government or administration of justice; under section 3(1)(e), seditious speech may operate 'horizontally' between private actors, by promoting "feelings of ill-will and hostility between different races or classes of the population of Singapore." It appears 'races or classes' has been broadly interpreted to include religious affiliation, primarily stemming from the conflation of ethnicity and religion, where Malays and Islam are concerned at least.[75]

The test is objective, based on the effects of the word, independent of intention or an actual likelihood of violence. The term "feelings" is inherently subjective and difficult to evaluate absent context, as a group of learned professors may react very differently from "an excited audience of young and uneducated men."[76]

Section 3(1)(e) of the Sedition Act was applied to cyber-speech in the case of *Benjamin Koh v PP*[77] where a blogger posted a *halal* logo next to a pig's head and insulted Islam, precipitating the exchange of some 200 comments and racial slurs between Chinese and Malays. This elicited a custodial sentence as general deterrence, given the "especial sensitivity" of race and religion issues, and how it affected not only the speaker, but the minority community and society at large. Senior District Court Judge *Richard Magnus* noted it was "only appropriate social behaviour, independent of any legal duty" for all citizens "to respect the other races in view of our multi-racial society" to avoid racial strife. In instructive tone, the learned judge stated:

> Young Singaporeans, like the accused persons before this Court, may have short memories that race and religion are sensitive issues. They must realize that

74 Fitzgerald J, *R v Sullivan* (1868) 11 Cox CC 44, 45.

75 Other ethnic groups, like the Chinese and Indians, are not automatically identifiable with a particular faith.

76 Coleridge J, *R v Aldred* (1909) 22 Cox CC 1 at 3.

77 [2005] SGDC 272 (District Court, Singapore).

> callous and reckless remarks on racial or religious subjects have the potential to cause social disorder, in whatever medium or forum they are expressed. In this case, it is the medium of the Internet and with it, its ubiquitous reach.[78]

A troubling case from the perspective of religious freedom is the successful prosecution under the Sedition Act of a Protestant Christian couple who randomly distributed evangelistic tracts to addressees with Muslim-sounding names in *Ong Kian Cheong v PP.*[79] District Judge *Neighbour* found that the judicial observations concerning race in *Benjamin Koh* equally applied to denigrating remarks about religion. Recipients of tracts such as that entitled 'Who is Allah?' felt variously upset as the publication "in promoting Christianity, denigrated his religion, Islam;"[80] one lodged a police report as he "felt that publication could incite religious tension between Muslims and Christians."[81] In deferring to the emotional man rather than the rational man (a rational response to receiving a publication one does not like is to throw it away rather than lodging a police report, in deference to the broader principle of free speech and robust intellectual inquiry), the district court demonstrated great solicitude for the feelings of the religiously offended to which free speech interests were subordinated. The public order 'trump' in the form of racial or religious harmony was raised without any serious negotiation that at least two constitutional rights were at stake: the article 14 right to free speech (not involving hate or any incitement to violence but merely propagating a view of religious truth) and the article 15 right of religious propagation. Oddly, Judge *Neighbour* had mentioned that a person was free to choose his faith and to practice it, but failed to note the third component of the article, that of religious propagation, which may have gone some way to adjust the balance of competing interests, or at least, as a mitigating factor in sentencing.[82]

It is certainly a matter of prudence that rights to religious propagation be exercised with sensitivity. Indeed, Prime Minister *Lee* in 1965 had

---

78 [2005] SGDC 272 (District Court, Singapore) at [7].

79 [2009] SGDC 163 at [81]. For an analysis of this case, see Lin, "Sedition and its New Clothes in Singapore," 2011, pp. 212-236; Thio, "Contentious Liberty: Regulating Religious Propagation in a Religiously Diverse Secular Democracy," 2010, pp. 499-500.

80 [2009] SGDC 163, [10].

81 [2009] SGDC 163, [11]

82 [2009] SGDC 163 at [79].

advised Christians that there were many people who might be in need of "some form of religious and moral guidance" such that there was "no need for going around looking for the 12 per cent Muslims to try and convert them."[83] Nonetheless, it is a matter of principle that religious propagation is a constitutional right which must be given full weight, lest it, as a form of religious free speech, be unduly chilled. The invocation of a constitutional right is not in itself determinative, as there are legitimate grounds for state regulation, but regulation must not render a right void of content and effect. What is also troubling is Neighbour's statement:

> As citizens of Singapore, both the accused cannot claim to be ignorant of the sensitivity of race and religion in our multi-racial and multi-religious society. Common sense dictates that religious fervor to spread the faith, in our society, must be constrained by sensitivity, tolerance and mutual respect for another's faith and religious beliefs. Both the accused by distributing the seditious and objectionable tracts to Muslims and to the general public clearly reflected their intolerance, insensitivity and ignorance of delicate issues concerning race and religion in our multi-racial and multi religious society. They both acted on their own accord without ensuring that the tracts were suitable for distribution to the general public.[84]

While it could be argued that the Protestant couple may have acted insensitively, even with ignorance or more fairly, naïveté to contextual sensitivities, they in no way acted in an 'intolerant' fashion, unless the very act of disseminating a religious viewpoint out of belief in its veracity is considered intolerant. This would be to privilege the viewpoint of moral relativism and to assert it, rather intolerantly against dissenters, as a dogmatic absolute. Such a reading of religious propagation would denude the right of any substance and has little to commend itself, being a form of anti-religious intolerance.

Though there is some degree of discretion in deciding on which case to prosecute under the Sedition Act, it is noteworthy that a person who published cartoons insulting to Christians on his blogs was let off with a police warning.[85] This may reflect a greater concern for the sensitivities of

---

83 Transcript of the Prime Minister's Statement to Religious Representatives and Members of the Inter-Religious Council, 30th September 1965.

84 [2009] SGDC 163 at [82].

85 "Government Drops Charges against Blogger who posted Jesus cartoons," *Reporters without Borders*, 20 July 2006 at http://en.rsf.org/singapore-

Malay-Muslims, whose interests the government is constitutionally obliged to safeguard and promote under article 152(2).

2. Legalistic Approach: Preventive Measures

There has been a fear that if religious disputes were litigated in a court of law, it may spark off racial and religious riots, as it did in the *Maria Hertogh* case[86] concerning a Dutch girl brought up by a Muslim woman as a Muslim during World War Two, whose Catholic parents sought custody of, after the end of the War. This sparked off race riots, given the close conflation of Malay identity and the Muslim faith. Indeed, this case was referenced as exemplifying inter-religious conflict between different religious groups, as, "where religious sensitivities are offended, emotions are quickly aroused", which could "destroy the good record of religious harmony built up in recent decades."[87]

The government also urges that problems a religious group might have with its policies be resolved not through litigation but through dialogue. For example, in relation to the '*tudung* controversy' which broke out in February 2002, when four Muslim primary schoolgirls were suspended for not conforming to the school uniforms policy by wearing *tudung* (Islamic female headscarf), the parents of the schoolgirls at one stage seemed intent on litigating this policy as a violation of religious freedom. While indicating that the government would abide by any judicial decision rendered, the government voiced its preference that the matter be

government-drops-charges-against-20-07-2006,18106.html. It is worth noting that a Christian pastor whose online sermons offended some Buddhists and Taoists was left off with a warning by the Internal Security Department and chastened by much print and online media reports. The pastor to his credit apologized sincerely, which Buddhist and Taoist leaders graciously accepted, being mature enough to appreciate the larger objective of maintaining good relations between religious communities. This was distinct from the childishly vindictive sentiments expressed by some netizens who wanted the pastor legally prosecuted for harming religious harmony; however, by inciting opprobrium and possibly ill-will towards Christians, these netizens may have be guilty of perpetuating disharmony between the relevant groups themselves by fostering ill-feeling rather than forgiveness. For an in-depth analysis, see Thio, "Contentious Liberty," pp. 501-505, 511-512.

86 *Re Maria Huberdina Hertorgh* [1951] 1 Malayan Law Journal 164.

87 Para 11, *Maintenance of Religious Harmony White Paper* (Cmd 21 of 1989).

addressed through the route of 'soft diplomacy' through quiet dialogue and negotiation rather than within the adversarial public forum of a court.[88]

Thus, the *raison d'être* for the introduction of the Maintenance of Religious Harmony Act (MRHA) (Cap 167A) in 1990 was to avoid judicial proceedings which "may themselves stoke passions further if the defendant turns them into political propaganda."[89] This empowers the relevant Minister to issue non-justiciable 'restraining orders' to religious leaders or those who incite religious personages to commit certain acts on four grounds listed under sections 8 and 9:

(a) causing feelings of enmity, hatred, ill-will or hostility between different religious groups;
(b) carrying out activities to promote a political cause, or a cause of any political party while, or under the guise of, propagating or practising any religious belief;
(c) carrying out subversive activities under the guise of propagating or practising any religious belief; or
(d) exciting disaffection against the President or the Government while, or under the guise of, propagating or practising any religious belief.

Only (a) relates to religious harmony while the other three relate to religious challenges to secular authority and public order. Under these orders, a religious personage may be restrained from addressing a religious group on any topic orally or in writing without prior ministerial position, being involved in religious publications or holding office in a religious group's publications committee without prior permission. These restraining orders last for two years and are renewable. This is designed to operate pre-emptively and promptly as a deterrent rather than in a punitive fashion. Non-compliance with restraining orders may attract a fine (up to

88 "Muslims urged to discuss tudung issue: Legal action is not the way to resolve matter," says MP Zainul Abidin Rasheed, adding "it's better to have more dialogue." *Straits Times* (28 January 2002). For a discussion of the tudung controversy, see Thio, "Recent Constitutional Developments: of Shadows and Whips, Race, Rifts and Rights, Terror and Tudungs, Women and Wrongs," 2002, pp. 352-355.

89 *Maintenance of Religious Harmony White Paper* (Cmd 21 of 1989) at [31].

$20,000) or a maximum three years imprisonment term. To date, no restraining order has been issued, though a Cabinet minister has indicated in a news report three instances when it was almost invoked, two of which involved one religious leader criticising another faith.[90]

3. Relational or Non-Legalistic Approach

What may be described as a relational approach towards handling religion-related disputes which threaten community harmony? A 'relational perspective' "seeks not only to affirm community identity, but also to affirm the identity of the transgressor and transgressed as valued members of that community, as an on-going relational enterprise."[91] It focuses on the quality of relationships between disparate groups in society, which is key to sustainable democracy. Adversarialism leads to alienation rather than rapprochement, which can heighten social tensions.

To promote a reconciliatory ethos, the Constitution has created certain processes which may promote dialogue between religious leaders, such as the Presidential Council for Religious Harmony (PCRH) established under section 3 of the MRHA. This provides that at least two-thirds of the PCRH (which may have between 6-15 members) must be "representatives of the major religions in Singapore" with the other members drawn from persons the Presidential Council for Minority Rights considers "have distinguished themselves in public service or community relations in Singapore." If the PCRH disagree with the minister's decision in issuing a restraining order, the President may override the ministerial order. Importantly, this forum allows religious leaders to develop relationships which can promote trust and confidence that facilitates dialogue, understanding and a reconciliatory approach which helps to defuse tensions. The Prime Minister in his 2009 National Day Rally speech indicated that he meets religious leaders regularly to "exchange views, discuss how to maintain

---

90 In 1992, a Christian pastor was warned to refrain from criticizing other faiths like Buddhism, Taoism and Catholicism through the pulpit and through publications, and in 1995, an Islamic religious leader was admonished for criticising a widespread Hindu belief that statutes of their deity, Ganesha, could drink milk offerings, which the leader had labelled not a miracle but the work of the devil. "Govt reins in religious leaders," *Straits Times* (Singapore), 12 May 2001, p. 1.

91 Thio, "Relational Constitutionalism and the Management of Inter-Religious Disputes: The Singapore 'Secularism with a Soul' Model," 2012, p. 15.

harmony, keep the line warm and the confidence on both sides so I know, you know me. If there is a problem, we are not dealing with strangers but with somebody we know and trust." Prime Minister Lee observed that he had also had to meet religious leaders out of publicity's eye, over "specific difficult cases." Thus, owing to "this active work behind the scenes, we have not needed to invoke the Maintenance of Religious Harmony Act for 20 years..."[92]

The recent nadir of ethnic relations was in the early 2000s, after a foiled bomb plot by the terrorist group, the *Jemaah Islamiyah*, general distrust against the Muslim community in Singapore was on the rise. The perpetrators of the plot were preventively detained under the Internal Security Act, their deprivation of liberty justified by reference to the threat they posed to national security.

The relational manner in which the government sought to deal with the fall-out is instructive, as it departs from the harsher, curt treatment of concerns raised in relation to other high profile detentions, most notably the 1987 'Marxist conspiracy' where linkages were drawn between the alleged conspirators and their apparent attempt to subvert the Roman Catholic church in order to establish a Marxist state. Certain Catholic priests preached against these detentions and declared that relevant government officials would face the punishment of God.[93] In response, the Law Minister *S. Jayakumar* declared that as a Hindu, he was "not frightened by Christian priests pronouncing an anathema or curse upon me", stating it was "a matter of grave concern that in Singapore any priest or religious leader, whatever his religious faith, should use his religious authority to work up feelings against Judges, Ministers and officials and to invoke the divine power of damnation upon secular authorities."[94]

At any rate, the Prime Minister in 1987 got the Catholic Archbishop to issue a public statement to the effect that the detentions of the alleged Marxists were unrelated to the Catholic Church.[95] Then, only a lone opposition politician, *Chiam See Tong* asked before a stony Parliament

92 PM Lee Hsien Loong, *National Day Rally Speech* (16 August 2009), text available online: http://www.pmo.gov.sg/News/Messages/%20National+Day+Rally+Speech+2009+Part+3+Racial+and+Religious+Harmony.htm.

93 Annex, *Maintenance of Religious Harmony White Paper*, id, at paras. 16-18

94 S. Jayakumar, *54 Singapore Parliament Reports, 6 October 1989* (Teaching of Religious Knowledge in Schools) cols. 584, pp. 635 ff.

95 Annex, *Maintenance of Religious Harmony White Paper*, id, at para. 15.

overwhelmingly dominated by the PAP what crimes the detained had committed, calling for officials to meet the concerned families and for a public inquiry. These were all rejected.

In stark contrast, in the post 9-11 era, the government put out a white paper on *The Jemaah Islamiyah Arrests and the Threat of Terrorism*[96] and provided extensive evidence and reasons for the detention of some 31 members of a fundamentalist Islamic terrorist group, who were Malay-Muslims, engaged in a bomb plot. To take some of the heat off the Muslim community at large, the white paper characterised the terrorists as "a small and isolated group of misguided Muslims" which mainstream, tolerant and law-abiding Muslims did not support.[97] The white paper detailed evidence of the bomb plot to make its case before the court of public opinion, despite there being no legal obligation to do so. It adopted a gentler, relational approach in meeting (and publicizing this) the families of the detained, holding consultations with Malay community leaders and even briefing schools on the detentions, in attempting to restore some trust through dialogue. The white paper underscored that the government's counter-terrorism efforts did not intend to "disrupt the legitimate practices and peaceful activities of the local Muslim community."[98] Rather than adopting a top-down coercive regulatory approach, the government sought to enlist the cooperation of the Muslim community in monitoring religious education to guard against extremist religious teachings. It stated that "all Singaporeans" should exercise vigilance in this regard. It urged that it would be "tragic" if this incident succeeded in sowing distrust and suspicious amongst Singaporeans. Consequently, the Muslim community set up a Religious Rehabilitation Group and Religious Teacher directory as a safeguard against radical religious teachers.[99]

Further, then Prime Minister *Goh Chok Tong* suggested the drafting of a Code on Religious Harmony as a hortatory statement of the rules guiding the relationship of religious groups within a multi-racial Singapore. Eventually, this was committed to the steerage of a junior

---

96 *The Jemaah Islamiyah Arrests and the Threat of Terrorism White paper* (Cmd 2 of 2003).

97 *The Jemaah Islamiyah Arrests and the Threat of Terrorism White paper* (Cmd 2 of 2003) at 23.

98 *The Jemaah Islamiyah Arrests and the Threat of Terrorism White paper* (Cmd 2 of 2003) at 23.

99 *The Jemaah Islamiyah Arrests and the Threat of Terrorism White paper* (Cmd 2 of 2003) at 22.

agnostic Minister who worked with parliamentarians and various religious leaders, conducting extensive consultations with national religious bodies and the public at large, to eventually produce the *Declaration on Religious Harmony* in 2003. Though without formal legal effect, the declaration reiterates 'soft' constitutional law standards which shape expectations and influence behaviour. Those involved in the collaborative process reported its utility in building consensus and developing social trust between the various actors, as well as its educative value in sensitivizing them to the concerns of other religious groups. At a time of heightened ethnic and religious tensions, "the drafting process facilitated nation-wide dialogue on religious faith, creating space for engagement among citizens, foreclosing insularity and helping to diffuse inter-communal suspicions."[100] While this promoted a model of consultative governance to some degree, notably, marginalized religious groups like the Jehovah's Witnesses were excluded from the process.

II. Claims for Religious Exemptions and Accommodations

Where a legal system contains religious exemptions to the general rule of law, it to some extent recognizes an alternative source of authority, which for reasons such as that of legal pluralism, warrant accommodation. A claim for exemption represents a claim to be insulated from general law, as a facet of recognizing and protecting religious diversity.

As discussed above, articles 152-153 of the Constitution provide for some degree of legal pluralism, mainly through AMLA, under the Muslim community in limited areas like family and inheritance law 'contract out' of the regulatory purview of the state. Where state security is concerned, the state and courts have refused to recognize an exemption from the compulsory military service regime in the form of conscientious objection. In a case before a military tribunal, the defence that in refusing to wear military attire the accused was only obeying his Bible which was "a higher law than any man-made law," was rejected, as secular tribunals do not consider divine law in their adjudicative processes.[101]

100 Thio, "Constitutional 'Soft' Law," p. 424.

101 *Pte Chai Tshun Chieh v Chief Military Prosecutor* [1998] SGMCA 3 (Military Court of Appeal) at [13].

1. Labour Law and the Religious Autonomy of Groups: Article 15(3)

Other jurisdictions have recognized religious exemptions from general labour law in relation to the employment matters.[102] This issue arose in Singapore when a Christian church decided to challenge the decision of the Minister for Manpower, made in August 2013, to the effect that its dismissal of a unrepentant church employee involved in administering the marriage preparation course, who had become pregnant as a result of an adulterous affair with another church worker, was without 'sufficient cause' under the terms of the Employment Act (Cap 91). The Manpower Ministry (MOM) asserted that labour laws had to be "kept secular to preserve harmony"[103] as employment legislation fell with the policy of preserving "a common secular space for people with other beliefs." The *Straits Times* produced an Op-Ed which sang the same chorus and effectively mocked the church's argument that there was an implied contractual term that church employees must live up to the moral teachings of the Church. It rather pompously opined: "Religionists should reflect on how a secular construct such as Singapore would unravel if any of its constituent parts claimed exceptionalism as a conferred right."[104]

What was astonishing was the complete absence of reference to article 15(3)(a) of the Constitution which provides that "Every religious group has the right ... to manage its own religious affairs." This is not an absolute right but subject to the article 15(4) which allows general law to restrict religious freedom rights to serve the interests of public order, health and morality. It is not surprising that in failing to consider the constitutional regime, the MOM treated the case as a simple employer-employee relationship, and failed to consider that the constitution might warrant taking into account the character and mission of the employer,

---

102 See, e.g., Evans and Hood, "Religious Autonomy and Labour Law: A Comparison of the Jurisprudence of the United States and the European Court of Human Rights," 2012, pp. 3-20; Durham and Scharffs, *Law and Religion: National, International and Comparative Perspectives*, 2010, pp. 407-413; Vyver, "Equality and Sovereignty of Religious Institutions: A South African Perspective," 2012, pp. 155-156, available at http://digitalcommons.law.scu.edu/cgi/viewcontent.cgi?article=1124&context=scujil.

103 Chuan, "Workplaces, labour laws, must be kept secular: MOM," *Straits Times* (Singapore), 28 August 2013.

104 "Safeguard secular nature of labour laws," *Straits Times* (Singapore), 17 September 2013.

where it is a religious institution, and the right of religious group autonomy to manage the internal affairs of the institution. The constitutional rights of a religious institution warrant special consideration, if that right is not to be a paper tiger.

The Faith Community Baptist Church (FCBC) was reported as seeking judicial review in October 2013 as it wanted judicial guidance "on where we stand with reference to the constitutional rights of religious bodies in the management of their religious affairs, which we believe include the hiring and dismissal of staff, the moral standards expected of staff at a level that reflects the ethos and values of the organisation."[105] This issue is not a claim for blanket exemption from general law, but may be framed as a claim for reasonable accommodation, bearing in mind the constitutional right to a religious group's autonomy, to which all decision-makers must give due weight to, in upholding constitutional supremacy. It does not involve a direct conflict, as in the case of substantive Islamic values and general law (e.g. prohibition on polygamy), but an indirect conflict insofar as the Church is not taking issue with the Employment Act regime protecting pregnant women, but with the means adopted to advance that statutory policy in the instant case and the failure to consider article 15(3). That is, the scope of religious autonomy does not conflict with public policy per se.

If leave for judicial review is granted, this would be the first time article 15(3) is being litigated which should shed light on the contours of religious group autonomy, the scope of self-administration and jurisdictional boundaries between the church and state. It is hoped that due weight will be given to the constitutional right and the communal dimension of religious life it safeguards; for, if a ministerial decision that its policy is constitutional is considered determinative, this would hark back to the unhappy categorical approach of *Colin Chan*, rather than a more nuanced process of balancing which takes the constitution seriously.

105 "Church seeks judicial review of Manpower Minister's order," *Today* (Singapore), 2 October 2013, available at http://www.todayonline.com/singapore/church-seeks-judicial-review-manpower-ministers-order.

2. Muslim Religious Headscarf: Tudung (2002) and Hijab Controversy (2013)

At periodic intervals, the issue of wearing religious dress in public spaces crops up, as an example of "diversity as inclusion." In 2002, in relation to the 'tudung' controversy, the government defended its policy of not allowing primary schoolgirls to wear tudung contrary to its uniform policy on various key grounds, as a qualification of the article 15(1) right to religious practises. First, it held that public schools were part of a "common space" which was to be free of religious expression, in order to emphazise the commonality amongst citizens rather than their differences and to promote integration, rather than assimilation.[106] Second, the government looked at the pragmatic concern that if *tudung* wearing was exempt from the uniforms policy, a deluge of religiously-based claims would follow, such as Seventh Day Advents request that examinations not be held on their Sabbath, Friday.[107]

In context, it must be appreciated that the Muslim community is divided as to whether wearing *tudung* is a mandatory aspect of religious practice; further, it is not a complete ban on wearing *tudung* per se, but a prohibition which is limited in time and place as it may be worn in tertiary institutes and most workplaces. Indeed, the current Speaker of Parliament, *Halimah Yacob*, wears *tudung*. The Mufti, as the highest Islamic religious authority in Singapore also advised parents to prioritize education over wearing *tudung*, being of the opinion that pre-teens did not have to wear it.[108] The Prime Minister also stated that the policy was not writ in stone and could be revisited if Singapore attains to a mature multi-racialism, as opposed to when suspicions are heightened towards religious communities which are aggressively assertive, particularly for Muslims in a post 9-11 world. This is an avowedly pragmatic approach, also reflected in the policy to allow Sikhs to wear turbans (which dates back to British colonial

---

106 See "Uniforms a way to stress common ties: Ministry gives parents the weekend to rethink sending daughters to school in headscarves, explains need for rule," *Straits Times* (Singapore), 2 February 2002, p. 1.

107 See "Why 'certain rules' in secular schools must be complied with," *Straits Times* (Singapore), 6 November 2000, p. 40.

108 See "Tudung Issue: Parents urged to put kids first," *Straits Times* (Singapore), 4 Feb 2002, p. 3; "Parents should heed Mufti's advice and move on," *Straits Times* (Singapore), 7 February 2002, at H3.

times) but not to carry around kirpan (ceremonial daggers).[109] A *Straits Times* editorial opined that despite these apparent double standards, all would be reconciled in due course as fewer Sikh children were wearing turbans.[110]

In September 2013, a public debate was sparked off by a question asked at a forum on race, as to why nurses could not wear Muslim headscarf to work, expanding into whether front-line officers like soldiers and police personnel should be allowed to display religious symbols on their uniforms or faces.[111] Muslim Affairs Minister *Yaacob Ibrahim* noted that while policewomen could not wear hijab while in uniform, they were free to wear it when they were out of uniform, "as indeed many do going to and from work." Indeed, for professions requiring their staff to be in uniform, wearing a Muslim headscarf at the workplace would be "very problematic."

Although this issue is potentially justiciable, the government preference is that the matter be handled through an open-ended deliberative process, with Malay MPs discussing the matter with the Cabinet and continuing to consult the community. The Muslim Affairs Minister also noted that "negotiating our common space in a way that all are comfortable with is a continuing work in progress. Muslims have to do this, as do people of other faiths."[112] The clear predilection is for an incremental approach through constructive dialogue, where all parties appreciate "the need for accommodation and compromise,"[113] with ministers noting that the peaceful and harmonious society Singapore had enjoyed was "because our communities understand the need to balance what each wants, and have been moderate and restrained in accommodating one another." Deputy Prime Minister *Teo Chee Hean* noted that the government had to balance

---

109 See "Ministers call for 'give and take' attitude," *Sunday Times* (Singapore), 17 February 2002, p. 26.

110 *Straits Times* (Singapore), 5 February 2002, p. 14.

111 See "Allowing hijab problematic for some jobs: Yaacob," *Today* (Singapore), 1 Nov 2013, at http://www.todayonline.com/singapore/allowing-hijab-problematic-some-jobs-yaacob.

112 "Allowing hijab problematic for some jobs: Yaacob," *Today* (Singapore), 1 November 2013, at http://www.todayonline.com/singapore/allowing-hijab-problematic-some-jobs-yaacob.

113 "PM Lee meets with MPs about hijab issue," *Today* (Singapore), 5 November 2013, at http://www.todayonline.com/singapore/pm-lee-meets-mps-about-hijab-issue.

"different community requirements" with the overall goal of maintaining social harmony. He urged that the reality of living in a multi-religious society was that communities pressing for their own concerns had to take into consideration "how that affects other communities and how others might see it."[114]

III. Consensus Building: Human Organ Transplant Act (Cap 131A)

Rather than impose a general law on a public health issue such as organ transplants, the government has sought to generate consensus within a dissenting religious community over a period of time until this crystallized to the point it was politically feasible to require their participation in a statutory regime.

This is evident in relation to the Malay community and its traditional resistance to organ donation for various religious reasons, such as the sacredness of the human body. In 1987, the Health Minister in introducing the Human Organ Transplant Act (HOTA) (Cap 131) noted that the Islamic religion specifically prohibits organ donation under the presumed consent system, but permitted donation of kidneys to save lives. In deference to Islamic religious teachings, Muslims were exempted from HOTA. In subsequent years, it was apparent in the series of *fatwas* issued by MUIS on human organ donation that what was once considered forbidden under Islamic law was later considered permissible to save life in cases of dire necessity and even encouraged as an act of charity.

In July 2007, the MUIS Fatwa Committee issued a fatwa stating it was *permissible* for Muslims to come under HOTA, to ensure that Muslims suffering organ failure had enhanced access to donated organs, consistent with the goal of saving lives. This reversed a 20 year ruling that enabled Muslims to come under the 'presumed consent' regime of the Human Organ Transplant Act (Cap 131A); in 2008, the Act was amended and the prior exemption of Muslims to HOTA, removed.

Under HOTA, a person between 21 and 60 is presumed to have agreed to donate various organs like his kidneys, liver and cornea when he dies, unless he has opted out. Only Muslims who opted in enjoyed priority where they needed organ transplants. The 2008 amendment to HOTA

114 "DPM Teo weighs in on hijab issue," *Today*, (Singapore), 5 November 2013, at http://www.todayonline.com/print/322766.

would increase the pool of donors and benefit the Muslim community, as a disproportionate number of them needed kidney transplants.[115] To allay doubts, the Ministry of Health prepared packages for all affected Muslims which explained the Act, Islam's position on organ donation and an opt-out form.

The government, in engaging with the Muslim community through consultation and dialogue over the issue of organ transplants, displayed respect for the autonomy of religious communities. It did not ride roughshod over religious reservations by imposing a uniform "one size fits all" policy, but provided space for the community to determine the issue internally. This demonstrated concern for religious sensitivities. Insofar as MUIS represents a comprehensive section of the Muslim community, this consultative approach reveals both prudent politics and shows fidelity towards the constitutional obligations under article 152. Dissenters were free to opt-out of the HOTA system, which safeguards freedom of conscience, while Muslims could not participate in mainstream society in relation to contributing to the pool of potential donors as well as enjoy greater access to organs where needed.

D. Conclusion

All constitutional orderings are an experiment, and the Singapore constitutional order's relationship with religious diversity is one driven by both principle and pragmatism. There is a conscious need to build a stable political community in which all citizens share membership, as well as protecting their distinct identity and autonomy of religious groups. In this experiment, the meaning of secularism, religious freedom, the scope and limits of legal pluralism and the boundaries of tolerance and accommodation of religious diversity are continually being negotiated.

Despite the pragmatic tenor of Singapore governance, there is a bedrock of constitutional principle that is evident in the constitutional design of religion-state relations, based on a voluntarist conception of religious identity. Within this secular democracy, the government strives not to coerce or suppress religious faith and there is a recognition of the role religious faith plays in society, through welfare, the cultivation of

115 See "Muslims to be included in the Act from Aug 1," *Straits Times* (Singapore), 22 Jan 2008.

personal, and social morality which shapes the tenor of public debate and community ethos. Everyone's faith perspectives are welcomed in the public square, with the government neither privileging a religious or secular belief system.

Religious diversity poses various problems to a constitutional order. First, the state must not discriminate between religious groups as this is a recipe for conflict and discontent. The government's policy is to be "neutral, fair. We are not against religion. We uphold sound moral values. We hold the ring so that all groups can practise their faiths freely without colliding with one another in Singapore."[116] Second, religious laws and values may conflict with 'secular' values embodied in law and policy. This relates to a competition between the authority of normative orders; the constitution in permitting legal pluralism under AMLA confirms that the rule of law may be qualified to serve other constitutional values, like accommodating religious difference. The Muslim-Malay community enjoys some degree of insulation from general law, where Islamic values in the field of personal and customary law are allowed expression, thereby protecting its collective identity. Third, the fact of religious diversity within a plural society also poses the problem of conflict between diverse religious groups within the same political space. Here, where religious harmony and civil peace between communities are at stake, where the rights of religious minorities are asserted or threatened, a heavy emphasis is placed on the public value of social harmony. While legal and punitive sanctions are available against those who disrupt religious harmony, there is a strong preference that where possible, religion-based disputes be diffused through a relational and dialogical approach rather than the judicial arena, with the focus on continual deliberation over stark resolution, the language of compromise over that of rights.

Ultimately, Caesar and God remain in an uneasy relationship, at various times partners, and other times, antagonists. The government accommodates some religious practices, such as religious processions in the public sphere, as a celebration of religious diversity. In other matters, it refuses exemptions and accommodations, especially where national security is seen to be imperiled. Here, religion is seen as a potential threat to state stability, as competition and a challenge to state authority, reflecting the modern state's antagonism to competing schemes of law and

---

116 Prime Minister Lee Hsien Loong, "Racial and Religious Harmony," National Day Rally Speech, 16 August 2009.

order. The management of religious diversity within a constitutional order is thus Janus-faced, with religious diversity simultaneously viewed as an object of celebration and identity, and as a subject to fear, to regulate and to control.

Works cited

Bari, Abdul Aziz, "Islam in the Federal Constitution: A Commentary on the Decision of Meor Atiqulrahman," *The Malayan Law Journal* 2 (2002): cxxix-cxlii.

Beer, Lawrence Ward, "Introduction," in *Constitutional Systems in Late Twentieth Century Asia*, ed. Lawrence Ward Beer, Seattle: University of Washington Press, 1992, pp. 1-39.

Constitutional Commission, Republic of Singapore, *Report of the Constitutional Commission 1966*, Singapore Government Printers, 1966.

Dane, Perry, "Constitutional Law and Religion," in *A Companion to Philosophy of Law and Legal Theory*, ed. Dennis Patterson, Cambridge, Mass.: Wiley-Blackwell, 1999, pp. 113-125.

Durham, W Cole Jr. and Brett G. Scharffs, *Law and Religion: National, International and Comparative Perspectives*, Austin: Aspen Publishers, Wolters Kluwer Law and Business, 2010.

Durham, W. Cole, "Perspectives on Religious Liberty: A Comparative Framework," in *Religious Human Rights in Global Perspective*, ed. Johan van der Vyver and John Witte Jr., The Hague: Martinus Nijhoff, 1996, pp. 1-44.

Evans, Carolyn and Anna Hood, "Religious Autonomy and Labour Law: A Comparison of the Jurisprudence of the United States and the European Court of Human Rights," *Oxford Journal of Law and Religion* (2012): 3-20.

Fernando, Joseph M., "The Position of Islam in the Constitution of Malaysia," *Journal of Southeast Asian Studies* 37, 2 (2006): 249-266.

Friedrich, Carl J., *Limited Government: A Comparison*, New Jersey: Prentice-Hall, 1974.

Hirschl, Ran, "Comparative Constitutional Law and Religion," in *Comparative Constitutional Law*, ed. Tom Ginsburg and Rosalind Dixon, Cheltenham, UK: Edward Elgar, 2011, pp. 422-440.

Hirschl, Ran and Ayelat Shachar, "The New Wall of Separation: Permitting Diversity, Restricting Competition," *Cardozo Law Review* 30, 6 (2009): 2535-2560.

Hirschl, Ran, "The Rise of Constitutional Theocracy," *Harvard International Law Journal Online* 49 (2008): 72-82.

Kadir, Suzaina, "The Role of Education in Ethnic/Religious Conflict Management: The Singapore Case," *International Center for Islam and Pluralism (ICIP) Journal* 2, No. 1 (2005): 1-18

Lin, Tan Yock, "Sedition and its New Clothes in Singapore," *Singapore Journal of Legal Studies* (2011): 212-236.

Mohamad, Mahatir bin, *The Malay Dilemma*, Singapore: Asia Pacific Press, 1970.

Nowak, Barbara S. and Singan Knən Muntil, "Btsisi', Blandas, and Malays: Ethnicity and Identity in the Malay Peninsula Based on Btsisi' Folklore and Ethnohistory," *Asian Folklore Studies* 63, No. 2 (2004): 303-323.

Rabb, Intisar "'We the Jurists': Islamic Constitutionalism in Iraq," *University of Pennsylvania Journal of Constitutional Law* 3 (2008): 527-579.

Tan, Kevin, "The Evolution of Singapore's Modern Constitution: Developments from 1945 to the Present Day," *Singapore Academy of Law Journal* 1 (1989): 1-28.

Thio, Li-ann, "Chapter 15: Freedom of Religion," in *A Treatise on Singapore Constitutional Law*, auth. Li-ann Thio, Singapore: Academy Publishing, 2012, pp. 869-924.

Thio, Li-ann, "Relational Constitutionalism and the Management of Inter-Religious Disputes: The Singapore 'Secularism with a Soul' Model," *Oxford Journal of Law and Religion* 2 (2012): 1-24.

Thio, Li-ann and David Chong, "The *Chan* Court and Constitutional Adjudication: 'A sea change into something rich and strange'," in *The Law in His Hands: A Tribute to Chief Justice Chan Sek Keong,* ed. Chao Hick Tim, Andrew Phang, VK Rajah and Yeo Tiong, Singapore: Academy of Law Publishing, 2012, pp. 87-119.

Thio, Li-ann, "Contentious Liberty: Regulating Religious Propagation in a Religiously Diverse Secular Democracy," *Singapore Journal of Legal Studies* (2010): 484-515.

Thio, Li-ann, "Soft Constitutional Law in non-liberal Asian Constitutional Democracies," *International Journal of Constitutional Law* 4 (2010): 766-799.

Thio Li-ann, "Courting Religion: The Judge between Caesar and God in Asian Courts," *Singapore Journal of Legal Studies* (2009): 52-79.

Thio, Li-ann, "The Cooperation of Religion and State in Singapore: A Compassionate Partnership in Service of Welfare," *Review of Faith & International Affairs* 3 (2009): pp. 33-45.

Thio, Li-ann, "The Passage of a Generation: Revisiting the 1966 Constitutional Commission," in *The Evolution of a Revolution: 40 Years of the Singapore Constitution*, ed. Li-ann Thio and Kevin Tan, New York: Routledge-Cavendish, 2009, pp. 7-49.

Thio, Li-ann, "Religion in the Public Sphere of Singapore: Wall of Division or Public Square?," in *Religious Pluralism and Civil Society: A Comparative Analysis*, ed. Bryan S. Turner, Oxford: Bardwell Press, 2008, pp. 73-104.

Thio, Li-ann, "Jurisdictional Imbroglio: Civil and Religious Courts, Turf Wars and Article 121(1A) of the Federal Constitution," in *Constitutional Landmarks in Malaysia*, ed. Andrew Harding and Hoong Phun Lee, LexisNexis, 2007, pp. 197-226.

Thio, Li-ann, "Apostasy and Religious Freedom: Constitutional Issues Arising from the Lina Joy Litigation," *The Malayan Law Journal* 1 (2006): i-cxvi.

Thio, Li-ann, "Control, Co-optation and Co-Operation: Managing Religious Harmony in Singapore's Multi-Ethnic, Quasi-Secular State," *Hastings Constitutional Law Quarterly* 2 and 3 (2005): 197-253.

Thio, Li-ann, "Constitutional 'Soft' Law and the Management of Religious Liberty and Order: The 2003 Declaration on Religious Harmony," *Singapore Journal of Legal Studies* (2004): 414-443.

Thio Li-ann, "Recent Constitutional Developments: of Shadows and Whips, Race, Rifts and Rights, Terror and Tudungs, Women and Wrongs," *Singapore Journal of Legal Studies* (2002): 328-373.

Thio, Li-ann, "The Impact of Internationalisation on Domestic Governance: The Transformative Potential of CEDAW," *Singapore Journal of International & Comparative Law* 1 (1997): 248-350.

Vyver, Johan D. van der, "Equality and Sovereignty of Religious Institutions: A South African Perspective," *Santa Clara Journal of International Law* 1 (2012): 147-169.

Walker, Graham, "The Idea of Nonliberal Constitutionalism," in *Ethnicity and Group Rights*, ed. Ian Shapiro and Will Kymlicka, New York: New York University Press, 1997, pp. 154-176.

The Development of Political Islam in Indonesia

Yon Machmudi

The face of political Islam in Indonesia went through significant changes throughout the 20th century. In general, political Islam in Indonesia has transformed and followed the development of democracy in Indonesia. It has become a major factor in strengthening the process of democratic consolidation. It is therefore not surprising that right now Indonesia is regarded as the most important model of democracy in the Muslim world. However, Indonesia's success in bringing about this consolidation of democracy was not without many challenges. To what extent has political Islam in Indonesia contributed to the development of democracy and how has it transformed into a new philosophy comfortable with democracy? In order to answer these questions, it is best to analyze the dynamics of political Islam in Indonesia from the early days of Indonesian independence to the present.

The important momentum that witnessed the transformation of political Islam in Indonesia began during the New Order era when political Islam groups exerted a new strategy in response to the repressive policies of the New Order regime. In the 1970s the generation of political Islamic groups started to adopt a new approach in their relation to the state. They tended to be more co-operative with the government, which differed from the old generation that would use more confrontational approaches. Since then, political Islam in Indonesia has embarked on a more comprehensive agenda, rather than simply promoting the formal and legal version of Islam. Therefore, this approach is more accommodating with democracy. This strategy, however, did not necessarily remove all radical and extremist tendencies within the Islamic community. There are many who reject this way of struggling for Islam through the promotion of Islamic values, and therefore they prefer to demand the application of formal Islamic law.[1]

---

1 See Jurdi, *Pemikiran Politik Islam Indonesia: Pertautan Negara, Khilafah, Masyarakat Madani dan Demokrasi*, 2008, pp. 181-192

Despite the transformation of political Islam into a more comprehensive approach, Islamic political parties also have shown interest in developments that are more accommodative to pluralism. Currently, there are two types of Islamic political parties in Indonesia: the Muslim mass-based party and the Islamic party. The first tends to use national ideology while the later only uses Islam as its ideological basis. The two parties differ only in terms of their ideological basis, and they are similar in their goals of Muslim values and support for democracy. In addition, many Islamic activists since the 1970s have joined secular and national parties that do not use religion as the basis of their political principles. This development has blurred the distinctions between Islamic and other nationalist parties.

A. Struggle for Islam

Islam appeared in the forms of social and religious movements before Indonesian independence as organizations demanding the freedom of Indonesia from Dutch and Japanese colonization. The Muslim resistance could be distinguished into two types. First, those Islamic movements that tended to wage war and other forms of confrontational resistance against the imperialists, and second, the Islamic groups which took cooperative strategies with the imperialists.[2] Cooperative groups were represented by the modernist Muslims, while the traditionalist Muslim groups tended to take non-cooperative methods in relation to Dutch and Japanese occupation in Indonesia. Largely the modernist groups received their education from colonial schools established by the Netherlands as part of that nation's humanitarian policy. In contrast, traditionalist groups were usually educated by clerics at local Islamic boarding schools (*pesantren*). Despite being dominated by traditionalist clerics, the non-cooperative groups were also supported by revolutionary Muslim youths who were influenced by the ideology of socialism.

Even though they were distinguished by cooperative and non-cooperative approaches, they were united by common Islamic ideals. They wanted to create an independent state that was based on Islamic teachings

2 See Fiederspiel, *Indonesian Muslim Intellectuals of the 20th Century*, 2006, pp. 27-44.

and envisioned the creation of a state based on Islamic ideology.[3] Among the well known Islamic leaders were *Achmad Dahlan*, *Hasyim Asy'ari*, HOS Cokroaminoto, and *Agus Salim*. Modernist Muslim groups represented the face of political Islam and usually confronted nationalist and socialist groups who had different views of the future of the Indonesian state. Leaders coming from the nationalist front were *Sukarno*, *Mohammad Hatta* and *M Yamin*. Among the prominent socialist figures were *Tan Malaka*, *Muso* and *Semaun*. Therefore, at the beginning of independence, Indonesian national movements were divided into three major groups, namely Islamists, nationalists and socialists.[4]

In preparing the ideology of the new state, the three groups of earlier Indonesian leaders fought each other to determine the national ideology of Indonesia to be established by the Committee to Prepare for Indonesian Independence (BPUPKI). At the center of the debate was the question of whether or not Indonesia's governing principles should be based on Islamic or nationalist ideology. This struggle pitted the nationalists and socialists against both the modernist and traditionalist Muslim groups.

After independence, the Islamist groups began to have disputes with each other. Political Islam included not only modernist and traditionalist groups, but also fundamentalist groups. Traditionalist Islamic groups constituted the majority of Muslims in Indonesia which were represented by Islamic groups such as Nahdlatul Ulama (NU), Mathlaul Anwar (MA), and the traditionalist group of Arab descendents, Jamiat Khair. Modernist groups, also known as the reformists, were represented by Islamic organizations such as Muhammadiyah, Persatuan Islam (Persis) and the reformist group of Arab descendents, Al-Irsyad.[5] While the fundamentalist group was small in number it, however, became a public concern because of its actions which were often at odds with the mainstream of Islamic groups. This group did not want to struggle for Islam through parliament but preferred to use more militant approaches in achieving its goal of establishing Indonesia as an Islamic state. This group was represented by the Darul Islam or the Islamic State of Indonesia that was led by *Kartosuwiryo* in West Java and *Kahar Muzakkar* in South Sulawesi. This

3 See Benda (trans.), *Bulan Sabit dan Matahari Terbit: Islam Indonesia pada Masa Pendudukan Jepang*, 1980, pp. 205-233.

4 See Crouch, "Islam and Politics in Indonesia," 1986, pp. 15-30.

5 For details on the development of Islamic mass organizations in Indonesia see Machmudi, *Profil dan Sejarah Profil-Profil Ormas Islam di Indonesia*, 2013.

fundamentalist group later came to be associated with the radical splinter group called Jemaah Islam (JI).

The hot debates among the Islamists, nationalists and socialists after Indonesian independence created strong tensions, and cooperation between them very difficult. The politics of stream (*politik aliran*) based on different political orientations and groups continued to develop and created wide polarization among Indonesian elites. The fundamentalist group under the banner of Darul Islam declared an Islamic State in West Java in 1948 led by Kartosuwiryo but failed to achieve its goal because it was destroyed by the Sukarno regime. However, traditionalist and modernist Islamic groups still continued to struggle for Islam and strengthened their role in the parliamentary arena.

Unfortunately during the Old Order when the various groups failed to come to an agreement, *Sukarno* took over the discourse of the state by issuing a presidential decree in 1959. This decree contains an order to dissolve the parliament and revert to the Constitution of 1945. This was the beginning of the authoritarian regime that imposed what he called Guided Democracy. To strengthen his power, *Sukarno* introduced a cross-ideological coalition involving three major powers; nationalists, Islamists and communists, called Nasakom (*Nasionalis, Agama dan Komunis*). The traditionalist group under the party of NU joined the coalition representing the religious front. Since *Sukarno* imposed his policy to include the communists in his governmental coalition, the modernist group represented by Masyumi refused to join the coalition and rejected the ideas of Nasakom. Some leaders from Masyumi such as *Syafruddin Prawiranegara* supported the resistance group Pemerintah Revolusioner Republik Indonesia (PRRI). A rebellion that took place in West Sumatra was successfully crushed by the central government. As a result of this rebellion, *Sukarno* dissolved the Masyumi and put some of its leaders into prison.[6]

Later, the involvement of communists in the government under the regime of Sukarno made the military and other Islamist groups unhappy. Therefore, when there was a rumor about the Communist Party's plan to conduct a military coup against the legitimate government, the army under Major General *Suharto* together with the Islamist groups was said to put down the bloody coup by the communist. The coup planned by the

6 See Syamsuddin, *Islam dan Politik era Orde Baru*, 2001, pp. 43-62.

Indonesia Communist Party (PKI) became known as the 30 September Movement (G30S PKI) and created a conflict that caused hundreds of thousands of casualties on both the Muslim and the communist sides. In the end, in the name of maintaining the stability of the country and to safeguard the security arrangements in Indonesia, *Suharto* and the army then took power from Sukarno. Since 1966 Suharto then consolidated his power by forming the New Order regime.

The modernist group under the leadership of *M. Natsir* hoped that the leadership of *Suharto* would bring good news for Masyumi since Muslim groups together with the army succeeded in thwarting the communists' coup. He demanded *Suharto* to rehabilitate Masyumi as a legal political party. Unfortunately for them, *Suharto* had no desire to do this and rejected *Natsir's* proposal. He tried to prevent former leaders of Masyumi from being involved in politics again. Since then *Suharto* began to implement hardline policies against his rivals by limiting their involvement in politics. Islamists and communists were defined as the enemies of Suharto, as well as enemies of the state.

B. A New Path of Political Islam

Suharto's background as an army commander who fought against rebellions in Indonesia made him cautious with political Islamic groups, and he sought to prevent the influence of Islamic groups in politics. In the early days of his rule, *Suharto* took harsh measures and actions against political Islamic groups. Therefore, the relations of the state and Islam in this era can be described as an antagonistic relationship.

The ban of the former actvists from Masyumi into politics forced Islamists to focus their activities in Da'wah. In order to maintain the spirit of political Islam, in 1962 they founded the Indonesian Islamic Propagation Council (DDII). DDII activists constantly leveled harsh criticisms against the regime through Islamic sermons in mosques. As a result, the New Order regime escalated their repressive policies against the Islamists. *Robert W. Hefner* stated that the only form of Islam that became the target of the regime's repressive policies was the organized Islam,

Islam that is institutionalized as political power while Islam as a cultural power was tolerated by the regime.[7]

In order to lessen the influence of Islamists, the regime proposed the principle of ideology called *Pancasila* to be adopted by all mass organizations and political parties, in particular Islamic social and political organizations. This of course led to further resistance from Muslim activists. However, since the regime was so strong and would not compromise on this issue, there was no option for Muslims unless they accepted the sole ideology of Pancasila. Any effort to reject the application of Pancasila would result in swift and decisive actions from the regime. In general the government was able to control the situation and forced all citizens to follow its policy. This led to the tragedy of Priok in 1984 in which thousands of Muslims were massacred by the military in a mosque led by *Amir Biki* in the north Jakarta because they opposed the government's policy. Other clashes between Islamists and the regime continued throughout the 1970s and 1980s.

In order to monopolize political discourse in Indonesia, the New Order regime also started to simplify political parties into three major groups, consisting of Islamic, nationalist, and secular parties. All former Islamic parties joined the United Development Party (PPP), the nationalists and the regime's fronts joined the Golkar, while socialist-leaning parties and Christians prefered to support the Indonesia Democratic Party (PDI).

In response to the policies of the New Order regime that tended to repress Islamic groups, the younger generation of Islamists tried a new approach, which *Bahtiar Effendy* described as an attempt to reconcile Islam and the state with a new theology of political Islam in Indonesia.[8] This approach gave birth to the important decision for Islamists to not only focus on the political struggle but started to develope more social, cultural and economic activities. They also sought to struggle for political Islam through nationalist and secular parties. Many of them then joined the ruling party and became part of the regime in order to carry out the islamization from within the system.[9]

---

7 See Hefner, *Civil Islam: Muslim and Democratization in Indonesia*, 2000, pp 175-180.

8 See Effendy, *Teologi Baru Politik Islam*, 2001, pp. 9-28.

9 See Ali and Effendy, *Pathfinding a New Path of Islam: Reconstruction of Indonesian Islamic Thoughts within the New Order Epoch*, 2011, pp. 151-164.

Although many observers considered this new strategy of political Islam in the New Order era as coopted Islam, in fact this approach was able to build better relations between Islam and the state. Politically, the Islamic parties suffered a setback, but Islamic aspirations began to be widely accepted on the level of political and bureaucratic power through collaboration with the regime. The emergence of the Association of Indonesian Muslim Scholars, Ikatan Cendikiawan Muslim Indonesia (ICMI) in 1990 was an important development in this struggle. Since then, if a person wanted to achieve power in government, they would have to embrace political Islam to some degree.[10]

Perhaps ironically, as Islam went mainstream in the government, the power of Islamic parties began to decline. At the grassroots and community level, Islamization was conducted by Islamic activists who focused on the propagation of Islam while at the elite level Islam was accepted by high level civil servants – even the ruling party was mostly dominated by Islamists.[11] This era also saw the awakening of Islam that occurred throughout urban areas. Many prestigious universities began to be filled with young Islamists, such as the University of Indonesia (UI), Bandung Technological Institute (ITB), Bogor Agricultural Institute (IPB) and Gajah Mada University in Yogyakarta (UGM).[12] Therefore, the Islamization process has occured not only within the ruling party (Golkar) but also within the party that had once been considered a secular party. Some examples that the government started to adopte as policies that were favourable to Islam were the enactment of several laws that favored the interests of Muslims. These laws were the national education law that requires all levels of schools to provide religious instruction in accordance with the religion professed by the pupils (1988), the Islamic Law Compilation (1991), the administration of Zakat through BAZIS (1991), the lifting of the ban on wearing headscarves for students in public schools (1991) and various government policies that clearly adopted Muslim aspirations.

---

10 For details about the development of ICMI see Anwar, *Pemikiran dan Aksi Islam Indonesia: Sebuah Kajian Tentang Cendekiawan Muslim Masa Order Baru*, 1995, pp. 235-240.

11 See Abdullah, "The Formation of a New Paradigm: a Sketch on Contemporary Islamic Discourse," 1996, pp. 47-64.

12 See Hasbullah, *Sejarah Sosial Intelektual Islam di Indonesia*, 2012, pp. 64-70.

C. Toward Post-Islamism

Islam has emerged as both a political and cultural force. Two parties that use Islam as the basis of their political ideologies are the Prosperous Justice Party (PKS) and the United Development Party (PPP). Islam-based parties with a more pluralistic ideology are the National Mandate Party (PAN) and the National Awakening Party (PKB). PKS is the biggest Islamic party that represents mainly students[13] while the PPP is the conservative Islamic party. PAN represents a modernist Islamic party while PKB represents a Muslim traditional party. Although both PKS and PPP claim to be Islamic party, they no longer focus their agenda on the formalization of Sharia and Islamic ideology in the state but rather try to focus on more common needs of the people in general.[14] This tendency enables them to unite with other Muslim activists from other different parties because of their strong commitment to struggle for the aspirations of Muslims. One example is the support of all parties except PDIP for the application of a new law regarding the regulation of pornography in Indonesia.

The possibilities of Islamic and nationalist parties in Indonesia to support the agenda of Islam in general results from the dominant role of Muslim activists in almost all political parties. The Golkar as the second largest party is historically known as the New Order's party since the 1970s. It welcomed many leaders from Islamic organizations to fill high positions in the party. The former chairman of the Indonesian Student Association (HMI), *Akbar Tanjung*, served as the chairman of Golkar in 1999-2004. In fact since the 1990s many members of ICMI held key positions in the Golkar. The succes of Islamist groups in Golkar is characterized by the emergence of *BJ Habibie*, the first chairman of ICMI, as vice president under *Suharto* in 1997 who was then appointed President in 1998.

The current ruling party, the Democratic Party (PD), also has experienced similar developments in which many Muslim activists have occupied central leadership positions in the party. *Anas Urbaningrum*, the former chairman of HMI, succeeded to lead the party even though he was

---

13 Further details about PKS see Machmudi, *Islamising Indonesia: the Rise of Jemaah Tarbiyah and the Prosperous Justice Party (PKS)*, 2008.

14 For further details on the charateristics of the political parties during the Reformation era see Amir, *Peta Islam Politik Pasca-Soeharto*, 2003, pp. 59-187.

later removed from the leadership because of charges of corruption. Now PD claims it is a religious-nationalist party. Likewise the PDIP, which is the party mainly supported by *Sukarno's* followers and their families, has set up a special Islamic organization as part of their political wing in order to attract Islamic activists and constituents. Many former leaders of Islamic organizations also joined the PDIP and still commit themselves to the struggle of Islam in the political sphere through modest means.

This varied approach of Muslims from all parties working towards the same Islamic goal can be seen as a post-Islamist strategy.[15] Their main effort is to struggle for Islam in harmony with social, political and cultural changes, in particular to follow the development of democracy. Why is this generation of Indonesian Islamists still considered as part of post-Islamism process? It is because they still are part of the history of Islamist groups of the past that have now transformed into more a accomodative type of Islam. Even though they are not formally organized but rather individually struggling for Islam, they share almost the same opinion that Islam should be promoted through politics in good ways which is compatible with democratic values. As a result, today we find that Islam is not only monopolized by Islamic political parties but also becomes agenda of nationalist parties. Here then the development of political Islam in Indonesia at the end is in accordance with democracy itself. Therefore, Islam is one of the important elements in the establishment of a consolidated democracy in Indonesia.

Marcus Mietzner gives a good analysis of the condition of post-reform Indonesia and how Muslims have played significant roles in the consolidation of democracy in Indonesia. He divides the Reformation era into two parts, the transition to democracy (1998-2004) and the consolidation of democracy (2004 till now).[16]

During the democratic transition period *Suharto* officially resigned from his position as president of Indonesia. After Suharto stepped down from his post on May 21, 1998, Vice-President *BJ Habibie* replaced him. Although *Habibie* served as President only one year, he was praised for his contributions in guiding the nation toward democratic elections in 1999. This transition was a most difficult and challenging moment. The

---

15 For further details about post Islamism see Bayat (trans.), *Pos Islamisme*, 2011, pp. 17-26.

16 See Mietzner, *Military Politics, Islam, and the State in Indonesia: from Turbulent Transition to Democratic Consolidation*, 2009, pp. 195-329.

new euphoria of freedom in all aspects of Indonesian lives was yet not supported by political stability and the rule of law and contributed to emergence of many social and political problems such as security issues, conflict and disintegration. In this time of transition Indonesia not only experienced the economic downturn but also faced problems concerning security issues, social conflict, as well as political and social disturbances. The conflict in Ambon, Poso, Aceh and the rise of terrorism were the most serious issues of that time. Although it faced sectarian violence in many corners, the new government was able to manage the issues and successfully created peace in Indonesia. The full commitment of Muslim groups who are both within political parties and religious organizations have contributed to make the nation of Indonesia united and no longer facing disintegration. The success of *Abdurahman Wahid*, the former leader of NU, in occupying the highest position as President of the Republic of Indonesia in 1999 was one of the Indonesian Muslim groups political achievements. Similarly, *Amin Rais*, the former chairman of Muhammadiyah was elected as chairman of the People's Consultative Assembly (1999-2004) while *Akbar Tanjung*, the former chairman of HMI, also was appointed as chairman of the House of Representatives (1999-2004). This development gives a strong indication that Islam has become an integral and significant part in the dynamics of Indonesian politics.

The success of the 2004 election was a milestone in the process of the democratic consolidation of Indonesia. The strong role of civil society backed by Islamic organizations and political parties marks the consolidation of democracy in Indonesia. Interestingly, Islamic parties began to develop into more inclusive and open parties, and moved to the middle spectrum. The former chairman of PKS, *Hidayat Nurwahid*, was elected as chairman of People's Consultative Assembly (2004-2009) replacing *Amin Rais*.

In addition, the 2009 elections saw eight political parties meeting the parliamentary threshold to gain reprensentatives in parliament. Among them are the Democratic Party (PD), the Golkar, the Indonesian Democratic Party Struggle (PDIP), the Prosperous Justice Party (PKS), the National Mandate Party (PAN), the United Development Party (PPP) and two parties run by retired generals, *Gerindra and Hanura*. Both Islamic parties (PKS and PPP) as well as two Muslim-based parties (PKB and PAN) formed a coalition with the Democratic Party and succeeded in supporting *Susilo Bambang Yudhoyono* and *Boediono* becoming President and Vice-President of Republic of Indonesia respectively for the period

2009-2014. It was the second time that the Indonesian President, *Susilo Bambang Yudhoyono*, was elected with the support of Islamic parties and Muslim-based parties such as PKS, PAN, PPP and PKB.

However, the main challenge of the Islamists right now is no longer associated with the ideology and radicalism but has more to do with the inability of Islamic parties to establish a good track record in combating corruption.[17] The issue of corruption as a chronic problem that has occurred in Indonesia and infected almost all political parties, and Islamist parties are no exception. Unfortunately, because of the high political cost in Indonesia many Muslim activists are entangled in corruption cases. The cases that hit several members of parliament and leaders from Islamic groups highlight the problem. The public begins to see that Islamic activists are also not immune to corruption such as *Anas Urbaningrum*, the chairman of Democrat Party and *Luthfi Hasan Ishaq*, the president of PKS. Both figures are representatives of Islamic activists in politics while in the same time many members of parliament from Islamic and Muslim based parties such as PPP, PAN and PKB have been long seen in corruption cases.

D. Conclusion

Muslims continue to contribute to the democratic consolidation of Indonesia. Muslims who have struggled for Islam in political parties have consistently supported the process of democratization in Indonesia by promoting the spirit of nationalism. Other mass organizations like Nahdlatul Ulama, Muhammadiyah, Persis, Persatuan Umat Islam, and Matlaul Anwar continually encourage and strengthen the civil society in order to create a more democratic Indonesia. Though the issue of terrorism is still emerging, in general it can be resolved by the government in cooperation with Islamic organizations and political parties.

Islamic parties continue to show the face of both poltical and cultural Islam. Neither face can be separated from the other. It is true that maintream Islam in Indonesia does not support the establishment of an Islamic state but it also resists the secularization of the country. That is the main portrait of the mainstream moderate Islam in Indonesia. Still, the

---

17 See Hefner, "Muslim Democrats and Islamist Violence in Post-Soeharto Indonesia," 2005, pp. 276-280.

main challenge for Indonesia is not radicalism or terrorism, but the need to stop the spread of corruption.

Works cited

Abdullah, Taufik, "The Formation of a New Paradigm: a Sketch on Contemporary Islamic Discourse," in *Toward a New Paradigm: Recent Developments in Indonesian Islamic Thought*, ed. Mark R. Woodward, Arizona: Arizona State University, 1996.

Ali, Fachry and Bahtiar Effendy, *Pathfinding a New Path of Islam: Reconstruction of Indonesian Islamic Thoughts within the New Order Epoch*, Jakarta: Puslitbang Kementrian Agama RI, 2011.

Amir, Zainal Abidin, *Peta Islam Politik Pasca-Soeharto*, Jakarta: LP3S, 2003.

Anwar, Syafii, *Pemikiran dan Aksi Islam Indonesia: Sebuah Kajian Tentang Cendekiawan Muslim Masa Order Baru*, Jakarta: Penerbit Paramadina, 1995.

Bayat, Asef (trans.), *Pos Islamisme*, Yogyakarta: LKIS, 2011.

Benda, Harry J. (trans.), *Bulan Sabit dan Matahari Terbit: Islam Indonesia pada Masa Pendudukan Jepang*, Jakarta: Pustaka Jaya, 1980.

Crouch, Harold, "Islam and Politics in Indonesia," in *Politics, Diplomacy and Islam: Four Case Studies*, ed. Coral Bell, Canberra: The Australian National University, 1986 pp. 15-30.

Effendy, Bahtiar, *Teologi Baru Politik Islam.* Yogyakarta: Galang Press, 2001.

Fiederspiel, Howard M., *Indonesian Muslim Intellectuals of the 20th Century,* Singapore: ESEAS, 2006.

Hasbullah, Moeflich, *Sejarah Sosial Intelektual Islam di Indonesia,* Bandung: Pustaka Setia, 2012.

Hefner, Robert W., "Muslim Democrats and Islamist Violence in Post-Soeharto Indonesia," in *Remaking Muslim Politics: Pluralism, Contestation and Democratization*, ed. Robert W. Hefner, Princeton and Oxford: Princeton University Press, 2005, pp. 276-280.

Hefner, Robert W., *Civil Islam: Muslim and Democratization in Indonesia,* Princeton and Oxford: Princeton University Press, 2000.

Jurdi, Syarifuddin, *Pemikiran Politik Islam Indonesia: Pertautan Negara, Khilafah, Masyarakat Madani dan Demokrasi,* Yogyakarta: Pustaka Pelajar, 2008.

Machmudi, Yon, *Profil dan Sejarah Profil-Profil Ormas Islam di Indonesia,* Jakarta: PKTTI UI, 2013.

Machmudi, Yon, *Islamising Indonesia: the Rise of Jemaah Tarbiyah and the Prosperous Justice Party (PKS),* Canberra: ANU E Press, 2008.

Mietzner, Marcus. *Military Politics, Islam, and the State in Indonesia: from Turbulent Transition to Democratic Consolidation.* Singapore: ESEAS, 2009.

Syamsuddin, Din, *Islam dan Politik era Orde Baru,* Jakarta: Logos, 2001.

The Other Pakistan: Special Laws, Diminished Citizenship and the Gathering Storm

Osama Siddique

A. Introduction

The historically strife wrecked Afghanistan and the destabilized neighboring Pakistani territories remain a primary global theater of war between competing international geo-political interests. For many, the most obvious explanation for this is embedded in the immediately preceding decades that witnessed the eventually defeated Soviet invasion of Afghanistan in the 1980s and the long subsequent years of vicious civil war amongst various warring factions that created the pre-conditions for the rise of the Taliban.[1] However, as is usually the case, there is much more to all this. More nuanced and deeper analyzes of this areas' complex history, culture and political economy do exist. However, they are routinely overwhelmed by staunchly statist national security evaluations of the more immediate triggers of violence. They are also meticulously overlooked by the exigencies of the identification, delegitimization and demonization of strategic targets that are held to neither deserve due process nor get any, in the decision-making that precedes their annihilation.[2] These are thus the terrains of choice for directly televised

1 For a persuasive analysis of the background factors that led to the emergence and strengthening of the Taliban movement see Rashid, *Taliban: Islam, Oil and the new Great Game in Central Asia*, 2000. *Rashid's* account is widely regarded as a fairly objective and at times even sympathetic treatment of the contributory role of various factors, such as the general lawlessness and anarchy created by the brutal warlords that ruled Afghanistan after the Soviet withdrawal, which in turn led to what was initially a natural and well-meaning reaction in the form of the Taliban movement. However, even *Rashid* cannot resist the temptation of some ethnic stereotyping. He describes the Afghans as, "[B]rave, magnificent, honorable, generous, hospitable, gracious, handsome..." who can also be "devious, mean and bloody-minded." Rashid, *Taliban*, p. vii. As if such contradictory characteristics don't exist in other nations of the world.

2 For a helpful discussion of the complex and multifarious factors that have molded the overall character of the five central Asian Muslim countries after the collapse of the Soviet Union in 1991 see Rashid, *The Resurgence of Central*

frontline landscapes of global ideological attrition. Against their backdrop, popular perception has regularly fed the images of a 'War on Terror' that is being visited by a grand alliance for freedom and democracy on a culture of pure evil – a culture whose cardinal article of faith is the export of wanton mayhem to the rest of the world. The mainstream international media's persistent 'othering' of a Darth Wader-like enemy is a narrative visually characterized by frequent grainy images of anonymous uncouth and half-crazed looking individuals crouching against a grey-brown, rock strewn moonscape, muttering inaudible doomsday dreams.

The ceaseless U.S. drone attacks on various Pakistani border territories under the justification of exterminating Al-Qaeda operatives and Taliban supporters is the most resonant recent example of a war that seems to transcend centuries and different governance eras – even if it has now taken on a form that is uniquely cold, calculated and seemingly impersonal. These ostensibly targeted killings remain the source of pitched debates in the academic realms of international law and politics; they are also the theme of highly divisive national and international discourses on the legality, suitability and ethics of a form of war that transgresses established notions of territorial sovereignty and conventional principles of legal culpability and due process.[3] While unmanned aircraft

---

Asia: Islam or Nationalism?, 1992. As a follow-up, the author analyzes the various reasons for the creation of militant Islamic fundamentalism and the formation of militant organizations in these countries in Rashid, *Jihad: The Rise of Militant Islam in Central Asia*, 2002.

3 The mainstream criticism in the Pakistani electronic, print and social media routinely castigates the drone attacks as a clear violation of Pakistan's airspace. Even as a tool of destruction, it describes the drones as recklessly inaccurate, the cause of many innocent deaths and thus the cause of much more damage than benefit. See for instance, "Over 700 killed in 44 drone strikes in 2009," *Dawn*, 2 January 1010 at http://archives.dawn.com/archives/144960, accessed on 13 July 2012. See also the story in the popular Pakistani website Buzz Pakistan, "Drone Attacks in Pakistan," Buzz Pakistan, 17 March 2010 at http://www.buzzpk.com/drone-attacks-in-pakistan/, accessed on 13 July 2012); and, Amir Mir, "60 drone hits kill 14 al-Qaeda men, 687 civilians," *The News*, 10 April 2009, at http://www.thenews.com.pk/top_story_detail.asp?Id=21440, accessed on 13 July 2012). The media also point out how these attacks make a fragile new democratic government in Pakistan look inept and compromising on territorial sovereignty to its electoral constituents, which in turn also impairs vital areas of international collaboration for investing in Pakistani democracy; the reform of its democratic institutions; the strengthening of tolerant, pluralistic social forces; the creation of economic opportunities; and the boosting of Pakistan's internal capacity to fight

hurtle death from the skies, huge questions remain on whether they prevent or promote armed radicalism and whether the anonymous deathly pay loads have some clandestine way of discerning between armed combatants and innocent civilians.

Meanwhile, the fundamentals of the underlying factors that have made these areas and its people vulnerable to a seemingly perpetual cycle of

---

terrorism, both socially and militarily. The drone attacks, they argue, sunder possible consensus and coalition between U.S. efforts to fight terrorism and the booming Pakistani public opinion against the brutalization of their country at the hands of religious radicals. These attacks force a crucible on the Pakistanis that coerces them to overlook the so-called collateral damage. In reality, most Pakistanis can't make any morally valid distinction between the slaughters of children, may it be in urban Lahore or rural FATA, and that for them is the very heart of the matter. Not only do they regard such a war as arbitrary and cruel but also a slippery slope as it helps recruit more suicide bombers and hinders possibilities of local, regional and national alliances against the radicals – the drones divide Pakistani public opinion to the detriment of all those who want to collectively confront radicalism. See for instance, David Kilcullen and Andrew Mcdonald Exum, "Death from Above, Outrage down Below," *The New York Times,* 16 May 2009, at http://www.nytimes.com/2009/05/17/opinion/17exum.tml?pagewanted=all, accessed on 13 July 2012; Rahimullah Yusfzai, "Drone attacks – where do we stand?," *The News International*, 29 March 2011, at http://www.thenews.com.pk/Todays-News-9-38778-Drone-attacks---where-do-we-stand, accessed on 13 July 2012; and Abid Mehsud, "Drone Attacks threat to our Sovereignty," *The Frontier Post*, 18 June 2012, at http://www.thefrontierpost.com/article/167257/, accessed on 13 July 2012. Pakistanis also regard the drone attacks as the latest in a long lamentable history of overt and covert meddling in Pakistani affairs and territory, usually in cohorts with military regimes and their agencies. The refusal by the U.S., on the other hand, to hand over the requisite intelligence and technology to their Pakistani political and military counterparts, is popularly seen as inexplicable. The increasingly loud mainstream criticism argues that the Pakistani people, their political parties, and now their elected governments and armed forces are keen on a larger dialogue and multi-pronged collective stra-tegy to fight extremism. They have the ideas, the will and the capacity but all they hear is the usual drone of 'do this or else.' For a dialogue to begin, they say, this drone too has to go. The Pakistani parliament has passed several resolutions calling for a halt to the Drone attacks. See for instance, Richard Leiby, "Pakistan calls for end to U.S. drone attacks," *The Washington Post*, 13 April 2012 at http://www.washingtonpost.com/world/pakistan-calls-for-end-to-us-drone attacks/2012/04/12/gIQAN1ZFDT_story.html, accessed on 13 July 2012). Local newspapers and social media regularly report the enormous body count of these attacks. See for instance the website *Pakistani Body Count* at http://www.pakistanbodycount.org/drn.php, accessed on 13 July 2012.

violence and mayhem remain largely academically unexplored.[4] The rabid faces of radicalism are so much more fascinating to the camera than the travails of a struggling democracy, retarded development and domestic access to services. As a result, we are hardly ever told of the genesis of this radicalism; the tell-tale story of its creation; and the genealogy of the angst that seems to grip it. Any attempt to discuss the actual necromancer behind the more visible forces of militant radicalism finds relatively little international attention. The bleak backdrop of economic and social disempowerment; the paucity of education and democratic space; and, above all, the historic use and abuse of Pakistani turf and many of its people by a coalition of international interests and local undemocratic regimes, in order to fight wars that the Pakistani citizenry was never consulted about, remains primarily unexplored.[5] Facing particular neglect

4 For one particular perspective on this issue see Siddique, "Of Judges and Drones: U.S. Policy alienates the Pakistani People," 2009.

5 See Siddique, "Of Judges and Drones," Contrary to the myth, Pakistanis have a keen sense of history. They remember persistent U.S. foreign policy support for its authoritarian military regimes of yore, as they do its simultaneous castigation of Pakistanis as a people incapable of self-governance and progress. General *Ayub Khan's* dictatorship in the 1960s was supported for Cold War era strategic justifications; and the pseudo-Islamist veneer of General *Zia-ul-Haq's* harsh dictatorship through the 1980s – an era most commentators blame for rapid democratic institutional decline, rights violations, and abuse of religion for political ends – was aided, financed and bolstered for running the Afghan Jehad. General *Musharraf* was thus only the latest in what is a long tradition. Equally evident to the Pakistanis is the fact that though Islamic political parties have invariably fared miserably in free elections, they were actively nurtured and strengthened under the *Zia* and *Musharraf* regimes, both desperate to carve out any legitimacy through manufacturing alternative political constituencies. The coalition partners for *Zia* and later *Musharraf* read like a veritable 'Who's Who' of forces of regression and political absolutism – their links to militant forces well known but strangely unmentioned. In late 2007, soon after *Musharraf* launched a second *coup* against the people of Pakistan, the author was in the U.S. to give some talks on *Musharraf's* latest. The author had left behind a country anguished and uncertain. A hapless regime running rampant, arresting the most 'odious threats' to domestic bliss and international peace – i.e., lawyers, university teachers, college students, judges, human rights activists, doctors, engineers, NGO workers, etc. Ironically, this was to bring about an iron order to better face the growing menace of the Taliban. The 'Taliban' is often used as a rather facile catch-all term for what is a complex and convoluted set of radical forces operating in the region in the new 'Great Game,' with multiple handlers, agendas, and financiers, but for paucity of space one will reluctantly stick to this term. In the following months, members of the diverse, burgeoning and highly vocal Pakistani civil society played hide and seek

are the variable and inconsistent administrative and legal regimes that have historically governed the troubled territories in Pakistan and their linkages with a mounting discontent with the State amongst the inhabitants of this area.

Given the above, this article endeavors to first of all closely review, analyze and distinguish the distinct administrative and legal history of these territories, as opposed to the administrative and legal system that prevails in mainstream Pakistan. Based on rigorous field work in the region, it then engages in a careful assessment of the ethos and operation of the vestiges of a fundamentally colonial legal system that continues to operate in these territories well into the twenty first century. The article then proceeds to highlight the aforementioned largely neglected issues and areas of inquiry through a coverage and discussion of recent developments in one specific area in the region – the valley of Swat – in the wake of an eventually quashed Taliban uprising against the Pakistani state. Swat in many ways is a highly illustrative example of why violence and radicalism in this particular region is inextricably knit with its inhabitants' highly differential access to rights that are at least theoretically available to other fellow Pakistani citizens. Thus, using Swat as a case study, the article sets forth to demonstrate the historical disconnects of this entire region with the larger polity, society and legal and governance frameworks that exist right next door – in other parts of the same sovereign country. Consequently, it postulates whether poor and disparate governance and not some Pseudo Social Darwinist notion of a mass genetic pre-inclination to violence, may be able to explain the cycle of destruction that has engulfed this region since at least the nineteenth century.

Without overstating one's case, it is nevertheless worth re-emphasizing that the valley of Swat and its larger surrounding area – for which, in order to illustrate the complex challenges and vagaries of this entire region, it serves as a leitmotif in this article – remains acutely ill-understood. After

---

to evade arrest and intimidation; or faced Kafkaesque court hearings while over sixty of the country's top judges had been packed off by *Musharraf* after his arbitrary and illegal sacking of Chief Justice *Iftikhar Muhammad Chaudhry*. And yet, at a time when additional draconian curbs were being introduced on all kinds of constitutional freedoms under *Musharraf's* 'enlightened moderation,' Pakistanis still retained their sense of humor. One popular quip was that *Musharraf's* new paradoxical strategy is to incarcerate the moderates and vanquish the radicals. But then who will be left for him to lord over, was the logical question. Siddique, "Of Judges and Drones,".

all, popular perceptions about Pakistan's north-western territories have changed but little from the colonial era. During the British Raj, such perceptions were predominantly molded by the foreign rulers' depiction of this terrain as the domain of barbaric, fickle, and habitually violent *jezail* bearing Pathans, Baluchis and other ethnic groups. Such monochromatic characterization escalated after the disastrous outcome of the First Anglo-Afghan War (1839-1842) and subsequent military campaigns waged by the British in the region. The motivation for these expeditions was to secure Afghanistan and the adjacent tribal belt in modern Pakistan as a center of influence in order to maintain heightened vigilance on British India's north-western border, beyond which lurked the looming specter of Russian expansionism.[6] Since they were not militarily subdued, the colonial policy position – both as a practical strategy as well as a handy slur – was that the tribals had to be bribed in order to persuade them to desist from attacking British expeditions and strongholds in the area. This fuelled a persistent stereotyping of the locals as capricious and dishonorable, while their multifarious aspects, diverse motivations and imperatives, and varying traits remained and were kept disguised. As Sir *Olaf Caroe* wrote in the introduction to his seminal work on the history of the Pathans: "… [A]fter a hundred years or more of close contact, the Pathan remains to the world, and even to himself, something of an enigma. Many have spoken and written of him and his country, but the surface has been scarcely scratched. There is need for a deeper ploughing."[7]

This article is indeed an endeavor to engage in such deeper ploughing. This necessarily entails scraping through the obfuscating patina and veneer of popular international reportage so as to explore whether there are clearly discernable links between the escalation of violent radicalism in these territories with their highly outdated and consistently poor administrative regulation, their disparate constitutional status, the asymmetric access of their inhabitants to fundamental citizenship rights, and their highly flawed justice system. All this unavoidably leads to another overwhelming question. One cannot but wonder whether much has really changed over the century and a half that separates the mildewed

6 For an insightful rendition of the main events and players in the Great Game and their imperatives see Hopkirk, *The Great Game: The Struggle For Empire in Central Asia*, 1992. For another fascinating account of the Great Game see Keay, *The Gilgit Game: The Explorers of The Western Himalayas*, 1993.

7 Caroe, *The Pathans: 550 B.C – A.D 1957*, 1958, p. xvi.

chronicles of the colonial imperatives of the 'Great Game' which mandated a particular governance model for this region, and, real-time, night-vision images of the post-colonial 'War on Terror' and its roadmap for regional pacification and oversight. In short, this article endeavors to showcase that which is never televised but which may hold the clues to diagnosing the particular malady of one of the most troubled regions in the world, events wherein continue to have deep and disturbing global reverberations.

B. The Special Territories and the Lesser Citizens

Pakistan's north-western 'special territories' could easily be conceived as small and significantly different neighboring countries. In contrast to the legal and administrative system in place in the rest of the country, they are characterized by different, complicated and, at times conflicting, administrative and legal regimes. They are administratively divided into regions called the 'Political Agencies' and the 'Frontier Regions' – these constitute what are collectively referred to as the 'Federally Administered Tribal Areas' ('FATA'); as well as the separately governed 'Provincially Administered Tribal Areas' ('PATA').[8] With a turbulent history shaped by the 'Great Game' in the nineteenth century; appeasement-driven administrative arrangements under British India to quell regular rebellions of local tribesmen; the location of some autonomous princely states of

8 See Kakakhel, *Integration of Fata Into NWFP: An Analysis*, 2010. The seven Political Agencies (also referred to as 'Tribal Agencies') constituting FATA are Bajaur, Mohmand, Khyber, Orakzai, Kurram, North Waziristan and South Waziristan. The Frontier Regions are FR Peshawar, FR Kohat, FR Bannu, FR Lakki Marwat, FR Dera Ismail Khan and FR Tank. See Kakakhel, *Integration of Fata*. PATA areas, on the other hand, are situated both in the provinces of Khyber Pakhtunkhwa (KP) and Baluchistan. The KP PATA areas are the former princely states and now districts of KP, which are: Chitral District (former Chitral State), Dir District (Upper Dir and Lower Dir, former Dir state), and Swat District (former Swat State including Kalam), as well as the Tribal Area in Kohistan District, the Malakand District, the Tribal Area adjoining Mansehra District (Battagram, Allai and Black Mountain of Hazara, Upper Tanawalormer) and the former Amb state. The Baluchistan PATA areas are: Zhob District, Loralai District (excluding the Duki Tehsil), Dalbandin Tehsil of Chagai District, Kohlu District (former Marri Tribal Territory in Sibi District), and Dera Bugti District (former Bugti Tribal Territory in Sibi District).

British India that retained their special status under treaty arrangements with the newly independent Pakistan; and, continuation of various colonial legal and administrative frameworks and policies of governance into the post-colonial era, this Pakistani region is unique in many ways. Largely tribal in nature and fiercely independent in parts, it is neither governed under Pakistan's mainstream legal and administrative frameworks nor subject to its regular formal justice system except for limited regions referred to as the 'Settled Areas.' Its development indicators, political evolution and socio-economic progress have consistently lagged behind the rest of the country. This is primarily because of tribal resistance to modernization and change; denuded citizenship rights under the Pakistani Constitution; lack of presence of and ownership by Pakistani political parties; international geo-political agendas and their turf management and financing of different local warring factions; and the consequent tumultuous history as well as uncertain present of this area. It, therefore, comes as no surprise that large sections of this area are currently in the international headlines for Taliban militancy; operations by the Pakistani military to overcome sedition and general lawlessness; relentless U.S. drone attacks; a heightened state of conflict between the State and various outlawed militant and terrorist groups, and recurrent violence and blood-feuds amongst many of its local political, ethnic, sectarian and tribal factions.

Geographically, FATA borders on its north and east with what was formerly known as the North West Frontier Province (NWFP) of the British Empire (now known as Khyber-Pukhtunkhwa' or 'KP'), which shares FATA's conflict ridden history due to the resistance of its inhabitants against British imperialism and its strategic use in the 'Great Game' as well as its cardinal transitory location during the various Anglo-Afghan Wars. FATA is bordered on its west by the highly unstable and perpetually war torn Afghanistan, and to its south by the Pakistani province of Baluchistan which is currently confronting a local insurgency as well as Taliban fuelled violence. The areas constituting PATA, on the other hand, are situated in the provinces of KP and Baluchistan.

FATA itself is an area of great diversity in terms of its administrative arrangements, land revenue regimes and legal systems.[9] The 'Political

9 See Kakakhel, *Integration of Fata,* p. 3. The 'Political Agencies' of the 'Tribal Areas' comprising FATA have not been subjected to land revenue settlement (except in Kurram valley of Kurram Agency), or to the regular system of

Agencies' under FATA continue to operate under the original colonial governance system introduced in the area through a treaty signed soon after Pakistan's independence in 1947. The treaty allowed the tribal elders or *'Maliks'* representing these areas to retain the same administrative arrangements as well as privileges as they enjoyed under the British Raj. As a result, FATA has had a special status under all Pakistani Constitutions so that ordinary Pakistani laws are not applicable there. These areas fall outside the jurisdiction of the Pakistani appellate courts; and their special legislative and legal arrangements are governed by distinctly separate sections of the Constitution.[10] The same holds true for their budgetary arrangements and overall administration.[11] The local system of justice is actually a hybrid of colonial regulations, tribal laws and piecemeal Pakistani legislation.[12]

---

administration of the 'Settled' districts of the KP province. The 'Frontier Regions' are smaller areas between the 'Political Agencies' and are administered by the District Coordination Officers of the Government of KP, with powers of the Political Agent for the area. In the 'Settled' Districts, land settlement has been carried out under the Land Revenue Act, 1878. Regular administration is conducted through an extension of normal laws and standard institutions such as the judiciary, magistracy, police and general administration. Id.

10 See Kakakhel, *Integration of Fata*, p. 4. Articles 246 and 247 of the Constitution of the Islamic Republic of Pakistan 1973 ('Constitution') provide the framework of the relationship between FATA and the Federal Government. The President of Pakistan is the Chief Executive of FATA and administers it through the Governor of KP as his agent. No act of Pakistani parliament can be enforced in FATA unless specially directed by the President. The President can make any regulation for the good governance of FATA. The jurisdictions of the Supreme Court and the High Courts have been barred in FATA. The President has the power to end the classification of FATA over any area provided he ascertains the views of the tribe through a *jirga*. FATA is represented in the National Assembly and the Senate by twelve and eight members, respectively, but has no representation in the KP Provincial Assembly. The Parliament is explicitly barred from legislating for FATA and related matters. So while parliamentarians from FATA can participate in legislation for the whole country they cannot legislate for FATA. See Kakakhel, *Integration of Fata*, pp. 5-6. For an overview of the political administration of FATA, see the official website http://www.fata.gov.pk/ index. php/link?33.

11 The Federal Government provides the development and non-development budgets for FATA. Since 2002, a separate FATA Secretariat handles its affairs and reports to the Chief Secretary of KP.

12 The 'Political Agents' are the chief administrators in the Political Agencies and wield judicial and police powers in their areas, deriving their authority from the Frontier Crimes Regulation 1901(the 'FCR') which is based upon the principle of

The Frontier Crimes Regulation 1901 ('FCR') enshrines and perpetuates the colonial model of crime control for the tribal areas that constitute FATA in Pakistan.[13] While seeking to both attract indigenous acceptance and justify itself on the basis of the particular socio-political context of the tribal areas, it co-opted certain features of local criminal dispute resolution such as the extended jury system implicit in the *jirgas*. However, beneath this socially-sensitive guise, the FCR was a blatant example of the colonial discipline and punishment regime that introduced highly intrusive modes of societal monitoring and surveillance and patently coercive mechanisms for control and punishment.

Two striking features characterize the FCR. First, the FCR introduced a framework for crime prevention and criminal adjudication that was distinct from and outside the ordinary administrative, policing and court system of British India. While ousting the jurisdiction of ordinary civil and criminal courts and the concomitant imperatives of due process enshrined in the procedural laws of the territory, it relied on the combined operation of colonial 'Political Agents,' deputy commissioners, district magistrates and tribal 'Councils of Elders' (*jirgas*). However, unlike the organic modes and indigenous mechanisms for the formation and operation of the traditional *jirgas*, the 'Councils of Elders' visualized under the FCR were purely the creatures of the regulation – their members

collective territorial responsibility for the tribesmen. The 'Political Agent' exercises his authority through tribal elders or *'Maliks'* and their tribal councils or *'jirgas'* which act as a jury in disputes of all kinds. The *Maliks* also assist the 'Political Agents' in matters of security and law and order and are paid an allowance by the 'Political Agents' for this purpose. Policing is performed by tribal levies (supplementary police drawn from the tribes. They are lightly armed, wear uniform and receive some basic training) and *Khasadars* (tribal police who patrol FATA and perform multifarious duties under the political administration. They are armed and wear no uniform). Since independence, the Pakistani government has administered only a small portion of Tribal Areas (confined to roads, schools, hospitals, residences and security buildings) and the rest of the area has been managed by the tribes themselves under their *'riwaj'* or local customs and traditions. See Murtaza, *USAID Court Efficiency Assessment Final Report*, 2010.

13 See *The Frontier Crimes Regulation 1901* (Regulation No. III of 1901), available at http://www.google.com.pk/url?sa=t&rct=j&q=the%20frontier%20crimes%20regulation&source=web&cd=2&ved=0CFAQFjAB&url=http%3A%2F%2Fwww.pakistansocietyofcriminology.com%2Flaws%2FTHEFRONTIERCRIMESREGULATION1901.doc&ei=kQL4T86DNsPQrQfzzN3QBg&usg=AFQjCNFi4cB01kde39ajZdrs9Gvq5Di_7Q&cad=rja, accessed on 7 July 2012.

were nominated and appointed and they were convened and presided over by the colonial government's administrative officers.[14] The FCR granted the administrative officers the discretion of referring particular civil disputes to the 'Council of Elders' for conducting an inquiry, holding hearings and coming to a finding. These were disputes that the administrators thought were likely to cause a blood-feud or murder, or culpable homicide not amounting to murder, or mischief or a breach of the peace, or in which either or any of the parties belonged to a frontier tribe, and regarding which they were of the view that a settlement through the 'Council of Elders' mechanism would tend to prevent or terminate the consequences anticipated.[15]

Once the 'Council of Elders' reached a finding, the colonial administrative officers were allowed several options apart from decreeing the finding of the 'Council of Elders' (or of not less than three-fourth of the members thereof), such as remanding the case for a further hearing, referring the case to a second 'Council of Elders,' referring the parties to a civil court, or declaring that any further proceedings were not required.[16] At the same time, while any such decree was to be a final settlement of the case and have the same effect as the decree of a civil court of ultimate resort, it could not give effect to a finding or a part of a finding of the 'Council of Elders' which the administrative officer found to be contrary to good conscience or public policy.[17] By precluding the jurisdiction of the ordinary civil courts, this new domain of administrative discretion thus created a parallel system of civil justice for the tribal areas.[18]

While the aforementioned framework encompassed any civil disputes that could potentially lead to crimes, the FCR also empowered the colonial administrative machinery to refer any criminal cases to the 'Council of Elders' where the administration felt that it was, "inexpedient that the question of the guilt or innocence of any person or persons accused of any offence, or of any several persons so accused," should be tried by courts under the Code of Criminal Procedure that was applicable in the rest of India.[19] Once again, the members of the 'Council of Elders' were

---

14 See *The Frontier Crimes Regulation 1901*, §§ 2, 8 (1).
15 See *The Frontier Crimes Regulation 1901*, § 8 (1).
16 See *The Frontier Crimes Regulation 1901*, § 8 (3) (a) (b) (c) (d) and (e).
17 See *The Frontier Crimes Regulation 1901*, § 9.
18 See *The Frontier Crimes Regulation 1901*, § 10.
19 See *The Frontier Crimes Regulation 1901*, § 11.

nominated and appointed by the concerned colonial administrative officer – any objections by the accused to any of the nominees were to considered and decided upon by the said officer in his sole discretion.[20] Upon receiving the findings of the 'Council of Elders,' it was up to the administrative officer to decide whether the question was to be remanded, or referred to a second 'Council of Elders,' or whether the accused was to be acquitted or discharged.[21]

Alternatively, the concerned administrator could convict the accused in accordance with the 'Council of Elders' finding(s) on any matter of fact (or the finding(s) of not less than three-fourths of the members thereof), of any offence of which the facts so found showed him or them to be guilty.[22] In case of conviction, the punishments ranged from fines, whipping, and simple or rigorous imprisonment to transportation.[23] Thus, barring some limits on when a criminal case could be referred to a 'Council of Elders' – in case it was already committed before a regular criminal court – the FCR enshrined a regime that allowed the colonial administration tremendous leeway to divert a wide range of criminal cases from the ordinary court system to one which was exclusively under its direct control. Furthermore, this special regime omitted many of the due process ingredients and requirements that the laws applicable in British India possessed.[24]

The other – and highly notorious – feature of the FCR was the wide-scale coercive powers that it bestowed upon the local colonial administration for controlling, blockading and taming a 'hostile or unfriendly tribe.'[25] These entailed individual and collective punishments such as the seizure of all or any members of such tribes and of all or any property belonging to them; their detention in safe custody; the confiscation of their seized property; debarring the same from all access to British India; and, the prohibition of all or any persons within the limits of British India from all intercourse or communication of any kind whatsoever or of any specified kind or kinds with such tribes or any

20 See *The Frontier Crimes Regulation 1901*, §§ 11 (1) and (2).
21 See *The Frontier Crimes Regulation 1901*, § 11 (3) (a) (b) and (c).
22 See *The Frontier Crimes Regulation 1901*, § 11 (3) (d).
23 See *The Frontier Crimes Regulation 1901*, § 12.
24 See *The Frontier Crimes Regulation 1901*, §§ 14 and 15.
25 See *The Frontier Crimes Regulation 1901*, § 21.

members thereof.[26] In addition, *inter alia*, entire communities could be fined or their remissions of revenue be forfeited upon being declared accessories to a crime for a whole host of acts or omissions or simply because a murder or culpable homicide was committed or attempted in their area.[27] At the same time, in a traditionally gun-bearing society, the FCR introduced a wide array of situations where a gun-bearing local could be found culpable of and punished for being in preparation to commit certain offences.[28] Concurrently, the colonial state also embarked upon certain modes of moral policing of certain acts, such as adultery, fearing their potential for stirring intra or inter-tribe violence.[29]

The FCR also allowed the colonial administration additional and far-reaching preventive powers that augmented its capacity for social engineering and control as well the promotion of its strategic military imperatives. Under the FCR, the colonial administration could prohibit the settlement of new villages, etc.; remove entire villages in the area; prevent the building of or the use of any existing building for public meetings and gatherings; demolish any buildings deemed to be used by criminals; operate local systems of watch and ward; and require entire classes of people to remove themselves from territories under the FCR (these were categorized as dangerous fanatics, those with no ostensible means of subsistence or who could not give a satisfactory account of themselves, those with blood-feuds, and, those involved in quarrels likely to lead to blood-shed); and punish those in breach of these regulations.[30]

Wide powers of inquiry, the availability of private citizen arrest, arrest by the police without any warrants – even allowing the right to cause the death of a person in certain stated situations – vast powers for providing security and conducting surveillance for purposes of prevention of murder, culpable homicide, or the dissemination of sedition, and for ensuring peace and good behavior amongst families or factions that were embroiled in blood-feuds or causes and quarrels likely to lead to blood-feuds through the execution of bonds, as well as a related regime of strict punishments, were additional notable features of the FCR.[31] In this context, the

26 See *The Frontier Crimes Regulation 1901*, § 21 (a) (b) (c) (d) and (e).
27 See *The Frontier Crimes Regulation 1901*, § 22, 23 and 25.
28 See *The Frontier Crimes Regulation 1901*, § 29.
29 See *The Frontier Crimes Regulation 1901*, § 30.
30 See *The Frontier Crimes Regulation 1901*, §§ 31 – 37.
31 See *The Frontier Crimes Regulation 1901*, §§ 38 – 46.

particular model of colonial administration and the special procedures laid down under the FCR ousted the ordinary courts as well as the applicable provisions of the civil and criminal procedure codes applicable in British India.[32] The idea of territorial responsibility and collective punishment was also extended in the form of recovery of fines from the relatives of the person(s) liable.[33] Significantly, the FCR prohibited any appeals from any decision given, decree or sentence passed, order made, or act done, under any of its provisions. Only the concerned colonial administrative officer could call for the record of any proceeding under the regulation and revise any decision, decree, sentence or order given, passed or made therein. He also enjoyed the power to direct the tender of pardon or enhance a sentence as well as additional powers that were reserved for the appellate courts under the ordinary criminal procedure of the country.[34]

Over the years, the FCR has undergone negligible modifications in terms of its geographical reach as well as the operation of its governance frameworks. In essence, it continues to operate unchanged from the colonial era. The ethos of its extant governance arrangements is based on the old colonial principle of pacificatory rule through local tribal leaders and chieftains, and the larger policy of the creation of a semi-independent, semi-lawless buffer between Afghanistan and the more settled areas to its east. It is administered by the Governor of KP as an agent of the President of Pakistan, under the supervision of the Ministry of States and Frontier Regions, and through the Political Agents and various additional lower tiers of administration – who have historically 'maintained the peace' through a combination of bargaining, cash gifts to the *Maliks* or the tribal leaders, and military force.[35] The FCR has come under sustained criticism from various quarters within the country for its violation of internationally accepted due process requirements, its highly differential treatment of the tribal people and their alienation from the rights and protections enshrined in the mainstream Pakistani political and legal system, and the notorious policy of territorial responsibility that attaches culpability to innocent women, children and male relatives or fellow tribal members of the

32 See *The Frontier Crimes Regulation 1901*, § 47 – 55.

33 See *The Frontier Crimes Regulation 1901*, § 56.

34 See *The Frontier Crimes Regulation 1901*, § 48 – 55.

35 See Ahmad, "Towards State-Building in Fata," 2011, at http://dprc.lums.edu.pk/components/com_publications/attachments/8-SSPB-Spring-2011.pdf, accessed on 20 July 2012.

accused.[36] It has been blamed for eroding three fundamental rights of the accused, namely, the right to appeal, the right to legal representation, and the right to present reasoned evidence in ones defense – or, as they are referred to by some, respectively as the rights to appeal, *wakeel*, and *daleel*.[37]

If FATA is complex and its laws discriminatory, PATA does not lag far behind. It is conspicuous for repeated governmental experimentation with different governance systems, ever since the areas therein ceased to be independent states. This shall be discussed in greater detail in the following section.[38] In many ways, the increasing fragmentation and violence in these 'special areas' are a direct function of their denuded constitutional status, maladministration, and unrepresentative governance. This has led to the extension of a clearly lesser sets of rights and remedies for their citizens, as also to much lesser opportunities for political growth and economic development. Continued disenfranchisement of local populations at several levels and governmental dependence on the selected elites as its sole constituency, has invariably led the latter to pander to the whims, demands and expectations of these elites. Paradoxically, such demands would be deemed retrogressive, anti-democratic and intolerable in the rest of the country.

The national debate on whether to fully integrate FATA – and also the semi-integrated PATA – into the rest of Pakistan, in order to extend normal legal and governance arrangements to the same is a highly complex and controversial one, with few clearly stated and rigorously

---

36 See Khan, "Justice Denied," *Newsline*, 6 December 2004, at http://www.newslinemagazine.com/2004/12/justice-denied/, accessed on 8 July 2012; and Rehman, "Dark Justice," *Newsline*, 14 August 2002, at http://www.newslinemagazine.com/2002/08/dark-justice, accessed on 8 July 2012.

37 See Ali, "Frontier crimes regulation: Centuries-old law will take time to reform," *The Express Tribune*, 2 December 2011, at http://tribune.com.pk/story/301002/frontier-crimes-regulation-centuries-old-law-will-take-time-to-reform/, accessed on 12 July 2012). See also Irfan Ghauri, "Political reforms: A century later, some rights for the tribals," *The Express Tribune*, 12 August 2011, at http://tribune.com.pk/story/229954/president-zardari-signs-fata-political-parties-order-2002-extension/, accessed on 12 July 2012.

38 Federal and Provincial laws have no applicability in PATA unless the Governor of the Province extends their operation under Article 247 of the Constitution. See West Pakistan Regulation I of 1969. Provincial Governors are also empowered to issue Regulations for the peace and good government of PATA areas situated in their Province. See PAK CONST. Art 246 (b) (i) and Art 247(3).

argued positions. This is primarily because such debate has been historically suppressed or ignored. The available literature emphasizes that discussing the future of FATA without extensive local engagement and meaningful allaying of local concerns – more particularly those of social development, political reform and economic progress – would be a self-defeating exercise.[39] Any evaluation of the legal and administrative challenges in PATA similarly requires not just a scrutiny of its historical experience with different laws, but also an honest appreciation of the various currents of popular resentment against this experimentation. The following snapshot of the valley of Swat – situated in the Swat District of PATA – and its specific set of historical experiences, legal and administrative regimes, and myriad current challenges, epitomizes in many ways the crisis that besets this entire area.

C. Swat and the Battle for a Different Kind of Justice

> Who, or why, or which, or what, Is the Akond of Swat…
>
> Do his people like him extremely well?
> Or do they, whenever they can, rebel,
> or PLOT,
> At the Akond of Swat?
>
> If he catches them then, either old or young,
> Does he have them chopped in pieces or hung,

39 See for instance, Justice (R) Mian Muhammad Ajmal (Former Judge Supreme Court of Pakistan, Ex-Law Minister, Government of NWFP), *FATA, its Constitutional Status and FCR*, (undated). While discussing various consultations with tribal elders and proposed changes to existing laws and regulations for FATA, the author emphasizes that without concerted efforts towards poverty alleviation, education and development in the region, a transition towards legal and administrative mainstreaming would be very difficult. There are perspectives that more strongly advocate full integration of FATA into Pakistan in order to address the backwardness and militancy in FATA which they attribute to its administrative and legal isolation, but even they stress the need for very careful steps based on extensive discussions and deliberations so as to not alienate the fiercely independent and culturally distinct Pashtuns of the area. See Kakakhel, *Integration of FATA.* A proposed draft of new regulations for FATA has also come into the picture that amends the FCR. See *FATA Regulation 2008* (Amended Frontier Crime Regulation 1901) by Reforms Committee headed by Justice (R) Mian Muhammad Ajmal.

or SHOT,
The Akond of Swat?

Do his people prig in the lanes or park?
Or even at times, when days are dark,
GAROTTE,
The Akond of Swat?

Does he study the wants of his own dominion?
Or doesn't he care for public opinion
a JOT,
The Akond of Swat? ...

(*The Akond of Swat*, Edward Lear, 1812-1888)

...the Akhund of Swat had two sets of progeny. On the one side were his disciples and deputies who collectively assumed the mantle of Sufi leadership. On the other were his own sons and grandsons, known by the title of miangul (flower of the saints), who took over the Akhund's position of political leadership in Swat and also inherited a degree of spiritual authority from him as well.

(*Heroes of the Age: Moral Fault Lines on the Afghan Frontier*, Edward B. Edwards, University of California Press, 1996)

Travelling north from the river fed hot plains, the lush mango groves and the timeless citadel cities of Punjab to the ancient, verdure and commercially vibrant valley of Swat also entails a drastic jump from the mainstream Pakistani legal system to PATA – a distinctively governed area under special laws and regulatory mechanisms.[40] The first half of

40 Although constitutionally part of Pakistan, PATA is subject to a separate system of governance. Article 246 of the Constitution defines the geographical scope of the tribal areas and Article 247 sets out the governance arrangement. Article 246(b) (i) defines PATA areas in KP to include: "The districts of Chitral, Dir and Swat (which includes Kalam) [the Tribal area in Kohistan district] Malakand Protected Area, the Tribal Area adjoining [Mansehra] district and the former State of Amb." Article 247 (1) provides: "... [T]he executive authority of a Province shall extend to the Provincially Administered Tribal Areas therein." Article 247(2) reads: "The President may, from time to time, give such directions to the Governor of a Province relating to the whole or any part of the Tribal Area within the Province as he may deem necessary, and the Governor shall, in the exercise of his functions under this Article, comply with such directions." Article

2009 brought to international attention the increasingly violent events in the valley. It also demonstrated the combustible potential of law reform as a felt issue, as well as a handy slogan for aspirants to political power with no qualms about using brutal force and wanton violence. Swat was historically governed by a local ruler (known as the *Akhunzada* or the *Akhund* of Swat; subsequently the title changed to the *Wali* of Swat). The *Wali* dispensed largely discretionary but affordable and quick justice by employing a tolerant amalgamation of Islamic as well as local customary law.[41] Edward Lear's enigmatic and misspelled 'Akond of Swat' in his nonsense verse with the same title refers to the same person, though perhaps equally enigmatic today to most Pakistanis except those living in Swat.[42] Nostalgia in the valley of Swat, however, for that bygone era when the '*Akond*' dispensed justice, is arguably not just romantic but also symptomatic of growing weariness with its replacement with multiple variations of an amalgam of Pakistani laws, cosmetic Islam and colonial principles of governance. To better understand recent events in Swat, one

---

247(3) provides: "… [N]o Act of [Majlis-e-Shoora (Parliament)] or a Provincial Assembly shall apply to a Provincially Administered Tribal Area, or any part thereof, unless the Governor of the Province in which the Tribal Area is situated, with the approval of the President, so directs; and in giving such direction with respect to any law, … the Governor, may direct that the law shall, in its application to a Tribal Area, or to a specified part thereof, have effect subject to such exceptions and modifications as may be specified in the direction." Furthermore, Article 247(4) provides: "Notwithstanding anything contained in the Constitution … [T]he Governor of a Province, with prior approval of the President, may, with respect to any matter within the legislative competence of the Provincial Assembly make regulations for peace and good government of a Provincially Administered Tribal Area or any part thereof, situated in the Province." Thus, federal and provincial laws have no applicability in PATA unless the Governor of the Province extends their operation under Article 247 of the Constitution. In 2009, the Governor of KP issued the Nizam-e-Adl Regulation.

41 For an interesting nostalgic description of his local justice, see an interview with the last *Wali* of Swat in Lamb, "The Wali of Swat mourns his lost land," *The Sunday Times*, 24 May 2009 at http://www.timesonline.co.uk/ tol/news/world/ asia/article6350519.ece, accessed on 10 January 2012). See also the illuminating memoirs of the last *Wali* of Swat that shed light on important aspects of the political and social history of the valle, in Barth, *The Last Wali of Swat*, 2008.

42 This is not to rule out that Edward Lear was deliberately poking fun at a local Indian ruler whose governance system stood apart from the legal system introduced by India's colonial rulers, making him sound like a comical and semi-mythical creature. It is worthwhile to read the rest of his limerick.

also needs to shift the scrutiny back to the nineteenth century and decipher the reasons for its historical affinity to radical Islamic ideologies and movements.[43]

The outbreak of violence in Swat in 2009 is more of a manifestation of the growing popular disgruntlement with the existing administrative and judicial system. There is less evidence that it denotes a deeper support for the ostensibly growing popularity of the Taliban brand of Islamic governance in certain parts of FATA, KP, and in adjacent Afghanistan. Part of the reason is that the substantive elements of the Taliban brand of Islam remain largely unarticulated and vague. Furthermore, since the Pakistani military operation in Swat in early 2010 to wipe out Taliban networks from the area, reports from the ground largely reveal a guardedly relieved local people. Thus, one has to be persuaded that many of them may have been coerced into subservience to the Taliban's power grabbing and expansionist agendas.[44] Importantly, Taliban exploitation of local class resentments between wealthy landlords and their landless tenants seems to have also played a major role; as have other grievances of the landless class with lack of employment opportunities, inequitable distribution of wealth and resources, and corrupt administration in the valley.[45]

The slogan of choice for the Taliban in Swat was that their brand of Islamic *Sharia* would provide quick and cheap justice, which the system it meant to replace had failed to do. While being reticent about the substantive ethos and facets of this *Sharia*, the Taliban interestingly put a premium on the 'speed' of justice. Before the situation got further out of

---

43 An insightful recent history that, *inter alia*, looks at Swat and surrounding areas and the fusion of jihad with a strand of anti-colonial nationalism is Jalal, *Partisans of Allah: Jihad in South Asia*, 2009. For a review of the famous anthropologist Fredrik Barth's classical works on the political anthropology of Swat and its critiques, see Edwards, "Learning from the Swat Pathans: Political Leadership in Afghanistan, 1978-97," 1998, pp. 712-728.

44 See e.g., the following Pakistani news reports: Yusufzai, "There is life after Taliban but fear lingers," *IPS NEWS,* 14 October 2009, at http://ipsnews .net/news.asp?idnews=48856; http://www.thenews.com.pk/edito rial_detail.asp ?id=190048, accessed on 10 July 2010; and Ayesha Ijaz Khan, "Clearing Misconceptions on Pakistan's War in Swat," 4 June 2009, at http://www.coun terpunch.org/khan06042009.html, accessed on 13 July 2012.

45 See Perlez and Shah, "Taliban Exploit Class Rifts," *The New York Times*, 16 April 2009, at http://www.nytimes.com/2009/04/17/ world/asia/17pstan.html, accessed on 13 July 2012.

hand and a military operation was ultimately unleashed in Swat, the battle lines were largely drawn around the structure and contours of a governmental proposal for legal and judicial reform – the *Nizam-e-Adl Regulation*, 2009 ('NAR').[46] They have persisted even after the insurgency was militarily defeated. The NAR was not a unique piece of legislation and, in many ways, drew upon earlier ineffective regulatory formulae for the region.[47] Once again motivated by immediate imperatives of appeasement rather than genuine reform, the government hastily generated this controversial law in order to placate the Swati public and their largely self-appointed Taliban spokespersons. Its underlying assumptions were that the Taliban led insurgency was essentially galvanized by two underlying grievances – that the existing legal regime in the area was both painfully slow as well as insufficiently Islamic. The NAR was put forward as the model of a quicker and more Islamic legal framework, and as a practical demonstration of the State's sensitivity to the sentiments of the Swatis who supported the Taliban uprising.

The timing was crucial as the Swat Taliban were more or less besieging the valley, blatantly running a parallel government, and committing human rights atrocities.[48] However, the government came under severe

46 See the contents of the *Shariah Nizam-e-Adl [Islamic Justice System] Regulation, 2009* ('NAR') at http://www.dailytimes.com.pk/default.asp?page=2009% 5C04% 5C15%5Cstory_15-4-2009_pg7_51, accessed on July 14, 2012. The legislative initiative, which literally means "system of justice" was proclaimed by the Pakistani government as an endeavor to bring peace to the region, and to also address local demands for making justice delivery more expeditious. See also the report from the Pakistani daily *The News International* at http://www.the news.com.pk/top_story_detail.asp?Id=20372, accessed on 10 July 2010.

47 The NAR is the latest of a series of justice system regulations issued for this area since 1975. It is evident that local pressures for introduction of a more Islamic law have influenced some of this legislation, though in all instances the Islamization is solely reflected in the official nomenclature rather than in any distinctively Islamic features of the law. These Regulations, in their order of issuance, are provided below:

(a) The PATA Criminal Law (Special Provisions) Regulation, 1975 and the PATA Civil Procedure (Special Provisions) Regulation, 1975;
(b) The Provincially Administered Tribal Areas (Nifaz-e-Nizam-e-Shariah) Regulation, 1994;
(c) The Shariah Nizam-e-Adl Regulation, 1999; and
(d) The Shariah Nizam-e-Adl Regulation, 2009 (the 'NAR).

48 The possibility of armistice with the Taliban through the NAR was hailed by the Pakistani government as a step welcomed by the Swati locals, weary of Taliban

criticism from international governments and media; as well as local political parties, media, civil society, and human rights groups for what they considered its capitulation to Taliban blackmail. They feared that an accord in the form of the NAR would be nothing short of an encouragement for the spillover of narrowly envisioned, harsh and repressive Taliban style Islam; and that it would exacerbate militancy and coercion in other parts of the country, leading to the creation of additional states within the State.[49]

As it turned out, the government's strategy to implement the NAR to forge an armistice with the Taliban failed.[50] This was largely due to two

---

presence and strong arm tactics, as well as wary of the cost of yet another military operation in the area in case a peace accord failed. See http://www.newspakistan.net/swat-peace-accord-welcomed-by-all-and-sundry-minister-009-26-02.php, accessed on 9 July 2010); and Khan, "The Return of Shari'a Law to Pakistan's Swat Region," 3 March 2009, at http://www.jamestown.org/single/?no_cache=1&tx_ttnews%5Btt_news%5D=34576&tx_ttnews%5BbackPid%5D=7&cHash=081b812552, accessed on 13 July 2012).

49 For an overview of both sides of the debate see the report "Grey Area in Nizam-i-Adl Regulations," *The Daily Dawn*, Pakistan, at http://www.dawn.com/wps/wcm/connect/dawn-content-library/dawn/news/pakistan/nwfp/grey-areas-in-nizam-i-adl-regulation-hs, accessed on 1August 2010). See also an overview of the critique of the NAR in *The News International*, Pakistan at http://www.thenews.com.pk/editorial_detail.asp?id=173260, accessed on 3 August 2010.

50 Once the possibilities of an accord based on the NAR failed and a military operation was launched to flush out the Taliban from Swat, the Pakistani media then went on to criticize the government for the crisis of internally displaced persons from Swat due to the military operation. See Amin, "Taliban big fish still alive – Swat IDPs question operation," *The Daily Times*, 4 June 2009, at http://www.dailytimes.com.pk/default.asp?page=2009%5C06%5C04%5Cstory_4-6-2009_pg7_26, accessed on 13 July 2012; and, Waseem Ahmad Shah, "Swat IDPs skeptical of return plan," *The Daily Dawn*, 2009, at http://archives.dawn.com/archives/15067, accessed on 13 July 2012. However, the Pakistani government as well as supportive sections of international media, maintained that an important shift in the political and popular mood had occurred in Pakistan in favor of the military operation due to blatant violation of the terms of the Swat peace accord by the Taliban. See Carlotta Gall, "Pakistan Army Poised for New Push into Swat," *The New York Times*, 5 May 2009, at http://www.nytimes.com/2009/05/06/world/asia/06pstan.html, accessed on 14 July 2012, as well as the report, "Gilani urges national consensus as APC convenes," *The Daily Dawn*, 2009, [hereinafter *Pakistan Army Poised for New Push into Swat*] at http://www.dawn.com/wps/wcm/connect/dawn-content-library/dawn/news/pakistan/16-gilani-urges-national-consensus-as-apc-convenes-hs-16, accessed on 15 July 2010.

fatal miscalculations on part of the Taliban. Unhappy that the key to controlling the legal and judicial system in Swat, i.e. the power of appointment of *'Qazis'* (judges), was not conceded to them under the NAR (which I shall shortly discuss), the Taliban publicly lambasted the government for bad faith and rejected the government legislation out of hand. However, simultaneously, they also exposed their own lack of commitment to bringing about a cessation of on-going violence. Unwilling to lay down arms (and to relinquish their effective rallying cry for a 'better' system of justice) as required by the armistice, they decided instead to test the waters for popular support for belligerence. Aggressive forays into surrounding areas followed, while the government's guns were temporarily averted.[51] The Pakistani government effectively used these two episodes to build public and political party support for sending in the army which eventually stamped out the rebellion.[52] The question remained, however, as to what would happen to the NAR.

A close examination of the design and details of the NAR is important, particularly as a specimen of how the Pakistani governments have traditionally responded to PATA's aspirations for reform in particular and to the aspirations of Pakistani citizens for a more efficient and equitable justice system in general. At one level, one can argue that the NAR addressed the Taliban's Islamic aspirations in a rather facile manner. For instance, the NAR essentially substituted the English titles of existing courts and law officers with more 'Islamic' sounding Arabic substitutes. In terms of applicable nomenclature, judges were transformed overnight into *'Qazis'* with no real change in their roles and responsibilities. Importantly, the actual brand of Islamic law to be applied by them in Swat and the rest of PATA was the one already defined, prescribed and anointed by the State. Furthermore, the *Qazis* were to be appointed by the government; their appointment qualifications were to be benchmarked by the State's standards and evaluated by its institutions; and their application and interpretations of *Sharia* law were to be consistent with the

51 See Yusuf, "Pakistani Taliban expand influence beyond Swat," *The Christian Science Monitor*, 15 April 2009, at http://www.csmonitor.com/2009/0415/p06s13-wosc.html, accessed on 5 August 2010; and Perlez, "Taliban Seize Vital Pakistan Area close to the Capital," *The New York Times*, 22 April 2009, at http://www.nytimes.com/2009/04/23/world/asia/23buner.html, accessed on 14 July 2012.

52 See *Pakistan Army Poised for New Push into Swat.*

methodology and interpretations already used by Pakistani judges. One can thus argue that the NAR did nothing to change the status quo, and in fact staunchly preserved the existing understandings of and mechanisms for applying *Sharia* law in the rest of the country.

Alternatively, one can argue that the NAR cleverly mitigated Taliban attempts to impose their hegemony under the guise of their brand of Islamic law, while genuinely attempting to address popular demands for a better legal and judicial system. According to this point of view, the real promise of the NAR, and a more concrete realization of the official commitment to the promised 'speed' of justice, lay not in the Islamic-sounding titles of judges, etc., but in the NAR's attempt to streamline and expedite disposal of legal cases.[53] According to this line of argument, delay reduction and better accessibility were thus the real hidden fruits in the promised basket, and not any substantively different laws. The official

---

53 The NAR sets out certain quantitative performance standards and enhances the mechanisms for judicial accountability of district court judges. The NAR put upper limits of six and four months each for the adjudication of such cases, and introduced certain measures for monitoring and penalizing court delays, in order to introduce greater efficiency to legal proceedings that typically last for years rather than months. Under the NAR, judicial officers/Qazis and Executive Magistrates must report the cause and reasons for any delay beyond the NAR prescribed periods to the District Judge/Zilla Qazi or the District Magistrate, or the presiding officer of the principal seat of Dar-ul-Qaza (High Court) who may, then, issue suitable directions. Furthermore, if the presiding officer of a court comes to the opinion that delaying tactics are being used, he may impose a cost on the recalcitrant party. If, on the other hand, the Qazi or the Executive Magistrate is found to be at fault, the relevant presiding officer may issue a 'letter of displeasure' that may lead to an adverse entry in the service record of the judicial officer. The presiding officer may also recommend disciplinary action for the latter. The NAR also mandates that no adjournment can be granted in a case unless the court is satisfied that the adjournment is unavoidable and is subject to costs. The restriction on adjournments is meant to ensure that the Judge/Qazi has more effective control over the pace of legal proceedings in court. The NAR also allows flexibility to the judges in the application of civil and criminal procedure in order to ensure expeditious decision in cases. Further, the NAR links the decision of allocation of a higher number of judges in a court with the level of case pendency in that court, 'to ensure expeditious dispensation of justice within the prescribed time schedule.' The provision of a consensual out of court settlement mechanism and additional mechanisms to discipline and galvanize police performance in the registration and investigation of criminal cases were also positives. Finally, a formal directive to introduce the option of conducting court proceedings in the local languages Pashto and Urdu, as well as in English, was an additional step towards making courts accessible to laypersons.

understanding of the Swat crisis thus held that public disillusionment with the existing legal system actually lay at the access and operational levels rather than in the Swatis looking upon the existing system as 'un-Islamic' in any way.

There is a third perspective as well. This perspective holds that the NAR not only duped the Taliban, but not unlike its many ineffectual predecessors, it duped ordinary Swatis as well. One justification for this view is that since the army operation there is little evidence that the NAR is being implemented.[54] The other justification is that hasty and purely efficiency oriented as it was, the NAR epitomizes the quick fixes of the past. It is not based on any serious engagement with the real underlying substantive justice issues faced by the citizens, and ignores the various vulnerabilities that debilitate vast sections of them. That the fundamental underlying dissatisfaction with the existing legal system may not be solely caused by delays in courts, but by the overall regime of rights and obligations that this system embraces and protects, was not even cursorily broached. Consequently, it did not contemplate any deeper and wider reforms. This highly flawed approach also permeates justice sector reform in the rest of the country. While a textual review of the NAR reveals the afore-discussed fundamental issues as well as the varying perspectives as to its achievements or failures, the following supplements NAR's textual review with some essential fact-finding on the ground. As it turns out, this fact-finding greatly bolsters the third perspective that has been discussed in this section.

D. A View From the Field – Detailed Feedback From Swat

To refer to the NAR as old wine in new bottles may sound rather bizarre since the topic of discussion is an Islamic law. But the metaphor still works. The author had the opportunity to visit Swat in 2010, soon after the Taliban insurgency had been more or less routed, though the area was still racked by sporadic violence. The visit offered a first-hand opportunity to observe the operation of the NAR in the post-insurgency era. Interviews

54 Detailed conversations with the Districts & Sessions Judge, Swat and additional judicial officers from the area in June and July 2010 revealed that the implementation of the NAR is piecemeal and less than satisfactory even a year after the end of the military operation in Swat.

with the judiciary operating in Swat at the time reveal the widely held perception that, as before, the legislative and administrative solution to the popular angst is a highly facile one.

As mentioned earlier, the NAR essentially comprises of a new set of court rules and procedural relaxations to expedite the time taken for decisions in civil and criminal cases, as well as certain penalties and accountability mechanisms for penalizing delay. It has nothing to do with *Sharia* other than in name.[55] As before, the judges appointed to function in Swat and elsewhere in the Malakand Division in the post-NAR era, belong to the provincial district judiciary – they merely have new 'Islamic sounding' Arabic titles.[56] Perceiving long delays in the adjudication and decision of cases under the preceding system to be the main political challenge for maintaining the writ of the State, immediate steps for delay reduction have, therefore, been the main focus of law reform in the area. Apart from introducing the NAR, at the time of writing, the Peshawar High Court had sent several additional judges to the area (mostly new appointees) in order to boost the capacity of the local judiciary to tackle the case backlogs.[57] The administrative decision-makers interviewed in

55 A typical reaction to the NAR from western observers at the time is embodied in the following evaluation: "Like other peace deals between the military and the militants in FATA, this accord, subsequently endorsed by Islamabad and Peshawar in April 2009, made major concessions to religious extremists." International Crisis Group, *Pakistan: The Worsening IDP Crisis*, Asia Briefing No. 111, 16 September 2010, p. 12, at http://issuu.com/crisisgroup/docs/196_reforming_pakistans_criminal_justice_system, accessed on 13 July 2012. There is however little evidence put forward to substantiate this assertion.

56 For instance, see the new designations of district court judges in District Swat as well as in the rest of the areas in which the NAR has come into play. See *Shariah Nizam-e-Adl [Islamic Justice System] Regulation, 2009.*

Former office/designation	**New Islamic office/designation**
Civil Judge/Judicial Magistrate	Illaqa Qazi
Senior Civil Judge	Aala Illaqa Qazi
Additional District/Sessions Judge	Izafi Zilla Qazi
District and Sessions Judge	Zilla Qazi

57 Interview with Syed Mussaddiq Hussain Gilani, Registrar Peshawar High Court, dated 30 June, 2010. According to him, "Give me an endless supply of judges in any part of Pakistan, and the case backlog will go away. However, obviously that cannot happen due to budgetary constraints. In the case of Malakand, we sent

the Peshawar High Court were quite happy with what they described as a positive public reaction to the NAR and a tangible resulting decrease in case pendency.[58] Whether this euphoria was sustainable and shared by the judicial officers functioning on the ground in the area required an evaluation of the actual situation in the district courts, which now follows.

The Swat district court complex is in an adequately operational condition, though cramped and overcrowded like other district courts in the country. However, at the time of writing, the court infrastructure in the rest of the district had undergone serious damage due to the clash between the Taliban and the Pakistan Army.[59] As opposed to the administrative spokespersons at the Peshawar High Court, the responses from the district judiciary in Swat about the impact of the NAR were considerably mixed and at times far less enthusiastic. The District & Sessions Court Judge, Swat, who is the administrative head for the district judiciary, for one, agreed with the decision-makers in the Peshawar High Court that the introduction of the NAR timelines for deciding civil and criminal cases, as well as the supply of additional judges from the Peshawar High Court, had shortened case proceedings and accelerated case disposals.[60] However, he admitted that the continuing lack of facilities and infrastructure constraints posed many impediments to the smooth functioning of the courts.[61] He

---

extra judges from other parts of the province and as a result the case backlog has come down." However, he agreed that this was obviously unsustainable and that the real test of the NAR would come when these extra judges were withdrawn. In his view, the local people had thus far reacted very positively to the NAR as it had effectively addressed the bottlenecks in the previous system.

58 Interview with Syed Mussaddiq Hussain Gilani, Registrar Peshawar High Court, dated 30 June, 2010.

59 For instance, at the time of writing, the Tehsil Court Complex in Matta Tehsil, which saw a lot of action between the Taliban and the Army, was badly affected and still unsafe for conducting everyday work, or for that matter even a visit. Hence the presiding officer of that court was actually interviewed in Saidu Sharif – the more secure, army protected capital city of Swat. Interview with Mr. Sajid Khan Additional District Judge, Matta, dated 8 July 2010.

60 Interview with District and Sessions Judge, Swat, dated 7 July 2010. According to the judge there were forty seven judicial officers serving in District Swat at the time of the interview.

61 Interview with District and Sessions Judge, Swat, dated 7 July 2010. Apart from the judges, various members of the court staff were also interviewed who said that the district judiciary continuously faced the problems of poor facilities, inadequate infrastructure, lack of opportunities for training, weak performance incentives etc., – and yet there had been no improvement in these domains

was of the view that the NAR had furnished the judges with a real power to resist delaying tactics by the lawyers. At the same time, he was also critical of the NAR as he felt that it had been introduced in a great hurry – the rushed introduction not only meant that the NAR had several lacunae and ambiguities, but also that it once again enshrined a 'special' legal regime for Swat and the rest of PATA. This, he said, was in violation of earlier judgments of the Supreme Court of Pakistan that had paved the way for mainstreaming the law in PATA in order to bring it at par with the rest of the country.[62] While he praised the initial dent made by the NAR on delaying tactics and case backlog, he was very cautious in taking a position on the prospect of a sustainable positive impact.[63] The NAR, he stated, was essentially a set of broad guidelines and instructions that

---

despite the rhetoric at the top in the wake of the Taliban uprising in Swat and also the various international donor driven justice sector reform programs. Interviews were conducted with two Reader Assistants, a Stenographer and two Public Prosecutors.

62 Interview with District and Sessions Judge, Swat, dated 7 July 2010. His main criticism was that the earlier system of district magistracy continued its autonomous operation in PATA whereby certain kinds of cases were decided by the district magistrates under local and special laws, despite the fact that such adjudicative powers had been taken away from the district magistracy elsewhere in the country and assigned instead to the judiciary. The latter, he said, reflected the government's decision to abide by several Supreme Court judgments that had mandated a complete separation of powers between the executive and the judiciary. Interview with District and Sessions Judge, Swat, dated 7 July 2010. This theme is an area of constant attrition between the judiciary and the district magistracy and hence the District & Sessions Judge's comments were not unsurprising as they stemmed from a certain entrenched institutional position on the debate.

63 Interview with District and Sessions Judge, Swat, dated 7 July 2010. The other main challenges faced by the district judiciary, according to the District and Sessions Judge, were budgetary constraints, the slow and cumbersome process of the release of funds by the High Courts to the District Courts, poor infrastructure and inadequate training opportunities for judges, especially for training abroad. As far as the training of court staff was concerned, the District and Sessions Judge thought that given the many other more serious challenges faced by the district judiciary, the decision of the justice sector reform donors to focus on the training of court staff was a naïve 'welfare state idea.' As to a contemporaneous USAID initiative for court process reforms for efficient case disposal through the introduction of better management techniques, he was not at all enthused. His view was that more effective case disposal was ultimately a function of personal commitment, dedication and of being God fearing. Interview with District and Sessions Judge, Swat, dated 7 July 2010.

allowed the judges the discretion to collapse the civil and criminal procedure in order to fit it into the tight new timeframes mandated under the NAR.[64] This, however, was not always possible or fair according to him, as the courts often came across complex cases that required additional time for fact-finding, evaluation of evidence, hearing all the pertinent parties, and just decision-making.[65]

The District and Sessions Judge was also explicit in declaring that the NAR was Islamic in name only and that it was no more or less Islamic than the laws in the rest of Pakistan.[66] It also emerged during the course of the conversation that the framework provided by the NAR for appeals from local district court decisions, i.e. essentially appeals to specified benches of the High Court and the Supreme Court (referred to in the NAR by new Arabic names – the *'Dar-ul-Qaza'* and *'Dar-ul-Dar-ul-Qaza'*) was as yet not in place.[67] Furthermore, the District and Sessions Judge candidly conceded that though the constant pressure from the judicial leadership to clear the backlog of cases had resulted in the district judges having 'disposed of' many of the cases before them, they had mostly not

64 Interview with District and Sessions Judge, Swat, dated 7 July 2010. According to him, though the standard civil and criminal procedure code of the country were still in place in Swat and other areas comprising PATA, the NAR had brought about a situation whereby the various steps and timelines therein were no longer binding. An additional tension, according to him, was between officially putting forward the NAR as based on *Sharia* and its specific time-lines for deciding cases. The *Sharia*, he said, provided no timelines for deciding cases but essentially furnished the method for making laws. Interview with District and Sessions Judge, Swat, dated 7 July 2010.

65 Interview with District and Sessions Judge, Swat, dated 7 July 2010.

66 Interview with District and Sessions Judge, Swat, dated 7 July 2010. The interviewed judge had received relatively extensive training in *Sharia* law, having undertaken the Dars-e-Nizami (a traditional course in Islamic jurisprudence) and having also attended short *Sharia* courses at the Federal Judicial Academy and at the Al Azhar University in Cairo. The interviewee was very uncomfortable with the categorization of the NAR as Islamic as opposed to the laws in the rest of the country and felt that neither were in violation of the *Sharia* and hence particularly different on the litmus test of Islamic/non-Islamic. He was firmly of the view that the NAR was titled as such purely because of political reasons in order to diffuse the Taliban militancy, which had been triggered due to successive years of bad governance in the area, as well as the government's strategic and political use of various radical elements in the past. Interview with District and Sessions Judge, Swat, dated 7 July 2010.

67 Interview with District and Sessions Judge, Swat, dated 7 July 2010.

yet written down the actual judgments.[68] He admitted that it was only when these judgments were written and became public; when they were accepted or appealed against; and, if appealed against, when the appeals were either upheld or struck down by the appellate courts, that the effectiveness of and the level of public satisfaction with the NAR's expedited case disposal regime would truly come to light.

The main operational shortcoming of the NAR, as stressed by many of the interviewed district judges, is that it does not exactly prescribe how the district judiciary in PATA is expected to collapse the complex and elaborate civil and criminal procedures in order to fit them into the tight confines of the NAR mandated case disposal deadlines. There was, as almost always, no deep and participatory engagement leading to the promulgation of the NAR in order to pursue efficiency without jeopardizing the various well-known imperatives of due process and natural justice, including, *inter alia*, adequate opportunities for the contesting parties to meaningfully plead their cases and for the judges to undertake a proper evaluation of facts and evidence.[69] The NAR is simply silent on how an optimal balance is to be struck between speed and due process. As a consequence, it leaves tremendous discretion to the judges and thereby increases the possibility of inconsistency of court practice as well as flawed trials.[70] This in turn can invariably lead to escalating

68 Interview with District and Sessions Judge, Swat, dated 7 July 2010.

69 This point was strongly emphasized in the interview with Mr. M. Asim Imam, Anti-Terrorist Court Judge, Swat, dated 6 July 2010; in the interview with District and Sessions Judge, Swat, dated 7 July 2010; and, the interview with Mr. Sajid Khan Additional District Judge, Matta, dated 8 July 2010.

70 On being probed, the interviewed judges spoke at length about the many problems triggered by the NAR's short timeframes for deciding civil and criminal cases. These included, *inter alia*, the problems of ensuring the availability of relevant witnesses and adequately recording evidence; the excessive focus on case disposals contributing to the growing gap between 'disposed' cases and actual 'decided' cases in view of written judgments; and, growing complaints from lawyers and even some litigants about their dissatisfaction with the excessively rushed pace of court proceedings. The interviewed judges were of the view that much greater legislative attention was required in order to revisit the legal problems of the people in Swat and the rest of Malakand. The mere collapsing of the procedural law or mandating broad and informal practice directions was simply not enough. They also suggested various areas that required concrete procedural law reform such as the introduction of additional formal disclosure requirements at early stages in the trial in order to weed out frivolous litigation. Interview with Mr. M. Asim Imam, Anti-Terrorist

appeals (and hence further delay) and also additional burdens for the higher courts – as well as for the district courts if the appellate courts decide to remand the cases back to them.[71]

The NAR is thus a good example of typically hasty legislation that aims to superficially (and one would venture to add, temporarily) address certain immediate and politically cumbersome symptoms of an inefficient and overworked judicial system. Since it sidestepped any serious engagement with PATA's historical experience with similar *ad hoc* laws; its rapidly changing context that divulges deep-seated popular resentment against various aspects of the operation of the legal system; and, the valuable feedback from the actual operators of the district court system as to the nature of problems that characterize the legal and court system, the NAR essentially offers the mere facade of reform instead of a real solution. It is a façade that is constituted of some Islamic rhetoric and a set of blunderbuss directives introducing some broad deadlines and targets. One may be persuaded to concede that the NAR's attempt to rationalize a cumbersome and delay-inducing procedure and to give more teeth to the courts in order to deter delaying tactics, are generic steps in the right direction. However, on available evidence, there has been no rigorous engagement with these reform themes – this in turn is likely to spawn a whole host of issues, which the interviewed judges warned about.[72]

Court Judge, Swat, dated 6 July 2010; interview with the District and Sessions Judge, Swat, dated 7 July 2010; and, interview with Mr. Sajid Khan Additional District Judge, Matta, dated 8 July 2010.

71 Interview with Mr. M. Asim Imam, Anti-Terrorist Court Judge, Swat, dated 6 July 2010; interview with the District and Sessions Judge, Swat, dated 7 July 2010; and, interview with Mr. Sajid Khan Additional District Judge, Matta, dated 8 July 2010.

72 For instance, the NAR is blind to the relative nature and complexity of the different kinds of cases before the district courts and endeavors to mechanically fit all of them within the tight timeframes provided by it, instead of being cognizant that delay reduction for different types of cases may require multiple case tracks with independent requirements and mandates. There also seems to be no recognition of the particular kind of litigation that takes place in Swat. This vital contextual dimension should ideally inform any special reform prescriptions meant to address immediate violent dissatisfaction, especially since the vehicle for reform can be *ad hoc* and more expeditiously context-specific. A review of the Swat district court data and interviews with the court staff revealed that in terms of civil cases, almost seventy per cent of the cases before the courts were land disputes. Whereas in the criminal domain, around forty per cent of the cases pertained to sexual offences, while the remaining were murder cases (once again

The most candidly critical and contextually nuanced assessment of the NAR came from the person arguably conducting one of the most dangerous jobs in Swat, if not the country, i.e. the Anti-Terrorist Court Judge for the entire Malakand Division.[73] A pleasant, soft-spoken man, he candidly mentioned that ever since his posting to Swat, his traumatized young son – who with the rest of his family lived in Peshawar – had taken to sleeping with a plastic toy gun under his pillow. The Judge's assessment laid bare the inadequacies of the government's reform engagement with the on-going political and legal challenges in PATA. Especially keeping in mind that the NAR was introduced in the wake of a very violent reaction to the prevalent legal system, in his view, various critical areas of reform starkly stood out for their omission. For instance, the Judge confirmed that there were two army detention centers operating in the district, where the ordinary criminal laws applicable in the area had no penetration. Not only was it legally unclear as to under what law the detainees had been arrested and detained – though a legal cover could be constructed owing to the extraordinary circumstances in the area and the consequent special ambit of the government approved army action – importantly, there were no mechanisms in place for handing over these detainees to the police and formally bringing them to a criminal trial. The *status-quo*, in his view, posed serious risks to the sustainability of peace and the public confidence in the criminal justice system.[74]

---

the majority of these stemming from long-standing land disputes). However, there has been no attempt in the NAR or thereafter to focus on these specific areas of constant attrition and contestation, and particularly the local land law regime. See interview with Mr. Hamid Iqbal, Superintendent to Court of District and Sessions Judge, Swat, dated 9 July 2010. The interviewee pointed out various gaps in the laws and regulations as well as their discordance with local practices and ground realities. These included, *inter alia*, the fact that certain areas in PATA had still not undergone formal land settlement which raised a special set of problems; the fact that women were historically not given their legal share in land also led to multiple disputes and crime; and the experience-based observation that most land disputes were linked to inadequate land record keeping, the corruption of *patwaris* or land record keepers, and various other shortcomings in the land ownership and transfer regime. Interview with Mr. Hamid Iqbal, Superintendent to Court of District and Sessions Judge, Swat, dated 9 July 2010.

73 Interview with Mr. M. Asim Imam, Anti-Terrorist Court Judge, Swat, dated 6 July 2010.

74 Interview with Mr. M. Asim Imam, Anti-Terrorist Court Judge, Swat, dated 6 July 2010. These were the army detention centers at Batkhaila and Fiza Garh.

Asked as to how he generally managed to adhere to the requirements of the criminal procedure given his vast territorial jurisdiction, the spate of terrorist activity in the area, and the much reduced timeframe for a criminal trial mandated by the NAR, the Judge admitted that it was a constant struggle. Given the aforementioned challenges, the biggest problems that he faced in his work – much as the inadequacy of his security, staff, facilities and equipment support were also evident [75] – were the ones posed by a weak and underdeveloped evidentiary law regime that did not allow an appreciation of circumstantial evidence, so

The army confined and investigated the 'most hardened militants' at these two facilities. Two anti-terrorist court judges were also present at these facilities. However, it was legally impossible for them to function at these detention centers, as they were outside their legal territorial jurisdictions – hence they were essentially conducting jail trials. Detention center inmates were not presented before any civilian courts or handed over to the police. According to informal sources, the detainees were categorized as 'Black,' 'Grey' or 'White' by the army, according to the culpability attached to them by army investigations – they accordingly met different fates. There was no indication of any formal evidence collection by the army, and also no certainty as to its appreciation of how a criminal trial took place. A rehabilitation center had been set up for underage militants – called *Subahoon* (which means 'Star of the Morning' or 'Morning Star' in *Pushto*) – but it was not easy to get the army to release them for induction into this center. There were several instances where the army presence in the area had precluded the engagement of the locals in traditional vocations such as stone-crushing etc., which persuaded or forced some of them to return to militancy. The on-going presence of the army in the area was a necessity of sorts. However, the continuing lack of civilian and army attention to developing a framework for the army to hand over detainees for criminal trials under the law, posed the threat of disenchanting many locals, including innocent detainees and their families, potentially influencing them to turn to militancy. Interview with Mr. M. Asim Imam, Anti-Terrorist Court Judge, Swat, dated 6 July 2010.

75 In a subsequent discussion, the judge also shared that the judicial leadership had not undertaken the necessary steps to provide adequate security to the judges in areas such as Swat. Financial incentives, risk allowances, housing, transportation, timely procurement and availability of good quality court equipment, the numerical strength and training of the court staff etc., were additional areas of neglect. The district judiciary had negligible access to any training abroad as well as differential access to training at local academies. It was very important, he emphasized, for judges working in special legal regimes such as anti-terrorism law to be exposed to special training programs in anti-terrorism related courses, collection of evidence, detention rules, and trial management; it was also highly necessary to introduce victim assistance and witness protection programs. Interview with Mr. M. Asim Imam, Anti-Terrorist Court Judge, Swat, dated 6 July 2010.

essential otherwise in terrorism cases.[76] Furthermore, according to him, additional problems germinated from the fact that various important amendments introduced to the country's anti-terrorism laws had not been extended to FATA and PATA – yet another example of the complications spawning from the multiplicity of legal regimes in the country and the slow legislative, executive and judicial responses to fast-changing social, political and security situations.[77] While certain new administrative arrangements – whereby the provincial finance departments had relinquished the responsibility for managing the court budgets to the provincial High Courts – had been hailed as a step towards greater judicial autonomy by the upper echelons of the judiciary, the judge on the ground had a very different take on this. He identified several new obstructions to the smooth and timely outflow of funds from the High Courts to the district judiciary, owing to the former's lack of experience in financial management, as well as the domineering attitude of the judicial bureaucracies towards the district judiciary – an attitude that also manifested itself in additional ways.[78]

---

76 Interview with Mr. M. Asim Imam, Anti-Terrorist Court Judge, Swat, dated 6 July 2010. The judge discussed at length the various aspects of the law of evidence, which, according to him, required urgent revisiting and meaningful amendment. He stressed that new situations like armed militancy and suicide bombings threw up important and urgent questions about, *inter alia*, the legal age for crime, the evidence required to get just convictions for new kinds of crime, and the legal definitions of 'complicity in crime' as well as of 'aiding and abetting,' etc. Yet, there seemed to be no real recognition of the actual challenges being faced by the police and law-enforcement agencies in such troubled areas, and hence no concomitant changes in the overall strategy, the laws and the regulations. Interview with Mr. M. Asim Imam, Anti-Terrorist Court Judge, Swat, dated 6 July 2010.

77 Interview with Mr. M. Asim Imam, Anti-Terrorist Court Judge, Swat, dated 6 July 2010. He further pointed out that anti-terrorism trials, not unlike other criminal trials, were acutely hampered by weak police investigations. This in turn was a function of lack of training, equipment, regulations and the scandalous inadequacy of reliable forensics facilities – the entire province had only one such facility. Interview with Mr. M. Asim Imam, Anti-Terrorist Court Judge, Swat, dated 6 July 2010.

78 Interview with Mr. M. Asim Imam, Anti-Terrorist Court Judge, Swat, dated 6 July 2010. According to the interviewee, it was imprudent for the High Courts to take up budget-making and financial responsibilities, given that the Chief Justices and the court administration hierarchies were already over-burdened. He also emphasized that the Anti-terrorist courts covered very large geographical areas and faced excessively high volumes of cases. In many such cases, the accused

In conclusion, the several judges and court staff interviewed in Swat attributed the Taliban led militancy to a series of historically ineffective regulatory frameworks for PATA that had created and fanned local resentment against the government and the legal/court systems. They were of the view – and this is remarkably bold feedback coming from state functionaries – that these regulatory frameworks had always been blind to the area's special history, its local context, and the factors that contributed to popular dissatisfaction and resentment with the legal/court system. Not the least of the main reasons for their unpopularity was that they were the output of non-participatory policy discussions and law-making. This made them, according to the interviewees, ideal targets for the convergence of multiple local and long seething social, political and economic resentments.[79] To the interviewees, there was nothing novel or particularly

managed to get bails from the High Courts. Thus, there was a need for greater dialogue and communication between different levels of the judiciary in order to rationalize the area of bail – the High Courts did not always seem to be cognizant of the ground realities faced by the district courts. Repeat offenders and highly dangerous individuals seemed to get routinely bailed out. Another area that in his view required urgent attention was the much-needed rationalization between the anti-terrorist laws and the laws for the protection of juveniles. As things stood, confusion and contradiction between competing policy imperatives prevailed in this area. However, there was simply no dialogue on this between the different levels of the judiciary. Interview with Mr. M. Asim Imam, Anti-Terrorist Court Judge, Swat, dated 6 July 2010.

79 Interview with Mr. M. Asim Imam, Anti-Terrorist Court Judge, Swat, dated 6 July 2010; interview with the District and Sessions Judge, Swat, dated 7 July 2010; and interview with Mr. Sajid Khan Additional District Judge, Matta, dated 8 July 2010. Contrary to popular reporting, the Taliban led resentment was not solely caused by dissatisfaction with the court system and its delays – the delays were no different from elsewhere in the country. In order to understand the deeper underlying reasons one needed to probe deeper and wider. The history and backdrop of a strong centralized state under the *Wali* of Swat, followed by various weak, poorly visualized and ineffective state mandated administrative systems; the unbridled allocation and use of powers by the State's administrative machinery under different regulatory regimes over the years; the cooption and strategic use of local radical elements by the State during different periods with the resulting weakening of the writ of the State; and elements of a class struggle emerging from land and resource distribution patterns in the area; were some of the main reasons behind the Taliban upsurge. These were essentially issues that required closer political and policy examination, negotiation and solutions, and could not simply be remedied by enforcing tight timelines for case disposal in courts – which was just one relatively minor dimension of the larger problem. The ineffective maintenance of law and order in the area had also contributed to

promising about the NAR solution in terms of its potential to address the complex challenges faced by the district judiciary in PATA. Under an Islamic veneer, it was, they felt, a largely ineffectual antidote for the recent violent challenge to the formal court-based legal system. Neither was it a substitute for deeper and more participatory political, policy and legislative thinking. Hasty patchwork was bound to once again expose the gaping holes in the area's political, economic, administrative and legal governance. Even in terms of dealing with delays, the interviewees stressed that the NAR did not systematically and meaningfully condense the civil and criminal codes in order to shorten the length of trials, while ensuring at the same time that the fundamental requirements of due process and a fair trial were met. It merely provided certain loose guidelines that led to a variety of interpretations and a high degree of variation in practice from court to court. Further, neither an improvement in infrastructure/facilities/resources nor the requisite clarity of direction and consequent deeper law reform had accompanied and supported the increasingly steep targets for monthly case disposals.[80]

---

the sustainability of safe havens for criminal elements, which were a strong component within the Taliban, and had their own vested interests in promoting anarchy. In the past, certain members of the local administration had also, at times, extended strong ideological support to the Taliban or were hand in glove with the criminal elements, but had evaded detection and accountability. Interview with Mr. M. Asim Imam, Anti-Terrorist Court Judge, Swat, dated 6 July 2010; interview with the District and Sessions Judge, Swat, dated 7 July 2010; and interview with Mr. Sajid Khan Additional District Judge, Matta, dated 8 July 2010.

80 Interview with Mr. M. Asim Imam, Anti-Terrorist Court Judge, Swat, dated 6 July 2010. According to him, there is nothing unique about the NAR. It is an old framework that has been tried again and again, i.e. an Islamic sounding law that makes some piecemeal amendments to the court processes in order to bring about relative operational efficiency. The NAR and its predecessors were not the result of any rigorous policy deliberations. In the case of the NAR, he divulged that it was the output of one senior bureaucrat in the provincial law department. The requirement in the NAR to conduct proceedings in Urdu was also onerous for judges trained in English. There was a growing recognition in the district judiciary that the hasty proceedings under the NAR would have serious ramifications for the quality of justice. At the same time, the judges felt that they needed more time to make sound decisions, as they did not want to be appealed against due to the inadequacy of their hastily delivered judgments. Interview with Mr. M. Asim Imam, Anti-Terrorist Court Judge, Swat, dated 6 July 2010.

Most of the interviewees specifically pointed out that the law of evidence, and the entire regime of criminal investigation, prosecution and forensic testing capabilities, were in dire need of modernization. They said that they also required advanced training for adjudicating the tremendous number of complex criminal cases generated by the rampant episodes of terrorism related violence in the area. Highly problematic also, they said, were the phenomena of the missing persons and the ambiguous status of terrorism and Taliban insurgency related detainees being held by the army, with no mechanism in place to formally transfer them to the police and the criminal justice system. Apart from the grave possibilities of the miscarriage of justice, the *status quo* could also lead to aggravating local sentiments. Yet, to the utter exclusion of these imperatives, as the interviewees reported, the sole emphasis from the judicial leadership was on the quick disposal of cases. Meanwhile, the judges confessed that they found it very hard to keep up with stiff case disposal targets. While case disposals had gone up on paper, they admitted that it was simply impossible to reason and write the final decisions at such an accelerated pace. It was only once the decisions were actually written and a number of them potentially appealed against, that one could objectively determine their quality as well as the nature of popular reception to the NAR led quick justice. As to the future, the feedback was highly uncertain. The interviewees displayed considerable anxiety about what the coming days held for the legal and court system in Swat.

E. Postscript

Shifting back to FATA, in August 2011, the President of Pakistan signed two Orders to aid towards the process of integrating FATA with the rest of Pakistan. The first Presidential Order extended the Political Parties Order 2002 ('PPO') – the primary law that regulates political activities in the country – to FATA, thus allowing for the operation of mainstream political parties in the region; while the second introduced certain important amendments to the FCR. The allowance of mainstream political activities in the region brings about much greater political freedom by opening up opportunities to the locals to form their own political parties, by lifting the restriction on the country's various political parties to operate in, recruit and organize themselves in the region, and by enabling the locals to engage with the larger political discourse and activity in the country and to employ national frameworks and platforms for propagating and advocating their rights.[81] This is a major step forward from the previous *status quo* where only independent candidates from FATA without any political party affiliation – invariably handpicked and anointed by the ruling government from amongst the local *Maliks* – were allowed to contest elections from the region and made their way (mostly uncontested) to occupy twelve and eight seats respectively in the country's National Assembly and Senate. Picked without any real political constituencies and competition, these tribal parliamentarians have historically been co-opted *en bloc* by one ruling national elite after another – the phenomenon of securing their loyalty through various kinds of financial and political incentives referred to locally by the term 'horse trading' – in the eventual national governmental set-up and used as pawns in a larger numbers' game for ensuring a ruling majority or coalition. This practice has consistently precluded any meaningful and wider political participation of the people of FATA and rendered their representatives bereft of the ability to effectively and autonomously showcase and advocate the concerns and demands of their constituents in the national legislative fora. The total control exercised over the elected representatives from FATA by whichever party was ruling the center, their use as mere powerless pawns in the larger political bloc-formation in the country, and the culture of visualizing any concessions or reforms for FATA as a handout rather than a politically advocated and negotiated right, have been the main banes of the extant political framework for the region. As it is, adult franchise was only granted to the people of FATA as late as 1997, and the extension of the PPO does promise to usher in a new era of political opportunity and freedom as well as greater linkages with Pakistan. Having said this, the new reforms still do not extend FATA any representation in the KP provincial assembly – or extend it the status of an

81 See Iram Khan, "FATA to see political activities soon," *The Dawn*, 9 August 2011 at http://dawn.com/2011/08/09/fata-to-see-political-activities-soon/, accessed on 12 July 2012). See also "Editorial, FATA Reforms," *The Daily Times*, 14 August 2011, at http://dailytimes.com.pk/default.asp?page= 2011\08\14\story_14-8-2011_pg3_1, accessed on 12 July 2012); and Irfan Ghauri, "Political reforms: A century later, some rights for the tribals," *The Express Tribune*, 12 August 2011, at http://tribune.com.pk/story/229954/ president-zardari-signs-fata-political-par ties order-2002-extension/, accessed on 12 July 2012.

autonomous province – and to that extent the lifting of the curtain has only been to extent of the national legislature.[82]

The second Presidential Order envisions certain important amendments to the FCR.[83] It visualizes a two-tiered appellate system comprising of the newly created FATA Tribunal (equivalent to a provincial high court) and an FCR appellate authority with a real right of appeal to the people of FATA against decisions under the FCR. The reforms, *inter alia*, also curtail the powers of arbitrary arrest under the FCR and preclude indefinite detention, introduce a requirement to produce a person accused of a crime before a magistrate within twenty-four hours of the arrest, incorporate the potential scenarios where an accused can be released on bail, stipulate a fixed time frame for the disposal of cases, and somewhat dilute the mischief of collective punishment by excluding women, children below the age of sixteen and elders above the age of sixty-five from its mischief as well as mitigate the ambit of such implication as to the other males of the tribe. Furthermore, any seizure of private property by the government would now entail the grant of compensation. Another amendment provides for the possibility of initiating an action for false prosecution in civil and criminal matters while the defendants are now also entitled to adequate compensation in criminal matters and compensatory costs in civil matters. The untrammeled powers of the 'Political Agents' to use state funds, ostensibly for promoting rule of law and for keeping the peace, are brought under check as the expenditure of state funds is to be subject to audit by the Auditor General of Pakistan. Certain reforms have also been introduced to promote and safeguard prisoners' rights in FATA.[84]

Despite these positive developments there is skepticism about the scope of reform and dissatisfaction with its pace. Critics point out that the archaic and draconian notion of 'collective responsibility' has been diluted but not fully erased, and neither has the judicial function been completely separated from the executive as is reflected by the fact that the new appellate bodies are still primarily manned by bureaucrats. They further

82 See "Editorial, FATA Reforms," (fn 81).

83 See *Frontier Crimes (Amendment) Regulation*, 2011.

84 See the *FCR Amendment Regulation*. See Ghauri, "Political reforms,"; see also Iqbal, "Major changes made in FCR: FATA people get political rights," *The Dawn*, 13 August 2011, at http://dawn.com/2011/08/13/major-changes-made-in-fcr-fata-people-get-political-rights/, accessed on 12 July 2012.

assert that any effective operationalization of these reforms and the resumption of normal political activity in the region is bound to flounder till such time that the governance policy for the area stops being dictated by security imperatives and the strategic tolerance of violent elements that such policy dictates. Unless the siege of terror by the militants is lifted the tribals, they argue, are not likely to enjoy their new-found rights; neither are they likely to gain from any investments in local development as such development projects are also increasingly controlled by militants – especially since they have been systematically wiping out the local *Malik* leadership and more moderate tribal elders in a series of suicide attacks. The introduction of a robust political and economic empowerment strategy, a much tougher stance against the local militants, and a complete abolition of the FCR is what many argue for.[85] Quite apart from these various points of criticism, observers also point out a marked lack of alacrity on part of the concerned authorities to roll out the newly introduced reforms. However, they highlight that while the reforms are welcome, they were preceded by negligible necessary groundwork in order to create an enabling environment and a robust absorption capacity. Given such lack of groundwork, others actually caution in favor of gradual and incremental reforms. Yet others persist that any legal reforms have no meaning without sincere concomitant economic and social reforms as what the people really need are schools, water, electricity and hospitals.[86]

The current reforms were initially visualized and publicly announced as a reform package in 2009. However, progress was stalled both because of the escalating violence in the area (reportedly on the military's request) as also due to the historically local levels of governmental direct engagement with the locals in FATA which undermines its overall ability to control conflict as well as to sensitively and comprehensively appreciate local grievances and aspirations for state-building and efficient service delivery.[87] State-building, political empowerment, service delivery, and peace-building are all inextricably knit imperatives which require a

---

85 See Taj, "Analysis: New FATA reforms – good but insufficient," *The Daily Times*, 20 August 2011, at http://www.dailytimes.com.pk/default.asp? page=2011 \08\20\story_20-8-2011_pg3_5, Accessed on 12 July 2012.

86 See Ali, "Frontier crimes regulation: Centuries-old law will take time to reform," *The Express Tribune*, 2 December 2011, at http://tribune.com.pk/ story/301002/frontier-crimes-regulation-centuries-old-law-will-take-time-to-reform/, accessed on 12 July 2012.

87 See Ahmad, "Towards State-Building in FATA," 2011, pp. 16.

cohesive, sustained and multi-pronged effort. However, the all too frequently interrupted democratic process in Pakistan; the resulting scarcity of democratic oxygen, political intent as well as executive autonomy and ability; and the inordinate influence exercised on local governance policies in the tribal areas by security concerns, military imperatives, and geo-political developments in the region, collectively ensure that FATA and the other special territories have never really received the holistic, participatory and unremitting reform attention that their highly convoluted state of affairs strongly merit. In the wake of popular elections that take place not all too frequently in Pakistan, weak and inept political governments stutter and fret for a while, and are then forced into a survival mode by the various endogenous and exogenous factors that perpetuate political instability in Pakistan. Soon enough they are heard of no more. Making highly infrequent appearances, FATA and the other 'special territories' linger for a while in the various extant national discourses, and then lose their limited moments of exposure to some other pressing national concern. The state of affairs since the FATA reforms were introduced in 2011 is no different.[88]

The continuing adverse security situation in FATA is of course a big reason for any lack of progress since the exciting presidential announcements in August last year; as is the fact that at the time of writing the government is utterly distracted by and embroiled in multiple other issues. These include, *inter alia*, the worst power crisis in the country's history, continued challenges posed by the devastation caused by the floods in 2011, several bitter contestations with a hyper-adventurous judiciary, frequent political brinkmanship with the powerful military, weak governance and poor service delivery in various sectors and a highly hostile and at times partisan media that loses no opportunity of taking the government to task, the general growth of lawlessness in the country as well as sustained acts of terrorism and suicide attacks in various parts, and the special constituency appeasement demands of the forthcoming elections which are just around the corner. Thus, while FATA has fortuitously appeared on the government's menu for reforms, the lack of local community participation while visualizing this recent reform

88 For an overview of the factors that have historically impeded sustained democratic political governance in Pakistan, see Siddique, "The Jurisprudence of Dissolutions: Presidential Power to Dissolve Assemblies under the Pakistani Constitution and its Discontents," 2006, pp. 624-636.

package impairs its ambit and outreach as well as the extent of local demand and ownership, thereby further eroding the legitimacy of the Federal Government instead of augmenting it. At the same time, when the initial excitement and spurts of activity are followed by long-periods of inertia, any momentum gained is soon dissipated.

Meanwhile, lack of security and deteriorating 'law and order' remain big concerns for the people of FATA as do low and differential access to schools, health services, hospitals as well meaningful political freedom.[89] The situation is not dissimilar in PATA. After the initial buzz around the NAR, one now hardly hears anything anymore about further reforms to address local issues with the courts as well as any steps to tackle the various issues with the NAR framework. At the same time, there are signs on the ground that as the NAR withers away, a storm may be gathering once more in Swat. The deep resentment against the existing legal and court systems – which overlays various additional historical discontents with how Swat has been governed – that preceded, triggered and characterized the Taliban-led uprising, is still seething. This may have been one betrayal too many.[90]

Works cited

Ahmad, Raza, "Towards State-Building in Fata," *Social Science and Policy Bulletin* (2011): 14-19.

Barth, Fredrik, *The Last Wali of Swat*, Bangkok: White Orchid, 2008.

Caroe, Sir Olaf, *The Pathans: 550 B.C – A.D 1957*, Karachi: Oxford University Press, 1958.

---

89 Important insights about popular perceptions and aspirations of the people of the region are provided by recent surveys and opinion polls in FATA and KP by the Community Appraisal and Motivation Program (CAMP), a research and advocacy focused NGO operating in Islamabad run by people belonging to FATA. CAMP also has various field offices in FATA. See Shinwari, *Understanding FATA: Attitudes towards governance, religion and society in Pakistan's Federally Administered Tribal Areas: Volume IV*, 2008; and Shinwari, *Understanding FATA: Attitudes towards governance, religion and society in Pakistan's Federally Administered Tribal Areas: Volume III*, 2009. See also CAMP's website at http://www.camp.org.pk/, accessed on 12 July 2012.

90 See Hammond, "The Situation in Swat: An Interview with Shahid R. Siddiqi," 2009, at http://www.foreignpolicyjournal.com/2009/07/09/the-situation-in-swat-an-interview-with-shahid-r-siddiqi/, accessed on 7 July 2012.

Edwards, David B., "Learning from the Swat Pathans: Political Leadership in Afghanistan, 1978-97," *American Ethnologist* 4 (1998): 712-728.

Hopkirk, Peter, *The Great Game: The Struggle For Empire in Central Asia*, New York: Kodansha International, 1992.

Jalal, Ayesha, *Partisans of Allah: Jihad in South Asia*, Cambridge, MA: Harvard University Press, 2009.

Kakakhel, Shakeel, *Integration of Fata Into NWFP: An Analysis*, The Forum of Federations Project in Pakistan by the German Ministry of Foreign Affairs, 2010.

Keay, John, *The Gilgit Game: The Explorers of The Western Himalayas*, Karachi: Oxford University Press, 1993.

Murtaza, Syed Ali, *USAID Court Efficiency Assessment Final Report*, 2010.

Rashid, Ahmed, *Taliban: Islam, Oil and the new Great Game in Central Asia*, London: I.B. Tauris, 2000.

Rashid, Ahmed, *The Resurgence of Central Asia: Islam or Nationalism*? Karachi, Oxford University Press, 1992.

Rashid, Ahmed, Jihad: *The Rise of Militant Islam in Central Asia*, Karachi: Vanguard Books, 2002.

Shinwari, Naveed Ahmad, *Understanding FATA: Attitudes towards governance, religion and society in Pakistan's Federally Administered Tribal Areas: Volume III*, Islamabad: Community Appraisal and Motivation Program (CAMP), 2009.

Shinwari, Naveed Ahmad, *Understanding FATA: Attitudes towards governance, religion and society in Pakistan's Federally Administered Tribal Areas: Volume IV*, Peshawar: Community Appraisal and Motivation Program (CAMP), 2008.

Siddique, Osama, "The Jurisprudence of Dissolutions: Presidential Power to Dissolve Assemblies under the Pakistani Constitution and its Discontents," *Arizona Journal of International and Comparative Law* 23 (2006): 624-636.

Constitutional Conflict and Restatement: The Challenge and Transformation of the Hegemonic Basic Consent in Thailand[1]

Henning Glaser

Among the numerous countries struggling for a sufficiently stabilized formula of political ordering,[2] as being expressed by the constitutional basic structure, the Kingdom of Thailand represents one of the most interesting cases in point. After the established political system based on the particular Thai form of royalist government had been challenged by the administration of Prime Minister *Thaksin* (2001-2006) the country started to increasingly split in two major political camps – commonly addressed with the colors *yellow* and *red* – since the military coup d'état of 2006. Since then the corresponding actors have been locked in a protracted zero-sum game with the 'red' *Thaksin*-camp being re-elected in all subsequent elections and the 'yellow' royalist camp repeatedly ending the rule of the respective governments through various non-electoral means. From its beginnings the constitutional crisis produced by this 'conflict of colors' amounts almost to what could be labeled as a *"deep play"* – a fierce struggle for domination about nothing less than the very identity of the political community, and the fundaments of the whole societal and political order: the country's fundamental consent and constitutional basic structure.[3] Despite massive attempts from the 'yellow'

---

1 The author would like to thank Ms. Shavaorn Wongcom for her assistance.

2 This 'formula' could also be addressed as the *'fundamental consensus'* partly defined as representing a general notion of acceptance of a vaguely perceived, yet preferable status quo and partly as a fabricated fiction, imposed and protected by those favored by its implications. In this sense, the fundamental consensus is essentially hegemonic rather than result of deliberate bargaining or choice on majority terms.

3 See for the term Geertz, "Deep Play: Notes on the Balinese Cockfight," 1973, pp. 412-453, distinguishing between normal and those competitions with 'existential' interests at stake. This latter kind of competition is the one along which lines the political community is – according to Carl Schmitt's distinction between friend and foe as the decisive criteria of the political community – defined. See Schmitt, *The Concept of the Political*, 2007 (1932).

side to consolidate its hegemonic position, the conflict had remained undecided for years until eventually being frozen by the military putsch of 2014 in favor of the 'yellow camp'.[4]

Surprisingly, residual space remains within the vast literature addressing the normative dimension of this conflict, despite its significance and impact. Yet, to appreciate it promises to be particularly interesting as both, the (hegemonic) social contract and the constitutional basic order, are strongly connected in Thailand and the contestation of one inevitably implies the contestation of the other. Thus, even beyond a genuine interest in Thai constitutionalism in general, in the actual process of political reform, constitution making or in the often observed judicalization of Thai politics, an understanding of the normative dimension of the conflict is necessary to explore elite and mass behavior in Thailand, the dynamics of social struggle and the developments of politics in general. Despite the fact that the country is known for having had a number of constitutions (and coup d'états), – the present interim constitution is the 19th since 1932 and awaiting to be replaced by the 20th which is currently in the making – the written constitution has always been a meaningful, yet limited instrument of political ordering. It is, in this sense, embedded in a much more meaningful and far reaching constitutional and political doctrine according to which the written constitution serves only as a part of a more complex and carefully differentiated concept of normative ordering whose unwritten parts frame

4 The extent of the conflict is reflected by its present toll during the eight years from 2006-2014: Two national elections annulled (2006, 2014), two governing political parties dissolved with their whole board banned from politics for five years by the Constitutional Court (2006 and 2008 affecting 246 politicians of the former governing coalition alone in 2006), not less than three elected governments terminated by constitutional court verdicts (two times in 2008 and in 2014), two military coup d'états (2006, 2014) which abolished two constitutions to be replaced by two newly formulated ones, two military crackdowns on 'red' demonstrations (2009, 2010), and two times a month long seizure of public places including central government buildings by 'yellow' demonstrators effectively being protected against decisive police action (2008, 2013/2014). All of these demonstration crack downs, dissolutions of governing parties, impeachments of prime ministers and terminations of national governments affected the 'red' camp indicating how total polity and politics have been captured by the 'war of colors'. Additionally, militant parts of both camp engaged in frequent mutual bloodshed in the context of 'street politics' from 2008 to 2014 with the 'red' militancy rarely also addressing the military directly and both sides commanding a considerable potential of armed militants.

the written ones. This hegemonic royalist or 'yellow' constitutionalism can only but fascinate the comparative lawyer with its originality as an autochthon, differentiated vision of good governance unfolding huge, practical impacts. Yet, it is heavily challenged, on the one hand by a highly personalized sort of populist, soft authoritarian leadership a la *Peron*, and an associated political movement in favor of progressive democracy and western-style constitutionalism on the other, which both combine together form the 'red camp'.

Though it is not possible to unravel the complex layers and lines of the Thai constitutional crisis as a clash of competing constitutionalisms in detail here, a basic overview shall be provided along two interrelated perspectives. The first view focuses on an ideal-typical distinction of the three competing conceptions of constitutional governance with particular attention paid to the hegemonic. The second perspective shall center on differentiating two phases of this hegemonic evolution, which will be analyzed with regard to its development from the 1970s until the escalation of the constitutional crisis in 2013 and vis-à-vis the two alternative 'red' conceptions in the first part of the paper while the second part deals with the eventual restatement of the hegemonic concept initiated by the post-putsch interim constitution of 2014 after the open conflict has been frozen by the coup and the subsequent implementation of a soft authoritarian regime. The hegemonic governance concept, legally defined as the country's constitutional basic order, is the "Democratic regime with the King as head of state"[5]. Most significant for the period from 2001-2013/14 is the growing 'red' *challenge* and corresponding 'yellow' *defense* of this concept, while the post 2014 coup period is particularly shaped by its *restatement*.

A. The Emergence and Challenge of the Basic Structure: Competing Concepts of Governance in Thai Constitutionalism and Politics

For the pre-2014 coup period three competing normative concepts of constitutional governance can be distinguished. The first is the hegemonic, positively stated constitutional basic structure, the "Democratic regime

5 The term is literally used by most Thai constitutions to label the form of government in Thailand but refers more widely to the constitution's basic structure.

with the King as head of state"[6], while the other two are challenging concepts advocated by the "red" camp.

The DRKS which has been described as a "liberal-conservative" project[7] is since its emergence in 1976 essentially marked by a deep-seated tendency to contain and discipline the mechanisms of representative or electoral democracy[8]. Since 2001 electoral democracy indeed became the basis of *Thaksin's* semi-authoritarian "electoral pluto-populist"[9] CEO-style democracy. Eventually, the resistance of academics, activists and citizens against the 2006 coup emerged in an increasing, counter-hegemonic claim for a sort of western-style constitutionalism based on representative democracy as the second 'red' challenge of the DRKS. While these challenging concepts are essentially different, it is difficult to keep them practically separated when it comes to their factually overlapping support base and the basically opaque nature of any political program in Thailand, to not speak of those who are challenging the hegemonic governance structure vis-a-vis its mechanisms of repressive reinforcement. This obfuscation is partly due to the fact that open promotion of alternative forms of government would amount to an illegal act.

I. The Constitutional Basic Structure: Democratic Regime with the King as Head of State

Acknowledging the DRKS as a hegemonic conception is the key for any appropriate understanding of the present conflict, as it forms the very centerpiece and legitimizing fundament of the *positive* constitutional order. The more surprising is the above mentioned desideratum pertaining to it. The difficulties in fully comprehending the issue start with the fact that the DRKS is not exclusively regulated by the written constitution but also existing beyond and above it. As such, it is part of a pre-positive

---

6 In the following abbreviated as 'DRKS'.

7 Connors, "Liberalism, Authoritarianism and the Politics of Decisionism in Thailand," 2010, p. 92.

8 See Glaser, "Thai Constitutional Courts and the Political Order," 2012, pp. 65-163; Yoshifumi, *Myths and Realities – The Democratisation of Thai Politics*, 2008, pp. 123, 125, 126, 135, 138, 144, 159, 166 and more.

9 Connors, "Liberalism, Authoritarianism and the Politics of Decisionism in Thailand," pp. 94 f.

normative order which sinks its roots in a heterogeneous normative ground encompassing religious, cultural and social orders of the political. This meta-positive dimension of the DRKS frames the written constitution in form of what has been called the 'cultural constitution'[10]. Both dimensions of the constitutional order, that of positive law and those of a pre-positive, partly non-legal one are centered around the King as the ever-present, totally good, and somewhat divine supreme institution who solely represents the people and the nation. This complex conception is reflected by the preamble of the constitution and differentiated by the dominating doctrine in constitutional law.

While it is understood by foreign observers of Thai politics that legitimacy within the established regime is defined and provided by far more than just law, it is often overlooked that *constitutional law* is explicitly, effectively, and nearly exclusively built on this fundament and especially how entrenched its whole design and dynamics are shaped by it: In fact, the whole architecture of the Thai Constitution[11] 1997 and 2007 can only be explained in the light of the DRKS as its basic structure determining the concept of sovereignty, the design and designation of all constitutional powers as well as the defensive mechanisms of the constitution.[12] This impact on positive constitutional law and practice and the fact that the DRKS concomitantly forms the center of the society's (hegemonic) fundamental consensus explain why any challenge to it implies a vital threat to the entire country's order. Nothing, thus, is more

---

10 See Nidhi Eoseewong, "The Thai Cultural Constitution," 1991, reprint 2003, available at http://kyotoreview.org/issue-3-nations-and-stories/the-thai-cultural-constitution/, last visited 12 November 2014: "For example, the king is the head of state, is the head of the armed forces, has sovereignty through all three powers, is the upholder of religion, and so on. But in the cultural constitution, the perspective on the 'institution' of the King is different. The Thai monarchy is 'sacred' *(saksit)* translated literally to mean having mystical power to maintain the peace and order of the world." See also Kittisak Prokati, "The Democratic Regime with the King as Head of State," published on 8th May 2014, at http://www.isranews.org/isranews-article/item/29235-kittisak-prokati.html, last visited 12 November 2014: "The King is the sole people's representative according to custom, morality and culture, the fundament of the legal system, good morals and the order of the nation."

11 In the following, "Thai Constitution" is abbreciated "TC".

12 Even the constitution's concept and practice pertaining to fundamental rights and elements of direct democracy can only be understood against the DRKS. See Glaser, "Multiple Constitutionalizations – 'Constitutionalism and Good Governance in European-Asian Perspectives'," 2014, pp. 50 ff.

suitable to indicate fundamental change in Thai politics and constitutionalism than a change of the DRKS.

Turning to the normative substance of the concept, it is already apparent that the term describes more than just the – quite impressive – range of single *positive* powers and prerogatives of the King in Thai constitutionalism.[13] First and foremost, in its positive dimension the DRKS defines not only the form of state but also the shape of government.[14] Only the appreciation of the DRKS as a *particular form of government* centered around the King opens up an understanding for the inherent tension between the two main terminological components of the formula, monarchy and democracy. In English translations, this is often bypassed or misunderstood by using the inadequate term "constitutional monarchy".

1. The DRKS' Double-Nature and the Constitution's Double-Structure

To understand the DRKS it is crucial to comprehend its complex normative structure, which originates from the fact that it is occupying *two normative dimensions* – positive constitutional law and the normative space which has been described as the 'cultural constitution'. Both blend each other in the meta-positive dimension of constitutional law which contains unwritten constitutional law that does not simply complementing

13 See for the TC 1997 according to which the King is the Upholder of religions (Sect 9), Head of the Thai Armed Forces (Sect 10), holding the prerogative to create titles and confer decorations (Sect 12). Furthermore, the King, according to the TC 1997, has the prerogative to issue a Royal Decree (Sect. 221), to declare and lift martial law (Sect. 222), to declare war with the approval of the National Assembly (Sect. 223), to conclude a peace treaty, armistice and other treaties with other countries or international organizations (Sect. 224), to grant pardon (Sect. 225), to remove titles and recall decorations (Sect. 226), and to appoint and remove officials in the military service and civil service who hold the positions of Permanent Secretary of State, Director-General and their equivalents (Sect. 227). Part of the Royal competences is it also to refuse to assent to bills and forcing the National Assembly for further deliberation (Sect. 94; the veto could be overruled by two-thirds of the total number of existing members of both Houses); to dissolve the House of Representatives (Sect. 116) and to convoke extraordinary sessions of the National Assembly.

14 See Kittisak, "The Democratic Regime with the King as Head of State." (Following the common usage, in citations Thai authors are referred to by their first name.)

but *framing* the written one. The borderline between this unwritten constitutional law and the 'cultural constitution', the narratives, myth and legally, insufficiently concretized social norms, often blurs.[15] Linking positive constitutional law, meta-positive constitutional law and the 'cultural constitution' the DRKS represents a vague, yet omnipresent and omnipotent meta-order of the constitutional order with very practical consequences.[16] Moreover, in its emanation as positive constitutional law, the DRKS forms a higher legal level than 'normal' constitutional law. In this sense, the double-nature of the DRKS which integrates meta-positive and positive norms also induces a double-structure of written constitutional law as well: the unquestionable and unchangeable level of the DRKS in its positive form and 'plain' constitutional law. This is reflected by the preambles of the TC 1997/2007:

> [The King] is graciously pleased to proclaim that whereas Constitutions have been promulgated as the principle of the democratic regime of government with the King as Head of the State in Thailand for more than sixty-five years; and there had been annulment and amendment to the Constitutions on several occasions, it is manifest that the Constitution is changeable depending upon the situation in the country.[17]

These words express a remarkable deal of relaxation towards the (in)stability of the codified supreme law of the land – apart from the

15 The 'cultural constitution' is a vague and fluid normative order considered to independently exist from written law while providing various normative effects. Basically it can be imagined as consisting of different interwoven elements including concepts of royal legitimacy based on traditional claims, notions of Theravada-Buddhism pertaining to the personal charisma of the reigning King whose merits cause his divination by his subjects, and generally the nature of social hierarchy and the traditional perception and use of different forms of power in Thai society preferring a notion of mitigation and tempering of power. See also Tongnoi, "The Role of the Monarchy in Modern Thailand," 1990, pp. 155 ff.

16 According to Kittisak, "The Democratic Regime with the King as Head of State,": "[...], the King is an essential part of the Thai 'Volksgeist'." The DRKS could also be labeled as something like the Thai equivalent to Western natural law. See Glaser, "Thai Constitutional Courts and the Political Order," pp. 65-163.

17 Preamble TC 1997. See also the very similar preamble of the TC 2007 and scholarly assessments like those of Seni Pramoj, "Father King Ram Khamhaeng's Stone Inscription: First Constitution of Thailand," 1990, p. 42; Tongnoi, "The Role of the Monarchy in Modern Thailand," p. 155.

DRKS – referring to its periodical nullification by coup d'états and strongly contrast it with the gravity and permanence of the DRKS which independently exists from its written form. In other words: The preamble explicitly displays the juxtaposition between DRKS and 'plain' constitutional law as well as between the codified and the unwritten constitution. It also indicates the doctrinal axiom that the DRKS has to be acknowledged by any new constitution as the "permanent, unchangeable and immortal" part of the constitutional order, which may not be affected or changed by 'man-made' constitutional law.[18] This overarching and untouchable supreme principle, however, is *totally built upon the person* of the reigning monarch who is thus the center and axis of both, the double-dimensioned DRKS and the double-structured written constitution.[19]

2. The Concept of Sovereignty in the Course of Thai Constitutionalism

Covering both dimensions, the meta-positive and the codified constitution, the DRKS, at heart, defines and organizes the sovereign power. This elaborated conception, more than anything else, reflects the originality and devotion of Thai constitutionalism in formulating an authoritative answer to the fundamental question of how to govern the country. Even if its complexity fully unfolds only in terms of its interpretation by the dominating doctrine and in relation to the grand political narratives, the constitutional text itself already reveals the striking differences to western constitutionalism. The relevant sect. 3 of TC 1997 and 2007 reads as follows:

---

18 See Bowornsak, "His Majesty the King and the People, Characteristics of Thai Democracy," 1996, p. 23.

19 See Kobkua, "The Monarchy and Constitutional Change Since 1992," p. 63: "It follows that the public powers of the King emanate not from a written constitution, but from the affection, devotion and trust that the Thai people have for him. These sentiments, as implied by the royal stand, form the very foundations of the King's legitimate right to intervene [...] in the affairs of the nation. This right overrides all other written legal authorities, be they the constitution or other man – made laws." And: "The King is [...] above all man–made laws in the land, but is under the law prescribed by the teachings of the Lord Buddha." He is therefore "definitely not a constitutional monarch of an ordinary kind" but the "highest authority in the land, towering over military, constitution and parliament".

> The Sovereign power belongs to the Thai people. The King as Head of the State shall exercise such power through the National Assembly, Council of Ministers and the Courts in accordance with the Provision of this Constitution.
>
> The National Assembly, the Council of Ministers, the Courts, other Constitutional organizations and State agencies shall perform duties of office by the rule of law.

Again, the constitution introduces a highly unusual distinction between the occupancy and the *exercise* of the sovereign power. This practically important exercise is allocated to the King. Obviously, this profoundly deviates from the principle of people's sovereignty. This becomes fully apparent with the clarification that it is the King who exercises the sovereign power via the three state powers whose legitimacy is thus cut off from the people as holder of the sovereign power.[20] Another important differentiation is provided in the third sentence of sect. 3. According to it the three state powers and the "other Constitutional organizations and State agencies" are bound to the rule of law implying that this does not affect the King as the one who ultimately exercises the supreme power. This distinction reflects once more the double-nature of the DRKS or King respectively at the top and above the constitution, as he alone is not exposed to any constitutionally stated principle which may limit his exercise of the sovereign power. Significantly, this differentiation appears not at all to be accidental. This follows from the evolution of the principle and its formulation in older constitutions and is approved by the ruling doctrine. Indeed, although the basic formulation that the king exercises the sovereign power has been used by earlier constitutions, its meaning and sometimes also its formulation has profoundly changed, especially with respect to *restrictions* of the King's power.

Completely different, even if only in force for some months, was Thailand's first, revolutionary constitution. In section 2 of this TC June 1932, the sovereign power was to be *exercised on behalf of the people* by the King, the Assembly of the Representatives of the People, the Committee of the People and the courts *together* and *as specified by the*

20 Though this makes sect. 3 TC 1997/2007 to be one of the most important provisions of the constitution it is rarely mentioned in English publications or, worse, even wrongly addressed as the normative foundation of (western-style) people's sovereignty in Thai constitutionalism.

constitution.[21] This changed with the 'permanent' TC December 1932 when the insofar formally equal status of the four constitutional organs[22] was replaced with a provision that gave the King the position to exercise the sovereign power through the other three state powers. This, however, was accepted by the revolutionary group as a mere formality to restore the dignity of the royal institution after the revolution which had ended the absolute monarchy some months ago and led to a pragmatic cooperation between the revolutionary group and the Palace, with the latter as the increasingly weaker partner. Correspondingly, the King had to exercise the sovereign power *by virtue of the provisions* or *in conformity* with the constitution, respectively as stated by the TC Dec. 1932. This set the model for the subsequent TC 1946, 1947, 1949, 1952. In this period from December 1932 to 1957 the dominating actor in Thai politics was the military – with two brief interruptions in the form of a short lived consolidation of conservative royalism in early 1933 and a temporary domination of a shaky progressive-royalist alliance in the postwar years 1944-1947.[23] Generally, during the years 1933-1944, the palace had been the relatively weakest power center periodically close to become totally eclipsed after the resignation of *Rama VII* in favor of a minor prince, the later King *Ananda.*[24] Against this backdrop the concrete formulation of the sovereign power reflected not so much any effective power of the Palace, but the need of a highly volatile political system to retain the monarchy as a dignified yet powerless if not periodically decorative part of the constitutional order. It was the calculus first of the revolutionary party and then the more apolitical military groupings to use the Palace to firstly structure and stabilize the polity by its mere existence in the wake of immense intra-elite competition and to secondly provide a point of

---

21 Similar was the exercise of the sovereign power regulated in the *French constitution of* 1791 (third title, Art. 1-5).

22 Even if they included the King it was the Assembly of the Representatives of the People which was the generally most important among them.

23 Until 1947 the second powerful center was the civilian progressive democratic faction of the original revolutionary group of 1932 and their followers, after 1947 the conservative-royalist Democrat Party until the balances of power were dominated by competing military factions from 1949 to 1957 when one of them took control under General *Sarit* who elevated the Palace to join the regime as the dignified center of the new constitutional order.

24 See Kobkua, "The Monarchy and Constitutional Change Since 1992," pp. 95-113, 118-132; Hewison, "The monarchy and democratisation" 2001, p. 63.

reference for vague regime legitimacy among the traditionally minded 'masses'.

This function of the Throne began to change after the coup led by Field-Marshall *Sarit*, a member of the then ruling 1947coup group against his former allies in 1957. In 1957, the young King *Bhumipol* already enjoyed a great popularity among the general population. As a result, the palace and the military formed a close alliance, for the first time in modern Thai history. The reason behind this was *Sarit's* need for someone to provide him with sufficient domestic and international legitimacy as he took control as a member of the disliked junta from his former allies who used to have strong ties to foreign powers which Sarit was lacking.[25] *Sarit*'s policy "to bring the King back into the national limelight" and to build up the full dignity of the monarchy in order to strengthen and widen his own political power base through popular support brought back an unprecedented level of "dynamism to the Throne and the personality of King Bhumipol".[26] In the resulting partnership, a strong bond of mutual respect and trust emerged between the leader of the junta and the monarch creating the necessary system-cohesion for *Sarit* to implement his new political philosophy. According to *Sarit's* philosophy, western constitutionalism had brought no benefits to Thailand while traditional patterns of national unity and 'fatherly rule' – at this time represented by *Sarit* himself – promised to be the right governance-formula when he abolished the parliamentary system to replace it with his Thai-style democracy.[27]

However, in *Sarit's* TC 1959, which followed his self-coup of 1958 to more independently rule as a benevolent dictator unhindered by western governance structures and with reference to the national ideology of "Nation, Religion, King" being symbolized by the Throne, sect. 5 regulates the concept of sovereignty as follows:

> The King shall enact laws by and with the advice and consent of the National Assembly. The Council of Ministers exercises the executive power and the Courts of Law exercise the judicial power in the name of the King.

---

25 See Thak, *Thailand – The Politics of Despotic Paternalism*, 2007, p. 82.
26 Kobkua, "The Monarchy and Constitutional Change Since 1992," p. 57.
27 See Kobkua, "The Monarchy and Constitutional Change Since 1992," pp. 61 f.; Thak, *Thailand – The Politics of Despotic Paternalism*, p. 106 f., quoting *Sarit*: "the Prime Minister is the father of a large family […]." And: "I still hold on to our ancient Thai traditional concept of father 'ruling' children."

The 1957 regime strongly supported the King's steadily growing importance within the equilibrium of power and the corresponding constitutional framework. However, for the first time since the very first constitution of June 1932, the TC 1959 used a new, comparatively restrictive formulation pertaining to the exercise of the sovereign power, explicitly limiting the King's role to a merely ceremonial dimension.

However, after *Sarit* had passed away in 1963, the King eventually emerged as the ultimate national arbiter when the remaining members of the junta fought for dominance. The King swiftly appointed one of *Sarit's* lieutenants, Gen. *Thanom*, to be the new prime minister stabilizing his position against his competitors in the military.[28] While the unique relationship between junta leader and King which marked the *Sarit*-era had come to an end and despite some quickly occurring frictions between the King and the remaining junta, the King grew in effective importance – especially when the junta's legitimacy eroded. However, even if the King had already become the most influential socio-political weight of the polity in 1968, the junta's TC 1968 provided the concept of sovereignty in its sect. 3 as follows:

> The sovereign power emanates from the Thai people. The King, who is the Head of the State, exercises it only in conformity with the provisions of this Constitution.

This crucial formulation allowed the King to exercise the sovereign power *only* in conformity with the provisions of the constitution. This novel formulation of the sovereign power would subsequently be repeated by the TC 1972, the last constitution under *Thanom*, and the TC 1974, the last constitution trying to balance the central role of the King and a more western-like notion of popular sovereignty after the TC 1946 (sect. 2 and 3 respectively).

The coup of 1976 ended the experiment to integrate the monarchy and a modest system of representative democracy on equal terms. Afterward, the King appointed the staunch anti-communist *Thanin* as prime minister who reestablished a civilian-authoritarian governance system which should become the nucleus for the gradual emergence of the DRKS. Different to

28 The first time the King had acted in this role to legitimate a post-coup junta was when he appointed *Sarit* "Defender of the Capital" after his putsch of September 1957. See Thak, *Thailand – The Politics of Despotic Paternalism*, p. 82.

those of *Sarit* and *Thanom* (1957-1973) it did not build on the military as the dominant group but tried to root itself in the monarchy as the decisive and supreme arbiter of the nation referring to notions of Buddhist governance embodied by the King. The corresponding constitution, the TC 1976 in its sect. 3 reverts to the older formulation of sovereignty, stating again that the King exercises the sovereign power (through the three state powers) by virtue of the provisions of the Constitution.[29]

This remained the standard formulation in the following TC 1977 which was introduced after the military had ended the *Thanin*-experiment by a putsch and reappeared in sect. 3 of the TC 1978 and 1991 until the TC 1997 eventually introduced another version, the one analyzed above. The disparity between the TC 1991 and the TC 1997 is remarkable as the former still repeats the model re-introduced by the TC 1976 while the qualitatively different formulation of the latter no longer binds the King but the three state powers instead (by the rule of law).[30] All in all, provisions which regulated how sovereign power was exercised had changed – in formulation and meaning – over the whole course of Thai constitutional development, reaching the highest level of appreciation for the King's position only with the TC 1997.

To appreciate this development it is useful to be aware of the shifting balances of power behind similar formulations in the different periods of Thai constitutionalism, namely the one from the TC December 1932 to the TC 1952 and the TC 1976 to the TC 1991. A notable fact is that the respective formulation in the period in between – the time of the TC 1959, 1968, 1972, 1974 – literally even limited the exercise of the sovereign power during a time in which the power of the King effectively rose until his position as the center of the polity was acknowledged by the TC 1976 with the return to the original formulation of the TC 1932 – with a completely different underlying constitutional doctrine.

This requires a brief – and necessarily selective – overview of the changing constitutional doctrine since the 1970s, the time when the DRKS

29 Interestingly, *Thanin*, who is now a Privy Councilor, suggested that it would be unnecessary for the King to follow the constitution, for it would be merely words on paper. See P. Heiecke, 1977, quoted in Hewison, "The Monarchy and Democratisation," p. 69.

30 The TC 1991 still states that the "power of sovereignty is derived from the Thai people, His Majesty the King as the head exercises that power *through the provisions of this Constitution for the Administration*" (sect. 2), through the three state powers (sect. 3).

emerged until it reached its climax after the last independent bid for power by the military had failed in the early 1990s.[31] A starting point is the position of one of the most influential Thai lawyers, *Yud Saenguthai,* and his writings on the Interim Constitution of 1972. *Yud* commented on the cornerstones of constitutional law in a time when the first period of royal emancipation came to an end awaiting a second dawn of the monarchy as the single most influential and most respected national institution. *Yud*, in the line with the wording of the respective constitutional provisions, distinguishes between the one who holds the sovereign power and the one who exercises it. Thus, between the people holding the sovereign power and the King exercising it. Based on the wording of sect. 2 TC 1972 the King "exercises it only in conformity with the provisions of this Constitution". *Yud* emphasizes that the exercise of the sovereign power *has to remain within the legal boundaries* created by the provisions of the Constitution. This clarification is accompanied by the acknowledgment that the King exercises the sovereign power like parents legally representing their children.[32] His comments indicate two tendencies in Thai constitutionalism short before the takeoff of the DRKS. Firstly, they show that the paternalistic concept of "father ruling children" which had been introduced by *Sarit* in 1958 was meanwhile already occupied by the person of the King and not the prime minister or junta leader anymore. Secondly, despite this increased role of the Throne, it was still *positive constitutional law* which drew the line for the legitimate use of state power, also legally defining the powers that fell under the King's exclusive purview. *Yud* explicitly stated that in any case which would raise doubts about the King's prerogatives it would have to be deemed that the respective prerogative was *not* given.[33]

Some years and a generation of lawyers later, two up-and-coming public lawyers confirmed *Yud's* account on the boundaries of the exercise of the sovereign power with respect of the TC 1977, short after the DRKS had started to take shape with the quickly abrogated TC 1976. For the decades to come both of these scholars, *Wissanu Krea-ngam* and

31 See Connors, "Liberalism, Authoritarianism and the Politics of Decisionism in Thailand," pp. 85, 89 and 92, who stresses that the monarchy during the 1990s was still an 'expanding' institution.

32 See Yud, *Lecture on the Interim Constitution 1972*, 1973, pp. 17-19, (Original in Thai).

33 See Yud, *The Interim Constitution 1972*, p. 18.

Bowornsak Uwanno, should form the inner circle of public lawyers repeatedly charged with the authoritative interpretation and alignment of Thai constitutional law. One of them would become a key framer of the current TC 2014, the other is currently charged with working out a permanent constitution for Thailand announced for 2015.[34] Their continuous work on Thai constitutional law offers a fascinating account of the evolution of the DRKS, starting with their joint account on the Interim-Constitution of 1977. The latter had been enacted following what could be labeled as the last successful coup by a military clique, attempting to independently dominate the political arena. The coup, which was informally led by General *Kriengsak Chamanan* who also became prime minister, put a quick end at the regime of *Thanin Kraivixien*, a loyal trustee of the King, and eased the very repressive stance toward oppositional groups *Thanin* had introduced.[35] In this political context *Wissanu* and *Bowornsak* explain the distinction between the ownership and the exercise of the sovereign power (sect. 3). They refer to the constitution drafters' intention to merely honor the King, who, however, would have to exercise the sovereign *within the boundaries of the constitution*. This doctrinal interpretation bears a striking resemblance to the context of the TC December 1932 which had introduced the model and acknowledged some additional royal prerogatives, however, "merely [as] a matter of compliment and honor to the King" rather than to really

34 *Bowornsak* studied and taught at Chulalongkorn University, received his PhD in France, is one of the framer of the TC 1997, 2006, 2007, and 2014, served several Prime Ministers as secretary or advisor and was member of the cabinet of Prime Minister *Thaksin* which he left before the coup 2006. Currently, he serves as First Vice President of the National Reform Council and Chairman of the Constitution Drafting Committee. *Wissanu* studied at Thammasat University and at Berkeley, taught at Chulalongkorn and Thammasat University, acted as chairman of the Judicial Council´s constitutional law section, is a cousin of *Bowornsak*, and worked with ten different administrations, most notably serving as Deputy Prime Minister during the *Thaksin*-administration and now again as Deputy Prime Minister in the junta-formed cabinet of General *Prayuth*.

35 *Thanin*, formerly president of the Supreme Court, like *Sarit* but with much more ideological furor, dissolved parliament, outlawed all political parties, started an anti-communist witch-hunt, burned tens of thousands of books including those of *George Orwell* and *Thomas Morus* and drove progressive activists into communist underground structures. After his ouster by the 1977 coup the King appointed him immediately to his Privy Council.

increase his power.[36] In sum, according to *Wissanu/Bowornsak* in 1978, the exercise of sovereign power had to remain within the limits of the constitution.[37]

As early as 1979 *Wissanu* provided a substantially modified concept of sovereignty already indicating a *shared sovereignty* between king and people stressing that the constituent power would be shared between King and people.[38] Eventually, in the 1990s, *Bowornsak* provided a fully differentiated and since then authoritative interpretation of the concept of sovereignty. It is, according to *Bowornsak*, not only to be exercised by the King alone but belongs also to *both*, King and people.[39]

At a first glance, this view might seem to deviate from the wording of sect. 3 of the TC 1991, 1997 and 2007, which state that the sovereign power emanates from/belongs to the Thai people.[40] However, the doctrine of the shared occupancy of the sovereign power is indeed supported by other parts of positive constitutional law, namely the preambles.[41] Their reading sheds a different light on the meaning of sect. 3 which, in teleological and systematic interpretation, seems indeed to define only one emanation of the sovereign power: the sovereign power within the constituted form of a codified constitution (whose elusiveness is underlined by the same preamble).

If the sovereign can be equated with the one who makes the constitution, it is indeed not the people but solely the King who alone acts according to the preambles[42] as sovereign. He is "graciously granting an

36 See Thawatt, *History of the Thai Revolution. A Study in Political Behaviour*, 1962, p. 124.

37 See Wissanu and Bowornsak, *The Interim Constitution 1977*, 1978, pp. 54-55.

38 See Wissanu, *Constitutional Law*, 1979, p. 23, (original in Thai).

39 See Bowornsak, *Public Law, Vol. 2, Separation of Public and Private Law and the Evolution of Public Law in Thailand*, 2005, pp. 182-183, (original in Thai).

40 Bowornsak, *Public Law, Vol. 2*, p. 182, concedes this too.

41 See on the normative and heuristic value of preambles respectively King, "Constitutions as Mission Statements," 2013, p. 84; Tushnet, *Weak Courts, Strong Rights: Judicial Review and Social Welfare Rights in Comparative Constitutional Law*, 2008, p. 12.

42 See only the relevant passages of the preamble of the TC 1997: "[…] May there be virtue. Today is the tenth day of the waxing moon in the eleventh month of the year of the Ox under the lunar calendar, being Saturday, the eleventh day of October under the solar calendar, in the 2540th year of the Buddhist Era. Phrabat Somdet Phra Paramintharamaha Bhumibol Adulyadej Mahitalathibet Ramathibodi Chakkri Narubodin Sayammintharathirat Borommanatthabophit is

audience to members of the Constituent Assembly for taking His Royal speeches" and blessings, then "thoroughly examining the draft" before "commanding" it into existence as to be the new constitution because he "deems it expedient to grant His Royal assent in accordance with the resolution of the National Assembly" and, in the case of the TC 2007, the public referendum on the draft respectively. In these preambles, the people is not the ultimate actor nor is the constitution made in their name. Dominantly acting, proclaiming, granting, and commanding, is the King for whom neither any popular nor national mandate is mentioned in doing so.

The normative substance which is at least implied in this reading of the preambles shall be differentiated with respect to the authoritative doctrine on constitutional key issues related to the sovereign power and some of the respective grand political narratives.

3. The Grand Narratives and Constitutional Doctrine: the Foundational Myth and the Uniqueness of the Monarchy in Thai Constitutionalism

What is described as 'grand narrative' is deeply rooted, orthodox interpretations of the historical foundation and substance of modern

---

graciously pleased to proclaim that whereas [...] and whereas the Constitution [...] established the Constituent Assembly [...] charged with the duty to prepare a draft of a new Constitution [...] and His Majesty the King graciously granted an audience to members of the Constituent Assembly for taking His Royal speeches and receiving blessings in carrying out this task, and, thereafter, the Constituent Assembly prepared the draft Constitution with the essential substance [...]; Having carefully considered the Draft Constitution prepared by the Constituent Assembly in the light of the situation of the country, the National Assembly passed a resolution approving the presentation of the draft Constitution to the King for His Royal signature to promulgate it as the Constitution of the Kingdom of Thailand; Having thoroughly examined the draft Constitution, the King deemed it expedient to grant His Royal assent in accordance with the resolution of the National Assembly;
Be it, therefore, commanded by the King that the Constitution of the Kingdom of Thailand be promulgated to replace, [...]. May the Thai people unite in observing, protecting and upholding the Constitution of the Kingdom of Thailand in order to maintain the democratic regime of government and the sovereign power derived from the Thai people, and to bring about happiness, prosperity, and dignity to His Majesty's subjects throughout the Kingdom according to the will of His Majesty in every respect."

constitutionalism commanding a nearly axiomatic quality. Their boundaries to constitutional doctrine are often blurred when they appear in terms of customary constitutional law or convention or the 'cultural constitution'.

Since ancient times, central in these narratives is the perception of the Thai monarchy as being exceptionally characterized by a direct and close bond between King and people, seeing both as always been united, with the King as the loving father of the nation.[43] This is, in the understanding of the canonical doctrine but also in the view of the Palace itself, in particular true for the reigning monarch as a cornerstone of the DRKS.[44]

This special bond, to come to another canonical narrative, has been reaffirmed in particular in the revolutionary year of 1932 for it was not the revolutionary force which founded constitutionalism in Thailand but the King himself who, following his own previous considerations, granted the nation her first constitution of his own will "out of paternal love"[45] and who placed himself voluntarily under it, thus becoming the "father of Thai democracy".[46] From this foundational act derives the 'shared' nature of

---

43 See Seni, "Father King Ram Khamhaeng's Stone Inscription: First Constitution of Thailand," pp. 17, 30, 33, 42 f.; Tongnoi, "The Role of the Monarchy in Modern Thailand," p. 152, and the doctrinal application of this narrative by Bowornsak, *Public Law, Vol. 2*, pp. 182-183; see also Pramuan, *Royal Prerogatives*, Bangkok 2005, pp. 31-45, (original in Thai).

44 See for the Palace, The Office of His Majesty's Private Secretariat, 1971, p. 26: "The King and the People become one. The Throne and the Nation become one, and a profound meaning is thus given to the Thai Throne. It becomes the personification of the Thai nationhood, the symbol of the Nation's unity and independence, the invariable constant above the inconstancies of politics, indeed, as it is written to be, the repository of the sacred trust of the whole nation." It is, in the interpretation of Kittisak, this unity of King and people which lays at the foundation of the DRKS, which legitimizes the King to use the sovereign power as their representative according to custom, moral and culture making him to be the basement of the legal system, the good public moral and the order of the nation. See Kittisak, "The Democratic Regime with the King as Head of State."

45 Seni, "Father King Ram Khamhaeng's Stone Inscription: First Constitution of Thailand," pp. 17, 28.

46 See the preamble of the Constitutions of 1978 and 1974 respectively, especially the latter: "Be it proclaimed by the King that He is advised by the National Legislative Assembly that the grant of the Constitution of Thailand on 10th December B.E. 2475 by His Majesty King Prachathipok […], His Majesty s Uncle, was the founding of democratic system of government in Thailand, it being His unwavering desire to grant to all the Thai people […] the power to

the sovereign power, which belongs to both, the King as its original holder and the people. Within this narrative frame scholars set different accents in detail where constitutional doctrine concretizes the sovereign power. While the earlier interpretation of *Wissanu* seems to stress the 'sharing' on more equal terms, *Bowornsak* and *Pramuan* stress a graduated concept in which the King is not only the original but also the *ultimate* holder of the sovereign power granting the people the position of the holder of sovereignty within the framework and under the conditions of the written constitution.[47]

4. Sovereignty, Constituent Power and Non-Written Royal Powers

According to *Bowornsak* it is the King alone who makes and embodies the (highest ranking) unwritten constitution which is not subject to the constituent power of the people. It is therefore the "permanent, unchangeable and immortal", thus the real constitution, which cannot be changed or amended by written law.[48] The drafters of any written constitution are just finding this real constitution and acknowledge it in their draft.[49]

---

administer the State affairs while the King was to be Head of State and to exercise the sovereign power emanating from the people, under the provisions of the Constitution." See also Kittisak, "The Democratic Regime with the King as Head of State."

47 See Bowornsak, "His Majesty the King and the People, Characteristics of Thai Democracy," 1996, pp. 11 ff., 23. The undeniable fact that the revolution of 1932 did happen is consumed by the respective doctrine in considering only the second constitution, the TC December 1932 as the very foundational document whose enactment is also celebrated as Thailand's Constitution Day. Significant is the change of language describing it in the earlier periods of Thai constitutionalism and the period of the established DRKS labelling the TC December 1932 a "Pact" between the King and the People's Party first and a "Charter" granted by the King by the 'crown lawyers' of the DRKS later respectively. See Kasian, "The Democratic Regime with the King as Head of State: Origin and Prospect," 2011, pp. 89-115, (original in Thai).

48 See Bowornsak, "His Majesty the King and the People, Characteristics of Thai Democracy," pp. 23 f.

49 See Bowornsak, "His Majesty the King and the People, Characteristics of Thai Democracy," p. 27. Arguing similarly, yet less differentiated in favor of the King as the ultimate source of the constituent power, Pramuan states that every constitution since 1932 had been given by the King who alone countersigned all

With striking resemblance to the preambles of the TC 1997/2007 he points out that while Thai politics are instable, the position of the King became firmer over the years. This acknowledges also the contingent character of the DRKS and its dependency on the person of the reigning monarch rather than the royal institution.[50]

In the light of this particular concept of sovereignty, the Royal powers and prerogatives cannot be regulated exhaustively by the provisions of the written constitution. Accordingly, those Royal powers which are not part of positive law continue to exist after a constitution has been promulgated including such powers as the appointment or removal of prime ministers from office or the dissolution of Parliament. And, as *Bowornsak* explicitly states, these decisions would have be to be accepted.[51]

5. The Sovereign Power and Coup d'états

Significantly the DRKS' concept of sovereignty reaches out even to the frequent phenomenon of coup d'états disciplining them as a class of regulated constitutional practice.

Drawing on the historical fact that the Revolutionary Party of 1932 requested the cooperation of the King after it had taken public power which was eventually leading to the more compromising TC December 1932, *Wissanu* points out that since then every leader of a coup group needed the consent of the King to establish a new constitution for the purpose of achieving the necessary legitimacy – domestic and international.[52] *Bowornsak* specifies that any junta which seizes power with 'good intentions' would return it back to the monarch as the ultimate holder of sovereignty who then starts another process of constitution

subsequent constitutions. Moreover, every amendment and even interpretation of the constitution would have to be made in the name of the King. See Pramuan, *Royal Prerogatives*, pp. 31-45.

50 See in this sense also Tongnoi, "The Role of the Monarchy in Modern Thailand," pp. 154 f., 159.

51 See Bowornsak, "His Majesty the King and the People, Characteristics of Thai Democracy," p. 29. See also Nidhi, "The Thai Cultural Constitution,": "Whether it is written or not, the king is in a position of revered worship and shall not be violated. If the section in the constitution on the king were totally removed, it would not shake the Thai monarchy at all."

52 See Wissanu, *Constitutional Law*, p. 23.

making as described. Referring to this normative script, *Bowornsak* introduces one more distinction of the sovereign power with the King as its *de jure* – and the junta as its temporary – *de facto* holder. The latter is legally and factually dependent on the King's endorsement of the coup to receive the necessary legitimacy and an amnesty for the violent overthrow of a lawful government.[53] Thus, similar to the 'civilian mode' of 'holding' the sovereign power, the *de facto* sovereign power of the military junta remains inescapable instable and dependent on the monarch as the ultimate source of sovereignty. Interestingly, in this conception the boundaries between the status of exception and the normal state of constitutional ordering blur in the same way as those between positive law and the unwritten constitution do. In other words: the coup is not an unleashed mode of naked force but it is tamed and framed by the unwritten constitution while people's sovereignty as being established by positive constitutional law represents just another mode of a merely ephemeral sovereignty.

6. People's Sovereignty and DRKS

Consequently there is no notion of representative democracy as direct expression of people's sovereignty which itself is insulated between those of the King as the one who ultimately holds and exercises the sovereign power. Moreover, people's sovereignty is widely regarded in Thai constitutionalism to have only been the treacherous claim for legitimacy by despots, revealing the concept as a sort of fatal mirage.[54] *Bowornsak* in this sense distinguishes between the principle of democracy in (western-style) written constitutions and democracy according to the customary or cultural constitution. While the first one would only create a form of governance without any substance, the latter represents a democracy

---

53 See Bowornsak, *Public Law, Vol. 2*, pp. 182-183. After the coup of General *Kriengsak* in 1977 against the royally appointed Thanin-regime which created serious tensions between the junta and the Palace, no other coup could be accomplished any more without royal endorsement. The two unsuccessful coup attempts in the 1980s mark the emergence of the respective constitutional practice according *to Bowornsak's* doctrine.

54 See Pramuan, *Royal Prerogatives*, pp. 31-45; Seni, "Father King Ram Khamhaeng's Stone Inscription: First Constitution of Thailand," pp. 30, 39 ff., 42 f., 46 f.

according to form and substance in the Thai way, which exists irrespective of any written constitution and is solely based on the bond between King and people, with the former as a "King of the people, by the people and for the people".[55] Thus, the Thai parliament does not represent the sovereign but serves as the body assigned with the exercise of legislative power under the King as the one who ultimately exercises the power.[56] Elements of electoral democracy are nonetheless built in what *Bagehot* would have called the efficient part of the constitutional order, namely to maintain the necessary balances of power in particular with respect to the military's ambitions to monopolize power, to ensure broad and dynamic elite integration, necessary mass participation, and external legitimacy. The electoral mechanisms are – from the perspective of the DRKS – however, naturally inhabited by a dangerous emancipatory potential, perceived as an abstract danger by the TC 1997 and a concrete one personified by *Thaksin* by the TC 2007/2014. This induces the establishment of a rigid disciplinary regime, attempting to control by an impressive ensemble of 'watchdog bodies' all elements of electoral democracy, especially political parties and political officeholders. It is completed by underlying narratives conjuring threats of bad politics and reinforcing the dialectics of 'dirty'politicians and 'clean' statesmen.[57]

7. The Royal Position Above Politics and the Positive Acknowledgement of the Unwritten Constitution

Finally, two more core provisions of the DRKS shall be briefly introduced. Firstly sect. 8 TC 1997/2007[58] stating that "the King shall be enthroned in a position of revered worship and shall not be violated" and that "no person shall expose the King to any sort of accusation or action."

---

55 Bowornsak, "The King and the People, Characteristics of Thai Democracy," p. 12.

56 See Kittisak, "The Democratic Regime with the King as Head of State," who underlines that this concept is essentially different from western-style representtative democracy in constitutional monarchies in which the king is just a symbol and the parliament is representing the sovereign power.

57 See Glaser, "Thai Constitutional Courts and the Political Order," pp. 65-163.

58 Sect. 2 TC 2014 is incorporating chapter II of the TC 2007 including its sect. 8.

This section, in the light of the DRKS[59], acknowledges one of the DRKS' secrets of success, namely the specific mode in which the King exercises the supreme power according to sect. 8 TC 1997/2007: *'above politics'*, meaning not only untouchable by any harm or by any legal responsibility but also untouched by and ritually separated from the sphere of electoral politics, hovering above those *actions* of power. It translates the dichotomous structure of sovereign power in constitutional politics under the sign of sect. 3 vesting the exercise of the sovereign power in the King who indirectly and discretely rules by model and allusion maintaining a form of higher and purer reality of power while his bond with the people is direct, intense and affective.

Similar important for the DRKS is sect. 7 TC 1997/2007 which states that:

> Whenever no provision under this Constitution is applicable to any case, it shall be decided in accordance with the constitutional practice in the democratic regime of government with the King as Head of the State.

This norm is of crucial importance in understanding the DRKS. While some older constitutions contained seemingly similar provisions sect. 7 TC 1997 was in fact introduced in the TC 1997 as a substantially new one. It has been significantly changed with the TC 2014, already indicating a transformation of the DRKS as such.

Before the enactment of sect. 7 TC 1997 the sect. 20, 22 f., 25, and 30 f. of the TC 1959, 1972, 1976 and 1991 respectively regulated that, in the case that no specific provision of the Constitution was applicable, this case should be decided in accordance with "Thai constitutional practices" (TC 1959), the "administrative practice of Thailand under the democratic regime" (TC 1972), the "traditional practice in Thailand in accordance with the democratic system" (TC 1976 and 1991).

It is noticeable that the DRKS is not point of reference but the general (unwritten) practice. Consequently, the respective sections are not regulated in the first chapter or among the first provisions of the constitutions. According to all these constitutions, in cases of any controversies about the respective resort to such unwritten practices (TC

59 The provision stems from the early days of Thai constitutionalism and significantly changed in meaning and impact over its development. See Thongchai, "Toppling Democracy," 2008, pp. 14 ff.

1959, 1976 and 1991) or about whether it would comply with the provisions of the constitution (TC 1972), the National Assembly was competent to decide on the matter.[60]

Rationale was to provide a methodological provision similar to sect. 4 of Thai Civil and Commercial Code to fill gaps of positive law. Subject of such a recourse were especially former constitutions and judicial interpretations of constitutional law or administrative practices.[61] However, the respective decision was not supposed to contravene either the letter or the spirit of the (codified) constitution.[62]

Contrary to the apparent similarity of these provisions with sect. 7, the latter represents a constitutional novelty, which expresses the full maturation of the DRKS. On closer scrutiny, both kinds of provision seem to have no more in common than their reference to an unwritten set of norms. Beyond that, they address substantially different normative orders, have a different addressee and are supposed to be applied to a different operational framework. While sect. 7 addresses (also[63]) the King himself acknowledging his unwritten prerogatives, the older provisions address and entitle only the 'simple' state organs to act in accordance with

60 See also the famous Supreme Court decision 913/2536 related to dispute between politician *Sanoh Tienthong* and the Attorney General after the *Suchinda* Coup pertaining to the confiscation and forfeiture of Sanoh's property according to declaration no. 26 sect. 2 and 6 of the National Peace Keeping Council establishing a judicial review based on sect. 30 TC 1991 particularly referring to the principle *nulla poena sine lege*.

61 See Likhit Dhiravegin, "Section 7 of the Recent Constitution," 2006, (original in Thai), available at http://www.manager.co.th/Daily/ViewNews.aspx?NewsID =9490000058417, last visited 13 November 2014; Banjerd Sangkaneti, "The Constitutional Practice under the Democratic Regime of Government with the King as Head of the State," *Thai Post Newspaper*, 19 May 2006, (original in Thai); Report of the Constitutional Drafting Committee No.14/1997, (original in Thai).

62 According to *Wissanu* and *Bowornsak* this applied even to former constitutions. Referring to sect. 30 TC 1977, Wissanu and Bowornsak, *The Interim Constitution 1977*, pp. 167-169, point out that the practice according to sect. 30 must not be contrary to the spirits and the provisions of recent constitutions, be it directly or indirectly.

63 Sect. 7, insofar, seems to have a double function or two different modes of application, to reserve the unwritten royal prerogatives and to open up the normative sphere of the unwritten dimension of the DRKS for the interpretation of plain constitutional law by the constitutional court. For the latter see Connors, pp. 143, 150.

established constitutional conventions and practices on the level of "plain" constitutional law enabling them to fill of gaps or provide guidance in cases of interpretative obscurity.[64] In other words: while the first kind of provision is a purely methodological one, sect. 7 is also a jurisdictional one in a certain sense. While the application of the older provisions allows for a review by the National Assembly, the application of sect. 7 is beyond the scrutiny of any established constitutional institution.[65]

This interpretation is in line with the genesis of this key norm, newly emerging in 1997. For this *Connors* gives a valuable account stressing that the provision was introduced very late in the deliberations of the Constitution Drafting Assembly (CDA). It coincided with a newly introduced reformulation of the crucial sect. 3. While the latter's older version read "the sovereign power *emanates from* the Thai people", the new version stated "the sovereign power *belongs to* the Thai people". Conservative members of the CDA and many of the so called "royal liberals" saw this new formulation as sharpening a problematic notion of popular sovereignty and fiercely opposed it.[66] They were highly concerned that the new formulation on sovereignty would challenge some key aspects of Thai constitutional thought and that the "King's power and prerogatives were being eroded" as "the new charter were moving away from traditional concepts of political order, in which the monarchy figured greatly".[67] The constitution making process took place during the economic crisis of the year 1997, which pressured the CDA to quickly conclude deliberations. The newly introduced sect. 7 was thus supposed to

64 See Pramuan, *Royal Prerogatives*, pp. 97-104. *Connor's* interpretation of sect. 7 in comparison as the "expression of the mythical belief of the mutuality of King and people" matches the context in which he examines the request of the 'yellow' protesters of the PAD in 2006 the King might replace Thaksin as prime minister based on his prerogative power according to section 7, but seems to be too narrow in general. See Connors, "Liberalism, Authoritarianism and the Politics of Decisionism in Thailand," p. 150. However, Connors is the only foreign scholar who started to interpret the positive legal basis of the DRKS at all.

65 This altogether proves the contravening explanation wrong that the provision was taken from previous interim constitutions. See Connors, "Liberalism, Authoritarianism and the Politics of Decisionism in Thailand," p. 150, quoting a member of the Constitution Drafting Assembly (CDA) 1997.

66 See Connors, "Liberalism, Authoritarianism and the Politics of Decisionism in Thailand," p. 150.

67 See Connors, "Liberalism, Authoritarianism and the Politics of Decisionism in Thailand," p. 150.

counter-balance the reformulated sect. 3 by acknowledging the unwritten Royal prerogatives.

Thus, sect. 7 does not pave the way for secondary considerations of constitutional customary law in cases of an unintentional gap in the law but confirms the unwritten super-constitution and thus gears two normative spheres of the codified constitution and the cultural constitution.

Moreover, it complements the regulation on the exercise of sovereign power according to sect. 3, not framing the exercise of this power by the positive constitution or even the rule of law (as it binds the 'normal' constitutional institutions acc. to sect. 3) but linking it with the unwritten powers of the King. This makes sect. 7 one of the most significant and important sections of the DRKS.

8. Short Summary

The DRKS in the rudimentary form presented here forms – as positive law – the core of the Thai Constitution. It emerged as a hegemonic regime since the 1970s and was fully consolidated during the 1990s until *Thaksin* challenged it. As much as the DRKS' canonical exposition by *Bowornsak* is common knowledge of every Thai lawyer, as much is it surrounded by a kind of taboo leaving the details more or less uncommented beyond *Bowornsak's* and very few other's iconic interpretation. This explains – at least partly – why most of the foreign observers discussing Thai constitutionalism and politics pay surprisingly rare attention to the constitution's basic structure which is prominently visible in the first two chapters of subsequent constitutions. This most notably pertains to the multi-fractured concept of sovereignty when foreign scholars identify a claim for people's sovereignty in sect. 3 TC 1991/97/07/14 by blending out the actually decisive second sentence of the provision which vests the exercise of power in the monarch. Just as misleading is the concept of 'shared sovereignty' which has been described as a mere policy goal of "the elite discourse on Thai-style democracy" [68] or "the conservative royalist discourse on governance for modern Thailand"[69] instead of being

---

68 Dressel, "The Struggle for Political Legitimacy in Thailand," 2011, p. 73.

69 Hewison and Kengkij, "'Thai-Style Democracy': The Royalist Struggle for Thailand's Politics," 2010, p. 190.

acknowledged as the normative fundament of constitutional law in force. However, there are reasons for the fact that the most important part of the Thai legal and political order remains a persisting desideratum in the English literature dealing extensively with Thai politics and constitutionalism. It is not only the difficulty to comprehend and qualify the vast normative ground of the DRKS beyond written law but in particular the general reluctance of the domestic legal science itself to reflect on the ever-present *numen* of the monarchy and the justified concern that it might be mistreated by foreigners. Notwithstanding, the 'red' challenge of the DRKS as well as its intrinsic transformation since 2014 will require more appropriate attention for this autochton conception.[70]

II. The "red" Challenge and its Conceptual Outline

Sociologically the 'red' challenge consists of very heterogeneous social and political groups forming a pragmatic alliance which is unified in its cognitive dissonance related to the DRKS and the more or less determined project to replace it by a different governance concept. There are indeed quite different elements joining hands on this platform, from staunch *Thaksin* supporters to some old adversaries, from people identifying with *Thaksin's* political vision to those demanding a form of western-style constitutionalism, from tightly organized groups to single voices of intellectuals, artists and professionals, from advocates of basically peaceful reform who comply with the legal requirements of the hegemonic regime to those resorting to militant resistance against what they perceive as taking away the electoral mandate by coup d'etats or court decisions and violent crackdowns on 'red' mass protests. 'Red' in this sense is not used here to describe a distinctive oppositional group like the *United Front for Democracy Against Dictatorship* (UDD), the main redshirt organization, but the whole spectrum of societal and political forces challenging the basic consent from this side.

---

70 See Hewison and Kengkij, "'Thai-Style Democracy': The Royalist Struggle for Thailand's Politics," p. 182, point to a kind of consensus among Thai people that there would not be the slightest hope that the DRKS could even be understood from a Western perspective – not to speak of a fair treatment might be added.

Ideal-typically, the 'red' challenge can be structured along three major distinctions: The first major distinction is between party organization and 'street based' mass movement. Precisely, between the *Thai Rak Thai Party* (TRT) and its successor parties *People's Power Party* (PPP) and *Pheu Thai Party* (PTP) on the one hand and the extra-parliamentary redshirt movement and its associates and sympathizers on the other. The second distinction is between *Thaksin* and his close followers and those who align with him against the same foe but with different policy preferences. The third distinction is between two ideal-typical normative concepts pertaining to the basic consent and the fundamental constitutional vision, namely *Thaksin's* "CEO-style populism" as developed and propagated during his premiership and a progressive version of representative democracy which took shape in different shades after the coup[71] displaying a strong accent on progressive democracy to be understood as predominantly based on the rights of the people in egalitarian and majoritarian terms and explicitly against the power of the great and the few. These two ideal-typical, subsequently emerging concepts of governance – inherently different and yet intertwined and mutually reinforcing their relevance against the constitution's basic structure – together form the 'red' counter-hegemonic discourse. Both are based on strong notions of *electoral democracy* and the *opposition to the coup* as legitimate constitutional practice as their common denominator.

While the focus here is directed at the competing governance models and normative visions rather than the different actors, groupings and campaign strategies, it lies in the nature of any counter-hegemonic challenge of a rigidly defensive regime that its normative contours and outlook appear much vaguer than those of governing constitutional law. In other words: while the DRKS can be approached via positive law and a set of canonical political narratives, the competing 'red' concepts barely appear extensively and explicitly formulated in public discourse.

Furthermore it has to be noted that organizational structures and personal affiliations within the 'red' camp often have blurred. For instance, not everyone in the leadership of the subsequent 'red' parties subscribes to the form and agenda of "CEO-style populism" personified

71 It is however reinforcing long existing counter-hegemonic discourses which were propagating equality and social justice since the 1932 revolution and surfaced prominently in the 1970 until they were suppressed and transformed into communist militancy.

by *Thaksin* while some, yet by far not all, of the extra-parliamentary redshirts did and still do.[72] Generally, the majority of those who challenge the status quo on the side of the 'red camp' seem to sway between the two ideal-typical main concepts, often between a deep seated conviction and strategic goals, between what they strongly perceive as wrong in their society and what they want to build instead. Others have to conceal their precise political vision due to the restrictions and potential criminal persecution by the hegemonic regime. In this respect it is important to understand the profoundly counter-hegemonic nature of the 'red' discourse at least after 2006. While *Thaksin's* government was periodically backed by a considerably powerful political position, which came close to deposing the hegemonic regime when he was prime minister, the redshirts have always remained a subaltern, counter-hegemonic force. It should be noted so far that the redshirts emerged only after the coup of 2006 which ended *Thaksin's* relative dominance who himself became both more open for the western-style rhetoric of constitutionalism and more openly radical in his stance against the established regime. Later on, especially in 2009 during the "Bloody Songkran" the joint *Thaksin*-Redshirt discourses blended with each other with notions of revolution.[73] Lastly, the relative weakness of any distinct normative or ideological programs and the corresponding overwhelming dominance of personalities in Thai politics have to be acknowledged to assess both, the hegemonic and the counter-hegemonic discourses in Thai politics. This background notwithstanding some elements of the two ideal-typical normative challenges of the DRKS might be highlighted.

72 Moreover, *Thaksin* himself, especially when his position was uncertain or shaky before being elected in 2001 and when his fortune as premier began to turn in 2004 and then again during the yellow administration 2009-2011, not only turned more decisive to "the people" but also resorted sporadically to the rhetoric of western-style constitutionalism which he formerly has had attacked. While these approaches seem to be strategically motivated they contribute to the ideological vagueness of the red discourse in general where it comes to concise political visions.

73 See Montesano, "Four Thai Pathologies, Late 2009," 2010, pp. 290 f.

1. *Thaksin's* "CEO-Style Populism"

The initial challenge of the DRKS came not on the wings of highflying political ideology but in the person of "CEO" *Thaksin Shinawatra*, the first Prime Minister to successfully claim to possess the popular mandate to effectively rule the country[74] – not as an administrative instrument in the sense of sect. 3 but on his own terms – and who inexhaustibly expanded his influence until the challenge he represented brought about his downfall. Conceptually, the challenge he represented might be circumscribed as follows. *Thaksin's* governance concept was opportunistic, eclectic and centered on his personality and thus lacked an elaborated program on normative terms. However, it proved to be appealing for many due to his responsiveness and efficiency to redress social problems and to simply perform. In this sense *Thaksin's* way resembles striking similarities with the visions of other strong leaders in their claim to directly respond to the people's interest, putting themselves at the very center of the political system, which they start to shape by entrenching their grip as much as possible. This endeavor regularly requires a maximum of personal power combined with a minimum of scrutiny: both based on the claimed popular mandate for the sake of national values beyond the petty yardsticks of formal constitutionalism. The leading maxim is a consequent reason-of-state approach equating the interest of the state with the leader himself. *Thaksin* within this leadership-model represented the modernist rather than the conservative or revolutionary version. Basically, his programmatic course was more or less marked by its open deviation from both, western-style constitutionalism and the DRKS.

To occupy and entrench a populist strong leadership position, as *Thaksin* did, regularly requires not only the sufficient personal qualities and resources but also a political system which is responsive to the emergence of such a leader who, after all, was inclined to transform the status quo. One of the conditions making the system prone to such an occupation is the existence of a latent, yet often hidden crisis of the social contract, an already initiated or awaited transformation and a lack of

74 The *Thaksin* administration holds three records indicating the *scandalon* 'Thaksin' already: For the first time in more than 70 years an elected government completed its parliamentary term, was reelected for the first time and could for the first time eschew the support of other parties to form a government.

opportunities to sufficiently redress these tendencies within the boundaries of the existing system. This might explain *Thaksin's* sustained success, despite the fact that he is no thoroughbred charismatic political leader or brilliant orator nor is representing a distinct ideology. Nevertheless, he remained the (comparatively) undisputed leader of the subsequent 'red' political parties and the outstanding personified 'red' challenge to the DRKS even in the eighth year after his ousting and subsequent exile. Such an outsized political persona overshadowing every other political actor in Thailand between 2006 and 2014 even from exile seems only to be explainable by a deeply ingrained crisis of the existing hegemonic social and political regime paving the way and securing a place for this type of leader. Three distinct qualities come together to make *Thaksin* 'different' within Thai politics: the ability to introduce an efficient management style imposed on cabinet politics and national administration, the absence of those scruples normally required by the unquestionable piety towards the DRKS combined with the obvious will to reach for the stars and the command of the necessary resources.

Means to accomplish his mission involved diffusing the rule of law as a counter-balancing mechanism to the political power of the prime minister, neutralizing all relevant competitors, and ensuring popular support. Thus he attempted to control a critical mass of public institutions, partly to free himself from the dense scrutiny they were supposed to provide, partly to streamline and rationalize the state apparatus enabling him to use it as an additional tool to his party to perform his policies as the major source of his legitimacy. These policies – as such a novelty in Thai politics – and the way and style he executed them meant an unprecedented challenge to the performance of the King by directly competing with him in crucial areas formerly solely occupied by the King and by presenting himself symbolically and effectively as the new center of the polity.[75] All in all, in doing so, he effectively "re-scripted the Constitution […] without changing a single word of it."[76] However, the conclusion that "the

75 See Hewiso and Kengkij, "'Thai-Style Democracy': The Royalist Struggle for Thailand's Politics," p. 196; Case, "Regime Types and Resilience in Thailand and Malaysia," 2010, p. 167. In particular *Thaksin's* national de-velopment and welfare politics attempted to make him increasingly appear as the benevolent leader the King had been since a long time before.

76 See McCargo and Ukrist, *The Thaksinization of Thailand,* 2002, p. 252.

people's Constitution has become the leader's Constitution"[77] might imply a clash of governance concepts which is neither supported by the subsequent development nor the basic structure of the TC 1997 itself – that one of *Thaksin's* 'model' and the supposed model of the TC 1997 shaped by popular sovereignty, representative democracy, and human rights. In fact, the TC 1997, against widespread misconception, was not dominated by a thick version of western-style democracy but – as suggested above – by a very distinct Thai version, the DRKS. Electoral democracy is in this conception an important mechanism to allocate, organize and legitimize *parts* of public power but in the same time, from the hegemonic perspective, inhabited by a dangerous potential of emancipatory forces evolving from the idea of representative democracy as the ultimate source of legitimacy. Consequently, it was the big project of the TC 1997 to carefully design it by retaining its function as merely a mechanism for dynamic elite inclusion and concomitantly for *disciplining* its actors and institutions to prevent both, its misuse by corrupt actors and its emancipatory potential. This constitution, fully governed and determined by the DRKS, became indeed increasingly domesticated by *Thaksin* who captured its plain apparatus and implicitly refused to comply with the most basic demands of the unwritten constitution. He even attempted to replace it with his own vision promulgating the political supremacy of his leadership based on *his* social contract with the people. It was the outcome of this clash, that the third concept emerged in the demands for a more western-style constitutionalism based on equality and majority will. *Thaksin's* own claim of legitimacy was based on his claim to offer the Thai people a better *performance* than any other political force could do, an offer he based on a *modernist agenda* stressing *administrative efficiency* and *social justice*, his successful *experience as a business-CEO* and, most crucial, the mentioned *social contract* between him and the Thai people reflected by *election results*. During the 2005-election campaign resembling somehow the King's style of speeches he declared:

> These past four years, this kind of change was not by chance […] but because of the power of your belief in me. I work hard, don't I? If I work hard, but you don't believe in me, there can be no trust. But if you believe in me, then when I speak, people listen, and bureaucrats are not stubborn, because they listen to the people. This is democracy […]. I have the same power as any person who becomes Prime

77 See McCargo and Ukrist, *The Thaksinization of Thailand*, p. 252.

> Minister, but beyond that I have special power because I do what I say I will do. People put faith and belief in me, don't they?[78]

To fulfill this new social contract *Thaksin* tried to implement his version of good governance by eradicating corrupt politicians (!), unresponsive bureaucrats and 'dark influences'[79] and concrete delivery with particular respect also of the lower middle and the lower classes. Neither the monarchy nor the bureaucracy or the notorious local patron-client-structures but the *politically led state with a distinct modernist agenda* under growing control of his party, the TRT, which in turn was solely ruled by *Thaksin* and the Prime Minister's team, became the decisive structure to deliver, expressed by village funds, agrarian depth relief, affordable health care, local economy development schemes, and in general better infrastructure for the rural areas. It was clear from the beginning, that this policy would challenge the established elites as he "offered himself as a leader, borne up by the direct support of the people, who would defy this elite [of old establishment bureaucrats and academics, Democratic politicians and old status families] and spread benefits more widely."[80]

In doing so and calling on his 'social contract' *Thaksin* denied to bow under the scrutinizing mechanisms of the constitution and thus, to obey the rule of law. Similarly he refused to respect fundamental rights as boundaries for his grand political project, especially when it came to the freedom of expression and the press or the execution of his national security policies, namely the war on drugs leading to a series of extra-legal killings. As early as in his first year in office, in 2001, he questioned the

---

78 Thaksin in 2005, quoted from Pasuk and Baker, *Thaksin*, 2005, p. 234.

79 "After the next election you will see a totally different scene from what you see now. What you see now is the last honeymoon for corrupt politicians." Thaksin, quoted from McCargo and Ukrist, *Thaksinization of Thailand*, p. 73. His fight against corrupt politicians and 'dark influences' was the most decisive attempt of this kind ever in Thai history even if it was motivated by *Thaksin's* interest to expand his direct control of the populace by eradicating the local networks necessary for political mobilization. It is somehow ironic that he now is the very symbol of corrupted politics in the hegemonic discourse. See for Thaksin's campaign and its strategic role in his power building project Prajak, "The Rise and Fall of Electoral Violence in Thailand: Rules, Structures and Power Landscapes, 1997-2011," 2014, pp. 395 ff.

80 See Pasuk and Baker, *Thaksin*, p. 234.

authority of the Constitutional Court to decide on an asset concealment case against him by claiming his popular mandate: "It's strange that a leader who was voted by 11 million people had to bow to […] the verdict of the Constitutional Court […]."[81] Generally "he suggested to his audience that the bundle of liberal democracy – rule of law, freedom of criticism, human rights, oversight by parliamentary opposition, checks and balances on the executive – had done little for them in the past."[82] The appropriate constitutional design *Thaksin* envisioned for the future was in fact a two-party system in which power, however, would not alternate between the two parties but in which his TRT would retain the monopoly of power with an impotent Democrat Party (DP) as the opposition keeping the democratic facade.[83] Among all the elites he challenged, including the armed forces and the royalist DP, the challenge of the Throne was outstanding. In the same time it meant to challenge the fundamental consensus and the constitutional basic structure. He did so by entrenching and re-defining the established conceptions of 'administrative performance' and the 'popular mandate', the latter by effectively tapping central sources of the King's legitimacy which amounted to an unprecedented violation of public piety and political moral as being prescribed by 'Thai-style-democracy' or the 'cultural constitution' respectively. With this challenge of one of the core assumptions of Thai-style-democracy, the "mutuality of king and people", he unmistakably marked his willingness to compete for power on tabooed ground.[84]

Thus, it seems not very realistic that "Thaksin may not have been entirely clear that he also challenged entrenched ideas associated with Thai style democracy".[85] For Thai politics *Thaksin* is most significant as the one who dared the unimaginable, nearly successful, with such benefits for those formerly excluded from national politics that they, for first time ever, realized their influence on the hegemony, a lesson they should not

81 Thaksin, cited in Pasuk and Baker, *Thaksin*, p. 2.

82 See Pasuk and, Baker, *Thaksin*, p. 234; see also Hewison and Kengkij, "'Thai-Style Democracy': The Royalist Struggle for Thailand's Politics," p. 196.

83 See McCargo and Ukrist, *The Thaksinization of Thailand*, p. 84; see also Pasuk and Baker, *Thaksin*, p. 240: "[H]e opened the hankered after the one man, one of" the strong leaders in Malaysia and Singapore where each only one political party ruled throughout the existence of the respective state.

84 See Hewison, "Crafting Thailand´s New Social Contract," 2004, pp. 503-522.

85 Hewison and Kengkij, "'Thai-Style Democracy': The Royalist Struggle for Thailand's Politics," p. 195.

forget henceforth. This altogether made him to become the very embodiment of the possibility of an alternative governance path and the political evil par excellence for those who were convinced to possess the best possible system exactly where *Thaksin* challenged it, at the very top, high above politics. His continuing presence in Thai politics despite his ouster and the subsequent crashes on his political 'infrastructure' left Thailand not only deeply split but made him to become the very personification of a vital threat to the DRKS and one of the most influential figures of modern Thai history. This effect is probably attributed to both, an already existing disposition of the hegemonic system marked by a hidden site of fracture when he became prime minister as well as his ability to effectively launch the challenge. Therefore, "the idea that Thaksin was 'sleepwalking' into history may be overdone"[86], given not only his unprecedented achievements in building a strong electoral machine providing the elected government with a hitherto unknown power but also the decisive attempt to recklessly challenge the grand taboo. On the other side, he was most probably not aware of the *independent dynamics* in which the shockwaves of his challenge should evolve. In consequence, yet unwittingly, he opened the doors for the redshirts and their supporters as "one of the most powerful social movements in recent Thai history"[87] which however, at least partly, advocate another model of political ordering competing with both, *Thaksin's* and the hegemonic one.

2. Progressive Democracy

The common denominator of the progressive 'red' challenge is the "desire to see full representative democracy"[88] not as a mere tool to enable *Thaksin's* CEO-style populism but as the fundamental normative principle

86 See Hewison and Kengkij, "'Thai-Style Democracy': The Royalist Struggle for Thailand's Politics," p. 195 f.; see also Montesano, "Four Thai Pathologies, late 2009," p. 281.

87 See Sinpeng, "Party-Social Movement Coalition in Thailand's Political Conflict (2005-2011)," 2014, p. 159.

88 See Jim Taylor, *Larger Than Life: 'Central World' and Its Demise and Rebirth – Red Shirts and the Creation of an Urban Cultural Myth in Thailand*, 2011, p. 3 quoted after Sinpeng, "Party-Social Movement Coalition in Thailand's Political Conflict (2005-2011)," p. 159.

and guiding political value of the political system and thus representing its hegemonic consensus and constitutional basic structure.

Proponents of this vision can be found among members of the subsequent 'red' parties, those of the different redshirt-groups and unorganized individuals. Some are (former) socialist, some humanists, some being convinced of the need to consider a western-like constitution as the untouchable fundament for the development of a mature polity and just society, and some are mainly motivated by what they perceive as constant injustice, applied double-standards and hypocrisy on the side of the hegemonic regime. Varying is also the degree of the concrete challenge towards the DRKS. There are notions of more or less progressive versions of western-style constitutionalism, calls for the abolishment of the differentiation between 'big' and 'small' people in the dominant social discourse and more or less articulated preferences to pursue the major sin of the hegemonic political discourse: the establishment of the republic.

To concretize the progressive mainstream vision two sources seem particularly suitable, the official *policy announcement* of the UDD, an umbrella organization of the redshirt movement and a proposed *draft constitution* of an independent group of law scholars, the *Nitirat* group.

The UDD despite being the biggest and most visible group voicing the progressive vision in the 'red' camp is not a homogenous, unified organization but comprising of several independent, sometimes loosely sometimes more closely knit oppositional groupings while *Nitirat* is a small group of legal scholars from the Thammasat University's Faculty of Law which is allied with a circle of activists and intellectuals and widely heard in Thailand by friends and foes.

Both groups' announcements are not necessarily representing the full spectrum of their policy preferences but rather the maximum they dare to openly declare 'from within' the borders set by the regime. Significantly in this respect, the UDP in 2010 formulated a *negative agenda* comprising the absolute refrain from touching at the monarchy issue and from engaging in verbal and non-verbal violence.[89] Positively the UDD announced the following six principles[90]:

89 See Naruemon and McCargo, "Urbanized Villages in the 2010 Thai Redshirt Protests. Not just to farmers?," 2011, p. 997.

90 See http://thairedshirts.org/the-movement/the-six-principles/, (*italics* in original), last visited 14 November 2014.

(1) To attain true democracy with *sovereignty truly in the hands of the people* of Thailand with the King as the head of state.

(2) To unify *grassroots masses* as the main social and cultural force together with people from every sector who seek democracy and justice *while resisting "aristocratic" forces that obstructs equitable and democratic development.*

(3) To promote *non-violence* as our modus operandi for all activities.

(4) To *fight against poverty* by tying economic policies on poverty reduction with political strategies which stresses that *economic policies must be formulated directly by an elected government.*

(5) To reinstate the "Rule of Law" through ensuring equitable and transparent judicial process for all, along with putting an end to the "double standards" policies which currently under control by aristocratic interests and elite networks.

(6) To revoke the 2007 Constitution along with its unjust laws that favor certain military and elite interest and to *draw up a new democratic Constitution.*

This progressive democratic policy agenda is complemented by the independent *Nitirat* proposal of an elaborated draft constitution. When the group began to take shape since 2009 around *Worachet Pakeerut* the room for maneuver for any open challenge of the hegemonic basic consent and the respective constitutional basic structure was so rigidly limited, that it chose to focus on one single point first: the law and practice of criminalizing critical commentaries on the King and certain members of the Royal family, sect. 112 of the criminal code. This proposition already enraged everyone who subscribed to the hegemonic basic consent and provided *Nitirat* immediately with the status of a barely tolerated dissident group with a kind of pariah image which was increasingly walking a tightrope.[91] The group, however, went eventually further on expanding

---

91 In 2011, short after *Thaksin's* sister *Yingluck* became prime minister, the group's campaign to amend the law in favor of a limitation of its scope and a reduction of the possible punishment of 15 years for every single violation provoked key figures in politics, the academia and the security forces to harshly address the issue resulting in warnings by all supreme commanders of the military forces. Squadron Leader *Prasong Soonsiri*, a key framer of the TC 2007, warned *Nitirat* explicitly that what they were doing could possibly lead to unrest and yet another military coup. The harsh reaction by the system-loyal forces of the 'yellow camp', which could be labeled as the "Nitirat shock" of the hegemonic regime, exemplifies the nature of the DRKS as the country's constitutional basic structure

their campaign to suggest the mentioned draft constitution, which expectedly draw similarly fierce criticism, personal attacks and warnings. Some crucial aspects of the draft and subsequent comments by core *Nitirat* members shall be highlighted.

Instead of drawing explicitly on western constitutionalism something what would provoke additional criticism of an unduly foreign influence, the group adopts the spirit and content of the Universal Declaration of Human Rights and declares especially the first and the third Thai C

onstitution, the TC June 1932 and the TC 1946, as sources of its inspiration. The proposed concept of sovereignty deviates substantially from the one of the TC 1997/2007, claiming that sovereignty does not only belong to the people but – as explicit fundament for the exercise of all state power – is also expressed by elections. Consequently and diverging from the status of the TC 2007 with its nearly half appointed Senate under TC2007, *Nitirat* proposes either a one-chamber parliament or at least a fully elected house. While representative democracy is the proposed form of government, the group acknowledges the monarchical form of state (yet not of government).[92] Accordingly, *Nitirat's* draft places the judiciary and the military under the effective supremacy and control of the people. As both powers are the ones closest related to the monarchy in the frame of the DRKS and considered to be the *avant garde* of its protection, this would substantially shift the existing balances of power. While higher judges shall be nominated by the prime minister to be approved by parliament, the lower instances shall be staffed with lay judges. Concerning the military *Nitirat* proposes the enactment of a strict civilian supremacy with the (elected) government appointing high-ranking military personnel while the parliament is supposed to appoint a military commissioner, a newly introduced office, who shall supervise the military's loyalty to the democratic regime. Tellingly are also two provisions pertaining to right of resistance against acts or orders

---

and hegemonic basic consent. - Not a single law had been attacked by *Nitirat* but *the* law, the whole of the social and political order far beyond any positive law.

92 Additionally, one group member, *Piyabutr Saengkanokkul*, in another publication, explicitly criticizes the idea of a "super-constitution" above the positive one and engages critically with the dominating doctrine pertaining to the constituent power. See Piyabutr, "Trivia about 'pouvoir constituant' or the Power to Establish Political Institutions," http://blogazine.in.th/blogs/piyabutr-saengkanokkul/post/3755, published on 10 November 2012, last visited 14 November 2014.

contravening the democratic regime. While soldiers shall have the right to disobey illegal and especially unconstitutional commands, every citizen shall have the right and duty to use any means to resist attempts to take away the supreme power from the people by a usurpation of power, or, to say it clearly, by a military coup. The draft specifies that such an usurpation is a criminal act, and that, after the supreme power of the people has been returned to them, the usurpers must be prosecuted a claim which is breaking with the classical doctrine and practice of legitimate coups.[93] One of the most critically received parts of the *Nitirat* draft completes the provisions pertaining to militant democracy when it states that the monarch has the duty to protect the Constitution and that a new head of state must swear an oath to abide and to protect the Constitution before he/she takes the position. This proposal proved not only to be provoking but appeared outright revolutionary for the proponents of the DRKS. Remarkably, not only system-loyal voices condemned the draft but also parts of the *Yingluck*-administration which was officially taking a distant stance to avoid any association with *Nitirat*. Some cabinet members concomitantly belonging to the Redshirt leadership remained

---

93 It is striking to compare these provisions providing for a militant democracy with the militant constitutionalism provided by the corresponding regulations under the DRKS in the TC 1997 and 2007 highlighting the essentially different basic structure in the respective visions. In the case of the TC 1997 and 2007, two identical regulations deal with threats to the constitutional order, sect. 69 and 70 TC 2007. According to Sect. 69 TC 2007 regulating in particular the scenario of a coup, "*a person* shall have the *right* to *peacefully resist* an act committed for the acquisition of the power to rule the country by a means which are not in accordance with the modes provided in this Constitution." Sect. 70 on the other hand states that "*every person* is under *duty* to uphold 'nation, religion and King' and the democratic regime of government with the King as Head of the State under this Constitution". While sect. 70 aims at the protection of the DRKS, does sect. 69 provide for the protection of an elected government like in the *Nitirat* proposal, yet with completely different impact: Is the protection of the DRKS a *duty* of *every* citizen and *not restricted* to any mode of action, are acts intended to protect electoral democracy *optional* and *restricted* to peaceful means. Especially the latter is practically decisive in the moment of a coup, which will regularly appear combined with the use of martial law or emergency powers effectively restricting such peaceful means like demonstrations etc. Thus, while electoral or representative democracy is the sole source of legitimate power in the *Nitirat* proposal and accordingly to be protected by all means against usurpation, electoral democracy in the TC 2007 (and the identical provisions of the TC 1997) is no integral part of the basic structure of Thai constitutional law which is formed by the DRKS.

surprisingly silent while *Nitirat's* proposal hit a nerve of many within the 'red' camp. In sum, the reaction to the proposal signals how much it had touched upon ultra-sensitive issues forcing even a 'red' government which was basically in power due to the electoral support of the Redshirts[94] to act very carefully if it did not want to endanger its priority project to bring *Thaksin* back home from exile before the basic consent was supposed to be re-defined by an amendment of the constitution.

B. The Preservative Restatement of the Basic Constitutional Order

The decade-lasting waving back and forth of the hegemonic system's defense battle against an ever increasing challenge of its basic tenets by an electorally backed, conceptually heterogeneous social and political force and the corresponding fight for dominance between the three described governance models reached a new level with the Interim-Constitution 2014 and its restatement of the DRKS. The latter has to be seen in the context of the 'yellow' anti-government unrest in the end of 2013 culminating in June 2014 when the military as a part of the pro-establishment camp staged a coup, assumed the position of an authoritarian arbiter, froze the conflict and started to re-define the constitutional basic consent, a project which continues with the current making of a permanent constitution. From this process the 'red' voice is virtually excluded while some basic conditions on the 'yellow' side seem to have shifted significantly, a shift which is visible mostly in form of constitutional law, precisely the Interim-Constitution 2014. The final part of the present paper will concentrate on this constitution while the broader 'yellow' discourse and its different shades and transformations cannot be considered here.[95]

---

94 See Sinpeng, "Party-Social Movement Coalition in Thailand's Political Conflict (2005-2011)," pp. 164 ff.

95 It should to be noted that the DRKS as the 'yellow' regime's normative manifestation in form of positive constitutional law is embedded in a far broader discourse whose principal tenets is shared by its proponents in the military, judiciary, senior bureaucracy, academia, economy, the Democrat Party and the yellow extra-parliamentary movements including the PAD and the PDRC. Taking up an old thread of the hegemonic negative-narrative of 'evil' politics it was mainly the PAD which stepped up to convert this underlying narrative on a mere abstract danger into a major agenda for the 'yellow' camp. Initially

Despite being just an interim constitution to be replaced by a permanent constitution earliest in 2015 the TC 2014 of July 2014 promises to be a highly important document insofar as it seems to reflect and anticipate the evolution of the DRKS heralding fundamental change. In this sense it could veritably be called revolutionary if it would not be such a pronounced expression of a conservative political agenda and not be led by such a preservative determination than it is. Accordingly, both, continuity and change mark the reformulated basic structure with the DRKS remaining at the heart not only of the TC 2014 but being even prescribed for the permanent constitution to come though it appears substantially modified in its already restated version in the same time. This change has gone mainly unnoticed by the majority of the western observers who focused on sect. 2 TC 2014 which states that Thailand adopts the DRKS and that the provisions of chapter II TC 2007/97 pertaining to the King would remain "in force as an integral part of this Constitution". This led to the common conclusion that the fundamental constitutional structure remained unaffected in the light of the new constitution. The reality deserves a more differentiated account. The more important chapter I of the former constitutions had indeed been changed at the central position, namely in form of the mentioned sect. 7 which appears in a substantially modified version in sect. 5 TC 2014. Introduced by the TC 1997 as an expression of the mature and differentiated DRKS acknowledging the constitution's double structure, sect. 7 had functioned in the constitutional debates since 2006 as the basis for subsequent calls for a Royal intervention to remove the respective 'red' Prime Minister (*Thaksin*, *Samak*, *Somchai*, *Yingluck*) and to appoint a new one, something which had eventually been achieved by decisions of the constitutional court or coup d'états. To understand the tectonic shift expressed by the

---

supposed to be an anti-Thaksin agenda it aims at electoral democracy at heart and is "going as far as rejecting" the western-style system of parliamentary democracy heavily attacking all its elements: elections as the fundament for political legitimacy, political parties as insofar necessary transformative mechanisms and the elected forms of government and parliament as trusted core institutions of the constitutional set up. This crusade is accompanied by nationalist notions and new interpretations of Buddhist governance in different versions and, like the 'red' discourse, abided by a heterogeneous alliance of different groups with partly competing political interests and preferences in terms of radicalism. See mainly for the PAD Nelson, "People's Aliance for Democracy: From 'New Politics' to a 'Real' Political Party?," 2010, pp. 122 ff.

recent modification of the provision it has to be remembered that it, according to the orthodox doctrine, did not necessarily refer to any already established or defined constitutional customary law rather than acknowledging a normative source *sui generis* which was directly linked to the monarch expressing his extra-constitutional prerogatives. It thus *provided for a vague yet central representation of the non- and meta-positive dimension of the DRKS within the codified constitution whose concretization could override positive constitutional law.* This totally changed with its new version in sect. 5 TC 2014. Repeating the formulation of sect. 7 TC 2007/1997 *it adds* like the predecessors of sect. 7 in older constitutions that the recourse to the DRKS shall *not be contrary to, or inconsistent with the constitution.* Furthermore, in the case that the thereby newly ordered compliance with positive constitutional law would be in question, the norm now provides for a *constitutional instance to decide* about it. If such a question arises related to the affairs of the National Legislative Assembly, it shall, according to sect 5, now be decided by the same. In any other cases the Constitutional Court shall decide. In other words: sect 5 firstly stipulates a *reservation* according to which positive constitutional law cannot be overruled anymore and secondly implements a constitutional *instance to decide* in case of doubts. This is completely changing the normative content and nature of this provision turning it from a competence norm rooted in meta-positive law to a mere methodological reference norm which is explicitly subjugated to positive constitutional law. Not the unwritten elements of the DRKS are now above the written Constitution but it is the other way round: confirming the *positivation and juridification of the DRKS* including the unwritten royal prerogatives and expressing nothing less than a tectonic shift in the constitutional order's normative fundament.[96]

---

96 Interesting in this context is the counter-hegemonic account of two key *Nitirat* scholars on the old sect. 7. TC 2007, *Worachet and Piyabutr,* who both stated each that sect. 7 refers only to regular customary law (by an established legal practice considered by the relevant actors as law) only serving as a secondary source of constitutional law to fill gaps in codification. Pertaining to the Royal prerogatives both agree that such prerogatives might exist beyond the written constitution but would have to be exercised strictly in accordance with the written constitution. See Worachet, *Lecture on State and Public Law*, 2012, p. 249 f., (original in Thai); Piyabutr, *Royal Prerogatives, the Privy Council and Charismatic Persons outside the Constitution*, 2007, p. 49 f., (original in Thai); see also the *Seminar of Nitirat* on "Coup d'etat and constitutional regime" at

This understanding finds a confirmation by the reading of two other sect. of the new constitution, sect. 27 and sect. 35.

Sect. 27 firstly prescribes the duties of the newly inaugurated National Reform Council which is charged with political and constitutional reforms while sect. 35 addresses the Constitution Drafting Assembly which is also established by the TC 2014. It prescribes the necessary content of the permanent constitution's draft. Both projects are explicitly linked to the basic constitutional order, the DRKS. Mission of the constitutional reform agenda according to sect. 27 is to "create a DRKS which is appropriate for the Thai society", and according to sect. 35 the permanent constitution in the making has to adopt "a DRKS which is appropriate for the Thai society". Both provisions strikingly express the coexistence of continuity and change. While the DRKS is acknowledged as Thailand's present and future form of government which has to lead national reform and constitution making, the TC 2014 adds for the first time in Thai constitutional history the auspicious phrase *"which is appropriate for the Thai society"*. In doing so it prescribes that the established DRKS has, in the same way in which it is re-adopted, to be adapted and restated dependent to the actual circumstances.

It might not be too speculative to understand this whole restatement project not as a reference to the political split and the eroding legitimacy of the DRKS expressed by the redshirt movement but in relation to the ailing of the reigning monarch who *personally embodies the heart of the DRKS* in the form it emerged in the 1970s and governed previous constitutions.[97] To put it in other words: the already initiated and further announced modification of this normative fundament, core and horizon of

---

Thammasat University, 30 September 2012, http://www.prachatai.com/journal/2012/10/42914, last visited 14 November 2014. In sum both suggest an interpretation which equates those of constitutional law and doctrine before the DRKS fully evolved, ironically the same position which is now expressed by the current TC 2014. Decisive in this inherently politicized discourse, however, is who makes which comment when and with which underlying constitutional policy.

97 Not for the time being but for the future succession to the Throne this might be highlighted from another perspective, too. The Thai understanding of ultimate royal sovereignty and the royal exercise of the sovereign power as well is defined by its Buddhist context. As such the Royal role and rule is highly dependent on the actual merits of the incumbent monarch in the sense of what could be called his *dhammic* quality as the embodiment of the sovereign power. It is, thus, not simply transferable by succession.

the whole legal-political order seems to be compellingly induced by the changed circumstances in person of the ailing monarch rather than a deliberate decision of the drafters. The impact of the changes reflected by sect. 5, 27 and 35 TC 2014 looms in form of the mainstay of the constitutional order's new architecture, precisely its efficient center, the point of concentration of the actual sovereign power.

Despite the rather indirect mode to exercise the sovereign power reflected by sect. 8, the King, additionally assisted by his Privy Council and a web of trustees throughout all societal segments, performed nothing less than the efficient center of the constitutional order as reflected not only by the DRKS' conception of the sovereign power based on sect. 3 but also by the positive acknowledgement of the unwritten constitution in sect. 7. Given that the Royal institution remains the unchangeable embodiment of the national values and virtues to be preserved under the coming constitution making it the dignified center of the constitutional order[98], the described modification of sect. 7, though, raises the question where the efficient center has to be located now and in future. While this question cannot be analyzed here for the future, the answer for the present TC 2014 lying in a remarkably significant provisionary efficient center of the constitutional order indicates at least the profound nature of the shift in Thailand's constitutional order which already reveals a tectonic one. Interesting is how consequent the coup group, in the way it assumes the concentrated sovereign power, temporarily occupies the position of the efficient center of the constitution.

In Thai constitutional practice the coup group usually forms a sort of national security council under a interim constitution which is supposed to guard the development back to a 'normal' constitutional status. Bearing in mind the highly regulated practice of coups in Thailand the current constitutional status of the coup group indeed offers a suitable subject of exploration for the question if the concept of sovereignty is already

98 The differentiation refers to *Bagehot* distinguishing an efficient and a dignified part of the English constitution and was already used by *Bowornsak* to describe the royal institution even with a different accentuation than proposed here. See Bowornsak, "Ten Principles of a Righteous King and the King of Thailand," available at http://www.thailandtoday.in.th/monarchy/elibrary/article /167, last visited 14 November 2014, and Bagehot, *The English Constitution*, 1963 (1867), p. 61.

affected by the actual project to restate the hegemonic basic consent even if only on a provisionary basis.

Under the TC 2014 the institutionalized junta, the *National Council for Peace and Order* (NCPO), is in fact stronger than any other coup group has ever been, and so is the position of its leader. The practice of a coup group to form such an institutionalized body in form of a "Guardian Council", which initially was supervising the cabinet in matters pertaining to national security, coincidently came up with the emergence of the DRKS, namely with the TC 1976.[99] The TC 1976 established in its sect. 18 an "Advisory Council" to the Prime Minister which comprised members of the coup group and was labeled "National Administrative Reform Council". It retained the supervision of the national security policy and the competence to authoritatively guide the cabinet on such issues. This model was repeated by the TC 1977 which established in its sect. 17 a "National Policy Council" consisting of members of the "Revolutionary Group" which had seized power. This Council had more far reaching authorities including those to "formulate policy guidelines of the state and to give advice to the Cabinet in order that the administration of the country is carried out in accordance with the policy guidelines of the state" (sect. 18). Concerning policies or actual problems the council's Chairman retained the authority to request a joint meeting with the cabinet which he would chair and whose decisions would bind the cabinet (sect. 19). With the third post-coup constitution, the TC 1991, the model became practice when the coup group, the "National Peacekeeping *Committee*", was constitutionally established as "National Peacekeeping *Council*" according to sect. 18 TC 1991. The fourth post-coup constitution since 1976, the TC 2006, follows the practice by institutionalizing the then junta, the "Council for Democratic Reform", in sect. 34 as the "National Security Council". The NCPO under the TC 2014 sets forth the practice with, however, some significant modifications. According to the established practice it is superior in relation to the Prime Minister as the King, according to sect. 19 para 3 TC 2014, has the prerogative to remove the

99 Before the 1976, coup groups did not regularly appear as constitutionally constituted bodies but remained informal power groups often shaped by sharp internal competition whose individual members partly occupied official positions. Before 1957 their members often hold only positions of secondary rank providing but real influence to them, while someone from beyond the inner circle served as Prime Minister.

Prime Minister on the initiative of the NCPO while there is no corresponding regulation pertaining to the NCPO chair.[100] Moreover, while it was up to the Prime Minister under the TC 1977 to appoint new members to the Advisory Council with the same's approval, it is the Head of the NCPO who, according to sect. 42 TC 2014, appoints new members and can for the first time explicitly also remove other members of the NCPO. Insofar, the NCPO basically follows the lines of the established model while applying its most robust version ever. In other respects the NCPO represents qualitatively new forms. Practically probably most significant is the power of the institutionalized junta to exercise special powers. The TC 1976 and 1977 retained such special powers in their sect. 21 and 27 respectively to counter broadly defined dangers for national security and good public morals by any necessary measure and requested the Prime Minister to gain the approval of the institutionalized coup group and to subsequently report to the parliament. By sect. 27 TC 1991 the typical special powers were given to the leader of the institutionalized coup group and the Prime Minister alternatively, both having the duty to report to the Speaker of the National Legislative Assembly in the case of their exercise. While the 2006 post-coup Constitution contains no such provision about special powers, the TC 2014 provides not only for the strongest version of these powers in Thai constitutionalism but also by a provision which transcends the boundaries of the previous models. According to sect. 44 TC 2014 the NCPO's special powers differ in two respects from previous versions. Firstly, the provision states that the head of the NCPO "shall have the powers to make any order [...] regardless of the legislative, executive or judicial force of that order". This *concentrates all state powers* in the end of the NCPO head eliminating any separation of powers.

Secondly, the *scope of application* of this absolute power is immensely extended. The provision allows decisions and measures in any case in which the head of the NCPO deems it necessary to act "for the *benefit of*

100 See in contrast sect. 14 para 2 TC 2006 dealing with both, the President of the National Security Council and the Prime Minister, and sect. 23 TC 1977 on the hand, stating the Chairman of the National Policy Council will countersign the Royal Command which is appointing or dismissing a Prime Minister. The regulation of the TC 2014 is most similar with sect. 22 of TC 1991 according to which the King holds the authority to strip the Prime Minister off his post on recommendation of the Chairman of the National Peacekeeping Council and to relieve a Minister of his post on the recommendation of the Prime Minister.

reform in any field or to *strengthen unity and harmony*". In this version the head of the NCPO effectively becomes the *commissarial gubernator of the supreme power*, the one who commands the totality of the sovereign power, nearly absolute.

Noteworthy in relation to the constituent power is sect. 46 TC 2014 which, for the first time, allocates the *sole initiative for constitutional amendments* to the NCPO (together with the cabinet) leaving the national assembly only the possibility to accept or refuse the bill without further debate. In this context it has to be mentioned that the TC 2014 as the NCPO's brainchild prescribes the necessary content of the permanent constitution to make in some detail in its sect. 35 related to eleven broadly formulated issues, thus *binding the constituent power* of the nation for the future in an unprecedented manner.

Another astonishing regulation which is new in Thai constitutionalism is sect. 45 TC 2014 which creates two new competences of the constitutional court. According to it the court is firstly competent to decide if an administrative or judicial application of the principles of the DRKS according to sect. 5 is in accordance with the constitution and secondly if a law is consistent with orders of the NCPO leader based on sect. 44 TC 2014. This seemingly procedural provision expresses two essential novelties of the new constitution, the juridification of the DRKS and the acknowledgment of the supreme power of the NCPO, whose orders are ranking above the law, being the constitutional measure for any law and thus cutting the NCPO off and placing it above the written law. – All in all, no other coup group enjoyed such a comparable constitutional position, either effectively or conceptually. An indication for the underlying shift represented by the position of the NCPO pertaining to the concept of sovereignty is represented by the terminology used to label the coup group. Since the practice to formally re-constitute the junta in form of a council which, as a body of the interim constitution, is wielding special powers emerged in 1976, a conceptual distinction has been made between the original coup-group which successfully seized power and its constitutionally established and institutionalized form. This terminological shift characterizes all post-coup constitutions after 1976 until the last one, the four subsequent post-coup constitutions of 1976, 1977, 1991, and

2006.[101] By applying this practice the constitution marked the fiction of a normative break between the coup group which was de-facto commanding the state of emergency and the constitutionally constituted and legitimized institution, between the normative unshaped and the normative shaped power.

This is totally different in the case of the TC 2014. The current charter is not only using the same term for the junta before and after the enactment of the constitution but explicitly states in sect. 42 that the NCPO – which seized state power – has the *power to continue its duty under the new constitution*. For the first time, an interim constitution renounces the terminological transformation of the junta and even orders institutional continuity between informality and formality, sheer force and legitimized rule. In other words: the distinction between the sovereign power de facto and de jure as well as the function of the interim constitution to *create* legitimacy are not accentuated or even acknowledged anymore.

In conclusion, the suggested reading of the TC 2014 exemplifies the start of a manifest restatement process of the basic constitutional order visible in form of three striking novelties in present constitutional design. With sect. 5 TC 2014 replacing the old section 7, a key provision of the DRKS has already been changed profoundly turning its normative (double-) structure upside down. This is accompanied by the ordered future alignment of the DRKS in the context of fundamental political reform (sect. 27) and constitution making (sect. 35) and thus expressing only the upbeat of an already initiated deep transformation. This overarching assessment is confirmed for the time being by the provisionary yet significant shaping of the sovereign power under the junta's command.

C. Conclusion and Outlook

After the military coup d'état 2014 the intense struggle over the basic consent which was unraveling Thailand for more than a decade remains frozen for the time being. Any actual challenge of the hegemonic regime's

101 Even after the coup of October 20, 1958, the coup group or military group (*kana thahan*) respectively was for the first time terminologically transformed into something else, the "Revolutionary Council" (*kana pattiwat*).

prerogative of interpretation is actually excluded by the effective yet not deeply repressive use of martial law and the practice of summoning non-compliant citizens for 'attitude adjustment' (instead of the detaining them). Nevertheless, the competing conceptions of governance envisioning the basic order of the social and political system on very different terms remain opposed to each other. They set forth normative threads running back to the dawn of modern constitutionalism in Thailand in the 1930s and will probably be revitalized in the future, especially since the current reform and constitution making process widely excludes the counter-hegemonic discourses. Given the fact that the competing conceptions of governance will most probably generally enjoy less impact of the central integrative figures, the King on the one hand and *Thaksin* on the other, the spectrum of interpretations might become more volatile on both sides probably providing a more diverse and dynamic development also within the major discursive lines when the current regime loosens its actual grip. Pertaining to the hegemonic discourse and corresponding constitutional basic structure it has to be highlighted that the dramatic adjustment is no result or expression of a compromise between the struggling camps. Rather it is the manifestation of the military's mission to preserve as much of the established system as possible, not only protecting the Royal institution against prospective republican tendencies but particularly the whole set of values and virtues attached to and embodied by it from the regime's perspective.[102] This is leading to a

102 The essence of this heritage is difficult to grasp from the outside. On the basis of a virtually ritual distinction between a 'good order' in the light of the DRKS and 'bad', yet to a certain degree necessary western-style constitutional elements in form of electoral democracy, the system governed by the DRKS allowed the emergence of a distinct socio-political superstructure. The latter proved to be able to integrate an unusual broad and diverse, stable and dynamic elite whose single segments were centered around the monarch in an unprecedentedly balanced equilibrium pacifying them internally and in relation to each other without recourse to repressive measures. In its mature form the DRKS eventually seemed to have been arranged the - formerly partly heavily competing - elites in a perfect *mandala* of the political guided by the royal model, a system which was supposed to represent everything 'good' in Thai society and culture. Everyone seemed to receive an important, secure, yet limited position within. Political ideologies in the western sense, never very strong in Thailand and often considered as potentially detrimental to the common good, seemed to be nearly completely melted down in favor of this Thai-style democracy which claimed to exclusively command the legitimate public faith. Whereas personal ambitions of the elite's members were successful channeled by the system's integrative

strong conservative notion of the currently authoritarian constitutionalism whose constitution making project is ridden by a rare determination to root out any uncontrolled space of electoral politics. Even more than before, electoral politics are perceived as highly dangerous, a tainted evil of modern constitutionalism, which, nevertheless, is to a certain degree unavoidable. On the side of the 'red' camp *Thaksin's* political infrastructure, in particular his future chances to mobilize party politics or to call on remaining confidants within the country's administrative structure, is battered more than ever before, while the decentralized Redshirts movement, currently staying nearly completely silent, seems to follow a wait-and-see policy from a hiding position. On the side of the 'yellow' camp where most energy seems to be invested in finding the optimal anti-electoral agenda within the narrowly defined frame of a constitutional project which is nevertheless taken seriously, the two biggest challenges seem to be the substantial preservation of the DRKS and the consequent execution of the regime's promised non-corruption and non-populism agenda.

In any case, Thai constitutionalism will remain one of the most interesting in the region with the new constitution to be expected in 2015 as the next major step in the project to adapt and restate the DRKS as the constitutional basic structure. If the DRKS becomes a unique normative conception to order the political in modern constitutionalism it remains to be hoped that the deep and highly charged conflict lines pertaining to Thailand's future ordering might be settled by a sustainable basic consent to be found and a suitable constitution to be made and that the country preserves its hitherto remarkable ability to refrain from slipping into protracted violence.

---

dynamics, partly secured by a high predictability of career paths and a vivid turnover of single career positions, the 'masses' seemed to peacefully arrange themselves in the framework of the King's self-sufficient-economy philosophy. Everyone one in this normative web was supposed to consider him- or herself as equally belonging to the grand family of the Thai nation with the King as its father and the Queen as its mother. Not only the vested interests in the social structure guaranteed by this system but also the normative, moral shock that this 'good' system and its fatherly ruler could be challenged by *Thaksin* explains the deeply seated hostility of most in the 'yellow' camp towards the 'red' challengers who in turn see their claim not only based on what they perceive as common sense but also on a legitimized thread of Thai constitutionalism itself which they see suppressed by the hegemonic discourse since the beginnings of Thai constitutionalism.

Works cited

Bagehot, Walter, *The English Constitution*, introduced and published by R. H. S. Crossman, Ithaca, New York: Cornell University Press, 1963 (1867).

Bowornsak Uwanno, "His Majesty the King and the People, Characteristics of Thai Democracy," (1993), in *Law and Solutions of the Thai Society*, ed. Bowornsak Uwanno, Bangkok: Nititham, 1996, pp. 11-31, (original in Thai).

Bowornsak Uwanno, *Public Law, Vol. 2, Separation of Public and Private Law and the Evolution of Public Law in Thailand*, Bangkok: Chulalongkorn University Press, 2005, (original in Thai).

Case, William, "Regime Types and Resilience in Thailand and Malaysia," in *Contemporary Authoritarianism in the Southeast Asia – Structures, Institutions and Agency*, ed. William Case, London: Routledge, 2010, pp. 162-173.

Connors, Michael K., "Liberalism, Authoritarianism and the Politics of Decisionism in Thailand," in *Contemporary Authoritarianism in Southeast Asia: Structures, Institutions and Agency*, ed. William Case, London: Routlegde, 2010, pp. 84-103.

Geertz, Clifford, "Deep Play: Notes on the Balinese Cockfight," in *The Interpretation of Cultures*, ed. Clifford Geertz, New York: Basic Books, 1973, pp. 412-453.

Dressel, Björn, "The Struggle for Political Legitimacy in Thailand," in *Political Legitimacy in Asia – New Leadership Challenges*, ed. John Kane, Hui-Chieh Loy, and Haig Patapan, New York: Pelgrave Macmillan, 2011, pp. 61-84.

Glaser, Henning, "Thai Constitutional Courts and the Political Order," *Seoul Law Journal* 2 (2012): 65-163.

Glaser, Henning, "Multiple Constitutionalizations – 'Constitutionalism and Good Governance in European-Asian Perspectives'," in *Constitutionalism and Good Governance. Eastern and Western Perspectives*, ed. Dirk Ehlers, Henning Glaser, and Kittisak Prokati, Baden-Baden: Nomos, 2014, pp. 13-61.

Hewison, Kevin, "The monarchy and democratization," in *Political Change in Thailand, Democracy and Participation*, ed. Kevin Hewison, London: Routledge, 1997, reprint 2001, pp. 58-74.

Hewison, Kevin, "Crafting Thailand´s New Social Contract," *The Pacific Review* 17 (2004): pp. 503-522.

Hewison, Kevin and Kengkij Kitirianglarp, "'Thai-Style Democracy': The Royalist Struggle for Thailand's Politics," in *Saying the Unsayable. Monarchy and Democracy in Thailand*, ed. Søren Ivarsson and Lotte Isagar, Copenhagen: Nordic Institute of Asian Studies Press, 2010, pp. 179-202.

Kasian Tejapira, "The Democratic Regime with the King as Head of State: Origin and Prospect," *Same Sky Magazine* 1 (2011), pp. 89-115, (original in Thai).

King, Jeff, "Constitutions as Mission Statements," in *Social and Political Foundations of Constitutions*, ed. Denis J. Galligan and Mila Versteeg, New York: Cambridge University Press, 2013, pp. 73-102.

Kobkua Suwannathat-Pian "The Monarchy and Constitutional Change Since 1992," in *Reforming Thai Politics*, ed. Duncan McCargo, Copenhagen: Nordic Institute of Asian Studies Press, 2002, pp. 57-71.

Montesano, Michael J., "Four Thai Pathologies, Late 2009," in *Legitimacy Crisis in Thailand*, ed. Marc Askew, Chiang Mai: Silkworm Books, 2010, pp. 273-302.

Naruemon Thabchumpon and Duncan McCargo, "Urbanized Villages in the 2010 Thai Redshirt Protests. Not just to farmers?," *Asian Survey* 6 (2011): 993-1018.

Nelson, Michael, "People's Aliance for Democracy: From 'New Politics' to a 'Real' Political Party? in *Legitimacy Crisis in Thailand,* ed. Marc Askew, Chiang Mai: Silkworm Books, 2010, pp. 119-159.

Pasuk Phongpaichit and Chris Baker, *Thaksin*, 2nd ed., Chiang Mai: Silkworm Books, 2009.

Prajak Kongkirati, "The Rise and Fall of Electoral Violence in Thailand: Rules, Structures and Power Landscapes, 1997-2011," *Contemporary South-East Asia: A Journal of International and Strategic Fears* 3 (2014): 386- 416.

Pramuan Ruchanaseree, *Royal Prerogatives*, Bangkok 2005, (original in Thai).

Saengkanokkul Piyabutr, *Royal Prerogatives, the Privy Council and Charismatic Persons outside the Constitution*, Bangkok: Opensbooks, 2007, pp. 48-70, (original in Thai).

Schmitt, Carl, *The Concept of the Political*, translated and with an introduction by George Schwab, with a foreword by Tracy B. Strong and Notes by Leo Strauss, Expanded Edition, Chicago: University of Chicago Press, 2007 (1932).

Seni Pramoj, "Father King Ram Khamhaeng´s Stone Inscription: First Constitution of Thailand," in *Development, Modernization, and Tradition in Southeaest Asia: Lessons from Thailand*, ed. Pinit Ratanakul and U. Kyaw Than, Bangkok: Mahiodol University, 1990, pp. 17-49.

Sinpeng, Aim, "Party-Social Movement Coalition in Thailand's Political Conflict (2005-2011)," in Contemporary Socio-Cultural and Political Perspectives in Thailand, ed. Pranee Liamputtong, Heidelberg: Springer, 2014, pp. 157-168.

Thak Chaloemtiarana, *Thailand – The Politics of Despotic Paternalism*, Ithaca, New York, Cornell University Southeast Asia Program Publications, 2007.

Thawatt Mokarapong, *History of the Thai Revolution. A Study in Political Behavior*, Bangkok, 1962.

Thongchai Winichakul, "Toppling Democracy," *Journal of Contemporary Southeast Asia* 1 (2008): 11-37.

Tongnoi Thongyai, "The Role of the Monarchy in Modern Thailand," in *Development, Modernization, and Tradition in Southeaest Asia: Lessons from Thailand*, ed. Pinit Ratanakul and U. Kyaw Than, Bangkok:. Mahiodol University, 1990, pp. 153-161.

Tushnet, Mark, *Weak Courts, Strong Rights: Judicial Review and Social Welfare Rights in Comparative Constitutional Law*, Princeton: Princeton University Press, 2008.

Wissanu Krua-ngam and Bowornsak Uwanno, *The Interim Constitution 1977*, Bangkok: Namaksorn, 1978, (original in Thai).

Wissanu Krua-ngam, *Constitutional Law*, Bangkok: Thiranusorn, 1979, (original in Thai).

Worachet Pakeerut, *Lecture on State and Public Law*, Bangkok: Duantula, 2012, pp. 249 ff.

Yoshifumi, Tamada, *Myths and Realities – The Democratisation of Thai Politics*, Kyoto: Kyoto University Press, 2008.

Yud Saenguthai, *Lecture on the Interim Constitution 1972*, Bangkok: Nitibanagan 1973, (original in Thai).

Political Values in Asia, the ASEAN Political Security Community and Confucius' Philosophy

Vicente Reyes, Charlene Tan

A. Introduction

In the ASEAN Charter, all member states are committed to common political values such as human rights, fundamental freedoms, democracy and the rule of law. These political values, as well as related political institutions and structures, are predominantly of Western origin. There is a need to recognize alternative models of organizing state and normative orders in Asia. One alternative is the political values that are derived and adapted from Asian philosophies. This paper critically discusses political values in Asia with a focus on the relevance of Confucius' philosophy to the ASEAN political security community. The paper begins by examining the formation of ASEAN, 'Asian values' and 'ASEAN Way'. This is followed by highlighting the key characteristics, challenges and future of the ASEAN political security community in the 21st century. The second part of the paper explores the political philosophy of *Confucius* and its potential contributions towards the flourishing of the ASEAN political security community.

B. ASEAN, Asian Values, and ASEAN Way

On the 2nd of July 2013, the ASEAN Regional Forum (ARF) convened its 20th meeting in *Bandar Seri Begawan*, Brunei Darussalam. This meeting was a remarkable accomplishment in the history of international relations. The ARF has no equivalent in any part of the world or in any epoch of human history. It exists as the longest and only multinational organization that includes key representatives of the Southeast Asian region (all the ASEAN member nations), countries of the modern western world (i.e. Australia, New Zealand, Canada, the European Union, and the United States), established East Asian economies (Japan, and South Korea) as well as the biggest nations that form part of the Non-Aligned Movement (i.e. Bangladesh, the People's Republic of China, India, North Korea, Mongolia, Pakistan, Papua New Guinea, Russia, East Timor and Sri

Lanka).[1] The longevity of the ARF is a testament to the distinctive set of international relations norms championed by its nerve centre – the ASEAN – and also the greater region of Asia.

Aside from its growing diplomatic influence, ASEAN and the greater region of Asia have also evolved into an economic giant. On the one hand, Asia has been described as an emerging "significant economic player" in the international arena of trade and business.[2] And on the other hand Southeast Asian nations, known traditionally for having "low income levels" accompanied by "relatively high stocks of human capital, and past success at improving labor productivity" were projected to eventually reach the economic levels of more developed East Asia.[3] At the dawn of the 21st century, these predictions have come to reality. The ASEAN and the greater region of Asia, otherwise known as the assemblage of nations described as belonging to Developing Asian economies,[4] has arisen to be an undisputed economic powerhouse in contemporary times:

> The region's real GDP in purchasing power parity (PPP) terms climbed from about $3.3 trillion in 1980 to an estimated $24.5 trillion in 2009. That is an increase of 7.5 times, compared with just three times for the world economy during the same period.[5]

With its diplomatic record evidenced by the enduring ARF and incipient economic might demonstrated by a steady and galloping GDP increase, how have these characteristics of Developing Asia been translated to political values and influence? More specifically, what is the status of fundamental political values in Asia namely: human rights, democratic freedoms and the rule of law in the world's most dynamic region?

---

1 See Association of Southeast Asian Nations, *Chairman's statement of the 20th ASEAN Regional Forum*, Jakarta 2013.

2 See Yeung and Li, "Theorizing economic geographies of Asia," 2003, pp. 119.

3 See Bloom, Canning and Malaney, "Demographic Change and Economic Growth in Asia," 1999, p. 34.

4 Developing Asia includes the People's Republic of China, Hong Kong, China, India, Indonesia, the Republic of Korea, Malaysia, Pakistan, the Philippines, Singapore, Taipei-China, Thailand and Vietnam. These economies account for about 95% of emerging Asia's GDP, and are thus representative of regional trends.

5 Lee and Hong, "Economic Growth in Asia: Determinants and Prospects," 2012, pp. 101-113.

One unmistakable feature of the region is that it is made up of "different mixtures of Confucian, Buddhist, Western, and other values"[6] such that Asian societies do not necessarily share similar levels of urgency and acceptance in relation to political and social concerns. The region portrays a very varied picture of how political values are played out. For instance, a developing country with a huge population like the Philippines, prides itself in upholding a vibrant democracy, yet suffers from "systemic corruption"[7] that has a debilitating impact on society. The small Singapore city-state that is known for its exceptional record of governance and its hard-nosed anti-corruption stance is typified by a wealthy society with one of the highest per capita GDP in the world that "blends almost seamlessly with stunted political activism."[8]

Systematic studies on the levels of civil and political rights in Asia provide interesting facets pertinent to the region. A comparative empirical survey on human rights in Asia, France and the US revealed that "Asian countries, especially East Asian countries, tend to do poorly on civil and political rights relative to others in their income group"[9]; this confirms what some scholars claim as the region's drab performance record in terms of upholding fundamental democratic entitlements. The same report states, however, that "Asian countries tend to do much better" in comparison to other nations with similar income groups on other valid human development measures such as "education, infant mortality, life expectancy, law and order and social stability."[10] The emerging gap between conventional political values – which are usually western-centric – as opposed to other values pertinent to a broader understanding of human development, becomes more pronounced in Asia. In fact, some commentators have attempted to describe this gulf as the basic opposition between (1) individual civil rights which are championed in the West and particularly in liberal democratic societies and (2) communitarian perspectives that recognize and accept certain "democratic rights" as long

6 Bell, *East Meets West: Human Rights and Democracy in East Asia*, 2000, p. 10.

7 Reyes, "The Impact of Automation on Elections: Case Study of the May 2010 Philippine Presidential Contests," p. 262.

8 Reyes, "Social Media Networks and Tactical Globalization: An Exploratory Case Study of Contesting Political 'space' in Singapore," 2013, p. 34.

9 Peerenboom, "An empirical overview of rights performance in Asia, France, and the USA: The dominance of wealth in the interplay of economics, culture, law and governance," 2006, p. 16.

10 Peerenboom, "An empirical overview," p. 17.

as these "contribute to strengthening ties to such communities as the family and the nation." [11] Other commentators have described this difference by using the terms 'liberal' (pertaining to full-fledged electoral democracies) and 'semi-liberal' or 'illiberal' (referring to electoral democracies that do not fulfill all the features of full-fledged electoral democracies). There are some others who have explicitly stated that "'illiberal' or 'semi-liberal' democracies" which possess "formal procedures of electoral democracy" combined pragmatically with "autocratic characteristics" are regimes that "are more accurately categorized as 'defective democracies'."[12] Given the great disparity which is characteristic of the nations in Asia and the intricate tapestry of political values in the region, would it be possible to describe a fundamental set of beliefs that sets the region apart? Would it be plausible to imagine a set of 'Asian values'?

I. Is There Such a Thing as 'Asian Values'?

The rhetoric of Asian values gained currency at the height of the Asian economic boom. It was identified as the ethos that explained the economic progress of the region that was characterized by strong regimes that were very different from the western notion of liberal democracies. The 'Asian values' purportedly represented aspects of western liberal beliefs of capitalism combined with features of autocratic rule that was the more prevalent mode of governance in the region. After the crippling 1997 economic crisis that started in Asia and spread like a crippling contagion worldwide, the rhetoric about Asian values receded. With the resurgence in the economic might of the region, revisiting the rhetoric around the Asian values may be imperative. Is there really such a thing as Asian values?

Given the wide diversity of religion, language and culture in Asia, it is doubtful that a set of common values could be devised. The proponents of the 'Asian values' argument imposed this concept upon the whole of Asia in order to give the West a holistic view of Asia. However, as not all Asian leaders support the argument, 'Asian values' as a concept is not a

---

11 Bell, *East Meets West*, p. 16.

12 Croissant, "From Transition to Defective Democracy: Mapping Asian Democratization," 2004, p. 159.

reality. It is merely a myth created by some Asian leaders as a political tool against challenges from both within and outside the states.[13]

Commentators have convincingly argued that the circumstances and chronicles of nations in the region have an immense variety. Most of the Asian region admittedly has strong links to Confucianism but these are not unanimous. Indonesia and Malaysia as well as the south of Thailand, the Philippines and Western China have very strong Islamic influences. Furthermore, communist China and Vietnam officially spurned Confucianism while "other philosophies such as Taoism and Buddhism have been interwoven"[14] into the history of peoples and societies in Asia. Another very compelling argument proposes that Asian values served as a powerful and normative creation used by elites – such as leaders, scholars and policy makers – to delineate Asia with the imagined 'Other' represented by the West. In this sense, Asian values emerged as a created mode of development that works well in the unique context of Asia.

'Asian values' as a doctrine of developmentalism can be understood as the claim that, until prosperity is achieved, democracy remains an unaffordable luxury. This 'Protestant ethic' form of 'Asian values' attributes high growth rates to certain cultural traits. These characteristics include hard work, frugality, discipline, and teamwork. Western democracy hinders rapid development, authoritarian rulers in the Asia Pacific claim, and thus must be delayed until substantial development has been achieved.[15]

This inquiry argues that one of the more analytically illuminating positions to take in relation to the question of Asian values is to see it more from a descriptive perspective. It may be more worthwhile to depict 'Asian values' not as a "particular set of attitudes, beliefs and institutions which all Asian people share in common but rather to refer to the great diversities which characterize Asian *values.*"[16] Shifting the focus from what is common and instead opening the gaze to various possibilities that may emerge from the great divergence of Asian values provides greater avenues for a deeper understanding of components that contribute to this

---

13 Hoon, "Revisiting the Asian Values Argument Used by Asian Political Leaders and its Validity," 2004, p. 162.

14 Dalton and Ong, "Authority Orientations and Democratic Attitudes: A Test of the 'Asian Values' Hypothesis," 2010, p. 4.

15 Thompson, "Whatever happened to 'Asian Values'?," 2001, p. 156.

16 Ho, "Asian values and modernisation," 1997), p. 13.

divergence. Scrutinizing the experience of the ten nations that form part of the ASEAN in its pursuit of understanding the differences in the histories and conditions of their member states reveals the emergence of a way to manage these differences: the 'ASEAN Way'.

II. The 'ASEAN Way'

The great disparity between the ASEAN nations is not something new. When the original ASEAN members consisting of the representative foreign ministers of Indonesia, Malaysia, the Philippines, Singapore and Thailand decided to group themselves together on the 8th of August 1967 to sign the Bangkok Declaration[17] that formalized the organization, each signatory was fully aware of the great divergence of each nation. In order to circumvent the potentially sensitive political economic dynamics that could arise in relation to how a diverse set of actors would operate in a regional grouping, a key foundational aspect of the ASEAN was institutionalized – the 'ASEAN way'. This is a *modus operandi,* a way of operating that governed ASEAN when it was first constituted some forty years ago, and which continues as the glue that binds its diverse members. To be more specific, this unique organizational mechanism consists of "*Mushyawara* (consultation) and *Mufakat* (consensus) and the foundational principle of non-intervention of ASEAN nation-states into each other's domestic affairs."[18] The history of the nation-states of Southeast Asia is excruciatingly mired in warfare and conflict emerging primarily from colonial experiences. As a result, the creation of the ASEAN needed to strategically take into careful consideration this troubled past:

> The founding of the Association of Southeast Asian Nations (ASEAN) was helped by the common desire of its members to ensure the survival of regimes which had by then retreated significantly from their postcolonial experiments in liberal democracy. This orientation was further institutionalised by ASEAN's doctrine of

17 ASEAN Secretariat, *The Asean Declaration (Bangkok Declaration)*, Bangkok: ASEAN, 1967.

18 Acharya, "Democratisation and the prospects for participatory regionalism in Southeast Asia," 2003, p. 376.

non-interference, which helped to shield its members from outside pressures towards democratisation.[19]

Ever since the creation of the ASEAN and the conception of its unique ASEAN Way, international relations scholars have criticized the organization and its ethos. The main reproach against the ASEAN Way was the absence of institutionally binding arrangements, unlike what can be found in the European Union. Consultation, consensus and non-intervention that distinguished the ASEAN Way from other operating processes of international alliances were often raised as evidence of the ineffectiveness of the Southeast Asian regional assemblage. Yet, more than 40 years after its foundation, ASEAN, notwithstanding its perceived flaw of not having institutionally binding power, remains unchallenged "as the hub of regional multilateral diplomacy"[20] in the entire Asian region. Nowhere is this prowess manifested clearly than in the experience of the ARF which political analysts claim "helped manage the demise of the Soviet Union, the rise of China, and the draw-down of U.S. military forces" and has also become instrumental in allowing regional political cooperation in the areas of "peacekeeping, disaster relief, and the further development of Confidence Building Measures (CBMs)."[21]

The continued and ever increasing political significance of the ARF, under the guidance of the ASEAN, paved the way for members of the regional organization to aspire towards the creation of an ASEAN Security Community "proposed in 2002 by newly democratic Indonesia and officially adopted by ASEAN a year later"[22] with the goal of promoting a just, democratic and harmonious Southeast Asia. This development was a portent of a future trajectory in the region: the emergence of an ASEAN security community.

---

19 Acharya, "Democratisation and the prospects," p. 375.

20 Acharya, "Asean at 40: Mid-life rejuvenation?," 2007, p. 1.

21 Garofano, "Power, institutions, and the Asean regional forum a security community for Asia?," 2002, p. 513.

22 Acharya, "Asean at 40."

C. An Emerging ASEAN Security Community

In 2012, the population of the ASEAN was nearly twice that of the United States of America, one fifth more than that of the European Union[23] and nearly five times that of Japan.[24] Among the ten very diverse countries of the ASEAN, six nations have emerged with more mature economies: These are the ASEAN 6 comprising of Indonesia, Malaysia, Singapore, Thailand, the Philippines and Brunei Darussalam. These six economies within the ASEAN have "grown rapidly and had become industrially competitive."[25] On the other hand the newest members of ASEAN, consisting of Cambodia, Vietnam. Laos and Myanmar, collectively known as CVLM, despite being unmistakably resource-rich countries continue to display various manifestations of economic vulnerabilities.[26] Despite these huge disparities in each one's economic standing, the ASEAN 6 and CVLM have joined forces to create one of the most durable regional groupings in the world – the enlarged ASEAN. The natural progression of the expanded regional organization was to go beyond its economic and diplomatic milestones and to move into a much more ambitious goal of greater cohesion. This vision was concretized in early 2000:

> To concretize the ASEAN Vision 2020, the ASEAN Heads of States/Governments adopted the Declaration of ASEAN Concord II (Bali Concord II) in 2003, which establishes an ASEAN Community by 2020. The ASEAN Community consists of three pillars, namely the ASEAN Political-Security Community (APSC), the ASEAN Economic Community (AEC) and the ASEAN Socio-Cultural Community (ASCC).[27]

The first and fundamental step in achieving the lofty vision for 2020 was the adoption of a regional charter. In 2007, during the 13th ASEAN

---

23 This corresponds to the European Union of 27 states or EU-27.

24 ASEAN, *Asean Community in figures (ACIF) 2010*, Jakarta: Association of Southeast Asian Nations, 2010.

25 Severino, "Beyond Forty: Towards Political and Economic Integration," 2007, p. 411.

26 See Coxhead, "A New Resource Curse? Impacts of China's Boom on Comparative Advantage and Resource Dependence in Southeast Asia," 2007, pp. 1099-1119.

27 ASEAN, *Asean Political-Security Community Blueprint*, Jakarta: Association of Southeast Asian Nations, 2009, p. 1.

Summit, a culmination of two years of consultation and consensus led to the ratification of the ASEAN Charter. The regional agreement is more than a reassertion of traditional practice. In addition to reaffirming the established principles that form part of the ASEAN rhetoric, the charter explicitly lists "to strengthen democracy, enhance good governance and the rule of law, and to promote and protect human rights and fundamental freedoms"[28] as goals to be attained by the organization.

Does the emergence of an ASEAN security community translate into a marked shift in the foundational ethos of the organization? Will the ASEAN move from its unique identity of consultation, consensus and non-intervention towards more institutionally binding arrangements?

In relation to a transformation of its ethos, commentators indicate that the ASEAN has consistently resisted the adoption of "post-sovereign regional norms" and has shied away from issuing official declarations espousing "commitment to democracy and human rights"[29] similar to those enshrined in regional institutions of the West. As to whether the region is moving towards greater obligatory agreements, scholars of the region emphasize that "there is little evidence of a sea-change in attitudes regarding the utility of force" which typifies security communities leading to the inevitable conclusion that "institutional enforcement is a non-issue"[30] in ASEAN's current state of affairs. An argument can be made that the foundational ethos, in fact, becomes more pronounced with ASEAN members practicing a "relational view of power" that accentuates "consensus among members"[31] while clearly acknowledging constraints this may place on the breadth and width of regional integration. The history of this unique regional organization is unambiguous: Despite the signing of accords, blueprints and action programs, the fact remains that consultation, consensus and non-intervention are still the operating mechanisms of ASEAN. Given the persistence of ASEAN to adhere to its foundational ethos and to avoid institutionally-binding arrangements, what kind of political security community can be envisaged to emerge in the 21st century? Corollary to this would be what are the emerging security threats that face ASEAN in the 21st Century?

---

28 Jones, "Security and democracy: The Asean Charter and the dilemmas of regionalism in South-East Asia," .2008, p. 737.

29 Acharya, "Democratisation," p. 387.

30 Garofano, "Power, institutions, and the asean regional forum," p. 520.

31 Jones, "Security and democracy, " p. 743.

D. Towards an ASEAN Political Security Community in the 21st Century

Alongside the economic strides experienced in Developing Asia, traditional and non-traditional security threats have similarly thrived in the region. Traditional security threats in ASEAN have made it one of the flashpoints of conflict in the 21st century. The increasingly militarized Korean peninsula and the shaky political detente in this part of Asia is a cause for grave concern. The South China Seas and the bickering among China, Vietnam, the Philippines and Taiwan over the Spratly Islands has been one of the critical issues in the region. The more than twenty years of war in Muslim Mindanao in the Southern Philippines has not abated and has even found similar occurrences in the South of Thailand. The increasingly distressing situation of the *Rohingya* people located in the borders of Thailand and Burma continue to be a hotspot not only for violence but for an escalating humanitarian crisis. These are just some examples of the increasing range of traditional security threats in the region. However, these critical issues are made much more acute with the spread of non-traditional security threats. The resurgence of terrorism particularly in Indonesia and the Philippines, the threats posed by the *Islamic State of Iraq and Syria (ISIS) fighters who have returned to their home countries in Asia*, the continued problem of transnational crime and its many forms (i.e. drug and human trafficking) that can be seen in developed states of Singapore and Malaysia as well as in the developing countries of Laos and Cambodia and the possibility of public health epidemics like the crippling Severe Acute Respiratory Syndrome (SARS) that devastated Singapore and Hong Kong and the newer strains of the Avian Flu and Ebola are a few examples of the emerging non-traditional security threats in the region. Given the increasing complexity of traditional and non-traditional security issues that face ASEAN, member states have seen the necessity of embracing a political security community.

In 2009, during the 14th ASEAN Summit held in *Cha-am* and *Hua Hin*, Thailand, the leaders of the regional grouping agreed to establish the ASEAN Political Security Community (APSC). One of the main diplomatic objectives of the APSC was to obtain the pledge of all ASEAN leaders to employ exclusively peaceful processes in settling differences in relation to security issues governing the region. The APSC becomes a timely and highly-relevant agreement particularly with the persistence of traditional security threats as well as the appearance of more complex non-security threats. The APSC identified three fundamental provisions:

> The ASEAN Political-Security Community envisages the following three key characteristics: (i) A Rules-based Community of shared values and norms; (ii) A Cohesive, Peaceful, Stable and Resilient Region with shared responsibility for comprehensive security; and (iii) A Dynamic and Outward-looking Region in an increasingly integrated and interdependent world.[32]

What is the future of the ASPC? On the one hand, there is overwhelming evidence that the ASEAN Way, typified by consultation, consensus and non-intervention, remains as the ethos of the member states of this regional organization. On the other hand, the APSC heralds a novel set of values that suggests increased integration and shared responsibility within a 'rules-based' scenario. It would appear that the ASPC attempts to steer the ASEAN known more for soft diplomacy towards a 'rules-based' or institutionally-binding arrangement. The proposed political security community in ASEAN is undoubtedly fraught with paradoxical tendencies.

A careful review of how ASEAN has addressed traditional and non-traditional security issues reveals how the regional organization manages to paradoxically combine formal rhetoric (i.e. formally signed agreements) with informal networking (i.e. the ASEAN Way). The continued mitigation of the Spratly Islands issue in the South China Seas is an example of how conflict and peace-building are maintained in this troubled region. One of the key mechanisms that helped diffuse the highly-volatile situation in this part of the world was the convening of South China Sea Workshops (SCSWs) that consisted of ASEAN, China as well as other pertinent stakeholders.[33] Formally convened as high-level diplomatic meetings, the SCSWs employed the ASEAN Way of informal networks – through consensus and the upholding of the principle of non-intervention among elite participants – in order to manage the highly-complex traditional security issues. The experience of the ASEAN in addressing the non-traditional security threat of transnational crime of terrorism provides another example of how a feasible balance between paradoxical consensus and change may be achieved. Scholars and practitioners have identified that the experience of Southeast Asia in addressing terrorism in the region has been met with a "broad general

32 ASEAN, *ASEAN Political-Security Community Blueprint*, p. 2.

33 See Weissman, "The South China Sea Conflict and Sino-Asean Relations: A Study in Conflict Prevention and Peace Building," 2010, pp. 36-69.

consensus"[34] among the ASEAN members. It has been suggested that this happened with the astute combination of "depoliticising terrorism" (treating terrorism as a technical problem rather than the more sensitive 'nation and ethnicity' problem and thereby arriving at a careful consensus) and the application of "ASEANisation" of counter-terrorism policies (the introduction of change via the well-known ASEAN Way).[35]

This chapter proposes that in order to better understand the nuances of Asian political values as represented by the ASEAN Way, adopting Confucius' virtue-centered political philosophy that attempts to balance paradoxical tendencies is analytically illuminating.[36] Furthermore, Confucius' ideas have the potential of providing a counter-hegemonic or at least an alternative narrative to the West in Asia. It should be clarified that our focus on Confucianism does not imply that this ideology is representative of or superior to other ideologies in Asia. On the contrary, as noted earlier, we are aware that Asia is made up of a diverse mixtures of Confucian, Buddhist, Western, and other values. The aim in this chapter is to highlight belief systems that originate from and are dominant across Asian societies that are relevant to our discussion on Asian political values and the ASEAN Way, using Confucianism as an example. The succeeding sections elaborate on Confucius' teachings and their potential contributions to the ASEAN Political Security Community (APSC).

E. Confucius' Political Philosophy

As noted earlier, common political values such as human rights, fundamental freedoms, democracy and the rule of law shared by the ASEAN member states originated from the West. But this does not mean that these political values are incompatible with or sidelined in Asian ideologies. One Asian ideology that has much to say about political ideals and issues is Confucianism. The rest of this chapter focuses on Confucius' teachings on the concepts of 'good government' and 'political

---

34 Soeslilowati, "Asean's response to the challenge of terrorism," 2011, p. 239.

35 See Gerstl, "The Depoliticisation and 'ASEANisation' of Counter-Terrorism Policies in South-East Asia: A Weak Trigger for a Fragmented Version of Human Security," 2010, pp. 48-75.

36 See Chen, "Transcending Paradox: The Chinese 'Middle Way' Perspective," 2002, p. 183.

participation'. The views of *Confucius* are based on the *Analects* – a collection of the sayings and conduct of *Confucius* and his disciples.[37]

I. Good Government

The first political concept is that of a good government – a topic that is close to the heart of *Confucius*. The Spring and Autumn Period (c. 722–468 BCE) that *Confucius* grew up in was a period rife with political and social turmoil, with rulers of different states vying for power and control. Appalled by the political and social chaos in his time, *Confucius* hoped to restore order and harmony by spreading his teachings and serving in the government. He desired to replace the prevailing harsh rule by law and punishment with the rule by virtue (*Analects* 2.3; all subsequent references refer to this text unless otherwise stated), through reviving the practices of the sage-kings from the Zhou dynasty (3.14, 8.20, 8.21, 9.5). He expressed confidence that he was able to improve the sociopolitical conditions in any state within one year and deliver results within three years (13.10).

At the heart of *Confucius'* political philosophy is his emphasis on virtue. He contrasts two types of government in the passage below:

> 2.3 The Master said, 'Lead [the common people] with policies, and keep them in line with punishments, and the common people will avoid punishments but will be without a sense of shame. Lead [the common people] with virtue, and keep them in line through *li* (normative human behaviors), and they will have a sense of shame and order themselves.'

Here, *Confucius* contrasts the rule by law through punishment and policies, and the rule by virtue through *li*. *Li* refers to the totality of normative human behaviors that are accompanied by corresponding attitudes and values for all aspects of one's life. *Li* covers every aspect of a human life, including looking, listening, speaking and moving (cf. 12.1). *Li* encompasses a wide spectrum of behaviors, ranging from activities of relatively narrow scope and rigid structure such as ceremonial rites, to activities of relatively broad scope and flexible structure, such as making

37 See Tan, *Confucius*, 2013. All translations are done by the second author, unless otherwise stated. The words in square brackets are not found in the original text of the *Analects* and have been added to provide greater clarity of meaning.

small talk. *Confucius* views the rule by virtue as effective for transforming not only the people's behavior, but also their character. Social order is obtained when the people are capable of and intrinsically motivated to order their lives in accordance with *li*. When people know and act according with *li*, they will naturally feel ashamed if their behavior deviates from *li*, with or without the fear of punishment. Besides this 'voice of conscience', the fact that everyone is able to evaluate and correct one another based on the common yardstick of *li* also produces an external pressure for everyone to conform to *li*.

According to *Confucius*, good government is based on *li*. Governing in accordance with *li* implies that a ruler should respect and promote the individual's human dignity, equality, learning opportunity and resources, as well as everyone's correlative rights. *Confucius* maintains that "if a person is able to govern a state through observing *li* and showing deference, what more is needed?" (4.13). *Confucius'* point is that a good ruler is one who manifests and models desirable attitudes, values and behaviors. On the specific qualities needed for government service, *Confucius* stresses the need for a ruler to be a *junzi*. The term 'junzi' literally means 'son of a lord' and was historically used to refer to aristocrats during *Confucius'* time. But *Confucius* re-interprets the term to refer to a noble or exemplary person that all human beings should aspire to be. In other words, *Confucius* adopted a broader and more inclusive definition of *junzi* – one that is based on merit rather than by birth. Everyone, not just the aristocrats, may succeed in becoming a *junzi* if he/she cultivates himself/herself in accordance to *Confucius'* teachings. A *junzi* is one who abides in and achieves *ren* (humanity or love) – the central quality that encompasses all other normative qualities of a *junzi*. *Confucius* avers that "a *junzi* does not violate *ren* even for as long as it takes to eat a meal; he is certain to be with *ren* even if he is in a hurry or distress" (4.5). *Confucius* further outlines five virtues of a ruler who is a *junzi*: 'The *junzi* is generous but not wasteful, works [the people] hard without their complaints, has desires but is not covetous, is at ease but not arrogant, and is awe-inspiring but not fierce' (20.2).

We see from the above that *Confucius* sees an ideal society as one that is defined by the allocation and performance of specific social roles. But this does not necessarily mean that such a society is paternalistic, authoritarian and elitist. It is not paternalistic in the sense of being interfering and controlling, since the *junzi*-ruler is supposed to govern not by law but by virtue. Far from being authoritarian, a *junzi*-ruler models and encourages the observance of *li* by not being arrogant (20.2), being generous in caring for the common people (5.16) and inspiring the common people to *ren* [humanity or love] (8.2). A *junzi*-ruler takes care of and leads the common people, not in a high-handed manner, but by giving them the necessary rights and freedom to live autonomously and participate actively in public policymaking according with *li*. This naturally entails consultation and consensus-building between the ruler and the subjects. It is noteworthy that a number of writers have argued that Confucianism is potentially compatible with democracy, civil society, human rights, equality and global justice.[38]

II. Political Participation

The second concept is that of political participation. Confucian traditions have been blamed (rightly or wrongly) for encouraging authoritarian and corrupt governments. In his survey of governments in the history of East Asia, *H. George Frederick* observes that "Confucian ideas came to be used to subjugate others, and less-than virtuous bureaucrats were much a part of the decline of government by the scholar-rulers"; and "by the 19th century, the common image of the Confucian was mostly negative, assumed to be the source of many of the ills of totalitarian government in East Asia."[39]

However, the charge that the Confucian tradition promotes authoritarianism and stifles individuality, personal autonomy and innovation applies more to Confucianism as an ideology than to the teachings of *Confucius*. The impression that Confucianism advocates the suppression of self-interest for the sake of societal welfare arises from the politicization of Confucianism where its selective teachings are utilized for political agendas.[40] *Confucius* himself expressed a strong interest in

---

38 For a good discussion of Confucianism and democracy, see Bell and Hahm, eds., *Confucianism for the Modern World*, 2003; Bary and Tu, eds., *Confucianism and Human Rights*; Bary, *The Trouble with Confucianism*, 1991; Tan, *Confucian Democracy: A Deweyan Reconstruction*, 2004. On Confucianism as a form of virtue ethics, see Norden, "Virtue Ethics and Confucianism," 2003, pp. 99–121; and Hutton, "Han Feizi's Criticism of Confucianism and Its Implications for Virtue Ethics," 2008, pp. 423–453.

39 Frederickson, "Confucius and the Moral Basis of Bureaucracy," 2002, p. 624.

40 See Tan, "'Our Shared Values' in Singapore: A Confucian Perspective," 2012, pp. 449-463.

current affairs and did not shy away from correcting the political leaders of his generation. For example, he laments as follows: "One who in occupying high office is not tolerant, who in observing *li* is not respectful, and who in overseeing the mourning rites does not grieve – how could I bear to look upon such a person?" (3.26). Here, *Confucius* lamented that the rulers (those who occupying high office) lacked the essential values and attitudes that should accompany the proper observance of *li*; namely, tolerance, respect and genuine grief (also see 3.1, 3.2, 3.6, 3.10, 5.18, 12.18).

Confucius also encourages his disciples to take up official appointments in states; in his words, "make yourself available when *dao* (the Way) prevails in the world, but remain hidden when it does not" (8.3). The *dao* or the 'Way' refers to the Way of heaven as exemplified in the exemplary behaviors, values and attitudes of the sage kings. In other words, the disciples should ensure that the state is one where the Way is valued and adhered to, as evident in the prevalence of stability and order. The expression 'remain hidden' reiterates the need to render one's service only in states where the Way prevails: to remain poor and lowly in a state that promotes the Way indicates that one is not doing one's part to realize the Way by taking up high official positions in that state. Conversely, to be rich and hold a high rank in a state that does not promote the Way is wrong as it implies that one is not doing one's part to realize the Way. In such a case, the only way to promote the Way is to leave that state.

Although *Confucius* counsels his disciples not to enter a state that is in crisis and to remain hidden when the Way does not prevail, he also teaches that they should speak up when they find a ruler saying something that is not right. When asked by Duke *Ding* if there is a saying that can ruin a state, *Confucius* replied, 'If what [the ruler] says is not good and no one opposes him, is this not almost a case of a saying ruining a state?' (13.15). But it should be clarified that this does not mean that one should criticize a ruler in an aggressive and confrontational way. Keeping in mind 12.1 about being guided by *li* (normative human behaviors) in everything we think, feel and do, *Confucius* is saying that one should speak up against a ruler *in accordance with li*. It is noteworthy that *Confucius* himself did not stage a public protest or start a revolution, but expressed his disagreements in a respectful manner and did not impose his views on any state. History also informs us that Confucius, in seeking political office and dissemination of his ideas in various states, chose to leave a state when he faced rejection or disappointment from the political leaders, rather than staying on to launch a coup d' état.

It is evident that *Confucius* propagates taking an active interest in political affairs. But it should be added here that this does not mean that he believes that the only worthy occupation for everyone is public office. Confucius, when asked why he was not involved in governing, replied: "The Book of Documents says, 'Filial – by being filial and friendly to one's brothers, a person is executing the work of governing.' Doing is being involved in governing. Why must one be 'involved in government'?." (2.21) As noted by Meng Peiyuan:

> Confucius was indeed very concerned about politics, very concerned about society, with strong practical concerns. Furthermore, joining politics was the main employment for someone who pursued studying in ancient society. This is unlike the current situation where there is a variety of occupations and avenues for one to attain life's value. But from Confucius' perspective, joining politics is an important avenue but not the only one, and one should not study for the sake of becoming an official'.[41]

Political participation, according to *Confucius*, may be expressed in different ways, encompassing not only holding an official appointment but also performing one's social roles in society. One is involved in governing as long as one demonstrates and promotes 'civic literacy' – participating effectively in civic life by staying informed and understanding governmental processes; exercising the rights and obligations of citizenship at a local, state, national and global level; and understanding the local and global implications of civic decisions.[42] Civic literacy is essential for the young and old to contribute actively and meaningfully in public policies, both locally and internationally, for the good of humankind. Commenting on constitutionally established democratic governments such as Japan and Korea, *H. George Frederick* observes that the "core Confucian ideas have already been modified to blend the rule of law with the rule of man" and that there is "good evidence that Confucian bureaucracy and democratic self-government are not only compatible with

---

41 Meng, *Meng Peiyuan jiang kongzi* [Meng Peiyuan talks about Confucius], 2005, pp. 143-144.

42 See Partnership for 21st Century Skills, *Framework for 21st century learning*, 2009. Available online at: www.p21.org/documents/P21_Framework.pdf, accessed 21 May 2012.

economic growth, but they may also be a powerful mix of economic, bureaucratic, and democratic ideas."[43]

The specific expression of civic literacy, of course, will depend on the localized social, political and cultural conditions. As discussed earlier, political values take place in Asia against a backdrop of Asian communitarianism and Asian values. The need to express political participation in the Asian contexts in a contextually sensitive manner is where the Confucian concept of *yi* (appropriateness or rightness) is pertinent. The quality of appropriateness refers to thinking, feeling and doing what is appropriate or right by exercising one's individual discernment and discretion. The exercise of appropriateness presupposes a certain level of independent thinking and rational autonomy for one to arrive at an acceptable judgment or decision in a particular situation. That explains why *Confucius* states that a *junzi* (noble or exemplary person) is "proper but not inflexible" (15.37), and "is not inflexible in one's studies." (1.8)

The quality of appropriateness is intricately tied to the concept of *li*. We have already learned that *li* covers every aspect of a human life, including looking, listening, speaking and moving (cf. 12.1). The ubiquity of *li* means that it is impossible for anyone to observe *li* by simply relying on a manual of rigid rules, even assuming that such a manual exists. What is crucial, if we wish to observe *li* accurately and intelligently, is to acquire the wherewithal to do what is appropriate without violating *li*. That is why the possession of the quality of appropriateness is important.[44]

The application of appropriateness should be role specific, in line with the idea of *zhengming* (rectification of names). A central passage to explicate the meaning of *zhengming* is as follows:

---

43 Frederickson, "Confucius and the Moral Basis," pp. 624–625.

44 *Cheng Chung-ying* suggests that we may analyze the quality of appropriateness (*yi*) in terms of two components relevant to the process of moral decision making: "First, there is understanding or perception of an end on the part of the moral subject. This is the subjective self-knowledge of good truth (or the way). Second, there is a potential state or situation which needs a fitting action to make it a moral state or situation. There is an objective quality in a situation which one must correctly perceive in order to make an appropriate decision and to take a course of action". Cheng, "On Yi as a Universal Principle of Specific Application in Confucian Morality," 1972, p. 272.

12.11 Duke Jing of Qi asked *Confucius* about governing. ***Confucius*** replied, 'Ruler ruler, minister minister, father father, son son.' The Duke said, 'Good! If the ruler be not a ruler, the subject not a subject, the father not a father, the son not a son, then even if there were grain, would I get to eat it?

Confucius explains the meaning of 'Ruler ruler, minister minister, father father, son son' in another passage where he claims that "when names are not correct, what is said will not be used effectively; when what is said is not used effectively, matters will not be accomplished" (13.3). The central idea here is that names are not just words for referents; they possess an intrinsic normative force. One who is given a title ought to live up to the expectations commensurate with the title. When titles are incorrectly and indiscriminately bestowed, people would fail to perform the social roles and responsibilities associated with the title. Hence, the phrase 'what is said is not used effectively' means that words or titles have lost their meanings and efficacy.

The rectification of names requires us to understand that our names or titles – as a ruler, minister, father, son and so on – come with specific roles and responsibilities that we are expected to fulfill. We should therefore exercise our discretion and judgment by doing what is appropriate for one another based on our respective social roles and as demanded by the occasion. Pointing out that *Confucius'* concept of appropriateness implies certain civil and political rights, *May Sim* correctly notes that

> on account of Confucius' emphasis on appropriateness (*yi*) in actions, which actions cannot be achieved without liberty and security, we can imagine his support for the first generation civil and political rights. The right to life, security and liberty are essential not only for acting fairly so that one does not unfairly profit oneself in material goods, honor, power or safety, but also for the other conditions on which Confucius insists for morality, namely, acting with *li*, proper intention, proper respect (*xiao*), and genuine self-investment.[45]

Overall, the quality of appropriateness serves to guide a person – whether ruler or subject – to participate effectively in civic life, exercise his or her citizen rights and obligations, and understand the local and global

---

45 Sim, "Rethinking Virtue Ethics and Social Justice with Aristotle and Confucius," 2010, pp. 206–207.

implications of civic decisions in a culturally sensitive and contextually appropriate manner.

F. Conclusions

Confucius' political philosophy has the potential to contribute towards the flourishing of the ASEAN political security community in two main ways. First, *Confucius'* philosophy supports the ASEAN Way of *Mushyawara* (consultation) and *Mufakat* (consensus). As mentioned, *Confucius* underlines the need of rulers to model and encourage others to observe *li* (normative human behaviors) by being generous in caring for the common people, inspiring the common people to *ren* (humanity or love), and giving them the necessary rights and freedom to live autonomously and participate actively in public policymaking. The above implies a process of consultation and consensus-building between the political leaders and citizens. Such a process is also salutary in building harmonious and peaceful relationships among the ASEAN countries by avoiding unnecessary intervention and conflicts, especially in the highly-complex traditional security issues. Underpinning consultation and consensus is civic literacy and active political participation by the citizens. As discussed, everyone, including both the ruler and subjects, need to possess and demonstrate virtue through *ren* (humanity or love), *yi* (appropriateness) and *zhengming* (rectification of names) in their common quest to become *junzi* (noble or exemplary person).

Secondly, *Confucius'* philosophy points to a possible shared political framework for the ASEAN political security – one that is *communitarian* in ideology. Communitarianism essentially highlights the importance of the community in the formation and shaping of the individual's values, behavior, and identity. Grounded in the communitarian aim to balance the rights of the individual rights with those of the society, Confucian ideas provide an alternative narrative and counter-hegemonic to individualism and individual civil rights commonly championed in the West. The Confucian self is not atomistic or solitary; it is intricately tied to one's social relationships and interactions with other human beings from one's family, community and the world. One learns to progressively observe *li* (normative human behaviors) in one's thoughts, feelings and actions, beginning with one's family through filial piety, before moving on to people in the community (peers, juniors, and elders) and the world. By beginning with the self and moving on to attachments to a particular family, ethnic group, religion, or neighborhood, individuals are able to develop 'civic virtue' – the requisite dispositions and actions that contribute to the good of the community and humankind. Researchers have noted that an Asian version of communitarianism exists in East and Southeast Asian countries such as China, South Korea, Malaysia, Indonesia, and Singapore.[46] This is reflected in their political leaders reminding their fellow citizens to fulfill their duties and responsibilities toward their family and community. The shared communitarian framework for the emerging ASEAN Political Security Community should be derived and adapted from not only Confucianism but also other indigenous ideologies such as Buddhism, Hinduism and Islam in Asia.

In conclusion, there is no doubt that the economic condition of each of the member of the ASEAN countries is not the only source of great differences in the region; in terms of political history and trajectory the ASEAN countries also possess wide variation. It may even be convincingly argued that the most outstanding distinguishing feature of the ASEAN is the immense diversity that encompasses the political and economic nature of its member countries. This is a distinguishing feature that creates paradoxes with respect to the ideal of achieving greater unanimity among the various member countries. However, a careful scrutiny of the history of the ASEAN in achieving unanimity reveals a careful balancing act of inherent paradoxes: On the one hand, the region seems to embrace a turn towards 'rules-based approaches' as evidenced by the creation of the ASEAN Charter and the blueprint for the ASEAN Political Security Community. But on the other hand, the practical application of how diplomacy and political maneuvering actually functions within the ASEAN is still very much governed by informal networks of consultation, consensus and non-intervention. The harmony and balance of paradoxical forces can be appreciated, as this paper has argued, by recognizing, among other worldviews, *Confucius'* virtue-centred philosophy.

---

46 See, for example, Tan, ''Creating 'Good Citizens' and Maintaining Religious Harmony in Singapore,'' 2008, pp. 133–142; Tan and Wong, ''Moral Education for Young People in Singapore: Philosophy, Policy and Prospects," 2010, pp. 89–102; Chua, *Communitarian Ideology and Democracy in Singapore*, 1995; Chua, "The Cost of Membership in Ascribed Community," 2005, pp. 170–195; Lee et al., eds., *Citizenship Education in Asia and the Pacific: Concepts and Issues*, 2004; Bell, *Beyond Liberal Democracy: Political Thinking for an East Asian Context*, 2006.

Works cited

Acharya, Amitav, "Democratisation and the prospects for participatory regionalism in Southeast Asia," *Third World Quarterly* 2 (2003): 375-390.

Bary, William Theodore de and Tu Weiming, eds., *Confucianism and Human Rights*, New York: Columbia University Press, 1998.

Bary, William Theodore de, *The Trouble with Confucianism*, Cambridge, Massachusetts: Harvard University Press, 1991.

Bell, Daniel A., *Beyond Liberal Democracy: Political Thinking for an East Asian Context*, Princeton, New Jersey: Princeton University Press, 2006.

Bell, Daniel A. and Hahm Chaibong, eds., *Confucianism for the Modern World*, Cambridge: Cambridge University Press, 2003.

Bell, Daniel A., *East Meets West: Human Rights and Democracy in East Asia*, Princeton, New Jersey: Princeton University Press, 2000.

Bloom, David, David Canning and Pia Malaney, "Demographic Change and Economic Growth in Asia," *Centre for International Development at Harvard University Working Paper*, No.15, 1999, pp. 1-47.

Chen, Ming-Jer, "Transcending Paradox: The Chinese 'Middle Way' Perspective," *Asia Pacific Journal of Management* 2 (2002): 179-199.

Cheng, Chung-ying, "On Yi as a Universal Principle of Specific Application in Confucian Morality," *Philosophy East and West* 3 (1972): 269-280.

Chua, Beng-Huat "The Cost of Membership in Ascribed Community,'' in *Multiculturalism in Asia*, ed. Will Kymlicka and Baogang He, Oxford: Oxford University Press, 2005, pp. 170-195.

Chua, Beng-Huat, *Communitarian Ideology and Democracy in Singapore*, London: Routledge, 1995.

Coxhead, Ian, "A New Resource Curse? Impacts of China's Boom on Comparative Advantage and Resource Dependence in Southeast Asia," *World Development* 7 (2007): 1099-1119.

Croissant, Aurel, "From Transition to Defective Democracy: Mapping Asian Democratization," *Democratization* 5 (2004): 156-179.

Dalton, Russel and Nhu-Ngoc Ong, "Authority Orientations and Democratic Attitudes: A Test of the 'Asian values' Hypothesis," *Japanese Journal of Political Science* 2 (2010): 1-21.

Frederickson, H. George, "Confucius and the Moral Basis of Bureaucracy," *Administration & Society* 4 (2002): 610-628.

Garofano, John, "Power, institutions, and the Asean regional forum a security community for Asia?," *Asian Survey* 3 (2002): 502-521.

Gerstl, Alfred, "The Depoliticisation and 'ASEANisation' of Counter-Terrorism Policies in South-East Asia: A Weak Trigger for a Fragmented Version of Human Security," *Current Research on South-East Asia* 1 (2010): 48-75.

Ho, Wing Meng, "Asian values and modernisation," in *Asian Values and Modernization*, ed. Chee-Meow Seah, Singapore: Singapore University Press, 1997, p. 1-20.

Hoon, Chang Yau, "Revisiting the Asian Values Argument Used by Asian Political Leaders and its Validity," *The Indonesian Quarterly* 2 (2004): 151-174.

Hutton, Eric L., "Han Feizi's Criticism of Confucianism and Its Implications for Virtue Ethics," *Journal of Moral Philosophy* 3 (2008): 423–453.

Jones, David, "Security and democracy: The Asean Charter and the dilemmas of regionalism in South-East Asia," *International Affairs* 4 (2008): 735-756.

Lee, Jong-Wha and Kiseok Hong, "Economic Growth in Asia: Determinants and Prospects," *Japan and the World Economy* 2 (2012): 101-113.

Lee, Wing On, David L. Grossman, Kerry J Kennedy, and Gregory P. Fairbrother, eds., *Citizenship Education in Asia and the Pacific: Concepts and Issues*, Hong Kong: Comparative Education Research Centre, University of Hong Kong, 2004.

Meng, Peiyuan, *Meng Peiyuan jiang kongzi* [Meng Peiyuan talks about Confucius], Beijing: Beijing University Press, 2005.

Norden, Bryan W. Van, "Virtue Ethics and Confucianism," in *Comparative Approaches to Chinese Philosophy*, ed. Bo Mou, London: Ashgate, 2003, pp. 99-121.

Peerenboom, Randall, "An empirical overview of rights performance in Asia, France, and the USA: The dominance of wealth in the interplay of economics, culture, law and governance," in *Human rights in Asia: A Comparative Legal Study of Twelve Asian Jurisdictions, France and the USA*, ed. Randall Peerenboom, Carole Petersen and Albert Chen, Abingdon, Oxon: Routledge, 2006, pp. 1-64.

Reyes, Vicente, "Social Media Networks and Tactical Globalisation: An Exploratory Case Study of Contesting Political 'space' in Singapore," *St Antony's International Review* 2 (2013): 33-46.

Reyes, Vicente, "The Impact of Automation on Elections: Case Study of the May 2010 Philippine Presidential Contests," *Journal of Developing Societies* 3 (2013): 259-285.

Severino, Rodolfo, "Beyond forty: Towards political and economic integration," *Contemporary Southeast Asia: A Journal of International and Strategic Affairs* 3 (2007): 406-423.

Sim, May, "Rethinking Virtue Ethics and Social Justice with Aristotle and Confucius," *Asian Philosophy* 2 (2010): 195-213.

Soeslilowati, Sartika, "Asean's response to the challenge of terrorism," *Masyarakat, Kebudayaan dan Politik (Society, Culture and Politics)* 24, No. 3 (2011): 228-241.

Tan, Charlene, *Confucius*, London: Bloomsbury, 2013.

Tan, Charlene, "'Our Shared Values' in Singapore: A Confucian Perspective," *Educational Theory* 62, no. 4 (2012): 449-463.

Tan, Charlene and Yew Leong Wong, "Moral Education for Young People in Singapore: Philosophy, Policy and Prospects," *Journal of Youth Studies* 13, No. 2 (2010): 89-102.

Tan, Charlene, “Creating ‘Good Citizens’ and Maintaining Religious Harmony in Singapore,” *British Journal of Religious Education* 2 (2008): 133-142.

Tan, Sor-hoon, *Confucian Democracy: A Deweyan Reconstruction*, Albany: State University of New York Press, 2004.

Thompson, Mark, “Whatever Happened to ‘Asian Values’?,” *Journal of Democracy* 4 (2001): 154-165.

Weissman, Mikael, “The South China Sea Conflict and Sino-Asean Relations: A Study in Conflict Prevention and Peace Building,” *Asian Perspective* 3 (2010): 36-69.

Yeung, Henry Wai-chung and George Li, “Theorizing economic geographies of Asia,” *Economic Geography* 2 (2003): 107-128.

List of Contributors

Maurice Adams
Professor of General Jurisprudence, Department for Public Law, Jurisprudence and Legal History, Tilburg Law School, Tilburg University

Robert Esser
Chair of German, European and International Criminal Law, Criminal Procedure and White-Collar Crime and Head of the Research Centre for „Human Rights in Criminal Proceedings" (HRCP), Faculty of Law, University of Passau, Member of the Supervisory Board, German-Southeast Asian Center of Excellence for Public Policy and Good Governance (CPG), Faculty of Law, Thammasat University

Henning Glaser
Lecturer, Faculty of Law, Thammasat University, Director and Member of the Supervisory Board, German-Southeast Asian Center of Excellence for Public Policy and Good Governance (CPG), Faculty of Law, Thammasat University

Jau-Yuan Hwang
Professor of Constitutional and International Law, College of Law, National Taiwan University

Sibel Inceoğlu
Professor of Constitutional Law, Faculty of Law, Istanbul Bilgi University

Jörg Luther
Professor in Public Law, Department of Law and Political, Economic and Social Science, University of Eastern Piedmont

Yon Machmudi
Lecturer at the Arab Studies Program, Faculty of Humanities, University of Indonesia

Vicente Reyes
Lecturer for Social Science, School of Education, University of New England

Osama Siddique
Associate Professor, Department of Law and Policy, Lahore University of Management Sciences

Charlene Tan
Professor, Policy & Leadership Studies Department, National Institute of Education Singapore

Li-ann Thio
Professor of Human Rights, Public and International Law, Faculty of Law, National University of Singapore

Gábor Attila Tóth
Associate Professor for Constitutional Law, Faculty of Law, University of Debrecen

Fabian Wittreck
Professor of Public Law, Faculty of Law, Westfälische Wilhelms University Münster